Straight to the Point

Tally 8.1

DINESH MAIDASANI

B.A., Dip. Comp. Sc.

FIREWALL MEDIA
(An Imprint of Laxmi Publications Pvt. Ltd.)
An ISO 9001:2015 Company

BENGALURU • CHENNAI • GUWAHATI • HYDERABAD
KOCHI • KOLKATA • LUCKNOW • RANCHI
NEW DELHI

1 Starting with Tally 8.1

INTRODUCTION TO TALLY 8.1

God bless the accountants. They were at one stage very lowly paid staff of the office, though they were the ones who knew more about the company than anyone else in the company. He used to have all the information about the strength and weaknesses of the company. How much the company owned and how much it had to pay out. But, alas, it still was a job equivalent to a babu of the office. There used to be a time when while tallying the various reports like Trial Balance, various ledgers, etc., he used to tear his hair out to match them. Well, he must be a happy man now. With the advent of computers and then of financial accounting packages, his life has really been made easy.

The accounts are tallied in a flash, the entries are done even faster and the balance sheet not even made but printed at any stage, when required. Among the various financial accounting software available in the market, the popular one is Tally. There are various versions of the software available in the market. The latest being 8.1.

Tally 8.1 empowers business owners to manage their businesses smoothly. Designed keeping in mind the needs of the Indian businessman, it has several key additions in terms of functionalities.

The multilingual capacity of Tally 8.1 gives you tremendous freedom of communication – you can maintain your business accounts in any Indian language, view it in another and print it in yet another language of your choice... all at the same time!

TallySilver/Gold 8.1 incorporate multiple language support at different levels. First, it allows the user to enter and display information in any unidirectional scripts. Available through 10 user interfaces in majorIndian languages like Hindi, Punjabi, Marathi, Gujarati, Oriya, Bengali, Telugu, Tamil, Kannada and Malayalam, TallySilver/Gold 8.1 help theuser to interact with the software using menu options that have already been translated into regional languages. Users can enter data through phonetic keyboards also. A typical usage of the phonetic keyboard will be to spell the term in English and the software will display it, after transliteration, in the language selected. For instance, on typing the characters "KAR", the software can render the word in Hindi using the Devanagari script...

You can send separate documents to suppliers, business associates, customers etc., in their language, while maintaining accounts in your language. In effect, you can conveniently transact business across the length and breadth of India, and language will no longer be a barrier. Freedom from dependence on accounting professionals is yet another clear benefit that Tally 8.1 enables... right from day one! You can let your accountant enter information in any Indian language that he is comfortable with and you can review it in your preferred language –at the click of a button.

Backed by the heritage of incredible simplicity, Tally 8.1 takes one more significant step towards ensuring that concrete business advantages are realised from accounting on computers.

The advanced technology empowering Tally 8.1 allows you to:

- Enter input data in the language of your choice
- Capture language-specific aliases for all masters
- Print reports, vouchers, invoices in any language, based on the information input in a language-specific alias through transliteration
- Enter data through normal as well as phonetic keyboards
- Interact with the menu options in a vernacular language, by choosing from the list of built-in interface languages

Value Added Features

Besides the unique multilingual capacity, Tally 8.1 comes with a host of beneficial features, such as:

- VAT Composition Returns
- VAT Composition Returns For All States
- Monthly / Quarterly Returns
- Annual Returns
- Excise For Traders
- Generation of Excise Invoice for Trader
- Tracking of Purchase Invoice during sales and ability to pass on Cenvat Credit
- Generation of Quarterly Returns (Form 2)
- Generation of Excise Stock Register (RG 23D)
- Fringe Benefit Tax (FBT)
- Accounting for FBT
- Computing FBT Payable
- Generating Challans (Quarterly)
- Filing FBT Returns (Yearly)

Installation

Installation of Tally is very simple, simply put the CD in the drive and let it run. It has a simple menu driven installation procedure. At the time of installation the user can opt to install the program files on any drive, i.e., if the hard disk has partitions, as well as specify the directory names where the program files are to be installed. The user can also specify the location of the data directory. It does not take more than 60 seconds to install Tally on the local hard disk.

Running Tally

Either by clicking at Tally from its icon on the Windows desktop or running it from Windows Explorer, you can run Tally to get the initial screen of Tally, which is shown next. We will talk about the details of the contains later, but first let us see what is new in the new version of Tally.

WHAT'S NEW IN TALLY 8.1

Release 1.0

Tally 8.1 - A Multilingual Business Accounting & Inventory Management Software provides support for Fringe Benefit Tax computation and VAT Composition returns generation in addition to its language capabilities.

New Features

Multilingual Support

Tally 8.1 is so technologically advanced that it can operate in all Indian languages concurrently! That means, you maintain accounts in any Indian language view it in another and print it in yet another language of your choice.... at the same time! With Tally 8.1 capture multiple language-specific aliases for all Masters and print Reports, Vouchers and Invoices in the language of your choice. What's more, Tally 8.1 supports transliteration of data for Indic family of languages.

Fringe Benefit Tax

FBT (Fringe Benefit Tax) is a one time, easy to enable configuration. Tally provides the complete tracking of expenses covered under FBT. It computes FBT based on the eligibility criterion and generates FBT Challan and returns.

VAT Composition Returns

VAT Composition Returns provides fast and error-free voucher entry with complete tracking of each transaction. The Composition Rate of VAT is automatically recognised based on the turnover. It prints VAT Composition Returns for VAT enabled states. The tax payable is calculated automatically and displays in the Return Form.

Excise for Dealers

Excise for Dealers provides complete tracking of duty credit availed and passed on. It supports printing of excise invoice and generates the required statutory reports.

Enhanced Functionalities and Features in Tally 8.1

Tally 8.1 is performance driven. Its enhanced features include:

- Language directory
- Ability to restore Tally 7.2 data within minutes
- Easy import and export of data
- User interface colours that are even more pleasing to the eye
- Speed of operation with extensive reduction of the Stat.900 file size
- Choice of multilingual options
- Multi-language printing options
- Ability to copy text from Tally to windows and vice versa
- Miscellaneous features

Language Directory

Language files (.dct) reside in the Language Directory. Specify this path at the time of installation or in the Tally.ini file.

- To change the Language directory path in the Tally.ini
- Open Tally.ini file from the Tally installed folder.
- Enter the path where the language files are present.
- Save and close the file.

Restore Process of 7.2 Data

Tally 8.1 does not recognise Tally 7.2 data backup files. You can restore Tally 7.2 data by clicking the tally72migration icon in the Tally 8.1 folder. Specify the destination and source files in Select Companies to Restore. The Migrate Data option completes the process. The 4 digit number 7.2 number is prefixed by 0, making it a 5 digit 8.1-compatible number.

Import of Masters and Vouchers

Tally now supports only the XML format to import Masters and Vouchers.

Export

If you select Multilingual from the language list during export, then Tally allows you to Export in three formats - ASCII (Comma-delimited), HTML (Web-publishing) and XML (Data-interchange). If you select English from the language list, then Tally allows you to Export in two formats - ASCII (Comma-delimited) and XML (Data-interchange). By default, Tally does not support SDF format. However, if you wish to use the SDF format, you can download the SDFExportImport.TCP utility from the Tally website.

Stat.900

Tally 8.1 has now been enhanced with features that speed up your operations.

The Stat.900 file size has now reduced extensively. This improves the performing speed while creating or importing a company.

Colours

The user interface has now changed to more appealing colours aimed at enhancing your use of Tally.

By default, Tally 8.1 screens display in a new colour as the colour quality is set to Highest (32 bit). However, to retain the usual display of Tally:

Go to Desktop > Display properties> Settings > Set the Color quality to Medium (16 bit) > Restart Tally

Tally's Phonetic Keyboards

Tally's Phonetic keyboard is useful for those who speak the language but do not know how to type it using the operating system keyboard. It is user friendly with the same layout as that of the English characters. You can spell the term based on its sound and the data is transliterated in the language selected.

Print Language

You can print documents and reports in the language of your choice in Tally. For instance, while printing the following voucher, select Alt+ L to bring up the Print Language Configuration prompt.

Select the language of your choice. The printed document displays as shown.

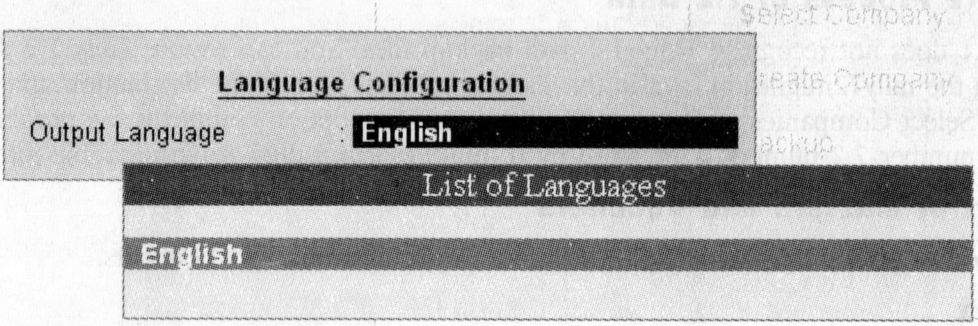

Major Changes and Enhancements

There may be minor variation in reports during migration of data from Tally 7.2 to Tally 8.1 due to the changes listed below:

LIFO and FIFO Valuation Method

Sales and Purchase vouchers passed on a single day now display in the Stock vouchers report in the order of their entry thus ensuring effective functioning of LIFO and FIFO Stock valuation methods.

For example, In Tally 7.2, A purchase invoice followed by a sales invoice and then again a purchase invoice will display in the stock vouchers report with all the sales entries listed first followed by all the purchase entries. Tally 8.1, however, displays the vouchers in the order of their entry –Purchase – Sales – Purchase.

Std Cost and Std Price Valuation Method

If you have not set Set Standard Rates? in Stock Item masters but have set Costing Method to Std Cost and Market Valuation Method to Std. Price. In Tally 7.2, the First Purchase cost was taken into consideration for the Std Cost Valuation and the First Sale price for Std Price valuation methods.

However, Tally 8.1 accurately considers the Last Purchase cost for Std Cost Valuation and the Last Sale Price for Std Price valuation

Average Cost

When Multiple Sales and Purchases are made against Receipt and Delivery Notes at a rate different from that specified in the Receipt and Delivery notes

For Example: Let us assume you have passed a Receipt Note for 100 nos. of an item @

Rs. 100 per item. Subsequently you pass a Purchase Invoice for 30 nos of the item @ Rs. 120 against the above Receipt Note. This means that some items are still pending against the tracking number.

In Tally 7.2, the difference in the rates would be incorrectly included in the original value The balance sheet viewed with Avg. Cost valuation method displays closing stock values at Rs. 10,600.

This has been resolved in the new Tally 8.1, which accurately displays the Avg. Cost closing stock valuation in the balance sheet as Rs. 10,000.

On Account values were being taken as 'overdue' in Ratio Analysis in 7.2

In Tally 7.2, On Account values were taken into consideration while calculating values for Due till today in Ratio Analysis.

Tally 8.1 has resolved this and displays only the outstanding values in Due till today. (for Sundry Debtors and Creditors)

Pending Tracking number values were approximate, even though quantities were accurate (causing few Paise difference depending on context)

Tally 7.2 used to display pending Delivery/Receipt with approximate values, causing a small difference in the values.

Tally 8.1 has resolved this and displays the pending Delivery/Receipt Notes values accurately.

Miscellaneous Changes and Enhancements

Tallysav.dat file

The Tallysav.dat file in the tally folder is now Tallysav.tsf.

Tally_req.slk and Tally_resp.slk files

The tally_req.slk file, which is generated while activating the Tally license, is now tally_req.lic.

Similarly, the tally_resp.slk file, which is generated as a response from the Tally Internet Services server, is now tally_resp.lic.

Tally Data files

The Tally 8.1 data file now consists of 5 digits. The numbering of a company created in Tally 8.1 starts with 10000. Additional companies created will be suffixed with 10001, 10002, 10003 and so on.

However, when you migrate Tally 7.2 data to Tally 8.1, the 4 digit-data file in the 7.2 folder is converted to a 5 digit-data file with 0 prefixed. Example: 00001, 00002 and so on.....

Loading Icon

The Tally Clock is now replaced with the Windows Wait icon

Close Button

To quit any Tally screen, you now have an option apart from the Esc key on the keyboard. The following button displays on the right of every screen in Tally. Click the Close button to quit the current screen.

Copying Text From Tally to Windows

Copying text to and from Tally to Windows is now a simple process. Use Ctrl+Alt+C to copy text from Tally and Ctrl+Alt+V to paste text into Tally.

Release 1.1

E-Mail Authentication

While mailing reports in Tally, the E-Mail Server now accepts the Authentication User Name and Password.

Multi-accounting Allocation

When you rewrite a company, the vouchers with multiple accounting allocations will be retained if Use Common Ledger A/c for Item Allocation is set to No.

Synchronization of Altered Transactions

Synchronization is possible even when data migrated from Tally 7.2 consists of cancelled vouchers.

Cost Centre Class in Stock Journal

In Tally 8.1 you cannot select Cost centre class while creating Stock Journals as it is not applicable.

Migration

The process of Migrating Data to Tally 8.1 is now effectively enhanced.

Migrating Currencies

Multiple currencies can now be easily migrated to Tally 8.1.

Forex Gain Loss Calculations

Tally 8.1 displays accurate Debit and Credit amounts in the Ledger Forex Gain/Loss report unlike Tally 7.2 in which Debit amounts were displayed as Credit and vice versa.

Some Unique Features

OpenTally

Tally 8.1 allows you to get the information you require in the format you need. Just create your format in any ODBC compliant software like MS-Word or MS-Excel, and pull data from Tally. To create any report you want. Like Audit Reports and Schedule VI forms. Or internal reports. You can even generate your export documentation by pulling data from Tally.

MailTally

Harness the power of the Internet! Tally 8.1 uses the SMTP protocol for e-mail. Now, e-mail invoices to your customer. Or your purchase order. In fact, e-mail any Tally report or document as easily as you print! Even reminder letters and statement of accounts need not be printed and posted. Simply e-mail them. It is not only postage cost that you save, you save on so much of your valuable time.

E-Tally

You can improve your company's efficiency by sharing information with your extended enterprise: your customers, your bankers, your business partners and other associates. Now publish all reports and documents from Tally 8.1 to a secure part of your website, using either FTP, HTTP or secure HTTP protocols, in HTML format. You can use this feature to inform customers the new price-range and stocks available for sale. Or publish reports that your CEO can access, while traveling, using any internet browser.

XML Tally

Tally 8.1 enables you to exchange information with non-Tally systems, using XML. You can now share data across locations, amongst business associates and partners, and make your workflow seamless. You can now collaborate with others and share information like never before.

On-line Help

Tally 8.1 has built in Context Sensitive Help. Press the Help button while in Tally, and it will bring up the relevant topic.

"Scenario" Management

The new "Scenario" Management capability allows you to plan, as well as analyse your business performance, under varying assumptions. You can get different views of your accounts and inventory information by selectively including Optional Vouchers and/or Reversing Journals and Memos. Use this feature for forecasting and planning. Prepare reports including provisional figures without affecting actual accounts using reversing journals that automatically reverse. This is useful for reporting interim statements.

Print Preview

This facility helps you check printed report formats and layouts before actual printing takes place.

Direct Access to the Internet

Tally 8.1 allows you direct access to Web Browsing from within Tally.

Cutting Edge Technology

Tally 8.1 has achieved major technological breakthroughs to enable you to benefit from collaborative technology such as protocol support for HTTP, HTTPS, FTP, SMTP, ODBC, and Raw Sockets with data interchange formats like XML, HTML, SOAP, SDF and related formats, rule-based collaboration supporting export, upload and synchronization.

Hardware Requirements

Minimum disk space: 10 MB (Excluding the help files)

Operating System Software: Microsoft Windows 98/ME/NT/2000.

ITEMS ON THE TALLY SCREEN

The Tally screen, which was shown earlier, has the following options:

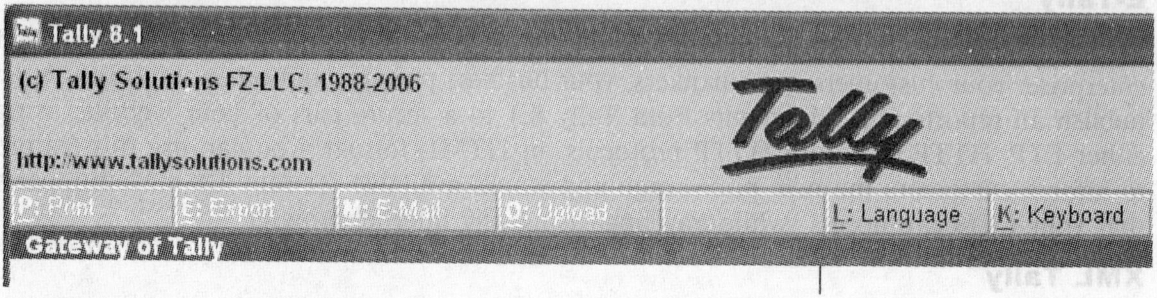

P: Print

Clicking at this button you can print the current information on the printer.

E: Export

Use Export option to export data (reports and statements) from Tally. The exported data can be rearranged on a spreadsheet, published on the web or exported to another company using Tally.

M: E-Mail

The E-mail is the most widely used facility on the Internet. It saves time and cost of postage. Use the email feature in Tally to:

- E-mail any Tally report or document like invoices or purchase orders
- Post reminder letters and statement of accounts.

O: Upload

All reports and documents generated in Tally can be published on your website. Tally can create reports in HTML format and upload the same directly to your website. For example, use this feature to inform your customers about the new price-range and stocks available for sale on your website. Tally uses the highest standard of data encryption methods to ensure security of data.

L: Language

Using this button you can select the installed language, other than the one which you are using.

K: Keyboard

Tally's Phonetic keyboard is useful for those who speak the language but do not know how to type the same using the keyboard.

This keyboard will allow you to spell the term phonetically based on how it sounds and Tally will display the data in the language selected after transliteration. The keyboard layout is the same as that of the English characters, which makes it user friendly and comfortable.

With a phonetically enabled keyboard, you can enter the information or data in any Indian language to generate bills, invoices and other reports.

H: Help

TallyHelp file is structured in such a way that it provides easy navigation between topics and facilitates easy search. The comprehensive Online Help covers basic and advanced operations. It is context-sensitive and extracts help on topics related to the current screen in Tally.

Buttons

These buttons are on the right hand side of the screen and can be activated using the keyboard keys mentioned against them.

F1: Select Cmp

Press F1 to select a company, among the companies which are there in the hard disk, by typing the name of the company.

F11: Features

The different features of a company can be selected or modified by F11: Features button. This button is available in almost all screens of Tally as you might wish to modify it as your requirements change. Company Features is specific to the current company only. Therefore, each company may have different features active. For example, a company in your group may need multi-currency whereas another company may not. Configuration options, on the other hand, affect all companies maintained in the same Tally directory and setting configuration for one company will affect other companies in that data directory.

F12: Configure

It allows you to configure various options, about which you will read later.

Gateway of Tally

Various options here are:

- Current period
- Current date
- Name of Company

- Date of Last Entry
- Company Info.
  - Create Company
  - Backup
  - Restore
  - Quit
- Status bar

Let us talk about them one by one.

Current Period

It shows the current period of the company on which you are working.

Current Date

The date as the records of the company.

Name of Company

Name of the company which has been selected.

Date of Last Entry

Date on which the last entry was made.

Company Info.

This has the following information:

Create Company

You can create a company using this. The details are explained later.

Backup

Tally has a flexible backup mechanism where in you can take a backup of the data from virtually any storage medium into any other medium.

The more commonly used media are floppy drive, hard disk drive, zip drive, tape drive, etc - installed either locally or on a network. In the backup screen, the source of the backup and the destination of where it has to be stored have to be given and Tally will do as required.

Restore

Restore literally means to bring back. Similar to backing up of data, Tally allows restoring of data from any medium into any other storage medium.

Quit

It quits the working of Tally.

Status Bar

This bar shows the various status of the working like the date, company, language used, etc.

Since you have not created a company, so you would not be able to select any company and neither you want to quit. So the only logical selection here would be to Create a Company.

Let us do it.

CREATE A COMPANY

To create the company, you would click at Create a Company, to get the screen shown below. Various items on the screen are described below:

Directory

This shows where in the hard disk, your data is being stored.

Name

Type here the name of the company you want to create. The name of your Company can exceed the space provided. Tally accommodates longer names by compressing the characters horizontally, so that the name is fully visible and you need not scroll sideways.

Mailing Name

Type here the mailing name of the company. By default this name is the same as the name of the company but it you wish you can specify a different, maybe a shortname, name here.

Address

Type here the address of your company. You can enter any number of lines for the address. This choice is optional in Tally. If you do not wish to fill any address, simply press the <Enter> key and move to next item.

State

Type here the State in which you are going to work. It is very important since VAT rates are different in different states.

PIN Code

It is the 6 digit code given by the postal authorities to the various areas in the country.

Telephone Number

Type here the telephone number.

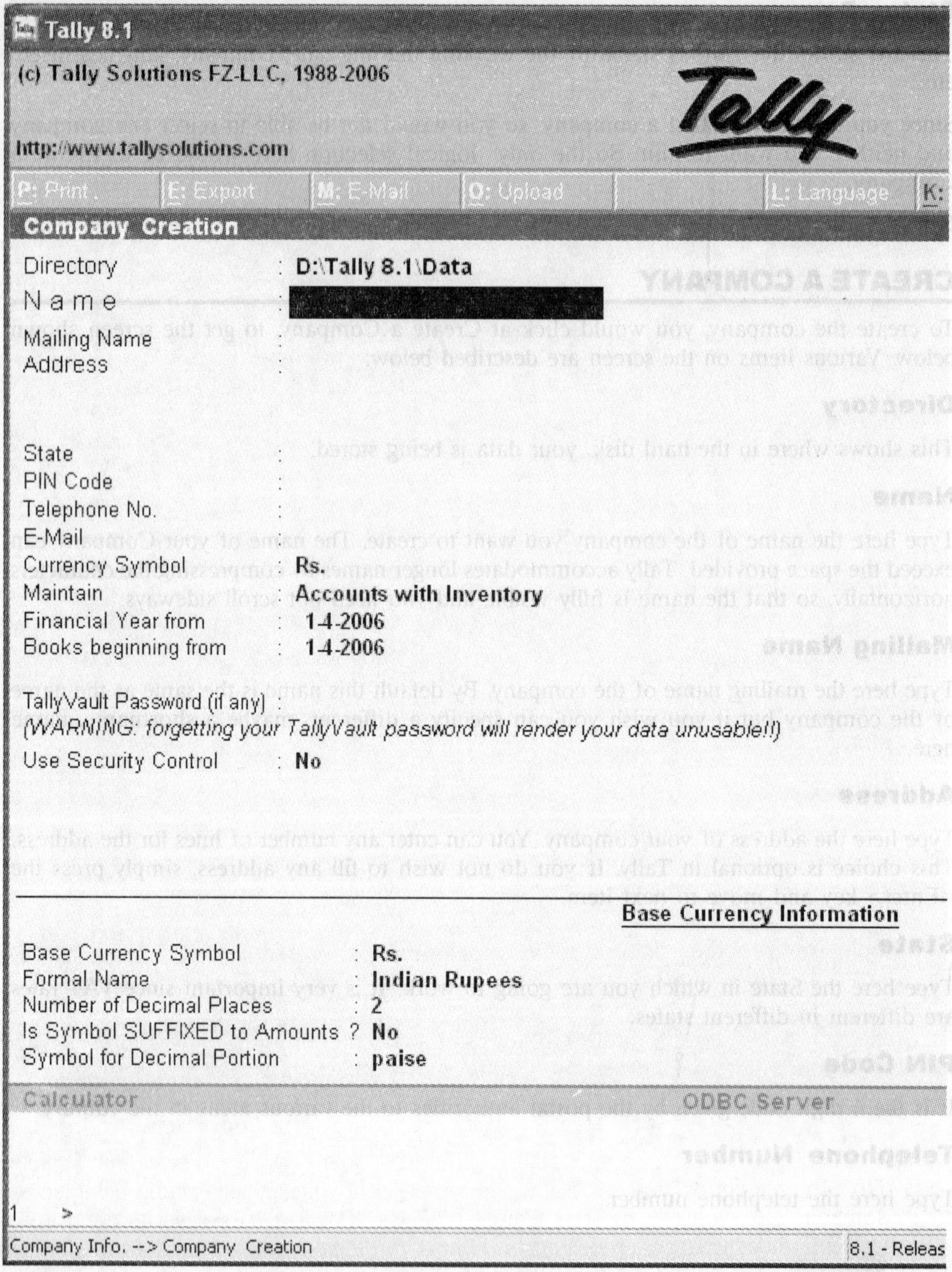
Tally 8.1

(c) Tally Solutions FZ-LLC, 1988-2006

http://www.tallysolutions.com

P: Print | E: Export | M: E-Mail | O: Upload | L: Language | K:

Company Creation

Directory : D:\Tally 8.1\Data
Name : [redacted]
Mailing Name :
Address :

State :
PIN Code :
Telephone No. :
E-Mail :
Currency Symbol : Rs.
Maintain : Accounts with Inventory
Financial Year from : 1-4-2006
Books beginning from : 1-4-2006

TallyVault Password (if any) :
(WARNING: forgetting your TallyVault password will render your data unusable!!)
Use Security Control : No

Base Currency Information

Base Currency Symbol : Rs.
Formal Name : Indian Rupees
Number of Decimal Places : 2
Is Symbol SUFFIXED to Amounts ? No
Symbol for Decimal Portion : paise

Calculator ODBC Server

1 >

Company Info. --> Company Creation 8.1 - Releas

E-mail Address

This is optional, if you want to give the e-mail address of the company, then fill it up or leave it blank.

Currency Symbol

Since you can use other than Rupees, this option can be used.

Maintain

There are 2 different ways you can use Tally. Remember, if you do not select Accounts-with-inventory, then you would not be able to run inventory. The options are:

Accounts Only

Use this option if you do not have any inventory transactions. Using this option you would not be allowed to have any inventory transactions.

Accounts-with-Inventory

Though this is selected by default, you can always differ to use your own option. Using this you would be able to use both Financial as well as Inventory Management.

Financial Year From

Type here the date from which you actually want Tally to maintain your accounts. By default it is taken to be the same date which you specify for beginning of the financial year, but you may however give any other date which is later to the date of beginning of financial year to maintain your books of accounts. If you give the date as 20-1-2001 then the accounts closing date will automatically will be taken as 31-3-2001.

Books Beginning From

Type here the date from which you actually want Tally to maintain your accounts. It is usually filled up by Tally when you specify from the date in the above column.

Tally/Vault Password (if any)

TallyVault is an enhanced security system, which allows for encryption of the company data. Encryption means converting normally accessible Tally information into unrecognisable information, which can only be reconverted by authorized persons. Give a password here and repeat the same. This basically results in the creation of an encrypted company whose information is not accessible to users other than the password holder.

Use Security Control

This option allows you to provide security control to your company. The default value here is "No". In case you wish to protect the information of your company from being accessed by someone else, you can use this feature of Tally. If you opt for security control, Tally offers a comprehensive pass-based access control to different parts of the information based on authority lists created by the system administrator.

BASIC CURRENCY INFORMATION

The best part of Tally is that you can work in any currency accounting system. You can infact use any foreign currency too. In this section you have to provide information related to this.

Base Currency Symbol

Specify the symbol of your base currency. For example for an Indian company the base currency is Rupees, whose symbol is "Rs.", therefore specify this symbol here. Tally uses this symbol in reports, whenever necessary.

Formal Name

Now that you have decided on the currency symbol, you can decide about the currency name too. Remember, Rupees is also available in other countries too, for example, Nepalese Rupees. If you wish you can write here Indian Rupees.

Number of Decimal Places

In this option you can specify a value from zero to four to denote the fractional part of the currency. For example, the fractional part of the Indian Rupee is Paisa for which the number of decimal places is two. The default option is also two.

Is Symbol SUFFIXED to Amount?

Most currencies have the symbol prefixed to the amount, for example, Rs.165.00 or $375.00, but some currencies take the symbol to the right of the digits, for example 600 Yen or 1000 Lira. Depending upon the currency you wish to deal in, choose an appropriate option. The default choice for the option is No. This means that the symbol be on the left hand side of the digits.

Symbol for Decimal Portion

Since you can use different currencies here, you can give the name of the fractional currency here. For example, Paisa for Rupees and Cents for Dollars.

Show Amount in Millions?

By default this option is No, which means that the amount will be displayed in lakhs and crores. In case you want the amount to be displayed in American system of millions, then select Yes.

Show Amounts in Millions	?	**No**
Put a SPACE between Amount and Symbol	?	**Yes**
Decimal Places for Printing Amounts in Words	:	**2**

Put a Space between Amount and Symbol?

In order to insert a space between the currency symbol and the amount choose Yes and to remove the space specify No.

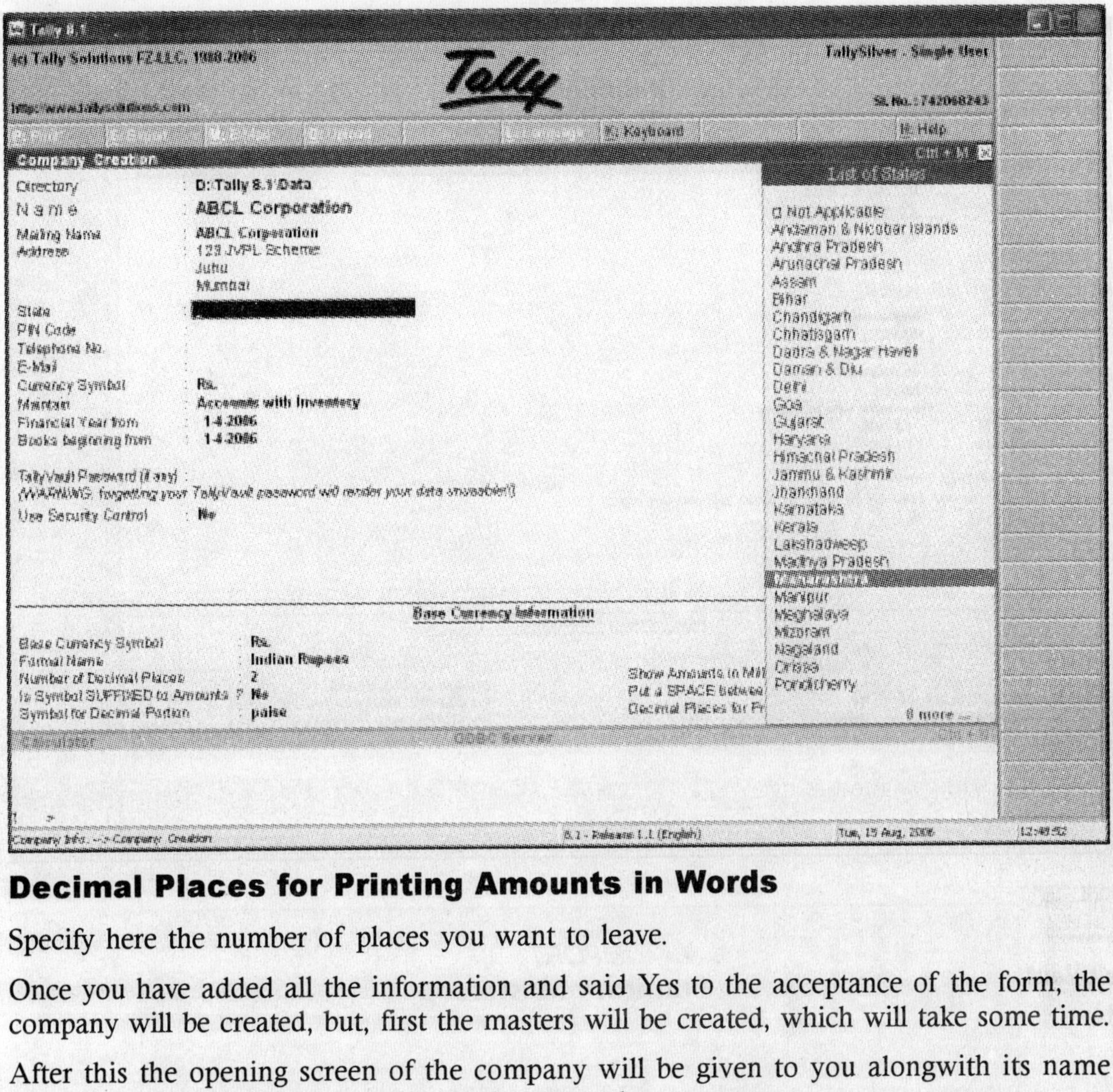

Decimal Places for Printing Amounts in Words

Specify here the number of places you want to leave.

Once you have added all the information and said Yes to the acceptance of the form, the company will be created, but, first the masters will be created, which will take some time.

After this the opening screen of the company will be given to you alongwith its name appearing in the list of companies, as shown on the next page.

We will talk about the various aspects of the company in a later chapter, but, let us look at the various features of the company.

For this click at F11: Features and you get the screen, as shown here. From here, click at Accounting Feature, which would result in the screen shown on next to next page.

ACCOUNTING FEATURES

Integrate Accounts and Inventory

Say yes, if you want to integrate accounts with inventory. You can maintain only accounts if you want to or even only inventory. In case you integrate accounts and inventory then

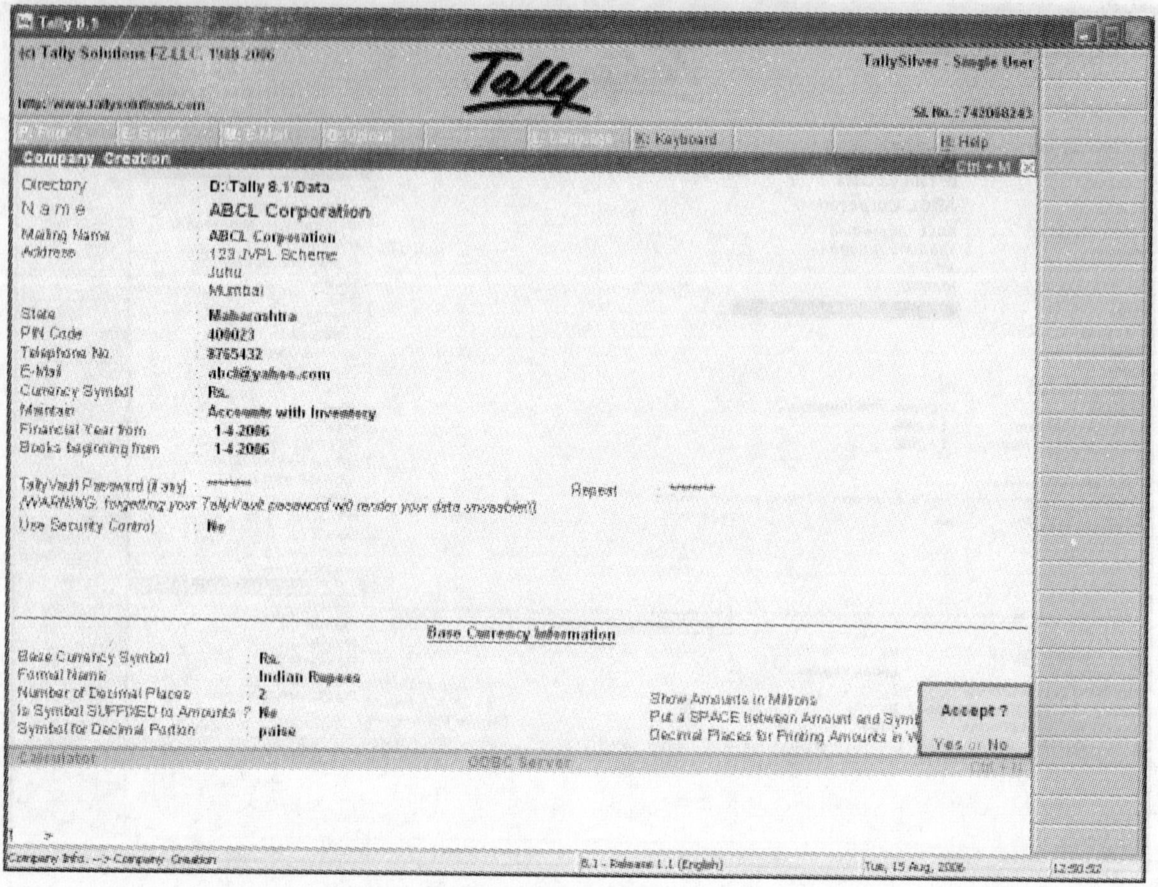
Tally 8.1
(c) Tally Solutions FZ-LLC 1988-2006
TallySilver - Single User
http://www.tallysolutions.com
Sl. No. : 742068243
K: Keyboard
H: Help
Company Creation
Ctrl + M
Directory : D:\Tally 8.1\Data
Name : ABCL Corporation
Mailing Name : ABCL Corporation
Address : 123 JVPL Scheme
Juhu
Mumbai
State : Maharashtra
PIN Code : 400023
Telephone No. : 8765432
E-Mail : abcl@yahoo.com
Currency Symbol : Rs.
Maintain : Accounts with Inventory
Financial Year from : 1-4-2006
Books beginning from : 1-4-2006
TallyVault Password (if any) : *******
Repeat : *******
(WARNING: forgetting your TallyVault password will render your data unusable!)
Use Security Control : No
Base Currency Information
Base Currency Symbol : Rs.
Formal Name : Indian Rupees
Number of Decimal Places : 2
Is Symbol SUFFIXED to Amounts ? No
Symbol for Decimal Portion : paise
Show Amounts in Millions
Put a SPACE between Amount and Symbol
Decimal Places for Printing Amounts in Words
Accept ?
Yes or No
Calculator
ODBC Server
Company Info. --> Company Creation
8.1 - Release 1.1 (English)
Tue, 15 Aug, 2006
12:50:52

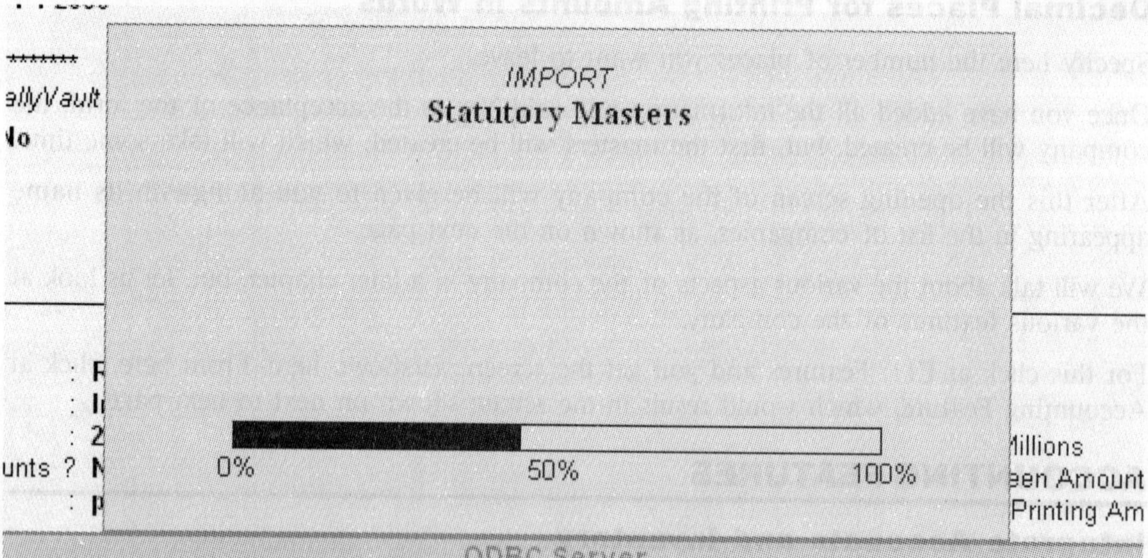
IMPORT
Statutory Masters
0%
50%
100%
ODBC Server

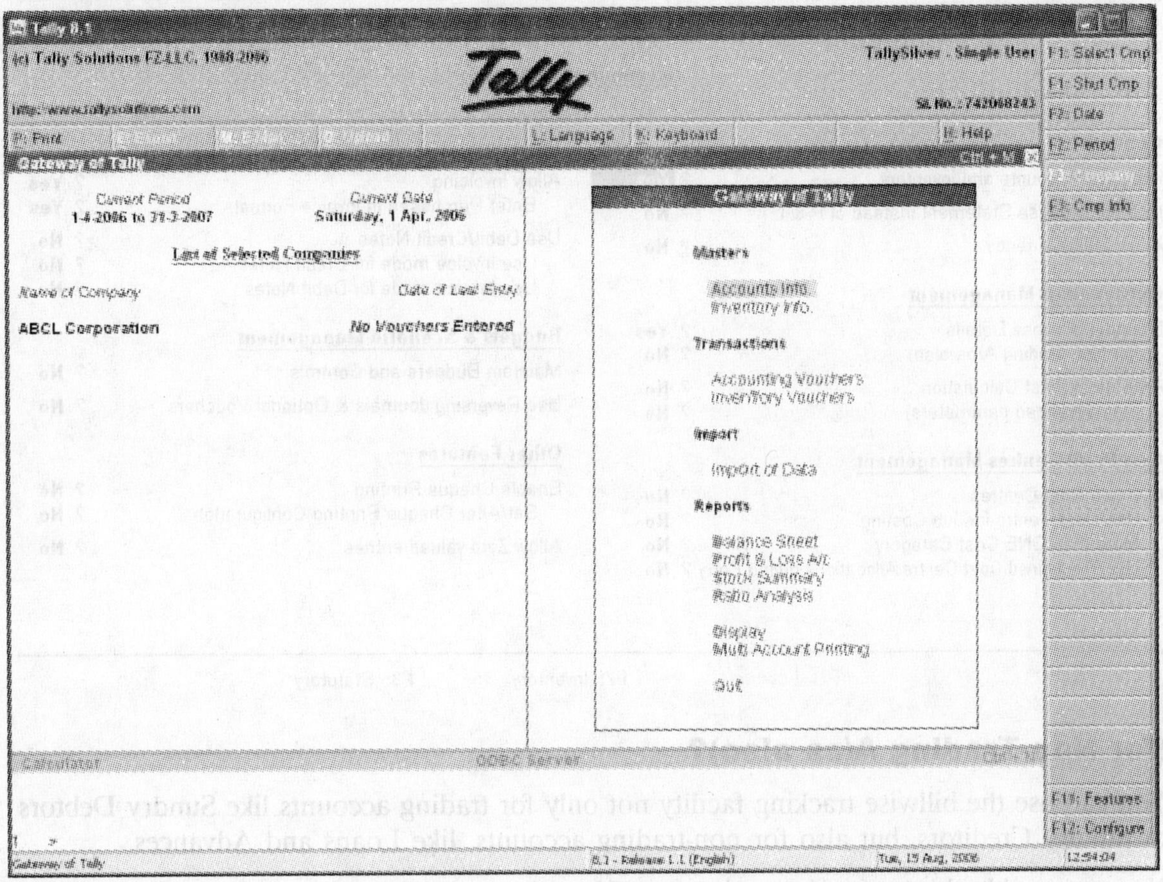

Gateway of Tally .....

Company Features

Accounting Features

Inventory Features

Statutory & Taxation

Quit

the profit and loss account and balance sheet reflect the closing stock according to inventory valuation. In case you do not integrate accounts and inventory then your profit and loss account and balance sheet do not reflect the closing stock according to inventory valuation.

Income/Expense Statement Instead of P & L?

You can opt to have this option by selecting it or not.

Allow Multi-Currency

Tally allows you to use more than one currency at a time specially useful if your company has accounts in more than one country.

Maintain Billwise Details

This option allows you to keep track of an account, on bill-to-bill basis. If you do not need bill-wise details, let this option be set to its default value which is No. In this case you will only get net closing balances of accounts, without any bill-wise details.

Company: **ABCL Corporation**

Accounting Features

General		Invoicing	
Integrate Accounts and Inventory	? Yes	Allow Invoicing	? Yes
Income/Expense Statement instead of P & L	? No	Enter Purchases in Invoice Format	? Yes
Allow Multi-Currency	? No	Use Debit/Credit Notes	? No
		Use Invoice mode for Credit Notes	? No
Outstandings Management		Use Invoice mode for Debit Notes	? No
Maintain Bill-wise Details	? Yes		
(for Non-Trading A/cs also)	? No	**Budgets & Scenario Management**	
Activate Interest Calculation	? No	Maintain Budgets and Controls	? No
(use advanced parameters)	? No	Use Reversing Journals & Optional Vouchers	? No
Cost/Profit Centres Management		**Other Features**	
Maintain Cost Centres	? No	Enable Cheque Printing	? No
Use Cost Centre for Job Costing	? No	Set/Alter Cheque Printing Configuration	? No
More than ONE Cost Category	? No	Allow Zero valued entries	? No
Use Pre-defined Cost Centre Allocations during Entry	? No		

F1: Accounts F2: Inventory F3: Statutory

(for Non-Trading A/cs also)?

You can use the billwise tracking facility not only for trading accounts like Sundry Debtors or Sundry Creditors, but also for non-trading accounts, like Loans and Advances.

You can enable this option by setting it to Yes.

Activate Interest Calculation

Using this feature you can set to have the interest calculation On or Off.

Maintain Cost Centres

This option permits you to allocate transactions of certain accounts to cost centres to determine unit-wise performance. Set this option to Yes to use this feature, otherwise let it be set to No its default value.

Use Cost Centre for Job Costing

You can skip this feature by clicking at No.

More than ONE Cost Category

In case you wish to maintain cost centres, you can also have more than one set of cost centres. Change this option to Yes to use more than one category of cost centres.

Use Pre-defined Cost Centre Allocations During Entry

You can skip this feature by clicking at No.

Allow Invoicing (Enter Purchase in Invoice Format)

You can opt to have the inventory through an invoice or otherwise.

Use Debit/Credit Notes?

Change this option to Yes to make separate debit and credit notes. If you use only journals for adjustment entries, let the option be set to No, its default value.

Maintain Budgets and Controls

Using this feature, you can create multiple budgets. There could be a budget for specific purposes, i.e., budget for your branch office, department budgets, realistic budget, etc. In case you wish to maintain budgets, set this option to Yes.

Use Rev. Journals and Optional Vouchers

In order to use reversing journals set this option to Yes, else let it be set to No, its default value.

Enable Cheque Printing

This option allows you to set the option of printing cheque or not.

Allow Zero Values Entries in Vouchers

It allows you to prohibit the entry of zero valued vouchers, as most of the time they are meaning less. However, if you wish to allow the entry of vouchers with zero value, set this option to Yes.

Now, we come to Inventory Features.

INVENTORY FEATURES

The following options are self explanatory regarding inventory. Set them to Yes or No depending upon your requirements.

Integrate Accounts and Inventory

Say yes, if you want to integrate accounts with inventory. You can maintain only accounts if you want to or even only inventory. In case you integrate accounts and inventory then the profit and loss account and balance sheet reflect the closing stock according to inventory valuation. In case you do not integrate accounts and inventory then your profit and loss account and balance sheet do not reflect the closing stock according to inventory valuation.

Allow Zero Values Entries

It allows you to prohibit the entry of zero valued vouchers, as most of the time they are meaning less. However, if you wish to allow the entry of vouchers with zero value, set this option to Yes.

Maintain Stock Categories?

Stock Categories offers parallel classification of items. You may create Stock Categories like Floppy Disks and Floppy Drives. If you want the facility, select Yes. The advantages of cost categories have been highlighted above. Even if you have selected No initially, you can always return to this screen and set it to Yes. Tally would internally assign stock groups to default Primary Stock Category. If you had initially selected No but now set it to Yes, you may want to alter all previous stock groups/items to properly catagorise them, else they would remain under Primary Stock Category.

Maintain Batch-wise Details?

This option is for maintaining batch information pertaining to stock items. The batch does not extinguish itself after it is disposed of, it remains on record and is quite like the ledger in behaviour. Hence, it is possible to view data like below: Stock Item – cloth, Batches – Red, white and blue. Hence you can extract all sales of blue cloth at any time.

Set Expiry Date for Batches?

This is useful for businesses that deal in goods that have expiry dates like medicines, food and other perishables. While voucher entry, date of manufacture of the product defaults to the date of the voucher is which can change but not to a date later than the voucher date. Expiry date cannot be a date prior to the voucher date. Batches should be used where they are small in number and remain constant. Do not use the batch option for tracking of lots

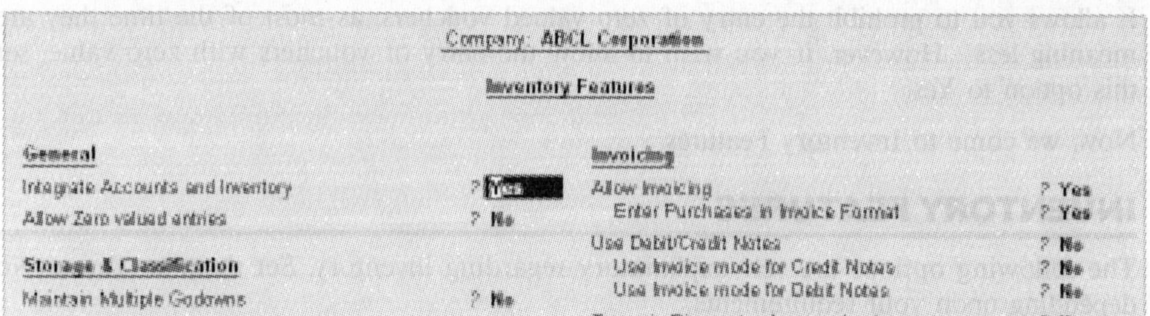

through manufacturing processes. If that is done, you will soon have a large number of batches which are not deleted. You will not be able to assign costs to particular lots as may be the intention.

Use Different Actual and Billed Qty?

This option enables you to specify quantities, that are different from that delivered, when invoicing and recording the fact. It is possible that you have delivered goods but some of them are in dispute and your customer wishes to be invoiced for only the quantity that he agrees to. He may consider the rest later and would then like to be invoiced. On the other hand, the rest is so bad that it is useless even for you to take back.

Hence, you can record the fact when raising the invoice without altering the delivery note or passing a rejection entry. Select this option if you have many such occasions.

Allow Purchase Order Processing

Order processing is the placing of orders with suppliers for purchase to be made from them or receive orders from customers for the purpose of selling. In Tally, Order Processing is linked to Inventories. This allows tracking of the order position for a Stock Item. Using this you can track arrival of goods ordered and also whether the ordered Stock Item are delivered on time etc.

You can create Purchase and Sales Orders in Tally. Purchase Orders (PO) can be created, printed and sent to suppliers. Goods received are linked with the POs and Invoices. Outstanding Purchase Orders should be monitored. Stock Summary displays order position of any item. The Purchase Order Book lists out all the Purchase Orders placed.

Allow Sales Order Processing

Likewise, Sales Orders received are recorded in Sales Order Entry screen. These details will be available during Delivery Note and Invoicing. The order position in the Stock Summary can be viewed. The Sales Order Book lists all Sales Order received.

Allow Invoicing (Enter Purchase in Invoice Format)

You can opt to have the inventory through an invoice or otherwise.

Use Debit/Credit Notes?

Change this option to Yes to make separate debit and credit notes. If you use only journals for adjustment entries, let the option be set to No, its default value.

Separate Discount Column on Invoices

Instead of standard discounts on the invoices you can use multiple format of discounts.

Track Additional Costs of Purchase?

If you enable this option, you are allowed to obtain a break-up of purchase costs, without the need to separately debit ledger accounts for expenses.

Use Multiple Price Levels

Set this option to Yes to create Multiple Price Levels.

Use Tracking Numbers?

Quite often businesses do not issue invoice (bills) along with the goods they deliver. Goods are accompanied by a document usually called a Delivery Note. Deliveries have to be related to invoices that may be raised on the customer later. It is important to track each delivery note to ensure that it is invoiced. It is only by invoicing that a financial liability is raised. Tally uses tracking numbers to maintain the relation between delivery notes and invoices/bills. This is available for both purchases as well as sales. Hence, if your business is affected by this situation either for goods received or goods sold, select this option. If you set it to No, you will not need the facility of separate delivery notes recording as your Purchase and Sales Vouchers would double up as delivery notes. Goods Receipt Note and Goods Delivery Note voucher types are not available if you do not use tracking numbers.

Use Rejection Inward/Outward Notes?

Yes, if you wish to record rejection of goods separately and not through a common Goods Receipt Note or Goods Delivery Note.

Next we have the Statutory and Taxation option.

STATORY AND TAXATION FEATURES

Enable Dealer – Excise (Set/Alter Dealer – Excise Details)

Set these options to Yes, to enable/alter the Excise for Dealers feature. Refer Excise for Dealers for further information.

Follow Excise Rules for Invoicing

Set this option to Yes, to follow Excise rules for invoicing. Provide the Excise information, for it to be printed on invoices and Accept, Yes to save.

Enable Value Added Tax (VAT)

Set/Alter VAT Details

Set these option to Yes, to enable the VAT features for the company. Refer Value Added Tax for more details.

Enable Service Tax

Set/Alter Service Tax Details

Set these option to Yes to enable the Service Tax features for the company. Refer Service Tax for further details.

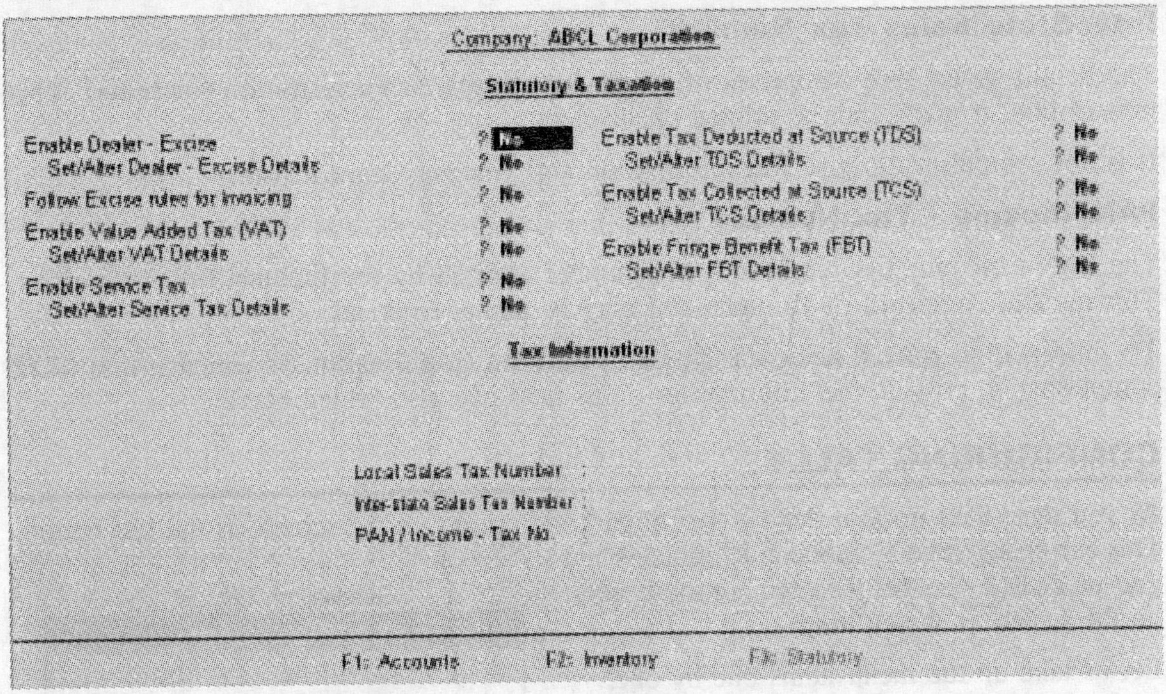

Enable Tax Deducted at Source (TDS)

Set/ Alter TDS Details

Set these option to Yes to enable the TDS features for the company. Refer TDS for further details.

Enable Tax Collected at Source (TCS)

Set/Alter TCS Details

Set these option to Yes to enable the TCS features for the company. Refer TCS for further details.

Enable Fringe Benefit Tax (FBT)

Set/Alter FBT Details

Set these option to Yes to enable the FBT features for the company. Refer FBT for further details.

Tax Information

Set this option to Yes to enter the Tax details of the Company.

Local Sales Tax Number

The Local Sales Tax Number entered during the Company Creation is automatically displayed in this field.

Inter-State Sales Tax Number

The details given here comprises of a number and date of registration (in India). This information, if given, can be printed on invoices.

It is not compulsory to give this information and you may leave it blank.

PAN/ Income – Tax Number

The PAN/ Income Tax Number is the number allotted by the Income Tax Authorities. This number comprises of 10 digits and may be alphanumerical.

The information entered here will appear in Account Confirmation Statements. It is NOT compulsory to provide this information – this field can also be left blank.

CONFIGURING TALLY

As you must have noticed there is a configuration option on the screen, as the last button. This can be accessed by pressing F12 too. When you press F12 you get the configuration menu on the screen as shown here:

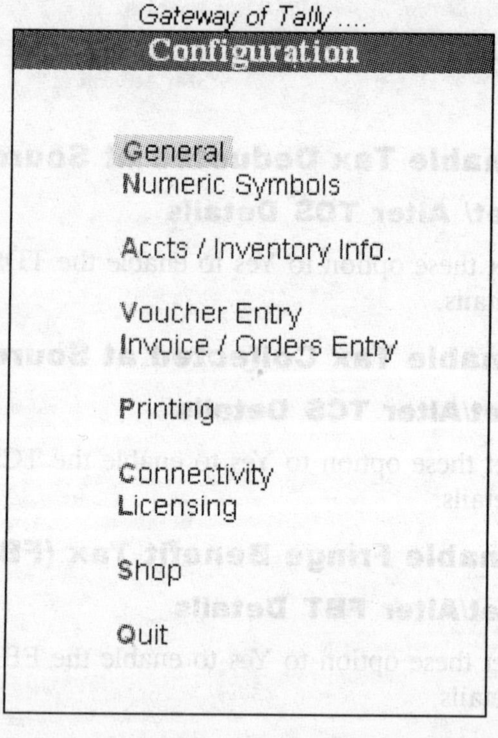

Let us take up the menu items one by one.

General

Click at General to get the General menu or press <G> to get it.

The various options of the screen are :

Use Accounting Terminology of

Tally provides the user with options of using either SAARC countries or International accounting terminology. Select an option according to your choice.

Default Appearance of Names in Reports

Tally provides you with the option of printing names with addresses of the parties or the names only. You can choose your option.

Default Appearance of Stock Item Names in Reports

Similar to above, you can choose here to print only the name of the stock item.

Style of Short Date

Tally provides you 3 options of specifying date in the format of: dd-mm-yy (Indo/British method), mm-dd-yy (American method) and yyyy-mm-dd (Japanese method). You can choose any one of these methods.

Separator to Use in Short Date

The default choice for separator in a date is a hyphen (-), if you wish to see the date in the format of dd/mm/yy format instead of dd-mm-yy, change the separator to (/). You can even change it to (.) to make the date look like dd.mm.yy. Please note that these options are only for printing, while entering data you can use any format.

Decimal Character to Use

Most of the countries use (.) to represent a decimal character, that is why it is the default value, but some use (,) to indicate the decimal point, depending upon your requirements you can select either of them.

Thousands Separator to Use

Normally in country like India (,) is used to indicate the thousand separation. For Four Thousand Five Hundred Sixty Five would be represented as 4,565. In some countries,

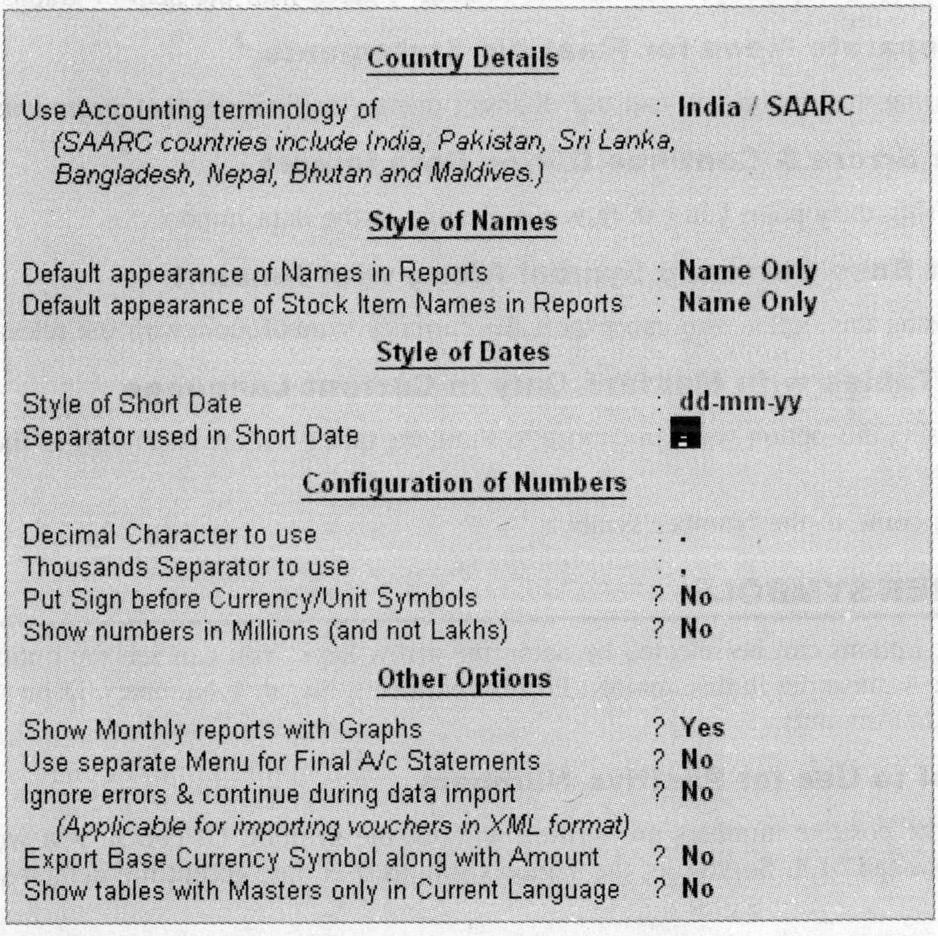

Country Details

Use Accounting terminology of : **India / SAARC**
(SAARC countries include India, Pakistan, Sri Lanka, Bangladesh, Nepal, Bhutan and Maldives.)

Style of Names

Default appearance of Names in Reports : **Name Only**
Default appearance of Stock Item Names in Reports : **Name Only**

Style of Dates

Style of Short Date : **dd-mm-yy**
Separator used in Short Date : **-**

Configuration of Numbers

Decimal Character to use : **.**
Thousands Separator to use : **,**
Put Sign before Currency/Unit Symbols ? **No**
Show numbers in Millions (and not Lakhs) ? **No**

Other Options

Show Monthly reports with Graphs ? **Yes**
Use separate Menu for Final A/c Statements ? **No**
Ignore errors & continue during data import ? **No**
(Applicable for importing vouchers in XML format)
Export Base Currency Symbol along with Amount ? **No**
Show tables with Masters only in Current Language ? **No**

however, a period (.) is used instead of a comma. So the above figure would look like 4.565. You can make the selection required by you.

Put Sign before Currency/Unit Symbols

This was discussed earlier too. You can use to represent Rs. to come before digits, i.e., Rs.250 or choose to have the sign on the right, i.e., 250 Yen.

Show Numbers in Millions (and Not Lakhs)

In India our counting goes like this: Units, Tens, Hundreds, Thousands, Lakhs, Ten Lakhs, Crores, Ten Crores, etc. Whereas in some countries like USA it is done like this: Units, Tens, Hundreds, Thousands, Ten Thousands, Hundred Thousands, Millions, Ten Millions, Hundred Millions, Billions, etc. So the amount of 12345678 in India would be shown as 1,23,45,678 (1 Crore, 23 Lakhs, 45 Thousands, Six Hundred and Seventy Eight) whereas in USA it would be shown as 12,345,678 (12 Millions, 345 Thousands, Six Hundred and Seventy Eight).

Show Monthly Reports with Graphs

By choosing this option you can see the monthly figures with the help of graphs.

Use Separate Menu for Final A/c Statements

By choosing this option you can use different menus for final account statements.

Ignore Errors & Continue During Data Import

By choosing this option you can ignore the errors in the data import.

Export Base Currency Symbol Along with Amount

By choosing this option you can export the currency symbol alongwith the relevant data.

Show Tables with Masters Only in Current Language

By choosing this option you can choose to show the tables with masters only in the current language.

Next we come to the Number symbols.

NUMBER SYMBOLS

Here the options can be selected by using the arrow keys. You can see the options here. There are 4 categories in this, mainly: Positive Numbers, Negative Numbers, Debit Amounts and Credit Amounts.

Symbol to Use for Positive Numbers

Mostly the positive numbers are written without the symbol. Of course you would not like +4 instead of 4. So you let the symbols stay as it is, i.e., accept the default values as such.

Symbol to Use for Negative Numbers

These use (-) as a prefix by default, and a blank suffix, that means using default setting –10.00 will be shown as (–)10.00, in case you wish to show it as (10.00)– which is a fast growing tradition to represent negative numbers, your settings will become prefix=(and suffix=).

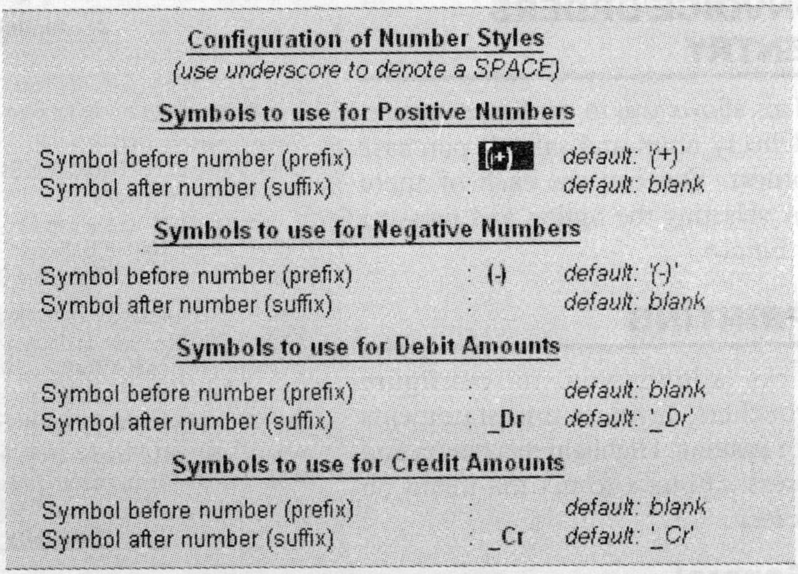

Configuration of Number Styles
(use underscore to denote a SPACE)

Symbols to use for Positive Numbers

Symbol before number (prefix)	: (+)	*default: '(+)'*
Symbol after number (suffix)	:	*default: blank*

Symbols to use for Negative Numbers

Symbol before number (prefix)	: (-)	*default: '(-)'*
Symbol after number (suffix)	:	*default: blank*

Symbols to use for Debit Amounts

Symbol before number (prefix)	:	*default: blank*
Symbol after number (suffix)	: _Dr	*default: '_Dr'*

Symbols to use for Credit Amounts

Symbol before number (prefix)	:	*default: blank*
Symbol after number (suffix)	: _Cr	*default: '_Cr'*

Symbol to Use for Debit/Credit Amounts

Here the default setting is prefix=blank, and suffix=_Dr, where the underscore _ denotes a white space, this will bring up the amount as 10.00 Dr. in order to obtain it as Dr 10.00, you should set prefix=Dr_ and suffix=blank, and finally to obtain it as 10.00 Cr, you would set prefix=blank and suffix=_Cr.

ACCTS/INV INFO MENU

This menu allows you to configure accounts and inventory masters. Various options on this menu are shown on the next page. Since most of the options are self explanatory, We are not taking them up one by one. In case you have any doubt about any option, just leave it as it.

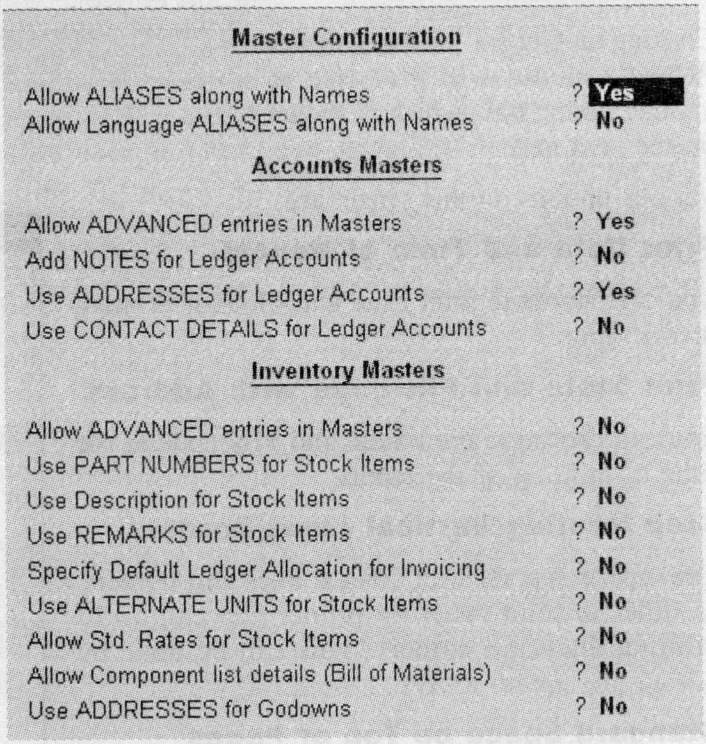

Master Configuration

Allow ALIASES along with Names	? Yes
Allow Language ALIASES along with Names	? No

Accounts Masters

Allow ADVANCED entries in Masters	? Yes
Add NOTES for Ledger Accounts	? No
Use ADDRESSES for Ledger Accounts	? Yes
Use CONTACT DETAILS for Ledger Accounts	? No

Inventory Masters

Allow ADVANCED entries in Masters	? No
Use PART NUMBERS for Stock Items	? No
Use Description for Stock Items	? No
Use REMARKS for Stock Items	? No
Specify Default Ledger Allocation for Invoicing	? No
Use ALTERNATE UNITS for Stock Items	? No
Allow Std. Rates for Stock Items	? No
Allow Component list details (Bill of Materials)	? No
Use ADDRESSES for Godowns	? No

VOUCHER ENTRY

This option allows you to configure the vouchers entries in Tally. Options are shown next.

INVOICE/ORDERS ENTRY

This allows you to configure invoice, delivery notes and sales & purchase orders. You can see each of them by selecting the option and pressing <Enter>.

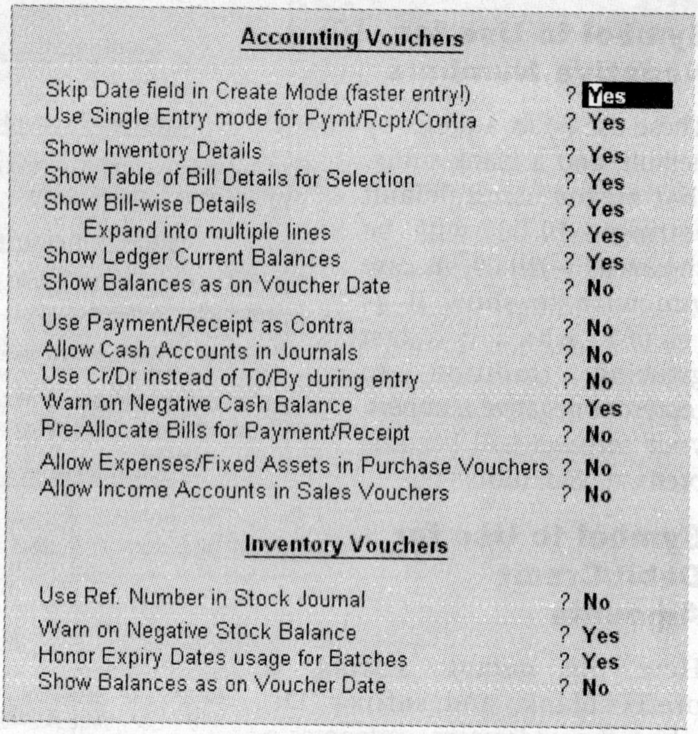

PRINTING

This allows you to configure vouchers, invoices and statements for printing. Highlight this option and press <Enter> to get the menu on screen.

General

Clicking on General on the Voucher Printing menu, will give rise to another dialog box, which is shown on the next page.

Gateway of Tally ....
Configuration ....

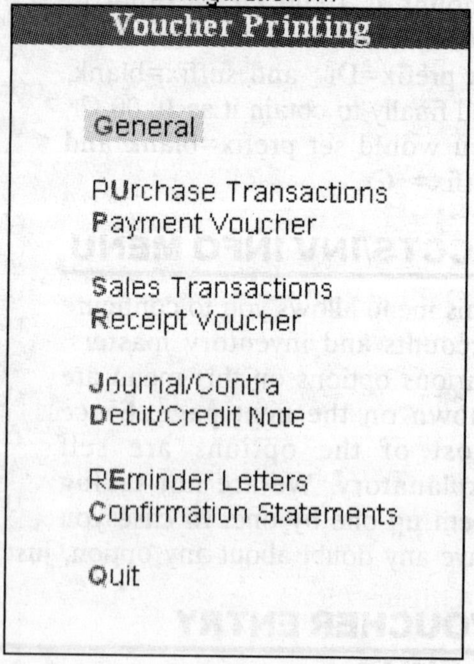

Various options on this screen are:

Print Date and Time of Report

You can choose to print Date and Time of printing of the report.

Print State and PIN code with Address

You can choose to print State and PIN code at the time of printing of the report.

Stop Printing Vertical Lines/Borders

This option reports with vertical lines and borders. In order to print faster on printer you can avoid printing lines and borders. This can be done by setting this option to Yes.

Standard Space on Top of Pages (Inches)

This option allows you to set top margin in inches.

Quick Format Printing

This option is mainly used when you are printing on dot matrix printers. Since speed here is the main criteria. The two options here are:

Split Long Names into Multiple Lines

Set this option to Yes to split long names into multiple lines. This will prevent the long names from being truncated.

Split Long Amount/Numbers into Multiple Lines

Set this option to Yes to split long amounts/numbers into multiple lines. This will prevent the long amount/numbers from being truncated.

Other options under printing can also be explored while working.

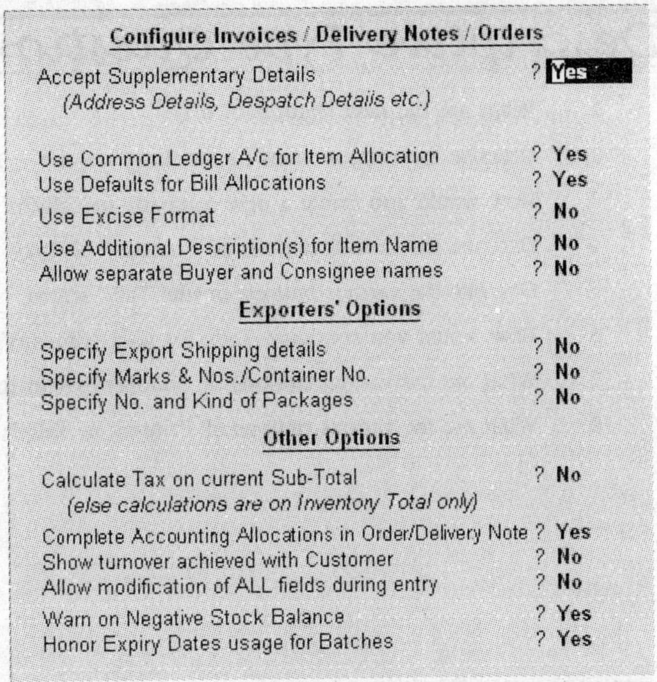

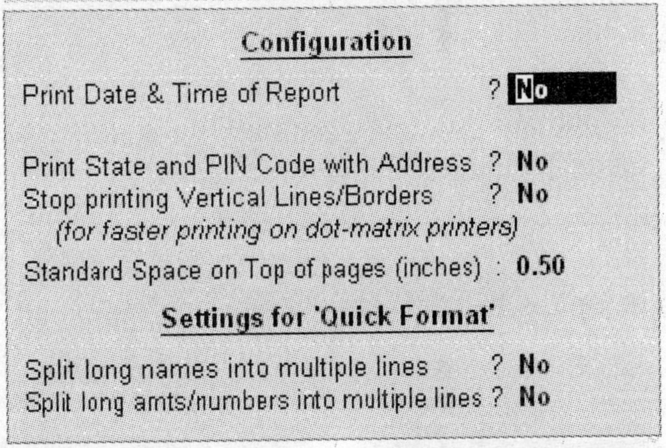

CONNECTIVITY

This option allows you to set up the configuration for connecting to Internet. The two options of the same are shown here.

Proxy configuration asks you whether you want to have the HTML connectivity while Auto-Dial asks for the specific dial up connection.

LICENSING

As can be seen here, the menu has Online, Offline and List Add-Ons. List Add-Ons shows the add ons being used with the software. Online takes you online to the web site of the company, making use of the options of either Updating or Surrendering.

You can Update or Surrender OffLine too.

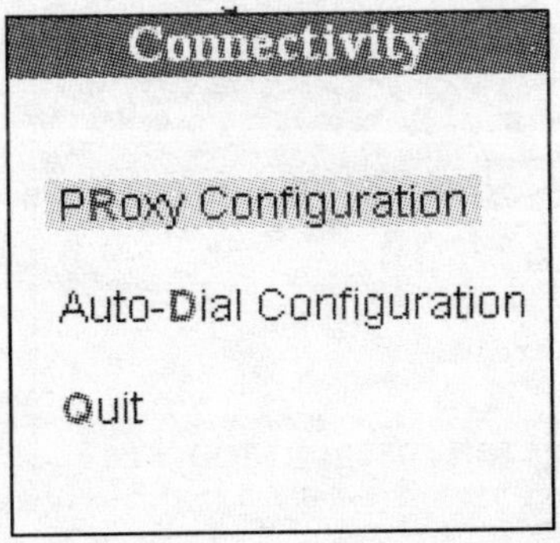

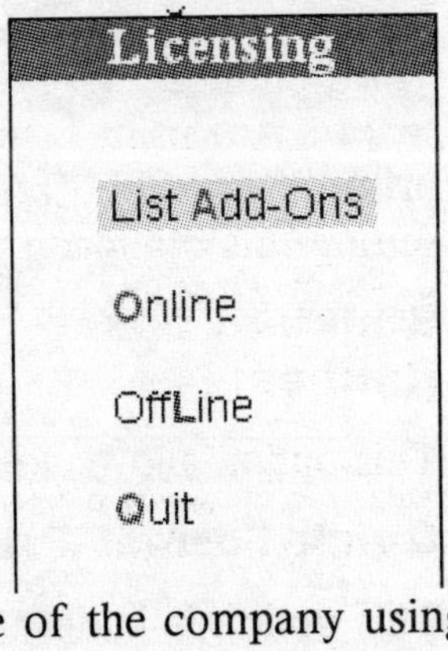

SHOP

You can shop for various updates and add-ons from the Web site of the company using this option.

Descriptive Type Questions

1. What are the new features of 8.1?
2. Describe the various items of the Tally screen.
3. How would you create a new company in Tally?
4. Describe the various options of Currency of Tally.
5. Describe the various buttons on the Tally screen.
6. How would you configure Tally for your company?
7. What are the various options of Number system in Tally?
8. What are the various options of Printing in Tally?

2 Creating Accounts Masters

CREATING ACCOUNT MASTERS

Masters are account heads which shows the transaction under that particular account. You can create masters for both Accounts as well as Inventory. Once you have the company selected, press Esc to reach the Master information menu, as shown here.

Gateway of Tally

Masters

Accounts Info.
Inventory Info.

Transactions

Accounting Vouchers
InvenTory Vouchers

Import

ImpOrt of Data

Reports

Balance Sheet
Profit & Loss A/c
Stock Summary
Ratio Analysis

Display
Multi Account Printing

Quit

As you can see there are lots of features which can be created from here. You can create Masters of Accounts, Inventory and Import Masters. Besides this you can create Transaction Vouchers like Accounting Vouchers, Inventory Vouchers and Import Transactions. On the Report side, you can print report like Balance Sheet, Profit & Loss A/c, Stock Summary and Ratio Analysis from here. You can also display the various information on the screen and print Multi-accounts.

The alphabet made capital and bold in between can be pressed to select that particular option, for example, pressing B would lead to Balance Sheet.

ACCOUNTS INFORMATION

This block has the following masters, Groups, Ledgers, and Voucher Types. Each one of them when clicked would lead you to Create (for creation of a new account), Display (for allowing you to view the information contained in that master) and Alter (for allowing you to change the information contained in that master).

So let us start with the first item, i.e., Groups.

CREATING AN ACCOUNTS GROUP

To create an accounts group, you must follow the following steps to create an accounts group. Click on Accounts Information from the Gateway of Tally to get the dialog box, shown here. Now, click at Groups to get the next box, which asks whether you want to Create, Display or Alter the Group.

Tally has some predefined groups available for you. You can either use them or create some more of your choice. These existing groups however, cannot be altered. Of the 28 pre-defined groups, 15 are primary groups and 13 are sub-groups.

These groups are shown below:

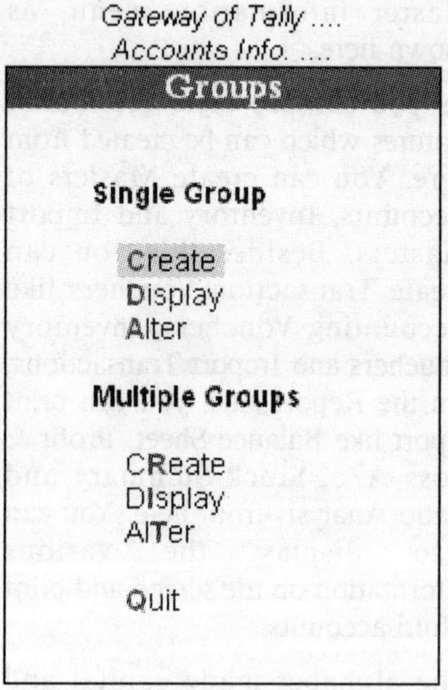

No.	***Main Group***	***Primary Group***
01	Capital Account	Reserves and Surplus or Retained Earnings
02	Current Assets	Bank Accounts
		Cash-in-hand
		Deposit or Assets
		Loan & Advances or Assets
		Stock-in-hand
		Sundry Debtors
03	Current Liabilities	Duties and Taxes
		Provisions
		Sundry Creditors
04	Fixed Assets	
05	Investments	
06	Loans or Liability	Bank OD Accounts or Bank OCC Accounts
		Secured Loans
		Unsecured Loans
07	Suspense Account	
08	Misc. Expenses	
09	Branch/Divisions	
10	Sales Account	

11 Purchase Account

12 Direct Income

13 Indirect Income

14 Direct Expenses

15 Indirect Expenses

16 Branch/Division

In the above case number 10 to 16 belong to the revenue nature.

These groups would be shown to you when you are creating an account to sort of asking you under which account the new account would be listed. Let us now see what these account heads or groups mean to you.

As seen from the above list these accounts are listed alphabetically and not in any particular order of the category.

In the following figure, we have created a new group called Production under Capital Account.

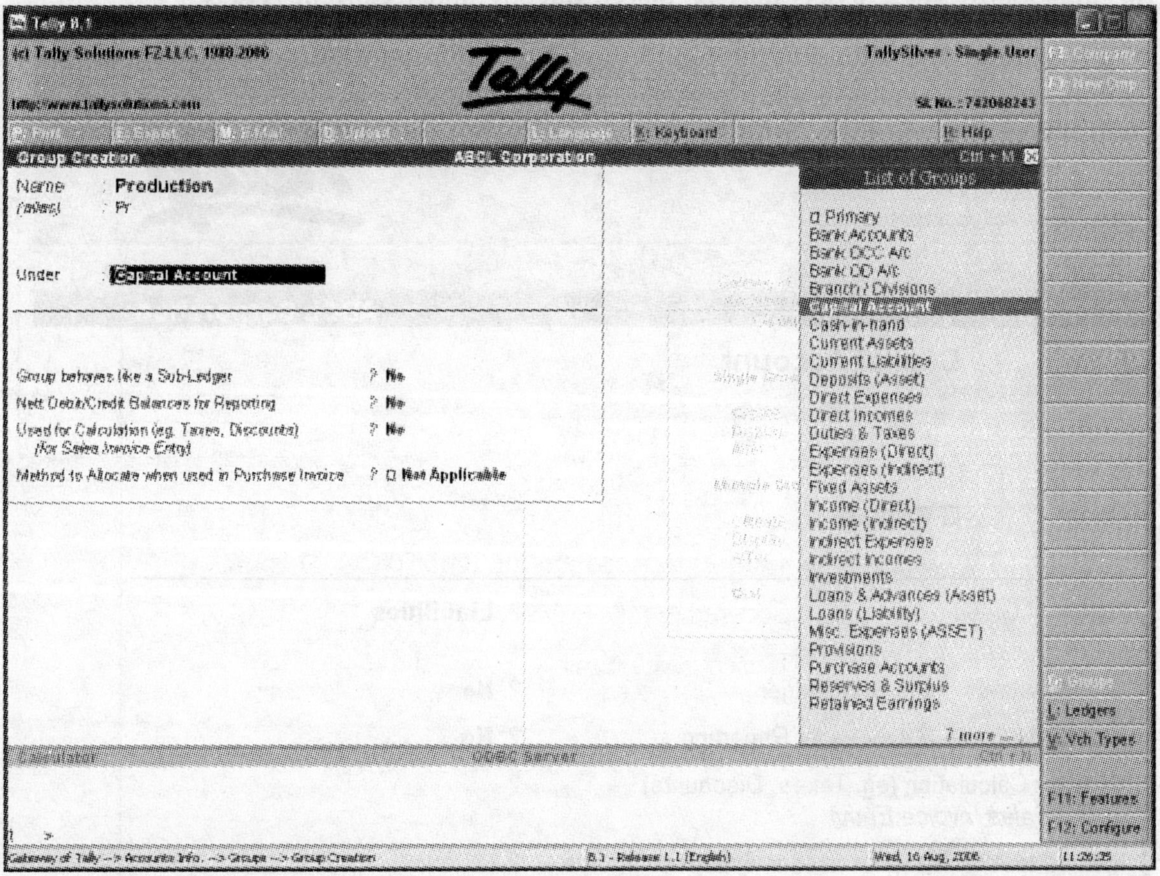

Capital Account

This is a primary group and is used to hold the capital and reserves of the company. You can open ledger heads like Partners Capital Account, Properties Capital Account, Share Capital Account, etc., under this group. You can see the properties of any group by selecting it and pressing <Enter>. For example, in order to see the properties of Capital Account group, select the group by using the arrow keys and press <Enter>. When you display the account you would see the following:

Reserve and Surplus

You can use this sub-group to open ledger heads like Investment Allowance Reserve, General Ledger and other such reserve accounts. The alias name for this sub-group is Retained Earnings.

Current Assets

This is a primary group and as the name of the group itself suggests that all the assets of the company can be placed under this head. This group has six sub-groups under it. Although you can place all your assets under these sub-groups, certain assets may not find place under the sub-groups. These assets may be placed directly under Current Assets.

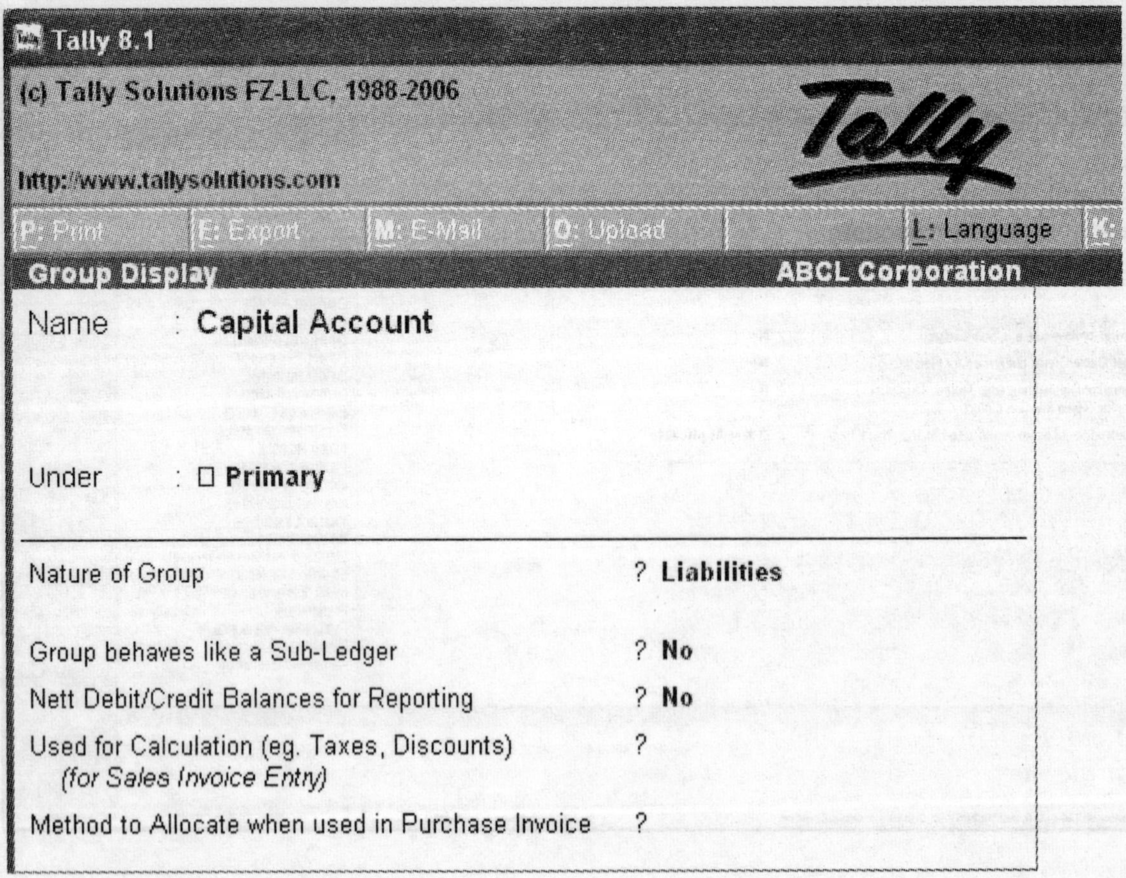

Bank Accounts

It is used to hold savings/current accounts and all other accounts of all the banks.

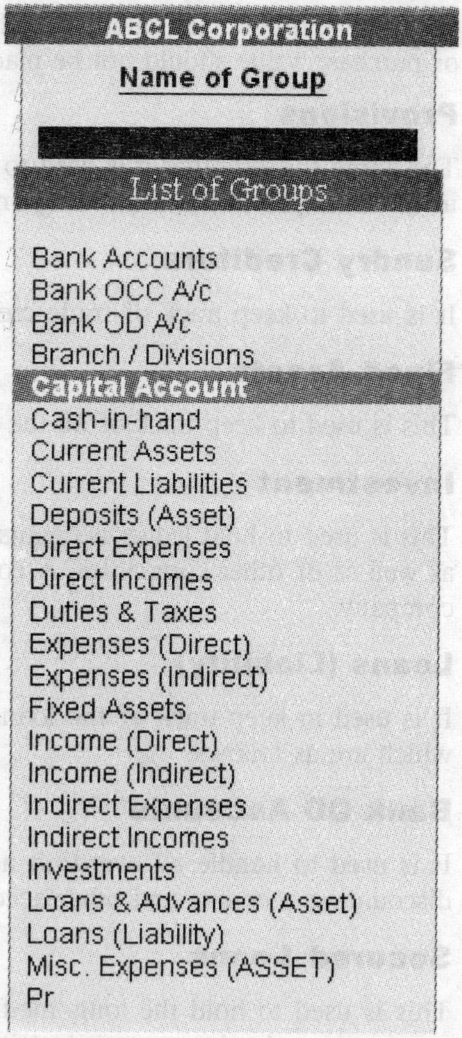

Cash-in-Hand

It is used to hold ledger account of cash. Tally by default opens one Cash A/c under this group. If required you can open more cash accounts.

Deposits or Assets

It is used to hold assets like security deposits, fixed deposits, rental deposits and all other such deposits made by the company (not received by the company).

Loans and Advances

It is used to hold all advances and loans of non-trading nature. For example advances against salaries, work contracts, or even purchase of fixed assets.

Stock-in-Hand

It is used to hold certain special accounts like raw materials, finished goods and work in progress. How the balances are controlled depends on whether you opted to maintain an integrated account-cum-inventory system or a non-integrated account-cum-inventory system in Company Features menu.

Sundry Debtors

It is used to hold accounts of companies and individuals to whom goods are sold on credit and money is receivable by the company.

Current Liabilities

This is a primary group and is used to hold outstanding and statutory liabilities of the company. Hence the liabilities like ESI, PF, and TDS find a place in this group. The group has 3 sub-groups under it which are as following:

Duties and Taxes

It consists of all types of taxes and duties like, Excise, Local Sales Tax, Central Sales Tax, VAT, MODVAT, etc. The duties and taxes falling under this group must be distinguished from the ones that fall under revenue account.

The accounts falling under this group constitute your balance sheet and are not a part of your sale and purchase value. Therefore, sales tax, excise duty, etc., if forming part of sales or purchase value should not be placed under this group.

Provisions

The name suggests that it is used to hold other tax provisions like income tax depreciation in it. Other provisions depending on operational method of company can be placed here.

Sundry Creditors

It is used to keep track of trade creditors of the company.

Fixed Assets

This is used to keep track of all the fixed assets, patents, trade rights, etc., of the company.

Investment

This is used to hold ledger accounts of shares, bonds and other securities of the company as well as of other companies. A convenient place to find all the investments made by the company.

Loans (Liability)

It is used to keep track of the loans taken by the company. This group has 3 sub-groups which are as follows:

Bank OD Accounts

It is used to handle all overdraft accounts with banks like, hypothecation accounts, bill discounting accounts and other accounts which are operated on day to day basis.

Secured Loans

This is used to hold the long/medium term loans taken by the company from financial corporations, banks, etc., against its fixed assets. Hence even if the company fails, these loans have to be returned from the fixed assets of the company.

Unsecured Loans

This is used to hold the loans taken unconditionally by the company. For example, loans taken by outside parties, including directors and partners fall under this sub-group.

Suspense Account

This is used by many companies to maintain a suspense ledger which keeps track of money received or paid by the company, whose nature of transaction is not yet known. The most common example is of money paid as travelling advance, the details of which will only be known after the submission of the TA bill.

Misc. Expenses

The loss of the company, which has not been written off but carried forward to the next year should fall here. However, Tally treats it as a negative profit and carries it to the Profit and Loss Account.

Branches/Division

This is used to keep the names of all companies which may be branches, divisions, sister concerns, subsidiaries of the existing company.

Let us now come to the revenue accounts.

Sales Account

It is used to hold all sales account of the company. Tally allows you to setup multiple sales accounts. You can bifurcate your accounts based on either of these factors: Tax slabs, Nature of trade, Geographical area, Product specification, etc.

In case you wish to see the net sales, you can either open a ledger account called Sales Return under this group or pass a journal entry for sales returns against the specific sales account.

Purchase Account

This is similar to sales account, except for the purpose of transaction.

Direct Income

This is used to hold ledger accounts of non-trade income accounts that affect gross profit.

Indirect Income

This is used to hold ledger accounts of indirect income of the company. For example, income from rent, interest, commission received, etc.

Direct Expenses

This is used to hold ledger accounts of those expenses of the company that determine its gross profit. Expenses like salary paid to labour, transportation, electricity bills, etc., fall under this group.

Indirect Expenses

This is used to hold ledger accounts of those expenses of the company, which determine its net profit. Expenses like advertising, maintenance of vehicles, administrative expenses, etc., fall under this group.

Display of Group Account

You can display any account on the screen by selecting Display from the menu. You would be next given a choice to display any of the above mentioned accounts, the list of which comes on the screen. Please remember the account is just displayed here. So as not to allow you to alter anything no cursor is provided, since it is only display.

Alteration of Group Account

You can display any account on the screen by selecting Alter from the menu. You would be next given a choice to select any of the above mentioned accounts, the list of which comes on the screen.

Now you are given the account format with cursor for you to change any information. You can change Name of any Reserved Group, but its characteristics will remain the same.

Deletion of Group Account

You can delete a group by pressing Alt+D in the Group Alteration screen. Your confirmation would be sought from you before deleting any record in the form of Yes or No. Click Yes if you are very sure of deleting.

Please remember that System Generated Reserved Groups cannot be deleted. Also user created groups cannot be deleted if any child group and/or ledger have been placed under the group. Thus, if you wish to delete a group under which child group or ledger exists, you should move the related ledgers and child groups to other groups first, then you can delete it.

Buttons on the Group Screen

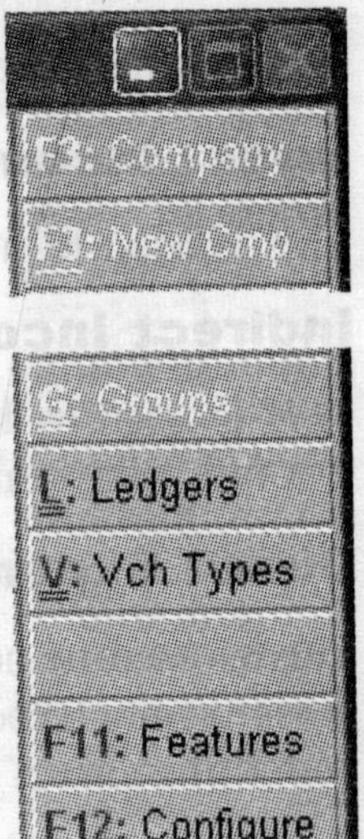

Following buttons are there on the side screen.

F3: Company

This button becomes active on selection of multiple companies. On clicking this button List of (selected) Companies is displayed to select the other company. In creation mode, you can Create a Group in another company you select from List of Companies upon pressing this button. On creation of one Group in the other Company, Tally brings back the previous Company to continue Group Creation for the first Company. In alteration mode, you can copy the group to a target company you select through this button.

F3: Company

This button becomes active in Display screen if multiple companies are selected, to enable to view Group of another company you select through this button.

G: Groups

This button appears in Alteration screen to alter position of group in report.

As per the requirements of the Company Law Board the groups of the accounts have been given an index value, according to which the groups are arranged in Tally. These groups with their index value are given here.

Name of group	*Index*
Capital Account	10
Loans (liability)	20
Current Liabilities	30
Fixed Assets	40
Investments	50
Current Assets	60
Branch / Divisions	70
Misc. Expenses (Assets)	80
Suspense Account	90
Reserves & Surplus	100
Bank OD Accounts	110
Secured Loans	120
Unsecured Loans	130
Duties & Taxes	140
Provisions	150
Sundry Creditors	160
Stock in hand	170
Deposits (Assets)	180
Loans Advances (Assets)	190
Sundry Debtors	200
Cash in hand	210
Bank Accounts	220
Sales Accounts	230
Purchase Account	240
Direct Income	250
Indirect Income	260
Direct Expenses	270
Indirect Expenses	280
Primary Groups (User Created)	500

L: Ledgers

These are actual account heads to which the transactions are identified. You make all your voucher entries in these accounts. As mentioned earlier, you have to classify all ledgers into groups. For most of the users, working with single ledger will suffice all their requirements. The advanced users can opt for working with multiple ledgers.

CREATING A LEDGER

You need to create ledgers for party/suppliers under the group Sundry Creditors for whom TDS has to be calculated automatically by the system.

The options Is TDS Applicable and the Deductee Type are available only for ledgers under the group Sundry Creditors.

You can either Create/Alter a ledger to specify your TDS account details.

Gateway of Tally > Accounts Info > Ledgers > Create

Various options of the screen are:

Name

Enter the Name of the account. You can provide the full name of the account. Tally fits it all in. Press Enter to move to the next field. Tally does not allow entry of duplicate names.

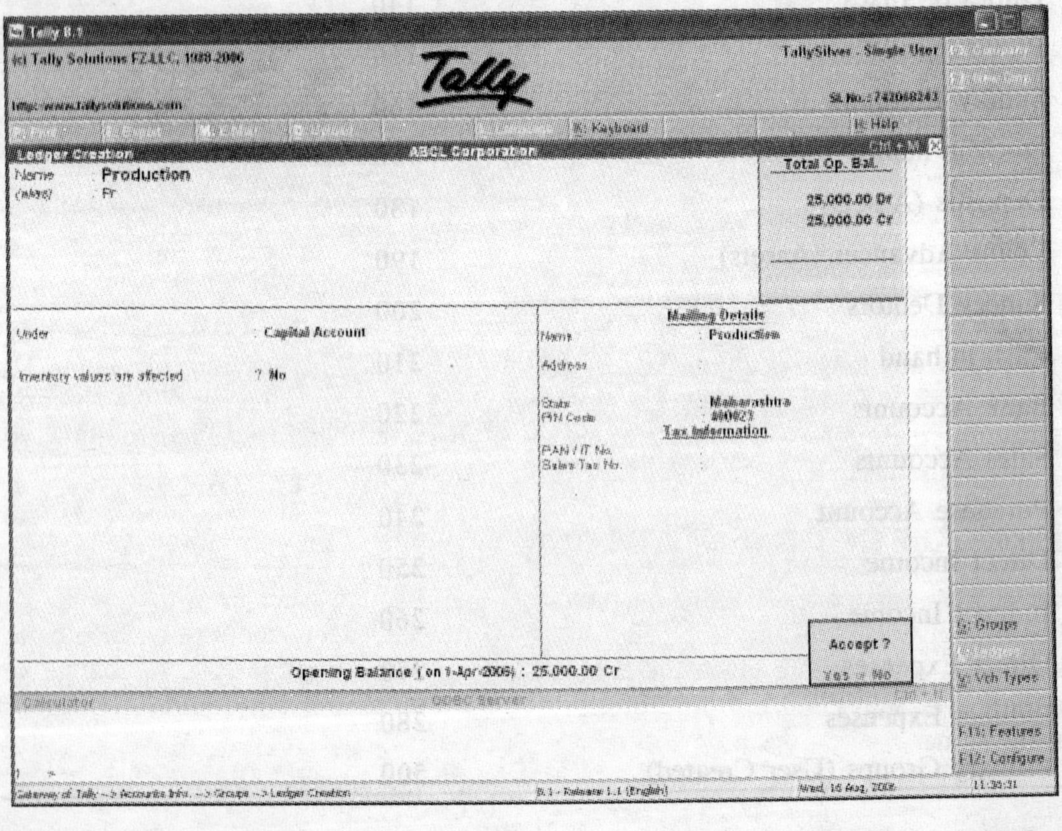

The uniqueness check is made here itself. Note that punctuation and other non-relevant information are ignored by Tally in its recognition of a name. Thus, CST, C.S.T. and C. S. T. are all considered as same. Tally converts the first letter of all relevant words to upper case, which helps you; speed up data entry. You need not bother about changing the case every time it is a different word.

Alias

Enter an alias name if required. You can access the Ledgers using the original name or the alias name.

Group

All accounts must be classified under their appropriate Groups. Select the Group under which the Ledger is created from the List of Groups. To create a new Group from this field press [ATL + C]. A Group is not important by itself, but because it controls the usage of Ledger accounts. A wrong classification would affect the treatment of the Ledger account in final statements and during voucher entry.

You can, alter a Ledger account to change its group classification at any time.

Opening Balance

If yours is an existing company whose books you are entering onto Tally, Opening Balance would be applicable in circumstances such as when the Ledger is an asset or a liability and if it has a balance in the account as on the date of beginning of books in Tally.

Tally recognises normal accounting principles of debit balances for Assets and credit balances for Liabilities. It accepts the reverse for obverse balances. Revenue accounts normally do not have balances. Tally, however, permits you to give balances even for such accounts - You may be transferring your books on to Tally in the middle of the year and may not have closed them in your earlier system. Hence, you may specify whether the balance is Debit or Credit. Simply D or C would suffice.

DISPLAY OF INDIVIDUAL LEDGER

You can display any ledger account on the screen by selecting Display from the menu. You would be next given a choice to display any of the ledger account, the list of which comes on the screen. Please remember the account is just displayed here. So as not to allow you to alter anything no cursor is provided, since it is only display.

ALTERATION OF GROUP ACCOUNT

You can display any ledger account on the screen by selecting Alter from the menu. You would be next given a choice to select any of the mentioned ledgers, the list of which comes on the screen. Now you are given the account format with cursor for you to change any information. You can change Name of any Reserved Group, but its characteristics will remain the same.

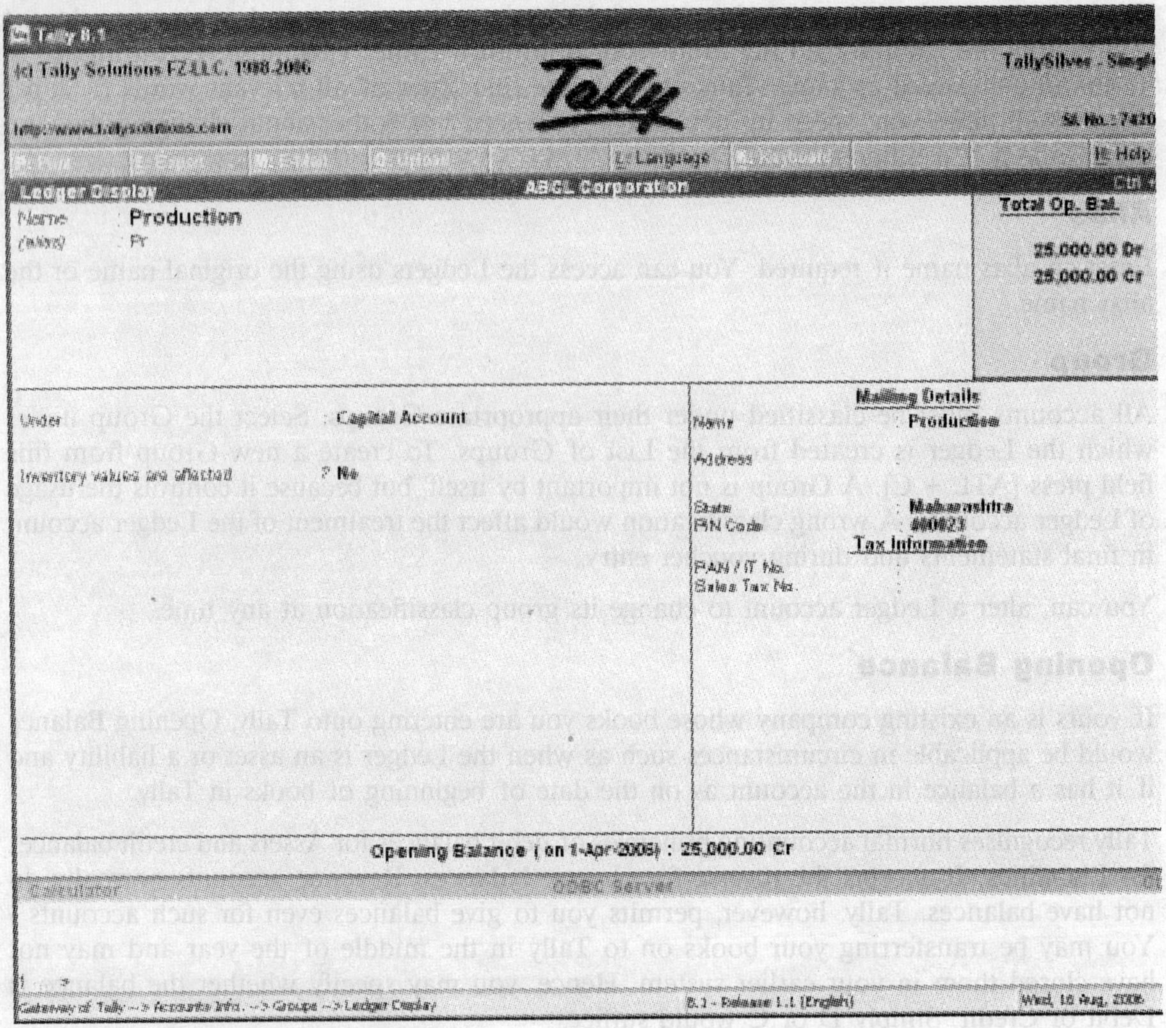

DELETION OF LEDGER

You can delete a ledger by pressing Alt+D in the Ledger Alteration screen. Your confirmation would be sought from you before deleting any record in the form of Yes or No. Click Yes if you are very sure of deleting.

However, if the ledger is transacted in any voucher, the message would not appear and you cannot delete the ledger.

CREATING MULTIPLE LEDGERS

Click at Create of the Multiple Ledger to create multiple ledgers.

On the next page, you would see the type of screen you would get for creating multiple ledger. This also allows you to set the following options.

Name of Group

Enter the name of the Group.

Under

If you select any group other than All Items in the Under Group field, then this column is filled in automatically with the selected Group name and the cursor skips this column. This speeds up data entry.

If you select All Items in the Under Group field, the cursor does not skip this field and allows you to enter the parent group of each of them.

To change individual group behaviour created using multiple groups, use 'single group/alter' option.

Buttons in Multiple Mode Group Creation

F3: Company

This button helps you to open a different company. In the creation mode, you can create groups in the other company. In alter mode, you can copy the information by accepting the

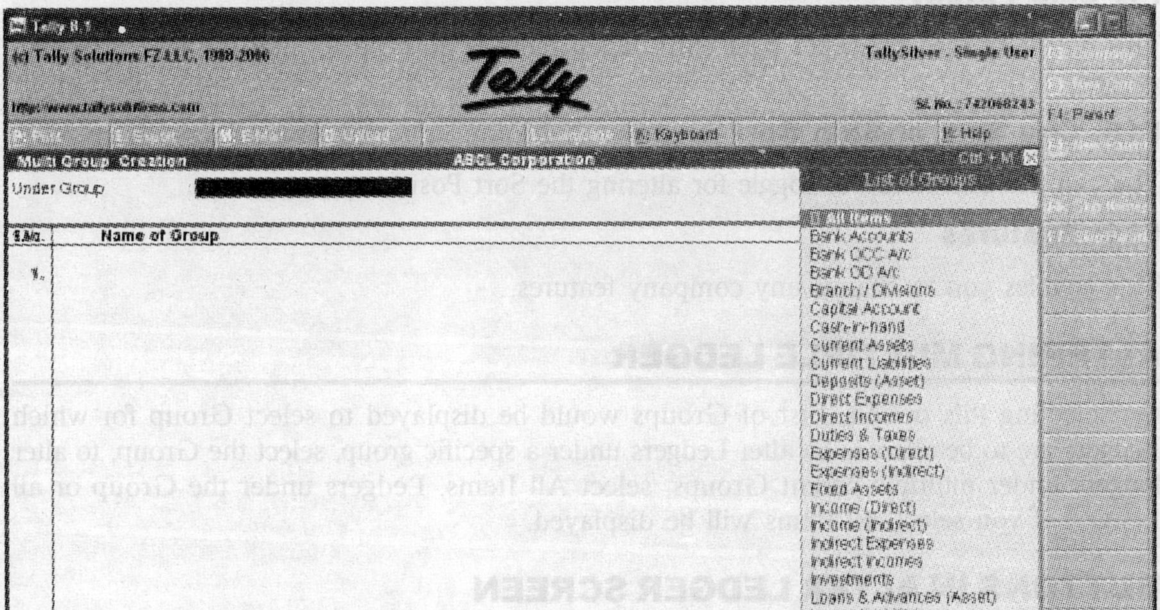

screen (enter or Ctrl+A). The old company's information remains. This feature is not available in Display mode.

Groups, Ledgers, Cost Categories, Cost Centres, Voucher Types, Currency, Budgets:

This button enables you to switch to the appropriate area without quitting from the current screen.

F4: Chg Parent

To change parent of the selected group, select the group from Names of Groups list.

For example, you are currently altering groups classified under Loans Liability and wish them all to be re-classified under 'Bank OCC A/c'. Instead of altering individual name, you can achieve this using F4:Chg Parent.

F4: New Parent

This allows you to quit from the current screen and modify a different group (relevant in Alteration/Display mode only). For example, you are currently altering groups classified under Loans Liability and now wish to ABANDON the current activity and alter groups under Bank OCC instead

F7: Skip Parent

This button is used for faster data entry when there is no need to alter the parent of sub-groups.

F10: Chg Sort or Skip Sort

You can use this button to toggle for altering the Sort Position

F11: Features

This enables you to change any company features.

ALTERING MULTIPLE LEDGER

On selecting this option, List of Groups would be displayed to select Group for which Ledgers are to be altered. To alter Ledgers under a specific group, select the Group, to alter ledgers under multiple parent Groups, select All Items. Ledgers under the Group or all Ledgers if you select All Items will be displayed.

BUTTONS IN ALTER LEDGER SCREEN

Following are the buttons on this screen.

F3: Company

To work with a different company. In the creation mode, you can create cost categories in the other company. In alter mode, you can copy the information by accepting the screen (<enter> or <Ctrl>+<A>). The old company's information remains. Not available in Display mode.

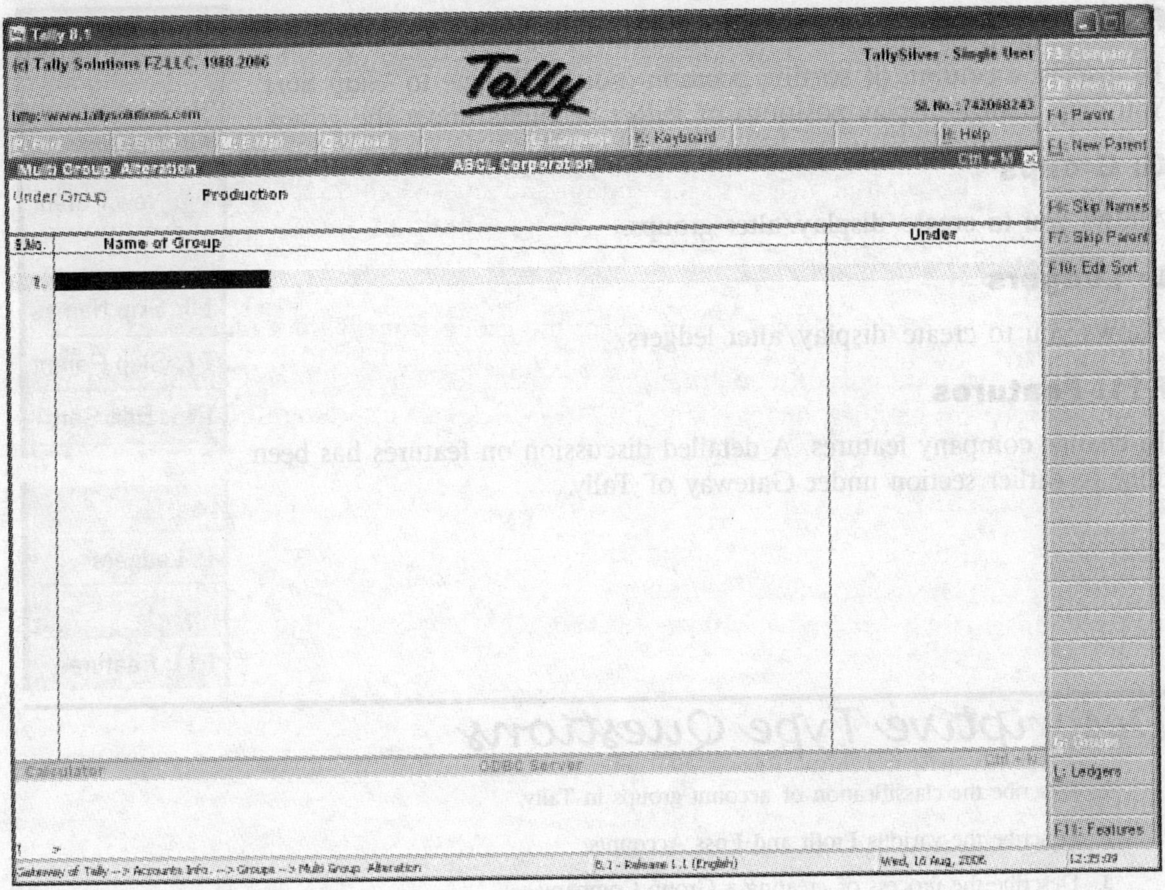

F3: New Cmp

To work on the same report of another company. Available only in display mode.

F4: Parent

To move the cursor to the field 'Under Group'

F4: New Parent

To bring up the list of Groups to select a new parent Group.

F6: Skip Names

For faster data entry when you do not need to the names of ledgers. The cursor will not go to that column. Toggle to 'Edit names'.

F7: Skip Parent

For faster data entry when you do not need to alter the parent Group. The cursor will not go to the column 'Under'. Toggle to 'Edit Parent'.

F10: Edit Sort

To display a column of sorting position indices. Toggle to 'Skip Sort'. You may change display positions of ledger accounts under the group.

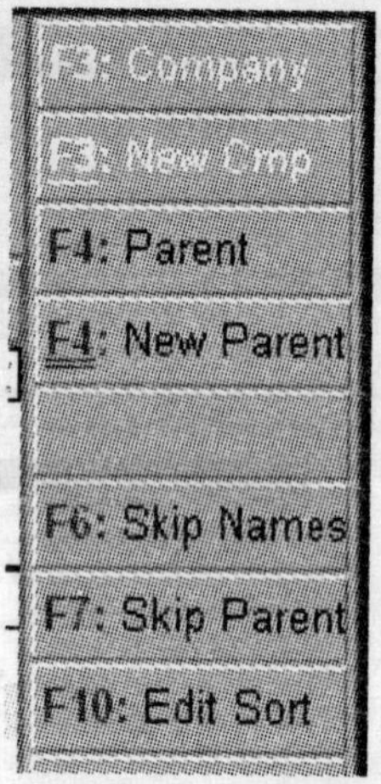

G: Groups

Allows you to create/display/alter groups.

L: Ledgers

Allows you to create/display/alter ledgers.

F11: Features

To change company features. A detailed discussion on features has been done in earlier section under Gateway of Tally.

Descriptive Type Questions

1. Describe the classification of account groups in Tally.
2. Describe the various Profit and Loss Accounts.
3. Describe the process of creating a Group Company.
4. How would you Display, Alter, Delete a Group account?
5. Describe the function of various buttons on the Group account screen.
6. How would you create a ledger in Tally?
7. How would you Display, Alter, Delete a Ledger from Tally?
8. How would you create a Multiple Ledger?
9. Describe the various options on Multiple Ledger screen.
10. Describe the function of various buttons on the Multiple Ledger screen.
11. Describe the various buttons on Alter ledger screen.
12. How would you set the credit limits?

3 Creating Inventory Masters

CREATING INVENTORY MASTERS

The different inventory information that you would provide to Tally by way of masters can be given by selecting the following options, Master, Inventory Info.

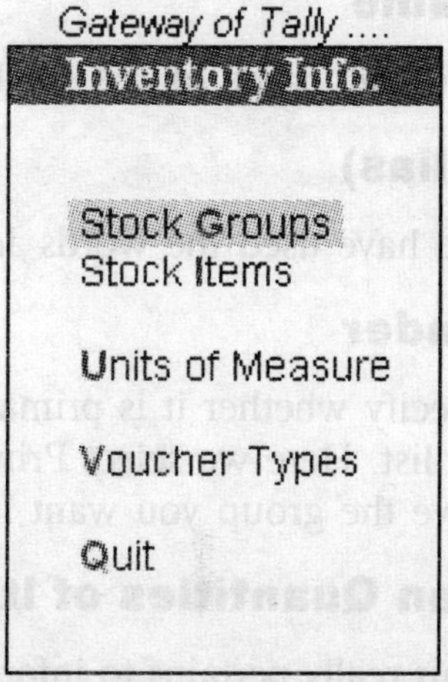

Various items on the screen are:

Stock Groups

Stock items can be grouped together under Stock Group to reflect their classification based on some community. Grouping would enable easy location and reporting of stock items in statements. Hence, items of a particular brand can be grouped together so that you can extract stock of all items of that brand.

Stock Items

Like Ledgers Stock Items are the primary inventory entity. You will use stock items while recording their receipts and issues. This is lowest level of information about your inventory. Each item that is required to be accounted for, needs to be created.

In fact, you will create a stock ledger account for each item and Tally calls this account 'Stock Items'.

Unit of Measure

Each stock has its own way of measuring. So you can set unit of measurement for each stock from here.

Voucher Types

You can set options for various types of vouchers.

Let us see each one of them.

STOCK GROUPS

For creating this press the following:

Gateway of Tally >>Inventory Info>>Stock Groups

You can create sub-groups of Stock Groups for deeper analysis

CREATING A STOCK GROUP

For creating a stock group, press the following:

Gateway of Tally>Inventory Info>Stock Groups>Single>Create

This dialog box, has the following information to be filled in.

Name

Give the name of the stock group. Here we wish to create a group Juices.

(alias)

We have used the words Jc, you can use something based on your name.

Under

Specify whether it is primary group or a sub-group of another group. Select from the pop-up list. Here we select Primary from the list. Use Alt + C to create a parent if you do not have the group you want in the list.

Can Quantities of Items be ADDED?

This really pertains to information on the stock items that you would create under this stock

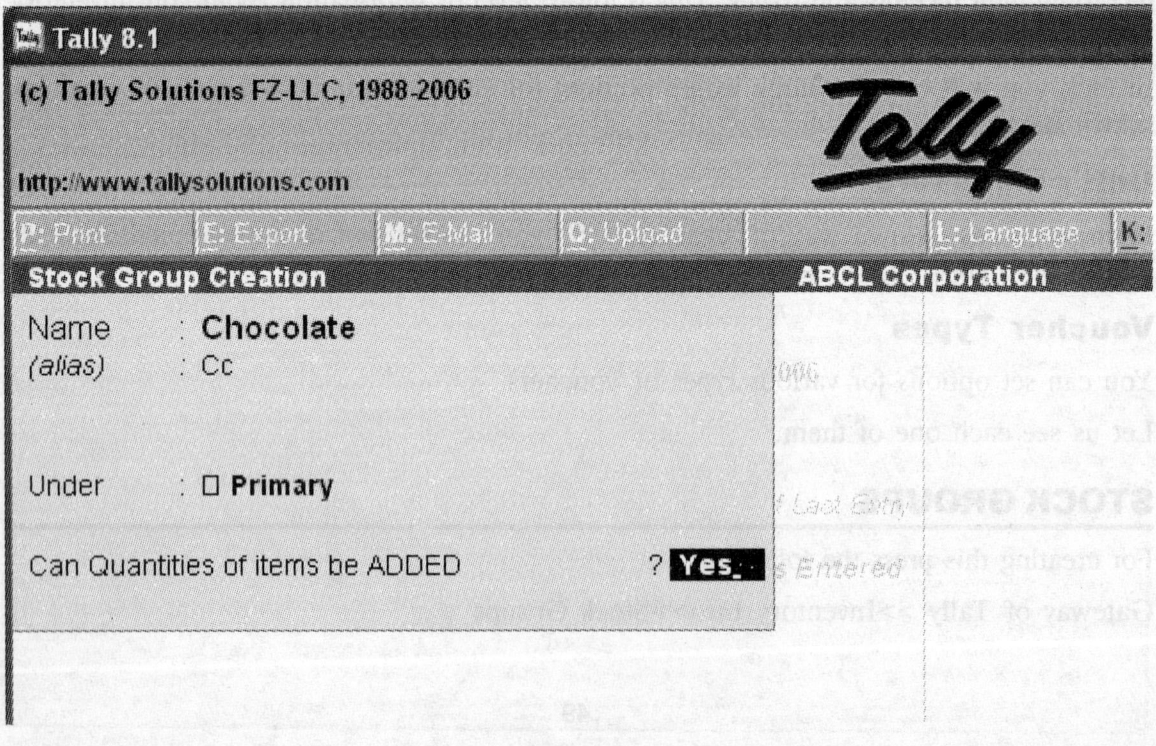

group. The stock items created under the group should have similar units to be 'addable'. It is, possibly, easier to set it to No initially and later set it to Yes on assessing the item units in the group.

CREATING MULTIPLE STOCK GROUPS

For this press the following buttons.

Gateway of Tally>Inventory Info>Stock Groups>Multiple Stock Group>Create

Select the parent group under which you want the new groups to fall. If you select any group other than 'All Items', e.g., Chocolates, you indicate that all new groups being created at this time will fall under the group 'Chocolates'. In that case, the column 'Under' is filled up automatically with 'Chocolates' and your cursor skips this column. This speeds up data entry.

Selecting 'All Items' allows you to specify the parent of each new group created and would give flexibility and the cursor moves to the column field 'Under' for the parent of each new group.

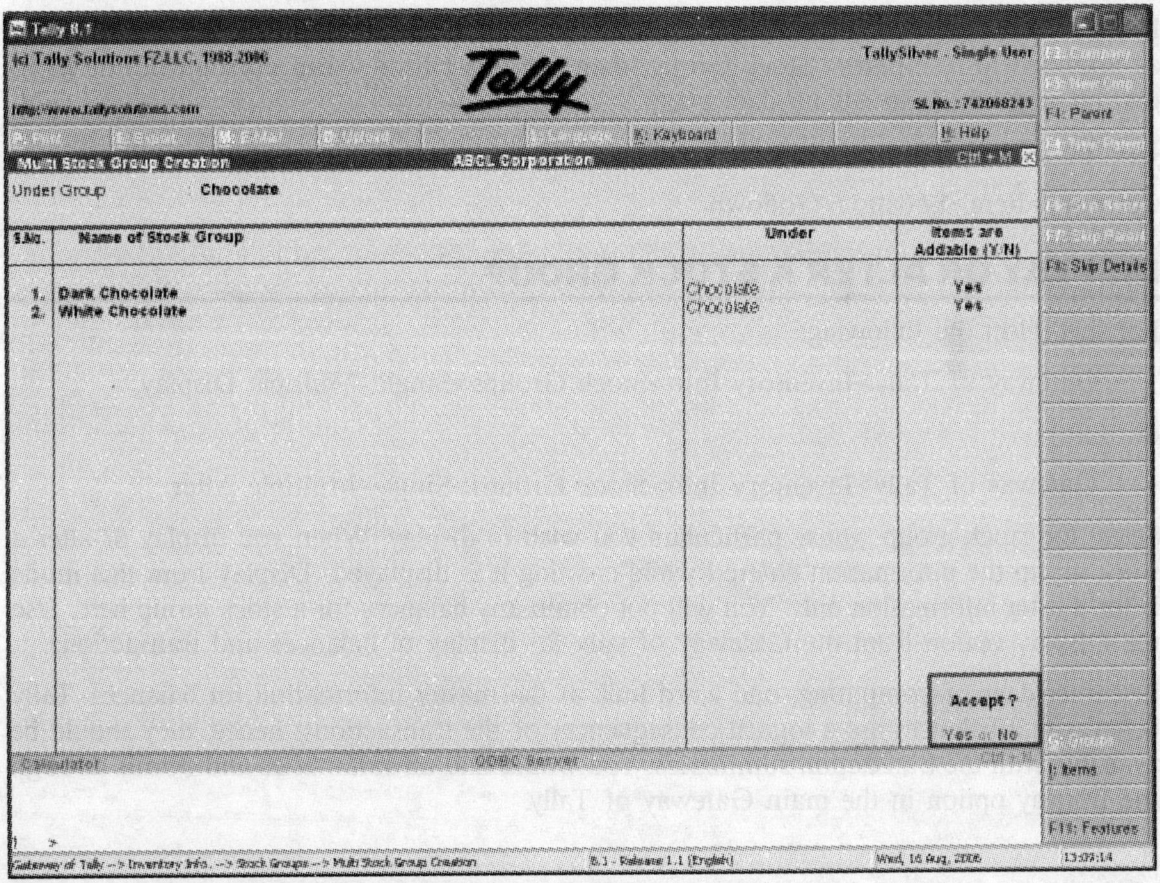

Name

Give the name of the stock group. In this case, we have give Orange Juice and Apple Juice.

Under

Since we selected 'Juices' in Under Group, we specify the parent here.

Items are Addable? (Y/N)

As explained under Single Stock Group Creation, this really pertains to information on the stock items that you would create under this stock group. It is, possibly, easier to set it to Yes initially and later set it to No on accessing the item units in the group.

Buttons

F4: Parent

To change the parent 'Under Group' when you may have created sub-groups under it. The change effects all the sub-groups created under the parent and they would belong to the new parent.

F8: Skip Details

If the answer to the question, "Items are addable' is to remain the default, i.e., remain same as Specified for the parent Stock Group, then use this button. Your cursor will not go to that column which speeds up data entry.

Use the following buttons to switch to the respective masters for creation.

Category>Item>Location/Godown

DISPLAY OR ALTER A STOCK GROUP

For this select the following:

Gateway of Tally>Inventory Info>Stock Groups>Single/Multiple Display

or

Gateway of Tally>Inventory Info>Stock Groups>Single/Multiple Alter

Select the stock group whose particulars you wish to display. When you display or alter a stock group the information entered while creating it is displayed. Display from this mode is for master information only. You will not obtain any balances for a stock group here. Use the Display option from the Gateway of tally for display of balances and transactions.

In earlier days of computing, one word look at the master information for balances. Tally believes that balances are a logical consequences of the transactions; hence, they should be available with the transaction summaries. You would find all summaries and details through the Display option in the main Gateway of Tally.

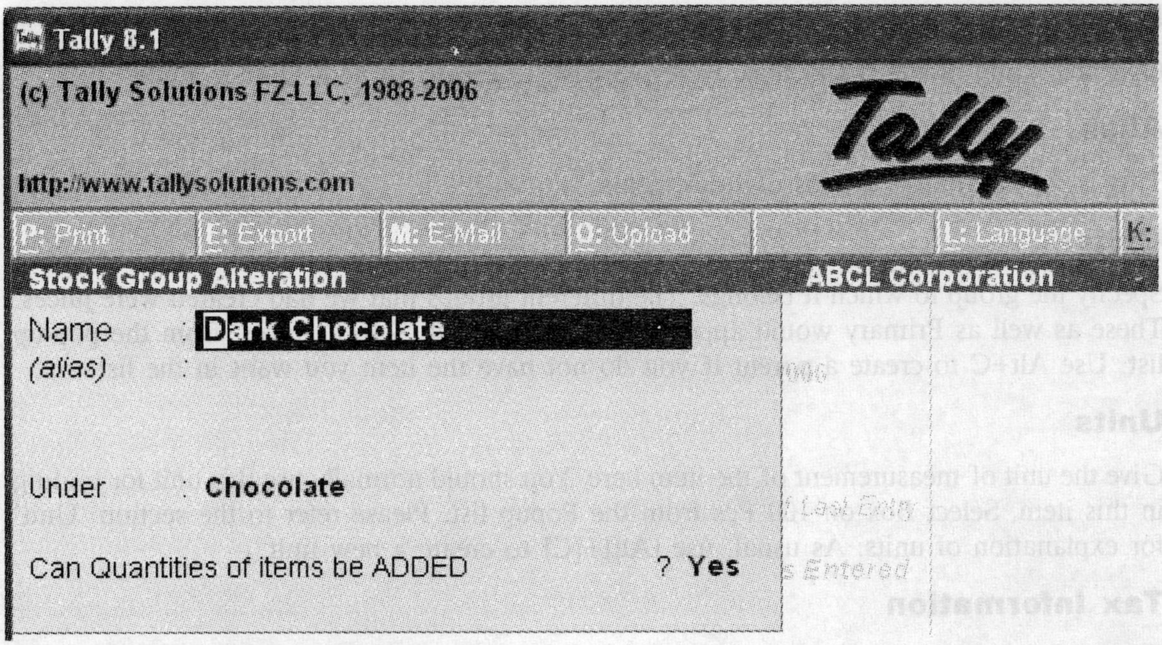

DELETE A STOCK GROUP

You can delete a stock group only if it does not have any children under it. The children could be stock group or stock item or both.

For this select the following:

Gateway of Tally>Inventory Info>Stock Groups>Single>Alter

Press [ALT]+[D] to delete the stock group.

You cannot delete a stock group from multiple mode.

STOCK ITEMS

For this select the following:

Gateway of Tally>Inventory Info>Stock Items

What is a Stock Item?

A stock item needs no explanation. However, what needs to be explained is how Tally uses it. Tally uses the phrase to include what traditional accountant would call a stock ledger account. All the stock items together would make up the stock ledger. So to display a stock ledger, display the stock items. You can draw a parallel to ledgers in accounting for stock items in inventory.

CREATING A STOCK ITEM

This gives rise to a dialog box as shown next. You have to fill the following information.

Name

Give the name of the stock item. Here we wish to create an item Orange Juice.

Alias

This is for alternative names of stock items.

Under

Specify the group to which it belongs. The different groups that we had created were juices. These as well as Primary would appear in the pop-up list. Select 'Juices' from the pop-up list. Use Alt+C to create a parent if you do not have the item you want in the list.

Units

Give the unit of measurement of the item here. You should normally use this unit for trading in this item. Select Box on 100 Pcs from the Popup list. Please refer to the section 'Unit' for explanation of units. As usual, use [Alt]+[C] to create a new unit.

Tax Information

Give the rate of tax applicable for the item. The rate specified here would be picked up when invoicing, if you selected the method of calculation as 'Tax Based on Item Rate' for your relevant accounting ledger account. Typically, this accounting ledger account would be 'VAT' Account' under the Group 'Duties and Taxes'. In such cases, the VAT or duty in invoice entry will be automatically calculated.

CREATING MULTIPLE STOCK ITEMS

For this press the following:

Gateway of Tally>Inventory Info>Multiple Stock Items>Create

This leads to the dialog box shown here. You have to fill the following information in it.

Under Group

Select the parent group under which you want the new items to fall. If you select any group other than 'Chocolates'. In this case, the column 'Under' is filled up automatically with 'Chocolates' and your cursor skips this column. This speeds up data entry. Selecting 'Juices' allows you to specify the parent of each new item created and would give flexibility and the cursor moves to the column field 'Under' for the parent of each new item.

S.Number

The serial number is automatically filled up.

Name of the Item

Give the name of the stock item.

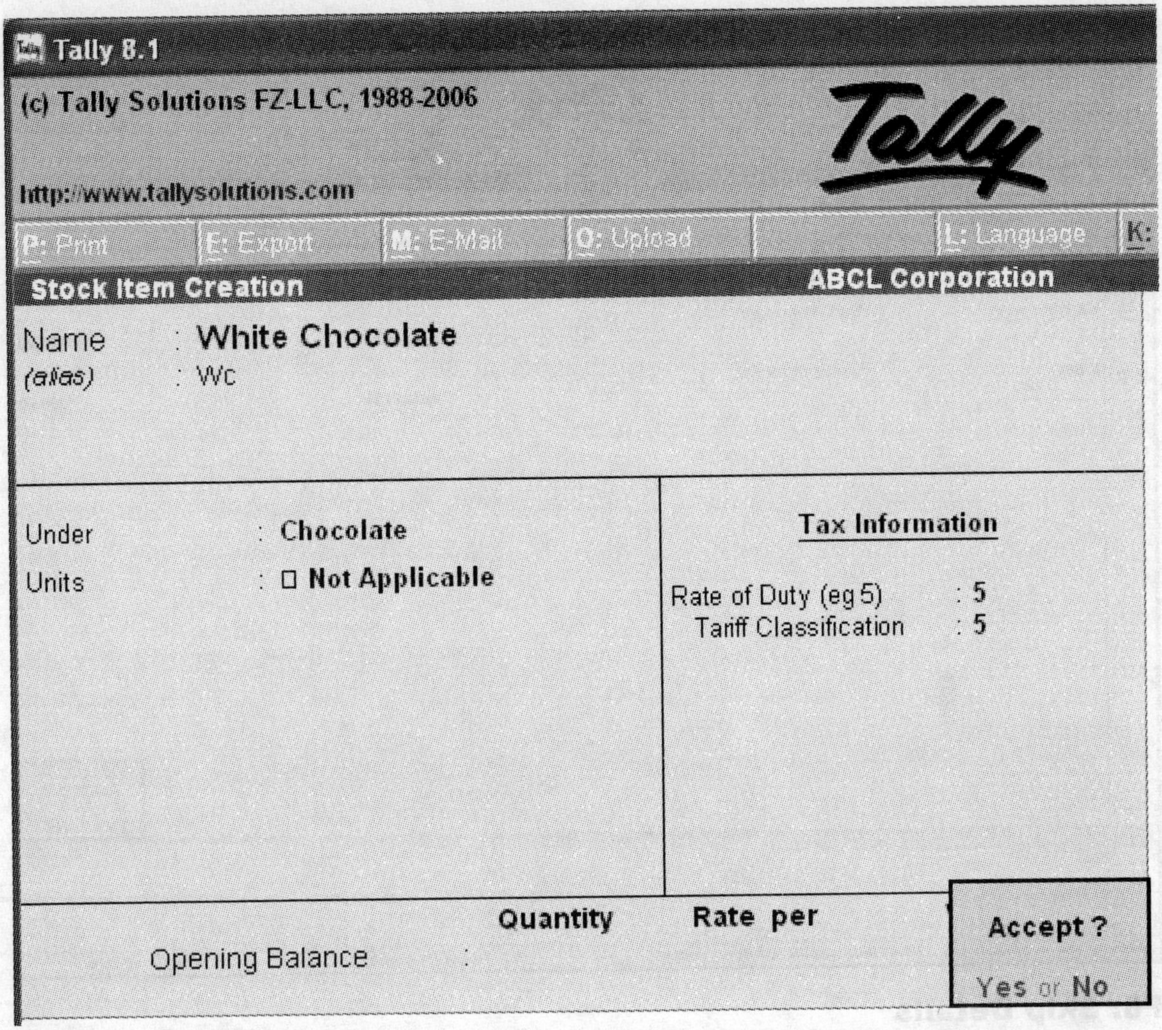

Under

Since we selected 'Dark Chocolate' in Under Item, we specify the parent here. We have picked up the parent from the group list. Use [Alt]+[C] to create a new parent.

Opening Balance

If you already have stock of this item at the time of creating its account in Tally, give its balance particulars, i.e., quantity, rate, unit and account.

Buttons

Various buttons under this screen are:

F4: Parent

To change the parent 'Under Group' when you may have created items under it. The change affects all the items created under the parent and they would belong to the new parent.

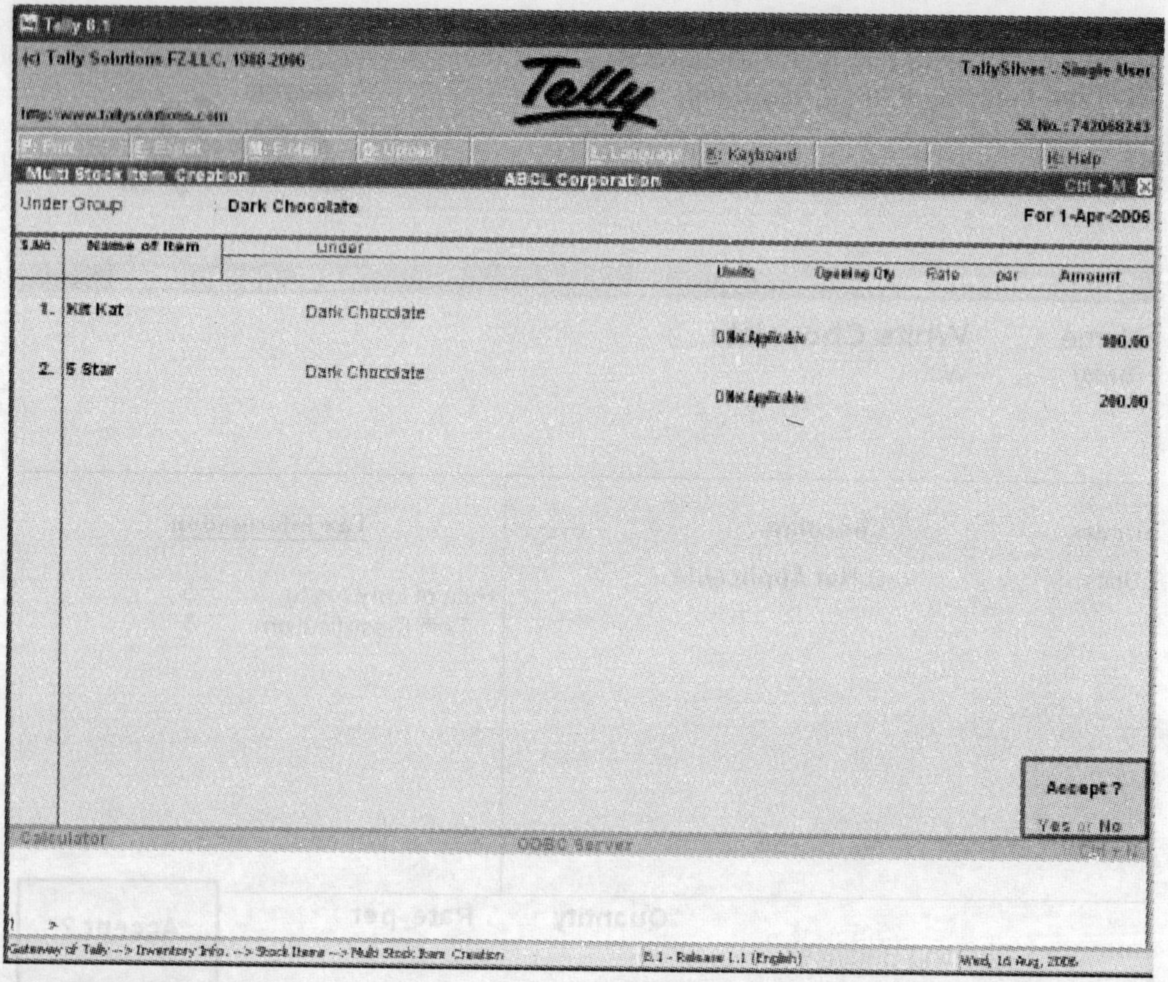

F8: Skip Details

To avoid the cursor going to the opening quantities fields, use this button. It toggles with Edit Details, which allows to entry of opening details.

F9: Skip Category

To avoid the cursor going to the Category field, use this button. It toggles with Edit Category, which allows entry of Category details.

Display or Alter a Stock Item

For this select the following:

Gateway of Tally>Inventory Info>Stock Items>Single/Multiple Display or Alter

Select the stock item whose particulars you wish to display or alter. When you display or alter a stock item, the information entered while creating it is displayed.

Delete a Stock Item

You can delete a stock item only if it has not been used form transaction entry.

For this press the following:

Gateway of Tally>Inventory Info.>Stock Items>SingleStock Item>Alter

Press [Alt] + [D] to delete the Stock Item. You cannot delete a Stock Item from multiple mode.

ADVANCED STOCK ITEM CREATION

We shall assume that all the advanced features of Inventory have been activated under [F12]: Configuration and [F11] Company Features. This section deals with the additional fields you would input during creation of a Stock Item. If you do not find a field that you are looking for, or if you want to remove some or all the extra fields, check configuration and/ or company features. Usually, you will be able to configure the information to your requirements.

For this press the following:

Gateway of Tally>Inventory Info>Stock Items>Single>Create

The additional information are:

Name

Specify the name of the Stock Item.

Alias

You can give aliases for the part number. There may be situations where, the manufacturer specifies his Part No., but you understand it better by its Bin Card number allotted to it.

Part Number

This is optional. Enter the Part No. of the item being created, for easy identification. (In certain industries, (e.g. Automobiles), various parts are better identified by their part numbers). You can alternatively use this field for Bin Card No., Code No., etc.

Description

Enter the description of the Stock Item that would appear in your invoices. This is optional.

Remarks

Remarks help to identify the product and its applications. You can give some particulars of the Stock Item created. When you post a query for the stock of this item, remarks help to decide if the item is suitable for a particular requirement.

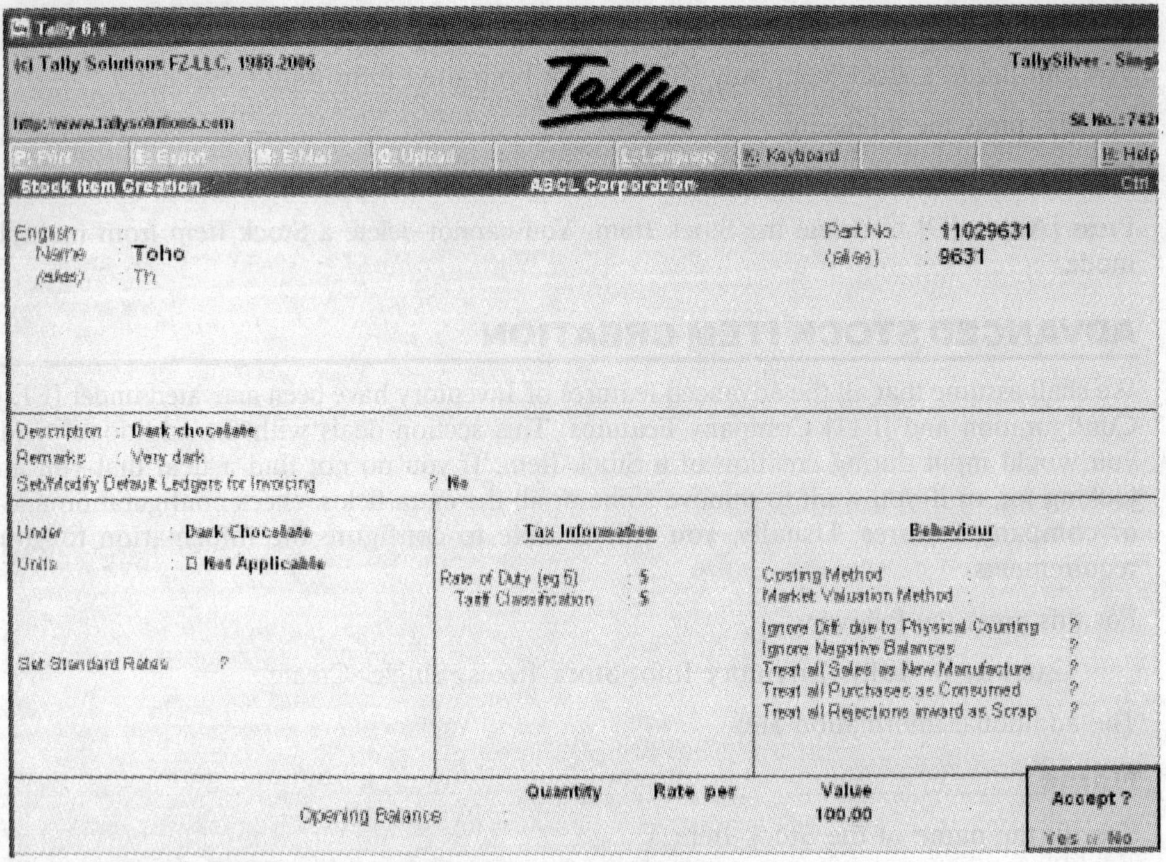

Set /Modify Default Ledgers for Invoicing

You can define the default ledger (usually the sales account), during alteration or creation of a Stock Item that will automatically be credited when you invoice the item.

Under

Select the group from the List of Groups. If you do not want to categorize it under any particular group that you created, choose Primary.

Press Alt + C to create a parent Group from this field.

Units

Give the unit of measurement of the item here. The item would be traded using this unit of measurement.

Alternate Units

This is another unit, apart from the main unit, which you can use for the Stock Item. This is particularly useful when you need to handle different units at different times. For example, you buy Data Cables in pieces but sell in packets of 5 pieces each. For alternate units, you are asked to give a conversion factor (e.g. 5) so that a link is maintained between the two.

What you give here is simply a conversion factor that comes up as default during voucher entry. You may specify a different factor during voucher entry.

Maintain in Batches?

Set this option to Yes if you want to maintain the batch information of Stock Items. The batch does not destroy itself after it is disposed; it remains on records and is quite like a Ledger in behavior. For example, Stock Item – Cloth, Batches – red, white, and blue. You can extract all sales of blue cloth at any given point of time.

Use Components BoM?

This has been dealt with in Bill of Materials section under Voucher Entry. It is however pertinent to mention here that BoM should be used only for items that have sub-assemblies or are manufactured.

Set Standard Rates?

Set this to Yes, if you want to specify standard purchase and sales rates for the item. Standard rates enable the valuation of inventory at standard purchase or standard sales price. Moreover, these prices come up by default during voucher entry (you may choose to override them if required). The standards are effective from the specified dates and they continue to be used at these rates until the next date, where the standard rate changes.

UNITS OF MEASURE

You will need to create units of measure for stock items. These can be simple units such as numbers, meters, kilograms, pieces or compound units, e.g., box, where, say, one box equals ten pieces.

Create a Unit of Measure

For this press the following:

Gateway of Tally>Inventory Info>Units of Measure>Create

This gives rise to a dialog box which has the following information to be filled in.

Type

Symbols are of two types: Simple and Compound. Simple units are considered as started by you and Tally just checks for duplication and nothing else. If you wish to give unit symbol that are single and not a combination of other units, select Simple. Tally defaults to Simple and if you want to change to compound, use Backspace from the Symbol field and select compound from the popup list.

Symbol

Give the symbol of the unit, e.g., No., Mtrs. This symbol given by you is used in all displays and printouts. We give the symbol 'no' for numbers.

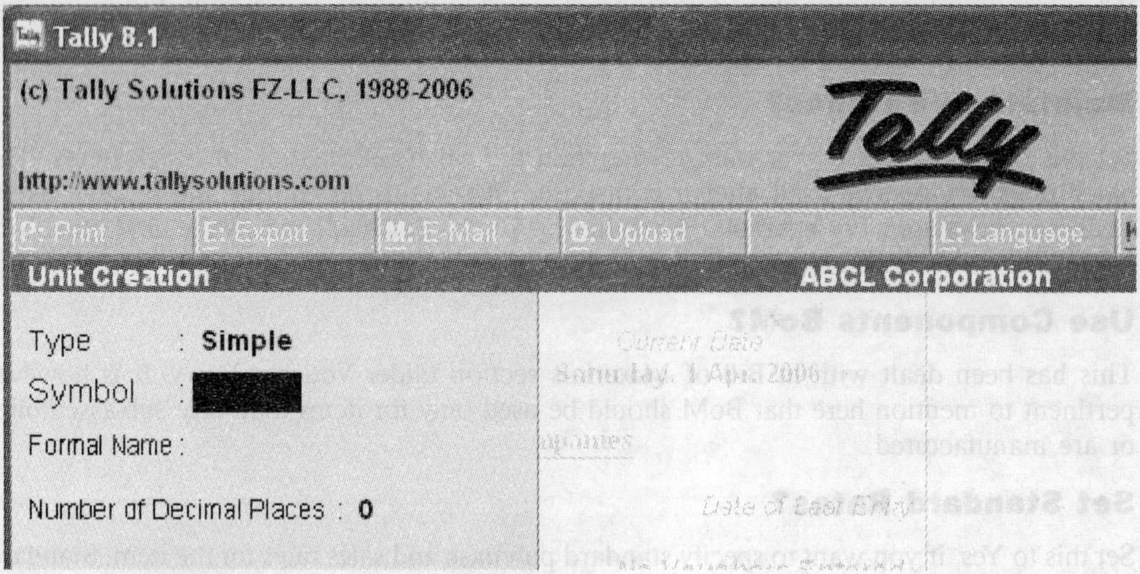

Formal Name

Give the formal name of the symbol. This explains the symbol, which is also used during consolidation of data of different companies where the symbols might be the same but are assigned to different Units.

The formal name will be used to match them. Here we type Number as the formal name for the symbol 'no'.

No. of Decimal Places

If the unit will be used in fractions, say for a kilogram you may have to use grams as well, give the number of decimal places. For kilograms, you would give 3 decimal places to accommodate upto 999 grams. Hence, a measure 1 kilogram 865 grams will be 1.865 kilograms. For units like numbers, you do not normally want a decimal place and you can specify 0 in such cases. You can specify 0 to 4 decimal places.

Descriptive Type Questions

1. How would you create the various stock items in Tally?
2. How would you create stock groups?
3. What are multiple stock groups?
4. What is Bill of Material?
5. How would you create a Unit of Measurement?
6. What are the different type of price lists that can be created in Tally?

4 Entering Accounts Vouchers

VOUCHERS THE MAIN INPUTS

Accounting is based on the vouchers that make. They form the main input for the accounting both for manual as well as for the computerized accounting. The output is the form of Reports. Tally recognizes a number of vouchers which can be used to enter data. First we would deal with accounts vouchers and then with the inventory vouchers.

VOUCHER TYPES

Tally is pre-programmed with a variety of accounting, each designed to perform a different job. The standard vouchers which includes inventory vouchers too are:

- Payment Voucher
- Receipt Voucher
- Contra Voucher
- Sales Voucher
  - ➢ Sales Orders
  - ➢ Sales Vouchers/Invoices
  - ➢ Delivery Notes
  - ➢ Rejection In
- Purchase Voucher
  - ➢ Purchase Orders
  - ➢ Purchase Vouchers
  - ➢ Goods Receipt Notes
  - ➢ Rejection Quit
- Journal Voucher
  - ➢ Credit Notes
  - ➢ Debit Notes
  - ➢ Journal
- Memo Voucher

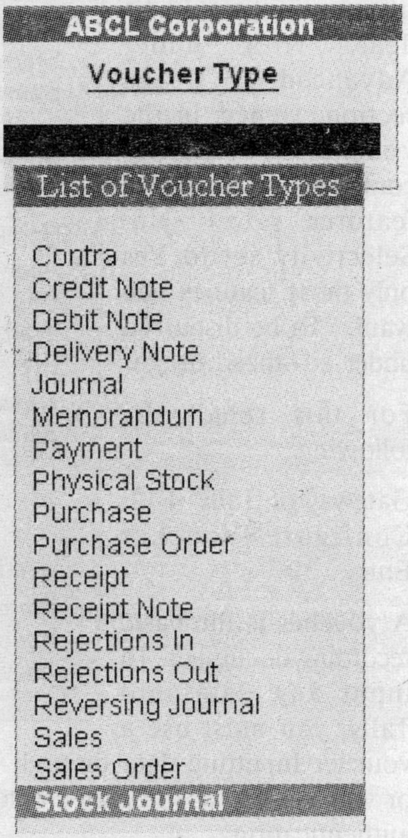

- ➢ Reversing Journal
- Stock Journal
- Physical Stock

You can enter these vouchers to suit your company and also create new ones. For example, if you wish to distinguish between cash and bank payments you can create vouchers to do this. Let us start with a simple voucher.

SIMPLE VOUCHER ENTRY

You should set the configuration for voucher entry so that only those features that you require appear when entering vouchers. We shall first learn simple vouchers, for accounting and inventory. Extra information would be dealt with under Advanced Usage section. Hence, in the voucher entry configuration set all the features to No. Selectivity set to Yes only those features you want. (To be discussed under advanced usage)

Accounting Vouchers

Skip Date field in Create Mode (faster entry!)	? Yes
Use Single Entry mode for Pymt/Rcpt/Contra	? Yes
Show Inventory Details	? Yes
Show Table of Bill Details for Selection	? Yes
Show Bill-wise Details	? Yes
Expand into multiple lines	? Yes
Show Ledger Current Balances	? Yes
Show Balances as on Voucher Date	? Yes
Use Payment/Receipt as Contra	? Yes
Allow Cash Accounts in Journals	? Yes
Use Cr/Dr instead of To/By during entry	? Yes
Warn on Negative Cash Balance	? Yes
Pre-Allocate Bills for Payment/Receipt	? Yes
Allow Expenses/Fixed Assets in Purchase Vouchers	? No
Allow Income Accounts in Sales Vouchers	? No

Inventory Vouchers

Use Ref. Number in Stock Journal	? No
Warn on Negative Stock Balance	? Yes
Honor Expiry Dates usage for Batches	? Yes
Show Balances as on Voucher Date	? Yes

For this select the following:

Gateway of Tally>F12: Configure>Voucher Entry

A voucher is the basic recording document. To input any data into Tally, you must use a voucher Inputting data through the voucher entry mode may be called created a voucher or voucher entry. You may create a voucher on-line on Tally and print it for hard copy and authentication.

THE VOUCHER ENTRY SCREEN

Here are the basic entries that you would be making while entering data into vouchers. Some vouchers may require additional information.

The Main Voucher Entry Area

This is where you enter your transaction. This screen contains fields for date, ledger name and amount as well as additional pop-up screens that are dependent upon your voucher configuration.

Direct Commands Area

Displays the commands you type into this area and the current version of Tally, is limited to calculator functions.

Button Toolbar

Displays buttons that provide quick interaction with Tally. Only buttons relevant to the current task will be visible.

Mouse Conventions

While working with Tally, please use the following conventions:

To	*Action*
Click	Press the left mouse button
double-click	Press and release the left mouse button twice, without moving the mouse pointer off the item
Choose	Position the mouse pointer on the item and click the left mouse button
Select	Position the mouse pointer on the item and double-click the left mouse button.
Press	Use the keys on the keyboard in the combination shown

Switching between Screen Areas

On selecting Voucher Entry from the Gateway of Tally, you are taken to the main voucher entry area. However, you may toggle between this and the Direct Commands/Calculator area at the bottom of the screen, by pressing [Ctrl] + [N] or [Ctrl] + [M] as indicated on the screen.

The active area of the screen is highlighted by a green bar. [Ctrl] + [N] to go to the Calculator/Direct commands area and [Ctrl] + [M] for the voucher entry area.

Use calculator by [ALT] + [C] when in amount field.

HOW TO ENTER VOUCHERS

You should have gone through the immediately preceding section for the concept of Tally vouchers. Different vouchers may be set up differently through the Voucher Types master maintenance. Hence, what appears in the voucher screen depends upon the voucher configuration, company features and the voucher type settings.

Gateway of Tally>Voucher Entry

The default voucher entry screen that is displayed the very first time you opt for it is the Payment Voucher. You do not need to get out of this screen for other vouchers. Simply switch the vouchers using the Button Bar or Function keys.

The screens for entering accounting vouchers are all very similar. Let us consider a simple payment voucher screen, as shown here.

Type of Voucher

You need to check, whether you are using the right voucher for the transaction. You change the voucher type by selecting the new type from the button bar. In some cases, Sales, Purchase and Journal as well as where you have created your own voucher types, e.g., under Payment, Tally will display a List of Vouchers for the type you select, from which you make a further choice.

Voucher Number

Tally will enter this for you if you have set-up the voucher type to do it. If it is to be entered manually, do so. There are basically 3 options of numbering the vouchers.

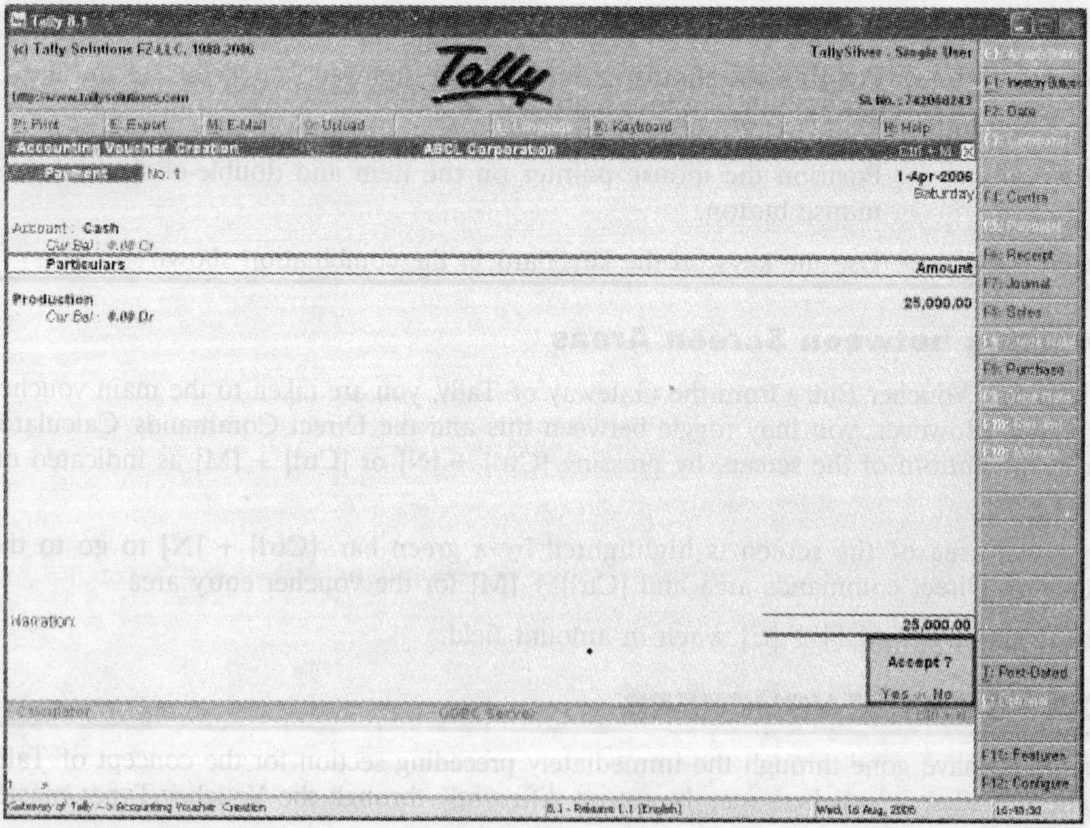

Automatic: Select for system-generated incremental numbering. On selecting it, you have to further specify:

Starting Number: Give starting number, normally 1, for the first voucher. You can restart number every month or year or continue the same for ever.

Width of Numerical Part: To get aligned look in Reports, specify maximum width.

Prefill with zero: Say Yes to fill-up the numbers with zeros to make up the width you enter at width of numerical part. No will leave the space blank.

Manual: Select manual to input Voucher Numbers during Voucher Entry.

Prevent Duplicates: Say Yes to trap if you enter an existing Voucher Number.

None: When you do not wish any Voucher Numbering, select None.

Reference (Not Available for Receipt and Payment Vouchers)

You can enter a reference such as Purchase Order Number or Invoice Number.

Date of Voucher

The date of the voucher you are entering at the top-right of the Voucher Creation screen. The date is taken initially from the Gateway of Tally Current Date and you may need to change it frequently to ensure vouchers are entered with the date you want. You change the date using the F2: Date button on the button bar.

Particulars – To/By or Dr/Cr

Tally defaults To/By but this can be changed to Dr and Cr by selecting F12: Configure in the Voucher Creation screen. Tab down to Use Cr/Dr instead of To/By during entry and type Yes. Each voucher line displays a prompt of Dr or By for debit entries and Cr To for credits. Depending on the voucher type, Tally selects either Dr or Cr for the first prompt, which you cannot change. Thereafter, you can change the prompt (if necessary) by typing over it with a D or C.

Particulars – Ledger Name and Amount

After To/By or Dr/Cr, you enter the ledger names and the debit and credit amounts. To select a ledger, type the first letter of its name (either case) and Tally displays a List of Ledger Accounts (the ledgers starting with the typed letter are highlighted). Only ledgers suitable for the voucher type are displayed. As you continue typing, the highlights reduce until a match is found.

The first ledger name prompt depends upon the voucher type. For example, in Payment Voucher, you are expected to debit first, a personal account like a creditor or a nominal account like Rent. Hence you are not allowed to center Cash or Bank as that would denote money received. (In the special case where in the Voucher Configuration you have activated the option Allow Payment/Receipt as Contra you are permitted to do so).

Likewise, in a Sales Voucher, you must first debit a personal account name like a customer and not a nominal account name. When you select the ledger, the current balance is displayed (if this option has been configured). When you enter the amount, the revised current balance is shown. After selecting the next ledger, Tally suggests the balancing amount as the value to enter, which may be accepted or typed over. You cannot complete the voucher entry until the debits equal the credits.

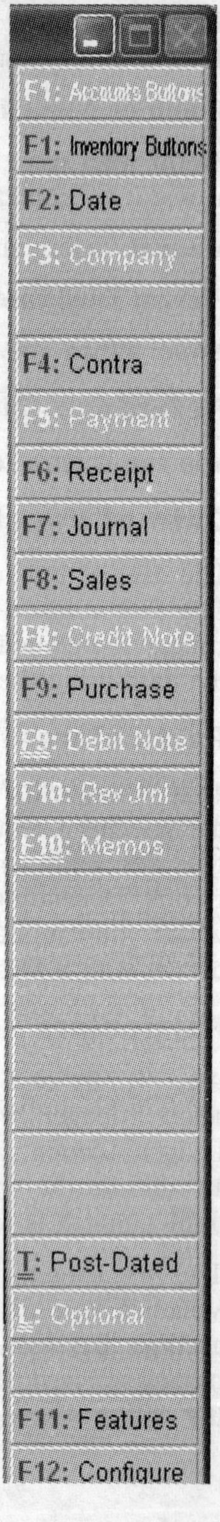

Narration

Here you type whatever is appropriate for the transaction. You can have a separate narration for each line of particulars, if you configure the voucher in that way.

Once you accept the data, Tally presents another blank data entry screen.

BUTTONS IN A TYPICAL ENTRY SCREEN

F2: Date

Use this button to change the date of the voucher.

F3: Comany

This would allow you to switch to another loaded company and enter a voucher in it. Therefore, you can, almost simultaneously enter vouchers for more than one company.

F4: Contra

To create a Contra Voucher

F5: Payment

To create a Payment Voucher

F6: Receipt

To create a Receipt Voucher

F7: Journal

This is split into Journal, Debit Notes and Credit Notes

F8: Sales

To create Sales Voucher/Debit Note Voucher

F8: Credit Note

To create a Cebit Note Voucher

F9: Purchase

To create Purchase Voucher Voucher

F9: Debit Note

To create Debit Note Voucher

F10: Rev Jml

To create Reverse Journal Voucher

F10: Memos

To create Memorandum Voucher

T: Post Dated

To mark the current voucher post dated.

L: Optional

To mark the current voucher optional. Toggles with Regular

F11: Features

To change Company Features.

F12: Configure

To check the accuracy of the voucher entered, one of the many ways is to select Day Book from the Display menu. Then Select F2: Period from the button bar and enter the period of display (it defaults to the current date only but you may display all the transactions for a particular period). Select F1: Detailed. Check the vouchers against what you were asked to do. If you find a mistake, position the highlight bar over the offending item and press Enter for Tally to display the voucher details for alteration.

The alteration facility is subject to security and access rights. All alternations are available for audit.

Display Voucher Type

To display a voucher on the screen, select the following:

Accounts Information>Voucher Type>Display

This will lead you to existing Voucher types, select the one which you want to get displayed. As in earlier cases, you get the voucher displayed here but cannot change it.

Alter Voucher Type

To alter a voucher on the screen, select the following:

Accounts Information>Voucher Type>Alter

This will lead you to existing Voucher types, select the one which you want to alter. Now you can change the voucher type.

Deletion of Voucher Type

To delete a Voucher Type, select it in Alteration mode and press Alt+D. If the Voucher Type has not been transacted in Voucher, you would be asked Delete ? Yes or No, respond Yes to delete. However, if the Voucher Type has participated in voucher transaction, you cannot delete it, nor can you delete any system generated Voucher type.

CONTRA VOUCHER

This voucher is used for the company when it withdraws cash from the bank or transfers funds from one bank account to another.

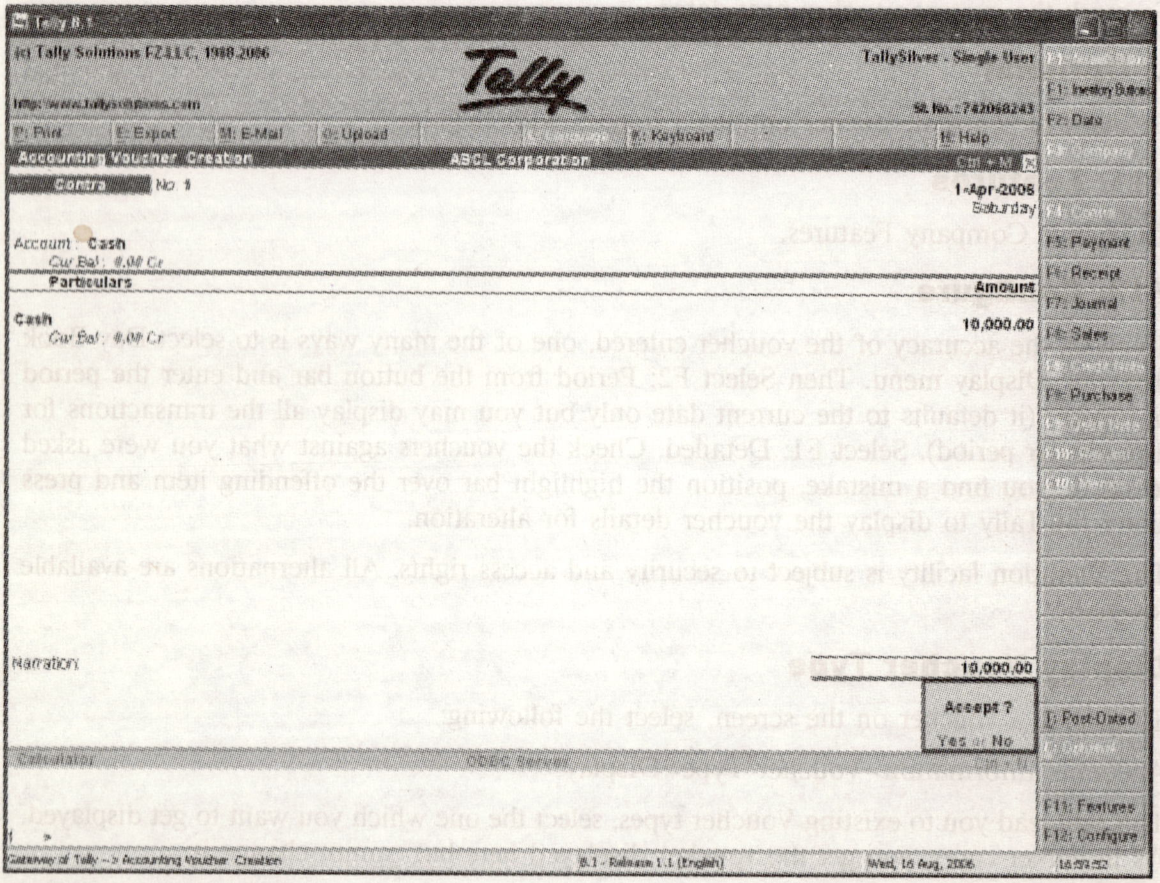

MEMO VOUCHER

This is a non-accounting voucher and the entries made using it will not affect your accounts. That is, Tally does not post these entries to ledgers but stores them in a separate Memorandum Register.

Some uses for Memo Vouchers

Making Suspense Payments

For example, the company gives an employee cash to buy office supplies, the exact nature and cost of which are unknown. You could enter a voucher for the petty cash advance, a voucher to record the actual expenditure details when they are known and another voucher to record the return of surplus cash.

However, a simpler way is to enter a Memo voucher when the cash is advanced and then turn it into a Payment voucher for the actual amount spent, when known.

Vouchers not Verified at the Time of Entry

It sometimes happens that you do not understand the details of a voucher you are entering. Enter it as a Memo voucher and amend it when you get the details.

Items Given on Approval

You will normally only enter completed sales into the books. Suppose items are given on approval. You can track them with a Memo voucher and convert it into a proper Sales voucher, or delete the memo voucher, depending on the outcome.

Memorandum Voucher Register

View all memorandum vouchers through

Display>Exception Reports

View them from the Day Book as well. You can enter and convert a Memo voucher into a regular voucher when you decide to bring the entry into your books. Use Scenarios to select the effect of Memo entries on reports and statements.

OPTIONAL VOUCHER

This is another non-accounting voucher. However, it differs from the Memo voucher in that it is not a separate voucher type. You mark an existing voucher, e.g., a payment voucher or a receipt voucher, as Optional. Press [Ctrl]+[L] or click on the button. This button toggles with Regular. By making it Optional the voucher does not get posted anywhere but remains in the have the Optional Register. You can make a voucher type default to Optional.

This is done during creation of a new voucher type or alteration of an existing voucher type.

Gateway of Tally>Accounts Info>Voucher Types

Use of Optional Vouchers

If a transaction has not been completed, you may not want it to affect the accounts. But if you want to record it so that you simply modify the voucher and remove the Optional mark by Regularising it. Display the voucher in Alter form and click on Regular. This way you can regularise the voucher and then post it, for example, Proforma sales invoice. In fact, an optional sales invoice is printed as a Proforma Invoice. You might want to see the impact of transactions without actually posting them. Optional vouchers allow you to do so. This not unlike the reversing journal. Use Scenarios to see the effect of Optional vouchers entries on reports and statements.

Forecasts

You may create new voucher types and make them default to Optional. Example: Create a New Voucher Type Sales Forecast. Record future sales projections using this voucher type. Use a Scenario to view Actual Sales against Forecasts. Normally, since these vouchers have no bearing on the books and statements.

Optional Vouchers Register

You can view all optional vouchers through

Display>Exception Reports>Optional Vouchers.

View them from the Day Book as well.

REVERSING JOURNALS

Reversing Journals are special journals that are automatically reversed after a specified date. They exist only till that date and are effective only when called for in reports like the Balance Sheet. These are used in interim reporting in the course of the financial year where accruals are required to be reported. These accruals are usually short term and are cleared in the subsequent period. However, to get a proper perspective, decision makers require the reports with full impact of all aspects and transactions. An example is the provision for depreciation. Depreciation is usually provided for at the end of the year. However, for monthly reporting including it would give a more accurate status.

Reversing Journal Voucher

Automatically reverses after a particular date — Applicable up to date.

Description	*Account*	*Amount*	*Amount*
		Dr.	Cr.
Voucher Entry	Depreciation	15000	
	Provision for Depriciation		15000

Another example: it is 30th June and you want to view the Balance Sheet as of today but June salaries are not paid until the first week in July. There is, therefore, a large liability, which would not be reflected in the Balance sheet. To overcome this, you would enter a reversing journal voucher dated 30th June, which would look something like this:

Dr.	Salaries	5,000
Cr.	Provisions (Current Liabilities)	5,000

When you view the Balance Sheet, you would ask Tally for the report with the reversing journals included. The voucher affects the report only for that day i.e., 30th June.

Applicable up to

This is the data up to which the reversing journal is available for inclusion in a scenario report. The Reversing journal can be created as of a particular date and made Applicable up to a different date. For example the depreciation entry could be dated 1st October 2000 and applicable up to 31st October 2000. The journal will be available for inclusion in a scenario for any day from 1st Oct 2000 till 31st Oct 2000. It will does not exist before 1st Oct and will be reversed automatically after 31st Oct and consequently not be available.

Reversing Journal Register

All reversing journal vouchers are maintained in a Reversing Journal Register. These are not posted to any books of accounts and are consequently cannot be included in a regular reports. They can only be seen through a scenario.

Post-dated Vouchers

While entering vouchers, you can post-date them and Tally will not update the ledgers until the date in question. This is most useful for entering transactions that take place on a regular basis. For example, if you pay for something by installments, you can set-up the payments in advance and Tally will only enter them in the ledgers as they fall due. Mark vouchers Post Dated by [CTRL]+[D] or click on the button. The button toggles with Regular.

Post-dated Vouchers Register

All Post-dated vouchers are maintained in a Post-dated vouchers Register.

Difference in theTreatment of Post-dated Vouchers and other Unconventional Vouchers

The major difference between Post dated vouchers and other Unconventional vouchers is that these actually affect regular books of accounts on the date of the voucher. Post-dated vouchers are not available for selection in Scenarios.

SALES VOUCHER

All the sales of the company, including cash sales are entered using this voucher. This entry would appear in both Sales Register and Cash Book. For this select the following:

Gateway of Tally>Accounting Vouchers>F8: Sales Voucher

Here you have to remember that the first entry must be a Debit involving any Debtor, or Creditor or Branch/Division, Cash or Bank Account. Second entry should be Credit to a ledger placed under Sales Account group. Rest of the accounts may be any Revenue Account (except Purchase) or Accounts under the Group Current Liabilities, other than Sundry Creditors. Thus you can include Duties and Taxes or other billing terms from 3rd entry onwards. A typical Sales Voucher involving several Billing Terms can be entered as follows:

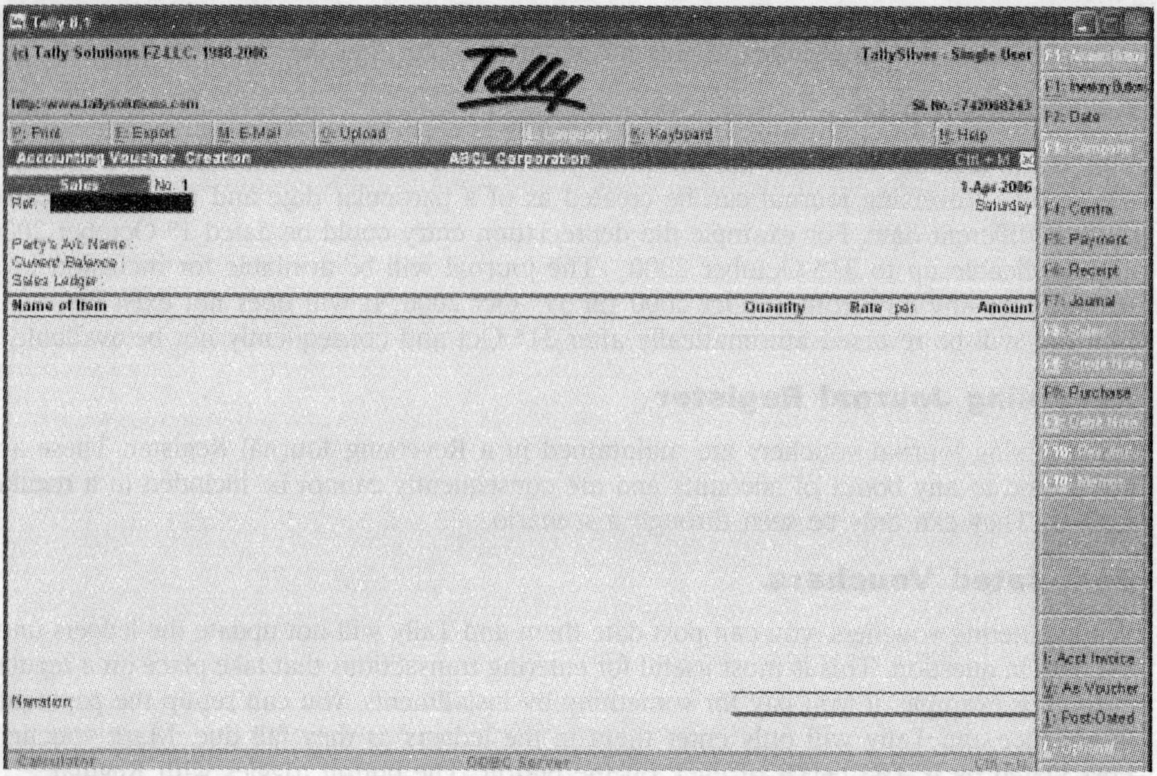

Particulars	*Dr/Cr*	*Debit*	*Credit*
Name of Buyer	Dr	(Total Bill Amount)	
Sales Account	Cr		(Sale Amount)
Duty/Tax	Cr		(Tax Amount)
Packing charges	Cr		(Expenses Amount)
Discount	Dr	(Discount Amount)	

If you have set Yes to Allow Income Accounts in Sales Voucher under F12: Configuration in Accounting Voucher under Voucher Entry, then you can select Income Account also in second entry.

PURCHASE VOUCHER

All Purchase transactions are entered in Purchase Voucher, including Cash Purchase.

For this select the following:

Gateway of Tally>Accounting Vouchers>F9: Purchase Voucher

Here you have to remember that the first entry should always be a Credit involving any Creditor, or Debtor or Branch/Division, Cash or Bank Account and second entry should be a Debit to a Ledger placed under Purchase Account group. Rest of Accounts may be

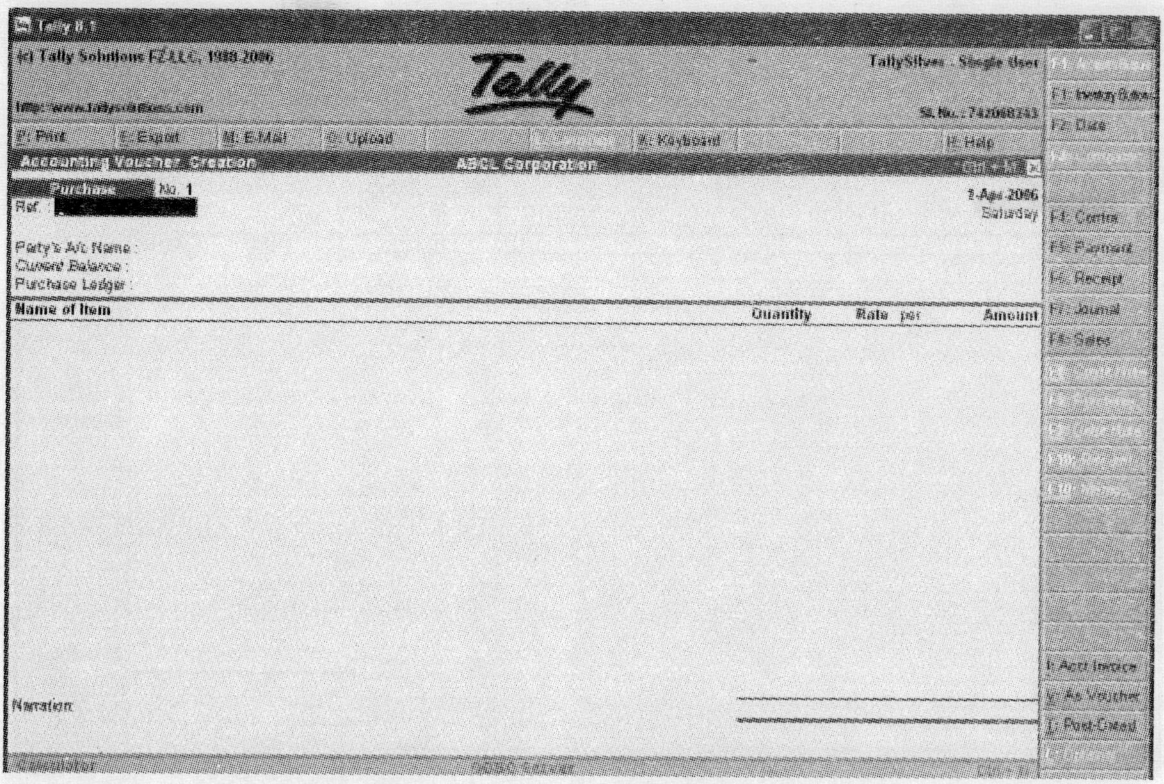

any Revenue Account, except sales, or any Account under the Group Current Liabilities, other than Sundry Creditors. Thus you can include Duties & Taxes or other billing terms from 3rd entry onwards. If you have set Yes to Allow Expenses/Fixed Assets in Purchase Voucher under F12: Configuration in Accounting Voucher, then you can select Ledger under Fixed Asset or Direct/Indirect Expenses also in second entry.

CREDIT NOTES

If you set Yes to the option Use Debit/Credit Notes in F11: Features, you can select this voucher upon clicking either F7: Journal or F8: Sales buttons. It is actually entered to credit Party Account. It is issued when a Buyer returns some goods that was sold to him (Sales Returns) or when you grant him credit due to rate difference or discount/rebate or due to some other reason you wish to credit Party Account. The first entry must be a Credit involving any Debtor, or Creditor or Branch/Division, Cash or Bank Account. Second entry should be a Debit to a ledger placed under Sales, Duties & Taxes and other revenue group, from 3rd entry onwards, you can Debit or Credit any account.

Debit Note

If you activate the option Use Debit/Credit Notes for the company under Features, you can select this voucher upon clicking either F7: Journal and F9: Purchase buttons. It is entered to Debt Party account. It is entered when you make Purchase Return or have short-billed a customer or your supplier have granted Credit to you on account of rate difference,

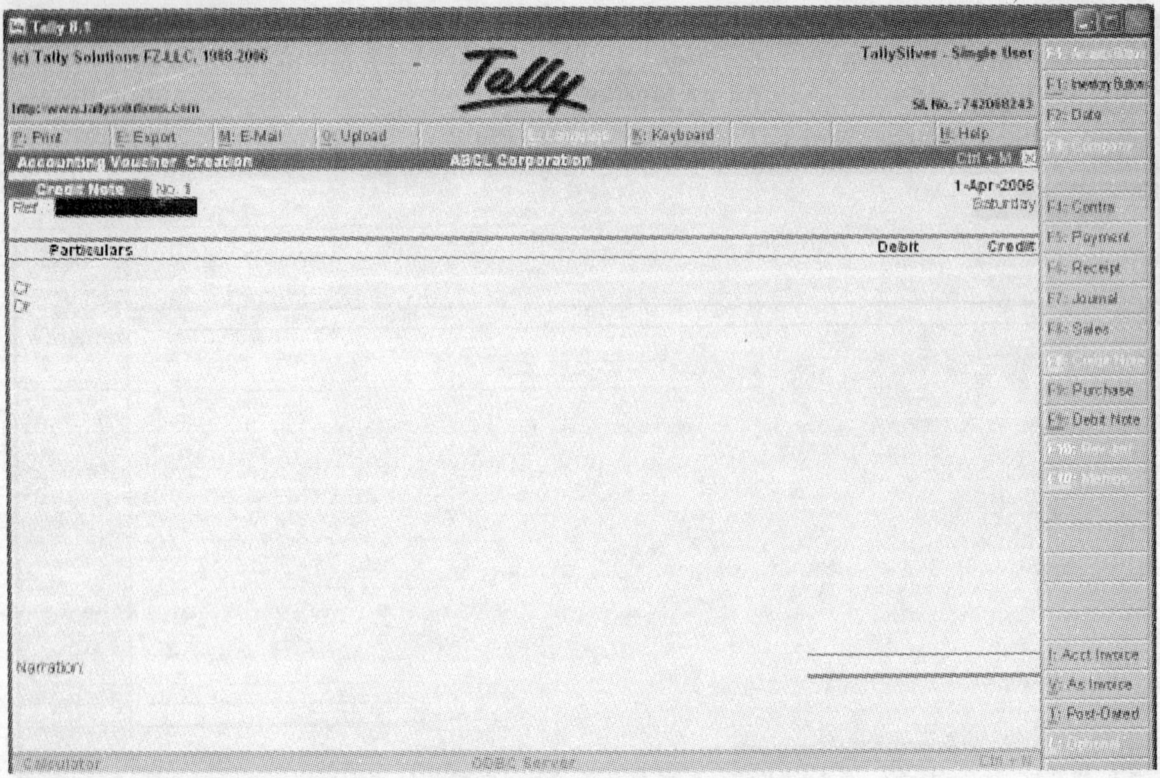

discounts, etc. The first entry must be a debit involving any Creditor, or Debtor or Branch/ Division, Cash or Bank Account. Second entry should be a credit to a Ledger placed under Purchase, Duties & Taxes and other revenue group, from 3rd entry onwards, you can Debit/ Credit any account.

Descriptive Type Questions

1. Describe the various options of Voucher entry screen.
2. Describe the process of entering vouchers.
3. Describe the function of various buttons on typical Voucher entering screen.
4. How would you Display, Alter, Delete the Vouchers?
5. Describe the process creating a Payment voucher.
6. How would you print cheques in Tally?
7. What is a Contra voucher?
8. What is a Memo voucher?
9. What are Optional vouchers?
10. What are Reversing Journals?
11. Describe Sales and Purchase vouchers.
12. How would you create Credit and Debit notes?

5 Entering Inventory Vouchers

ENTERING INVENTORY VOUCHERS

Let us now concentrate on the vouchers which are purely for the inventory purposes. As in the case of accounting vouchers, these can also be created, displayed, altered or even deleted.

SALES AND PURCHASE VOUCHER ENTRY

In Accounts-with-Inventory Companies when Tracking Numbers is NOT activated. We shall use sales as our voucher for discussion. The same applies to Purchases. You do not get the voucher types Receipt Note and Delivery Note in the Sales and Purchase Voucher sub-menus.

In addition to the above particulars that are applicable for all types of vouchers, sales and purchase vouchers have special inventory considerations for accounts-with inventory companies. Sales and Purchase ledger accounts must have the option Are Inventory Values Affected set to Yes for this section.

Inventory Allocations

Inventory items need to be considered in financial vouchers in cases where you use ledger heads that have stated Yes to the question Are Inventory Values affected? Display your Sales and Purchase affecting inventory. Hence, when you enter a voucher (usually a Sales or Purchase Voucher) a sub-screen pops up after the concerned ledger head and amount requiring you to give inventory item details.

The inventory details that you give in an accounting voucher (like Sales and Purchase Voucher), affects stocks by immediately updating them, only if Tracking Numbers are not activated in [F11]: Features.

The information that you need to give in the inventory allocation sub-screen depends upon the features enabled for the company.

A typical inventory allocation sub-screen would look like this:

Inventory Allocations for : Purchase of Disks

Name of Item	Tracking Document No.	Quantity	Rate per	Amount
Sony Disks	Sony35	250.00	5.00	1,250.00

Name of Item

Pick the item from the list of items (or create a new item by [ALT]+[C]

Location

If you have more than one location, you must specify the location to which this item relates. Hence, a sub-screen would come up after the tracking number to enable you to specify the location quantity, rate and amount for the item. You can give multiple locations for example.

Item Allocations for: Sony Disks 3.5"

Godown	Quantity	Rate per	Amount
CWC	250	5.00	1,250.00
Godown	200	5.00	1,000.00

Batch Number

In the locations sub-screen itself, the batch number can be given, if batch numbers have been activated in Company Features. Select a batch number from the list of existing batch numbers, or give a new number for a new batch.

Manufacturing Date

Again, it appears only if it has been activated. Give the date of manufacture. This enables you to set expiry date for the batch as a period form the date of manufacture, e.g., three months from the date of manufacture.

Expires on

It appears only if it has been activated. Give the date of expiry or a period from the date of manufacture. If, for the item, you had disallowed the use of expired goods; you cannot issue them after the expiry date. (Check item master).

Quantity

Normally, no explanation is required. However, you can set Company Features to allow Actual and Billed quantities. Then, you have to give both quantities here. The actual quantity updates stock and the billed quantity affects the accounts. Give the quantity either in the main unit or the alternate unit. You may even specify quantities in both units, e.g., 100 bars = 150 kgs.

Rate

Give the rate for the stock item. If you have entered Standard Rate for the item (Standard Cost and Standard Selling Price – see item master), the voucher will pick the relevant standard rate for that date by default. You may, however, modify it while entering the voucher.

Per

Give the unit of measure for the quantity of the item here. This can be the main unit or even the alternate unit.

Amount

The quantity multiplied by the rate per unit is the amount.

End of List

In all multiple allocations or selections, you must either be required to select the option End of List or press [Enter] at the first blank field. This would accept the multiple allocation and take you back to the present screen, for example, Multiple locations, batches or items.

VOUCHER CLASSES

Voucher Class is the novel way of automating accounting allocations during Invoice entry. It is a table for predefining the entries that you wish to automate to make Invoice creation a breezy tasks. This is particularly useful in sales invoicing where you can define once, the nominal ledger account to be credited for each item of sale. Then during voucher entry, the accounting credits for items sold are done automatically.

The automation is taken a step further; the additional accounting entries (that fall below the stock items line) like Tax, freight and other charges can also be predefined to be carried out untouched during actual invoicing.

The benefit of this approach is that decision is taken out of the hands of the data-entry operator and control rests with senior management who can set the class parameters. It also reduces chances of errors during voucher entry. Of course, you can still continue to use Tally as before without classes if you do not require it.

Classes can also be used to automate the rounding off of values. Rounding method can be present when defining a class for a single line or for the entire voucher or invoice.

Hence, Voucher Class permits:

- Automation of entries to predefined ledger accounts
- Automatic rounding off to preset value limits.

Another feature that has been added is the ability default sales ledger account to be affected for each stock item. This capability is available for companies maintaining accounts with inventory. Activate it through

1. F12: Configure
2. Accts/InvInfo.

Now when you alter or create a stock item, you can define the nominal ledger account (usually the sales account) which should automatically be credited when you invoice this item.

For example, you might have sales ledgers broken up as Sale of Finished Goods and Sale of Intermediates. Let's assume that your finished goods are Computers and intermediate goods are CD ROM drives. Against the stock item Computers, you will specify Sale of Finished Goods as the Sales Ledger account to be affected. Against CD ROM drive you will select Sale of Intermediates. These will be the default sales ledger accounts that will be affected only when invoicing. They can be overridden by the account that you may set in the Class table.

The dual facility of ledger allocation with stock item and ledger allocation defined in a class provides the flexibility to permit allocation of different stock items to different sales accounts as set up in the class table. You can either alter the existing Sales Voucher Type or create a new voucher type based on Sales. From Gateway of Tally > Accounts Info > Voucher Types. The item Name of Class is below Position Index on Reports and above the Numbering Table.

Give a name by simply typing it, e.g., Taxable, VAT, Local or Export. You may create more than one class. Hence, you might want to have one Taxable Class and another Export Class. The Class table for that name is created. The Class Table is split horizontally for accounting allocations and additional accounting entries.

DEFAULT ACCOUNTING ALLOCATIONS

Ledger Name

Select the ledger to be credited for each item sold in the invoice. More than one ledger can be affected for each item, e.g., for Tax-inclusive items, the ledgers to be credited will be Sales and Tax in a definite proportion. This is where percentage comes in.

Percentage %

Useful in tax-inclusive price cases, you can specify the sales ledger account, as say, 82.5% and in the next line the Tax account with the balance 17.5%. Normally, for tax-exclusive prices, you will give 100% for the Sales account. The % symbol is required to be mentioned.

Rounding Method

This may be used only where the sales account is NOT 100%. Calculated amounts may be required to be rounded off upwards or downwards or normal. Normal is rounding to the number of decimal places specified for the currency based on the less than 5 & greater than 5 rule. You can set your own rounding off rule, e.g., round off to the next whole number. In such a case, you will give Upwards.

Rounding Limit

For the previous example, you will set it to 1 to achieve the amount to the next whole number. To round off upwards to the nearest 50P, you will set it to 0.50.

Override Using Item Default?

This question to be answered Yes or No. Item default refers to the Sales Ledger account that you may have set for a stock item, e.g., for Computers – Sale of Finished Goods. If in the Class Table here, you mention Sales – Local and set No to this question, then Sales – Local will be the account affected and not Sale of Finished Goods. Setting it to Yes will affect Sale of Finished Goods. The advantage of this is that you can use different classes to affect different sales accounts.

Additional Accounting Entries

This part is relevant for Tax and other charges like freight and insurance.

Ledger Name – this is self explanatory. You can give more than one ledger.

TYPES OF CALCULATION

Different class methods are provided and select the one suitable. The Value Basis that you will provide in the next column will calculate using the Type of calculation specified. See below for an explanation of each Type of Calculation.

Value Basis

Give the amount which is to be used for the Type of Calculation. For percentage, you must use the symbol %. Hence Tax on Sales is 17.5% on Item Rate to use the rate give in the stock item. The method Total Amount Rounding will round the total invoice and put the difference in the Ledger name mentioned here.

Hence, the account Rounding Off will contain the sum that essentially rounds off the invoice to the desired level. Rounding Method and Rounding Limit have been explained already.

Remove if Zero?

This is a question to be answered Yes or No, essentially to permit Tally to ignore the account and not to make any entry in it if its value is zero. If Yes, ensure that you are permitted to make Zero value entries in F11: Features. No will record the invoice in the ledger account with nil amounts.

Under normal circumstances, you will probably wish to set this value to Yes. However, in cases such as Zero Rated VAT, you may wish to retain the Ledger Account line, even though the calculation yields a nil amount.

Effects on Cost Centres

Cost Centres will remain un-allocated when classes are used to allocate account entries. Cost centres can also be predefined under Cost Centre Classes. Refer to Cost Centre Classes for further information.

EXPLANATION OF TYPES OF CALCULATION

As Additional Excise

In the Indian sub-continent, a manufacturing tax, or Excise is levied. For some products, a supplementary levy on the Basis Excise Duty is charged or Additional Excise Duty. This is a surcharge calculation. For example, an Additional Excise duty of 10% on the Basic duty. While the calculation method is identical to As Surcharge (see below), the result is to provide a Total Excise Payable calculation accurately during Invoice printing.

As a Flat Rate

When you wish to specify a standard mark-up/down on an invoice. For example, 100.00 for every invoice, independent of the qty/value of the invoice.

As Surcharge

When you wish to calculate the value based on the immediately preceding figure. For example, a Sales Tax of 10% is applicable on an invoice, which would be calculated on the value of goods sold. On this, a Surcharge of 5%, i.e., 5% of the Sales Tax value is applicable.

As Total Amount Rounding

Typically, the last line in an invoice. You would need to create an account which would carry the rounding difference. Now, as the other values of the invoice are calculated, this account would automatically get adjusted to keep the Total Invoice Value to the desired rounding limits. Normally, you would also mark this invoice as Remove if Zero? Yes, so that the account head is not retained in the invoice print-outs if no rounding was applicable.

As User Defined Value

This allows you to specify a value while creating the invoice itself. Normally, you would use this when the basis of calculation is neither Value nor Qty dependent and therefore, needs to be entered every time you create an invoice.

Based on Quantity

In case of calculations based on the Total Qty supplied. For example, you may have Freight or Forwarding charges as 2.00/Kg. and if the total qty supplied in the invoice is 200.00 Kg, then the amount should become 4001.00. The Value Basis will also need to be provided as 2.00/Kg or 0.50/Pc as the case may be.

On Current Sub Total

In certain environments, taxes are applicable on the Total Goods Value as well supplementary charges such as Excise Duty, Packing Charges, etc. Normally, when the tax calculation method is specified as On Total Sales (see below), the calculations are based on the Total Goods Value only. When you wish the supplementary charge to be included, then you would set On Current Sub Total as the type of calculation.

On Item Rate

Typically used for both VAT as well as Excise Duty style calculations. Here, you would have specified the Rate of Tax applicable for each Stock Item and you would want only those items to be used for calculation purposes which equals this Rate of Tax. The advantage is to be able to mix multiple Tax Rate products in the same Invoice and yet get the correct ones picked up for each Tax bracket.

On Total Sales

The most common basis of Tax Calculation in on the total value of goods/services. This method would calculate using the sum of Stock Items used in the invoice.

PURE INVENTORY VOUCHERS

Pure Inventory vouchers perform the same function in the inventory system as accounting vouchers in the accounting system, i.e. they too, are means of entering transactions. In this case, the vouchers record the receipt and issue of goods/stock, the transfer of stock between locations and physical stock adjustments.

If you have chosen not to integrate accounts with inventory, inventory vouchers will not have any impact on the Balance Sheet stock figures. They will maintain the stock balances. However, you can configure Tally so that the inventory entries would automatically update the Balance Sheet stock figures. (By choosing to integrate Accounts and Inventory in F11 Company Features). Remember, you can trace an entire transaction right from the goods transfer stage to the financial accounting of it, irrespective of integration status. For example, the purchase of stock can be tracked form the purchase voucher through to the receipt note, through to the invoice from the supplier and on through to the eventual payment.

Types of Inventory Vouchers

Tally is pre-programmed with a variety of inventory vouchers, each designed to perform a different job. The standard vouchers are:

- Receipt note voucher (F9: Purchase)
- Rejections-in voucher (F8: Sales)
- Delivery note voucher (F8: Sales)
- Rejections-out voucher (F9: Purchase)
- Stock journal voucher (F7)
- Physical stock voucher (F10)

Unless you have Tracking numbers activated in F11 Company Features, the Goods In Receipt Note and Goods Out Delivery Note vouchers will not be activated. Tally will assume that goods are received along with Purchase Vouchers and Goods are delivered along with Sales Voucher/Invoices. When Tracking Numbers are activated, you inform Tally that you may receive goods that are not accompanied by Supplier's invoice – the invoice will arrive separately. Also that you may not deliver goods together with your invoice – you may invoice later.

You are allowed, however, in a voucher, to select Not Applicable when the Tracking Number sub-screen comes up. This would update inventory right away without the need to pass a separate inventory voucher. The vice-versa is also true. You can alter these vouchers to suit your company, as well as create new ones. For example, if you wish to distinguish between delivery notes for stock delivered from different locations, you can create vouchers to do this. This function of each voucher type is now explained.

Receipt note Voucher

For recording goods received. For example, the company receives new stock from a supplier. If a Purchase Order exists for that Supplier, selecting it will bring up the order particulars.

Receipt note voucher	
Description	Records receipt of new stock from suppliers
Details recorded	Reference, ledger account, supplier's name and address, name of stock item, stock location, quantity, rate, amount, narration

Rejections-in Voucher

For recording goods received back that was rejected by a customer. For example, the company takes back into stock items rejected by a customer.

Rejections in voucher	
Description	Records returns of goods by customers
Details recorded	Reference, ledger account, customer's name and address, name of stock item, stock location, quantity, rate, amount, narration.

Delivery note Voucher

For recording goods delivered to a customer. For example, the company delivers goods from stock to a customer. If a Sales Order exists for that customer, selecting the appropriate Sales Order will bring up the relevant particulars.

Delivery note voucher	
Description	Records the delivery of goods to customers
Details recorded	Reference, ledger account, customer's name and address, name of stock item, stock location, quantity, rate, amount, narration

Rejections-out Voucher

For recording of goods that are rejected and returned to a supplier. For example, the company returns items that had previously been taken into stock to the supplier.

Rejections out voucher	
Description	Records return of goods to suppliers
Details recorded	Reference, ledger account, supplier's name and address, name of stock item, stock location, quantity, rate, amount, narration

Stock Journal Voucher

For recording stock transfers from one location to another. For example, the company transfers items of stock from the warehouse to the shop.

Stock journal voucher	
Description	Records the transfer of stock from one location to another
Details recorded	Names of from and to locations, name of stock item, quantity, rate, amount, narration

Physical Stock Voucher

For recording actual stock as physically verified or counted. For example, stock found on conducting a stock-check. It is not unusual that the company finds a discrepancy between the actual stock and the computer stock figure. If you have configured your inventory vouchers to Ignore physical stock difference, these physical stock vouchers will really be for recording purposes only. However, if you have configured the vouchers not to ignore physical stock difference, then all transactions subsequent to the physical stock voucher will use the balance as mentioned in that voucher.

How to Enter Pure Inventory Vouchers

There are three different types of screen for entering inventory vouchers. The screens for Receipt notes, Rejections-in, Delivery notes and Rejections-out are the same except for the voucher name and whether the voucher relates to a customer or supplier. The other two types are for the Stock journal and Physical stock vouchers.

Unlike accounting vouchers whose advanced usage is being discussed separately, we shall include advanced usage of inventory vouchers here. Vouchers involving pop-up screens depend upon configuration settings and it will be assumed that these settings have been activated.

Gateway of Tally>Voucher entry

The basic process to enter each voucher is:

Change the date if necessary.

Select the voucher type from the button bar menu:

- F7: Stock journal
- F8: select Delivery Note or Rejections-out
- F9: select Receipt Note or Rejections-in
- F10: Physical Stock

Type in the details and check they are correct before accepting.

A typical inventory voucher screen appears.

The screen is split into three sections:

- The type, reference and date of the voucher.
- Party's particulars
- Inventory item details.

Types of Voucher

You need to check you are using the right voucher for the transaction. You change the voucher type by selecting the new type from the button bar. In some cases, like receipt notes (where you have opted for Use rejection notes in F11) you will see a pop-up screen from which you select the right voucher.

Voucher Number

Tally will enter this for you if you have set-up the voucher type to do it. If it is to be entered manually, do so.

Reference Number

This is optional. You can enter a reference such as Purchase Order Number or Supplier's Delivery Note Number.

Date of Voucher

The date of the voucher you are entering is displayed at the top-right of the Voucher Creation screen. The date is initially the Current date and you may need to change it to ensure vouchers are entered with the date you want.

You change the date using the F2: Date button on the button bar.

Ledger Account

There are no To/By or Dr/Cr in inventory vouchers.

To select a ledger, type the first letter of its name (either case) and Tally displays a List of Ledger Accounts, (the ledgers starting with the typed letter are highlighted). Only ledgers suitable for the voucher type are displayed. As you continue typing, the highlights reduce until a match is found. Here you usually need a supplier's ledger account.

Supplier's Name and Address

Give the supplier's name and address. This could be different form the ledger name (but, on the other hand, could be the same). This information is useful when printing out the Goods Receipt Note.

Name of the Item

From the popup list of Stock item, select the stock item that is being received. If it is not in the list, create it using [Alt]+[C]

Tracking Number

You will use the tracking number to link this receipt note with the Supplier's Invoice that will be received later. (You will record the Supplier's Invoice through the Purchase Voucher). Hence, select the number you think will help maintain the link. Tally gives you two numbers that are default of the Receipt Note number and the Reference. However, you may opt to give your own number, in which case select New Number. If you do not wish to give a tracking number at all, select Not Applicable.

An explanation on the four options in the list is necessary. Tracking numbers link the different accounting and inventory vouchers as follows:

- Receipt Note/Goods In vouchers with Purchase vouchers
- Goods Out/Delivery Note with Sales Voucher/Invoice
- Rejections-In with Credit Note
- Rejections-Out with Debit Note

New Number

Give a number not in the list. You will use this number to reconcile, when making a Purchase Voucher entry.

Not Applicable

If you do not want a tracking number. This may be resorted to in cases where you want to update stocks immediately with this entry and no goods inward entry will be needed. When in an inventory voucher if you select Not Applicable, that will update stocks and you do not want to make a separate accounting/invoice entry. Not applicable option is important and hence we repeat the cases where you would use it:

1. When you raise a sales voucher/invoice that accompanies the goods and you do not want to pass Goods Out entry. Not Applicable will update stocks without the Goods Out entry.

2. Likewise, when you record a purchase voucher and wish to update inventory without a separate Goods In entry, select Not applicable for the tracking number.

3. The same applies to Debit Notes-Rejection Out and Credit Note-Rejection In.

4. When you send out samples for approvals, where you do not want to raise an invoice. Likewise when you receive samples but no invoice will be forthcoming.

DEFAULT VOUCHER NUMBER

Reference Number

The reference field if field in becomes the default. Tally also lists the voucher number and the reference number of the current voucher for selection. Select the one that is easy to track later.

Pending Tracking Number

If you have a pending tracking number from a previous voucher, it will be listed here together with details like location, quantity, rate and amount. You will select a pending tracking number to adjust that with the current voucher entry. This could be a Purchase Voucher received and recorded, for which the goods are now being received.

Order Details (in Case Purchase Order Processing is Active)

If, however, Purchase Order Processing is activated (Company Features), an order field is now available. Select Not applicable if there were no orders particulars to adjust to record. If the order existed, by selecting the order number from the pop-up list of orders, the rest of the fields are automatically filled up. These are, however, available for editing (can alternatively be set so that editing is not permitted – through F12: Configuration). Otherwise, select a new number to input details.

Location

If you have more than one location, you must specify the location to which this item relates. Hence, a sub-screen would come up after the tracking number to enable you to specify the location quantity, rate and amount for the item. You can give multiple locations also.

Batch Number

In the locations sub-screen itself, the batch number can be given, if batch numbers have been activated in Company Features. Select a batch number from the list of existing batch numbers, or give a new number for a new batch.

Manufacturing Date

Again, it appears only if it has been activated. Give the date of manufacture. This enables you to set expiry date for the batch as a period from the date of manufacture, e.g., three months form the date of manufacture.

Expires on

It appears only if it has been activated. Give the date of expiry or a period from the date of manufacture. If, for the item, you had disallowed the use of expired goods, you cannot issue them after the expiry date. (Check item master).

Quantity

Normally, no explanation is required. However, you can set Company Features to allow Actual and billed Quantities. Then, you have to give both quantities here. The actual quantity updates stock and the billed quantity which affects the accounts. Give the quantity either in the main unit or the alternate unit. You may even specify quantities in both units, e.g., 100 bars = 150 Kgs.

Rate

Give the rate for the stock item. If you have entered Standard Rate for the item (Standard Cost and Standard Selling Price – see item master), the voucher will pick up the relevant standard rate for that date by default. You may, however, modify it while entering the voucher.

Per

Give the unit of measure for the quantity of the item here. This can be main unit or even the alternate unit.

Amount

The quantity multiplied by the rate per unit is the amount.

End of List

In all multiple allocations or selections, you must either be required to select the option End of List or press [Enter] at the first blank field.

This would accept the multiple allocation and take you back to the parent screen. For example, Multiple locations, batches or items.

Narration

Here you type whatever is appropriate for the transaction. Once you accept the data, Tally presents another data entry screen.

STOCK JOURNAL

For this select the following:

Gateway of Tally>Voucher Entry>[Alt]+F7 or Click on Stock Journal

A stock journal is used to transfer materials or stock from one location to another location. Stocks could even simply be shown as consumed. Or even only produced without both

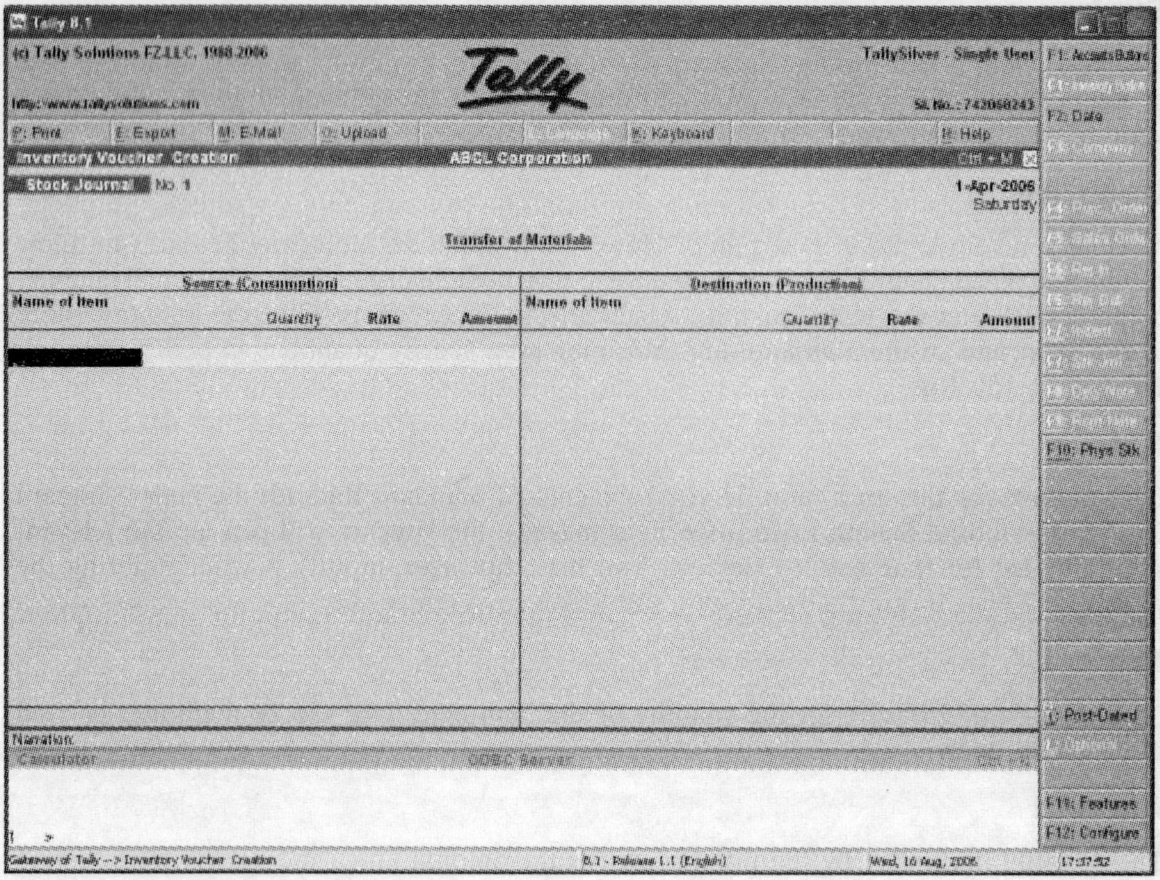

consumption and production. Hence, it is not like other journal where debits and credits must match. You can specify quantities that do not move and their rates and amounts do not change. If standards rates have been entered in the stock item masters, they will appear. In the target location, you can specify additional costs incurred without actually affecting accounting at all. Only the stock values goes up. Hence, it is technically correct where an expense incurred on production or inward has been accounted for in the cost of that item. The Stock Journal Screen has three parts – the top part accepts general information, the left hand side is the Source location or Consumption Part and the right hand side is the Destination location or the Production Part.

While you must furnish the common information required in the top part, you may elect to give information for only the left or right part or both.

COMMON INFORMATION

Reference, Date and Voucher Number

If activated for this voucher, reference field will come up. Give a reference number, if required. Voucher number depends upon the settings in Voucher Type.

Source (Consumption)

Here give the name of the item and the location form which sit moves or where it is consumed as well as the rate and amount. If the rate is specified in the stock item master, it will be brought up when you indicate the item name. The effect of entry in this part is of reducing stock of the items specified.

Destination (Production)

Here give the name of the item and the location into which the named item moves. It is not necessary that the item names should match the names in the source part. This is because of a totally new item could be produced out of materials consumed. You can specify the rate of the item and amount. If the rate is specified in the stock item master, it will be brought up when you indicate the item name.

The effect of entry in the Destination Part is of increasing stock of the items specified in this part.

Additional Cost Details

Another interesting facility is available for the Destination location (Production). You can specify what additional costs were incurred in moving goods into the location or for producing them. Though these costs are strictly accounting heads, they do not get posted in the relevant nominal ledger accounts but add to the cost of the item. In the target location, you can specify additional costs incurred without actually affecting accounting at all. Only the stock value goes up. Hence, it is technically correct where an expense incurred on production or inward has been accounting for in the cost of that item.

After entering the amount for an item, the additional cost details entry box pops up.

You may specify additional costs for transferring or producing the item. These would, typically be wages, power freight etc. Remember that you must have ledger accounts opened for the additional costs. Moreover, additional costs entered for the ledgers, do not reflect in the relevant ledger with the amount but only add to the cost of the item.

Percentage (%)

You can specify the additional cost by the way of a percentage of the cost of the item, in which case give the number, e.g., 2 for 2% of the cost of the item. You may, alternatively, skip the percentage field and input an amount directly.

Actual

This displays the total additional cost for the item and the effective cost per unit of item/ product produced.

BILL OF MATERIALS

Introduction

A Bill of Materials contains a list of items that make up another item. In other words, it is a list of constituent items.

Enable bill of materials facility

This is relevant for manufacturing organizations and can be set up through configuration. For this select the following:

Gateway of Tally>F12:Configure>Accts/Inventory Info

A Bill of Materials should be available while manufacturing an item. Hence, first enable

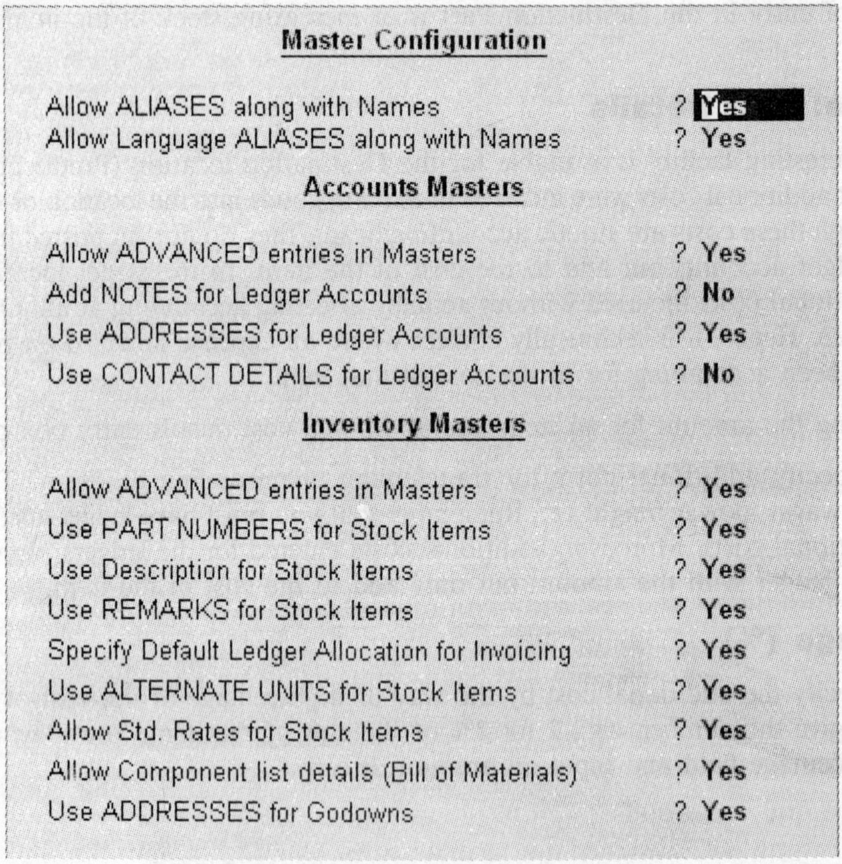

manufacturing entries. This is done through a stock journal. It is wise to create a new voucher type say, Mfg Journal which is based on Stock Journal.

Stock Journal as Manufacturing Journal

Stock journal vouchers can be accessed as:

Gateway of Tally>Accts Info>Voucher Type>Display>Stock Journal

When you use a stock journal as a manufacturing journal, the stock journal voucher entry screen would then be modified to accept name and quantity of the product being manufactured, its list of components and additional costs of manufacture associated with it. If, for an end-product item, you have specified a bill of materials that contains the list of components, this list is brought up automatically and filled in for the quantity of the end product.

How to Create a New Manufacturing Journal

For this select the following:
Gateway of Tally>Accts Info>Voucher Type>Create

You have to fill the following information:

Name

Give a new name to the voucher type, e.g., Mfg, Journal. It could be any other name.

Type of Voucher

This must be Stock Journal. Pick it up from the pop-up list.

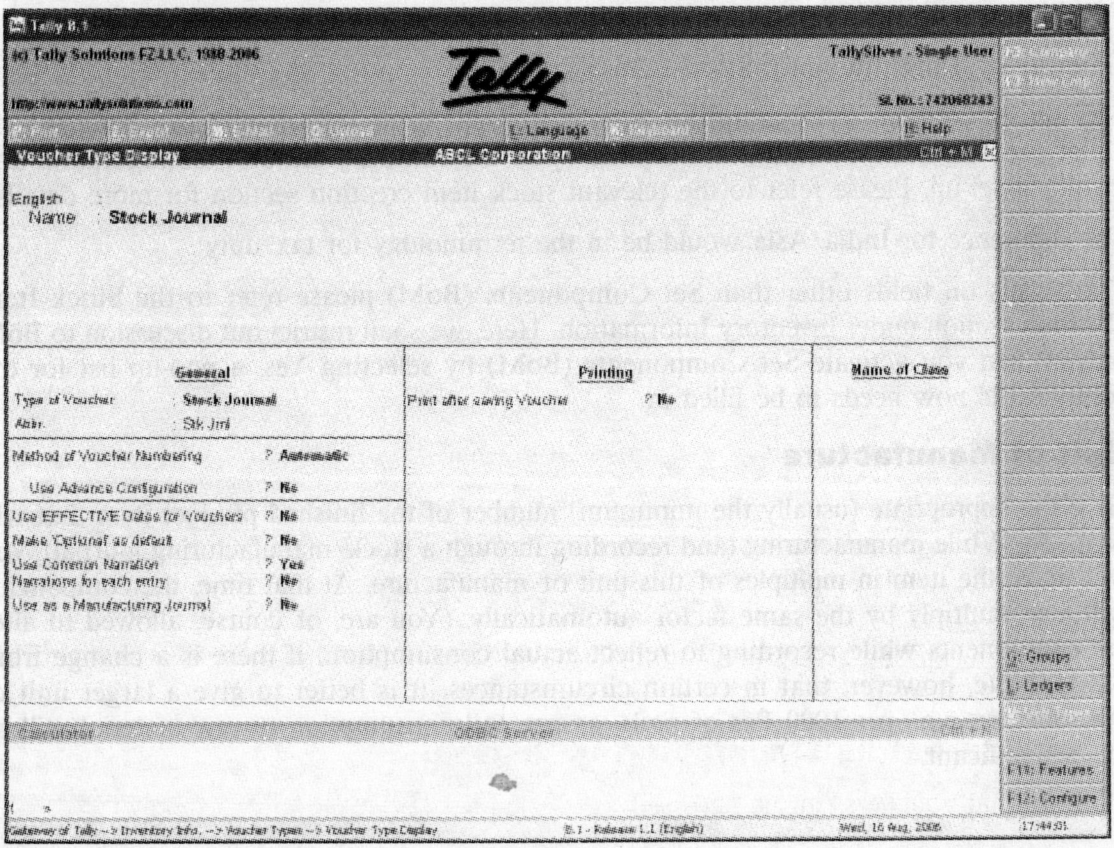

Abbr.

The abbreviation to the voucher type name. Type in a suitable abbreviation, e.g., Mfg. or mfg. jrnl.

Method of Voucher Numbering etc.

Follow the normal voucher type creation.

Use as a Manufacturing Journal

Select **Yes**.

The other areas of voucher type screen have been discussed under voucher type section. Please refer to that section for any assistance.

How to Create a Bill of Material

You can create a Bill of Material (BoM) for any stock item. Typically, you would like to create a BoM only for those items that are being assembled in-house. For trading items, you do not need a BoM. Therefore, we need to specify a BoM at the time of creating a stock item (or altering its master)

Let us create a new stock item and specify its BoM.

For this select the following:

Gateway of Tally>Inv. Info>Stock Items>Create

This screen contains information for Britain/Europe. Some information like Batches, Alt. Units and Intrastate Classification depend upon the company features, configuration and invoicing set-up. Please refer to the relevant stock item creation section for more details.

The difference for India/Asia would be in the terminology for tax/duty:

For details on fields other than Set Components (BoM) please refer to the Stock Item Creation section under Inventory Information. Here, we shall restrict out discussion to BoM only. When you activate Set Components (BoM) by selecting Yes, a pop-up list for the components now needs to be filled in.

Unit of Manufacture

Give the appropriate (usually the minimum) number of the finished product item that will be made. While manufacturing (and recording through a stock/manufacturing journal), you will make the item in multiples of this unit of manufacture. At that time, the components will also multiply by the same factor automatically. (You are, of course, allowed to alter the components while recording to reflect actual consumption, if there is a change from BoM). Note, however, that in certain circumstances, it is better to give a larger unit of manufacture, e.g., per 1000 Pcs of nails, as per nail consumption or raw material will be too insignificant.

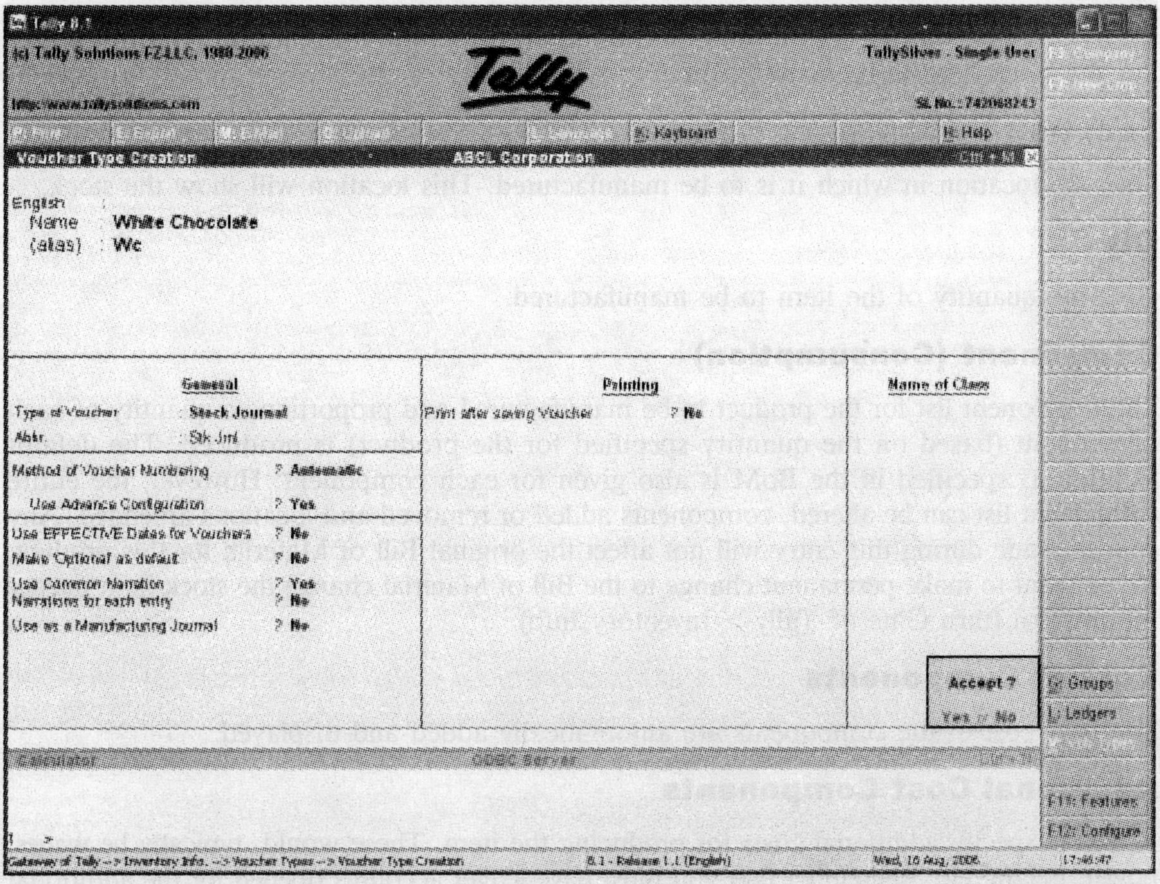

Item, Location (Godown) and Quantity

Give the component name and quantity and if multiple locations (godowns) have been set up, the most likely location for the item. Again by specifying the location here, you are not restricted to that location during transaction/voucher entry. The locations would default to these but you can opt for another. Input your options for other questions for the stock item and accept the screen.

The Stock Journal/manufacturing Journal Entry Screen

For this select the following:

Gateway of Tally>Voucher Entry>Click on Stk. Jrnl

If you had created a new voucher type Mfg Journal, a pop-up menu will show both the default Stock Journal and the Mfg Journal.

Input fields for the Mfg. Journal:

Reference

Give a reference number, if required.

Name of Product

For the stock item to be manufactured.

Location

Give the location in which it is to be manufactured. This location will show the stock.

Qty

Give the quantity of the item to be manufactured.

Component (Consumption)

The component list for the product to be manufactured and proportionate quantity of each component (based on the quantity specified for the product) is produced. The default location as specified in the BoM is also given for each component. However, the entire component list can be altered, components added or removed and locations amended. Any change made during this entry will not affect the original Bill of Material for this product. If you want to make permanent change to the Bill of Material change the stock item master information (thru Gate of Tally > Inventory Info)

Cost of Components

The base cost of the components are automatically added and displayed.

Additional Cost Components

You may specify additional costs for producing the item. These would, typically be wages, power, freight, etc. Remember that you must have ledger accounts opened for the additional costs. Moreover, additional costs entered for the ledgers, do not reflect in the relevant ledger with the amount but only add to the cost of the item.

Percentage

You can specify the additional cost by way of a percentage of the cost of components, in which case give the number, e.g., 2 for 2% of the cost of components. You may, alternatively, skip the percentage field and input an amount directly.

Total Additional Cost

This displays the total additional cost for the item.

Effective Cost

This is the sum total of the cost of components and additional costs.

Effective Rate

Effective cost per unit of item/product produced.

Advanced Usage

You may create a stock or manufacturing journal directly while creating a sales invoice. The need often arises in situations where the manufacture has not been recorded but the invoice is being prepared. While creating an invoice, when the cursor is at the quantity field of the stock item (manufactured product), press [ALT]+[V] to bring up the manufacturing stock journal screen for the product/item. On completing the mfg journal, you are brought back to the next field in the invoice screen. Thus, the item would be manufactured, its components reduced from stock and also invoiced in a single transaction entry.

[ALT]+[V] creates a new stock or manufacturing stock journal transaction voucher and is not to be used as an allocation screen. Therefore, if [ALT]+[V] is pressed again, (say during alternation of the invoice), one more manufacturing journal will be created and will not alter the previous manufacturing journal. The principal is the same as [ALT]+[C].

If you want to alter the related manufacturing/stock journal, you must alter it separately, in the normal manner. It will be available through Display > Inventory Books > Stock Items or through Statistics > Mfg or Stock Journal.

Buttons in a Typical Voucher Entry Screen

F2: Change Date

Use this button to change the date of the voucher.

F3: Change Cmp

This would allow you to switch to another loaded company and enter a voucher in it. Therefore, you can, almost simultaneously, enter vouchers for more than one company.

Post Dated

To mark the current voucher post dated.

Optional

To mark the current voucher optional.

F11: Features

To change the features.

F12: Configure

To check the accuracy of the vouchers entered, one of the many ways is to select Day Book from the Display Menu. Then select F2: Period from the button bar and enter the period of display (it defaults to the current date only but you may display all the transactions for a particular period). Select F1: Detailed. Check. Check the vouchers against what you were asked to do. If you find a mistake, position the highlight bar over offending item and press Enter for tally to display the voucher details for alternation. The alternation facility is subject to security and access rights. All alterations are available for audit.

Purchase and Sales Orders

Tally permits you to produce Purchase and Sales Orders form the system. Purchase Orders may be produced, printed and sent to suppliers. Goods received are linked with the POs and Invoices. Outstanding Purchase Orders should be monitored. In the Chapter on Voucher Entry, we have shown how orders are linked with delivery notes and invoices. Hence, we will only consider creation, alteration and deletion of Purchase Orders here. Display order position of any item form the Stock Summary. The Purchase Order Book will list out all the Purchase Orders placed.

Likewise, Sales Orders received are recorded in Sales Order Entry Screen. The details are available during Delivery Note and Invoicing. You may view the order position in the Stock Summary. The Sales Order Book lists all Sales Order received. Activate Purchase and Sales Order Processing in F11: Company Features.

We shall first take up purchase orders.

How to Create a Purchase Order

Purchase Order details will also depend on configuration settings. Hence, have a look at the configuration and voucher types.

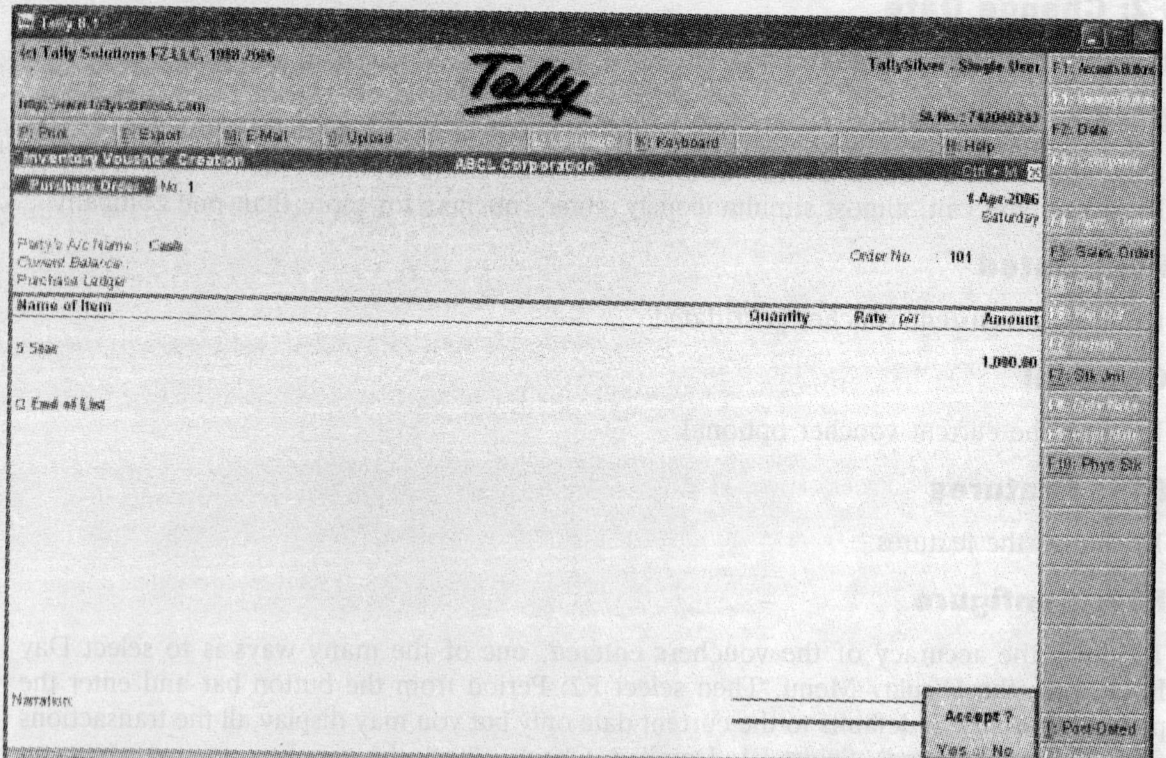

Gateway of Tally>Voucher Entry>F9: Purchase>Select Purchase Order

Give the supplier's name. Type in the same manner as voucher entry and select from list of Ledger Accounts. Use [Alt] + [C] to create a new account.

Order No

The voucher number can be treated as your Purchase Order number. You may configure the voucher type through Acct. Info > Voucher Types to set prefixes and suffixes for Purchase Orders. This particular Order No. field is an additional field to record order number if different from the voucher number.

Name of the Item

Give the name of the stock item for which the order is to be placed. Once the name is given the Item Allocations sub-screen pops-up that needs to be filled in.

Due on

The due date for delivery of the item. This will enable monitoring of outstanding deliveries. The order can be split for delivery on different dates.

Location

In case multiple location features is active, this field is required to be given, else it does not appear.

Quantity, Rate and Amount

Give the quantity of the item required and its rate. The amount is calculated but is modifiable to enable rounding off.

Additional Cost Details

Additional cost on the item may be incurred which can be mentioned here. Give the way of percentage of the item cost or a flat amount. If not, select end a list. Additional costs increase the value of the item and do not independently appear in the nominal ledger account or expense.

Next Item

The cursor then comes to the Item field again and you can enter another item to order. If no other item is required, press [enter] on the blank field to take the cursor to tax/expense field.

Expense/Tax

Once the item details have been entered, you might specify tax to be charged and other expenses like freight, if any. The tax or expenses has to exist as a ledger account or it may be created using [Alt]+[C]. We shall select tax @ 17.5% to be charged on the item values. The order entry screen would then appear thus:

Narration

Optional. You may give some particulars about the order.

ALTER A PURCHASE ORDER

You can alter a Purchase Order by displaying it from a variety of place but is easier through the Purchase Orders Book or the Day Book.

For this select the following:

Gateway of Tally>Display>Day Book

or

Gateway of Tally>Display>Inventory Books>Purchase Orders Book

Delete a Purchase Order

Alter an order and use [Alt]+[D] to delete it.

HOW TO CREATE SALES ORDERS

Sales order entry is exactly like Purchase Orders.

Sales Order details will also depend on configuration settings. Hence, have a look at the configuration and voucher types.

Gateway of Tally>Voucher entry>F8: Sales>Select Sales Order

This screen has the following information to be filled in.

Party's A/c Name

Give the customer's name. Type in the same manner as voucher entry and select from list of Ledger Accounts. Use [Alt] + [C] to create a new account.

Order No

The voucher number can be treated as your internal serialised order number. The field Order No. is advised to be used for customer's order number.

Name of the Item

Give the name of the stock item for which the orders is placed. Once the name is given the Item Allocations sub-screen pops-up that needs to be filled in.

Due on

The due date for delivery of the item. This will enable monitoring of outstanding deliveries. The order can be split for delivery on different dates.

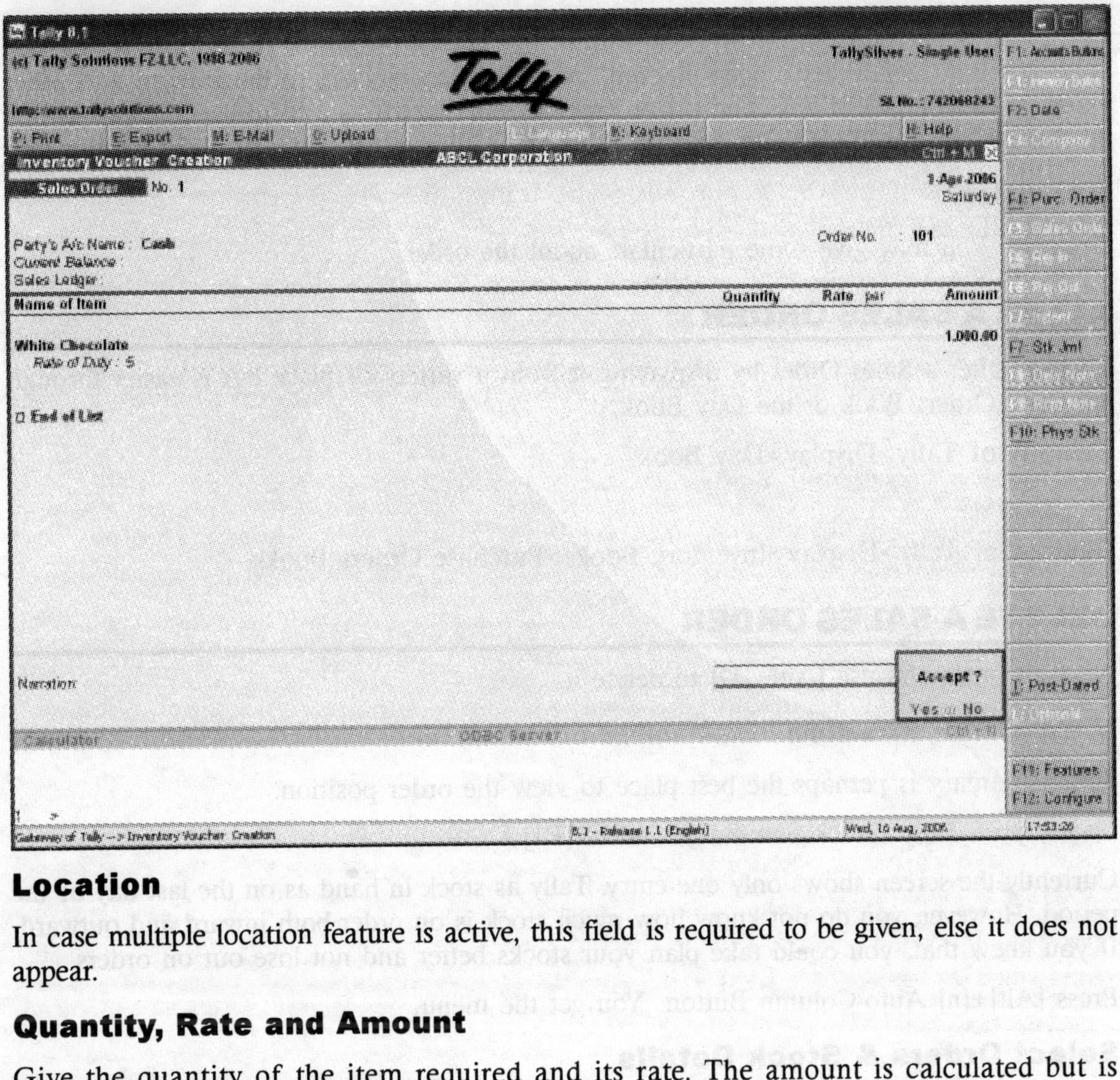

Location

In case multiple location feature is active, this field is required to be given, else it does not appear.

Quantity, Rate and Amount

Give the quantity of the item required and its rate. The amount is calculated but is modifiable to enable rounding off.

Additional Cost Details

There is no additional cost details for sales orders. They exist only for Purchase as the values are added to the cost price. In case of sales, additional cost need to be entered along with tax.

Next Item

The cursor then comes to the Item field once again and you can enter another item to order. If no other item is required, press [Enter] on the blank field to take the cursor to the tax/expenses field.

Expense/Tax

Once the item details have been entered, you might specify tax to be charged and other expenses like freight, if any. The tax or expense has to exist as a ledger account or it may be created using [Alt]+[C]. We shall select tax @ 17.5% to be charged on the item values.

Narration

Optional. You may give some particulars about the order.

ALTER A SALES ORDER

You can alter a Sales Order by displaying it from a variety of place but is easier through the Sales Orders Book or the Day Book.

Gateway of Tally>Display>Day Book

or

Gateway of Tally>Display>Inventory Books>Purchase Orders Books

DELETE A SALES ORDER

Alter an order and use [Alt]+[D] to delete it.

View Order Position

Stock summary is perhaps the best place to view the order position.

Gateway of Tally>Stock Summary>Delete [F1]

Currently the screen shows only one entry. Tally as stock in hand as on the last day of the period. However, you do not know how much stock is on order both inward and outward. If you knew that, you could take plan your stocks better and not lose out on orders.

Press [Alt]+[n] Auto-Column Button. You get the menu.

Select Orders & Stock Details

Remove Rate and value from display by configuring it using F12.

This will enable all columns to fit in one screen.

Sales Order Reports can be accessed through [Alt]+F7 of the stock summary or Alt + C of the Stock Summary. They can also be accessed through ALL other reports by pressing F9 or F10 (Accounting/Inventory Reports).

Invoice Entry

Invoicing or Sales invoicing is not very different from sales voucher entry. In fact, you use the same voucher but select As Invoice option to turn it into sales invoice. Purchase invoices are recorded through normal Purchase Voucher entry and it does not have the provision of being converted into an invoice format for entry purpose.

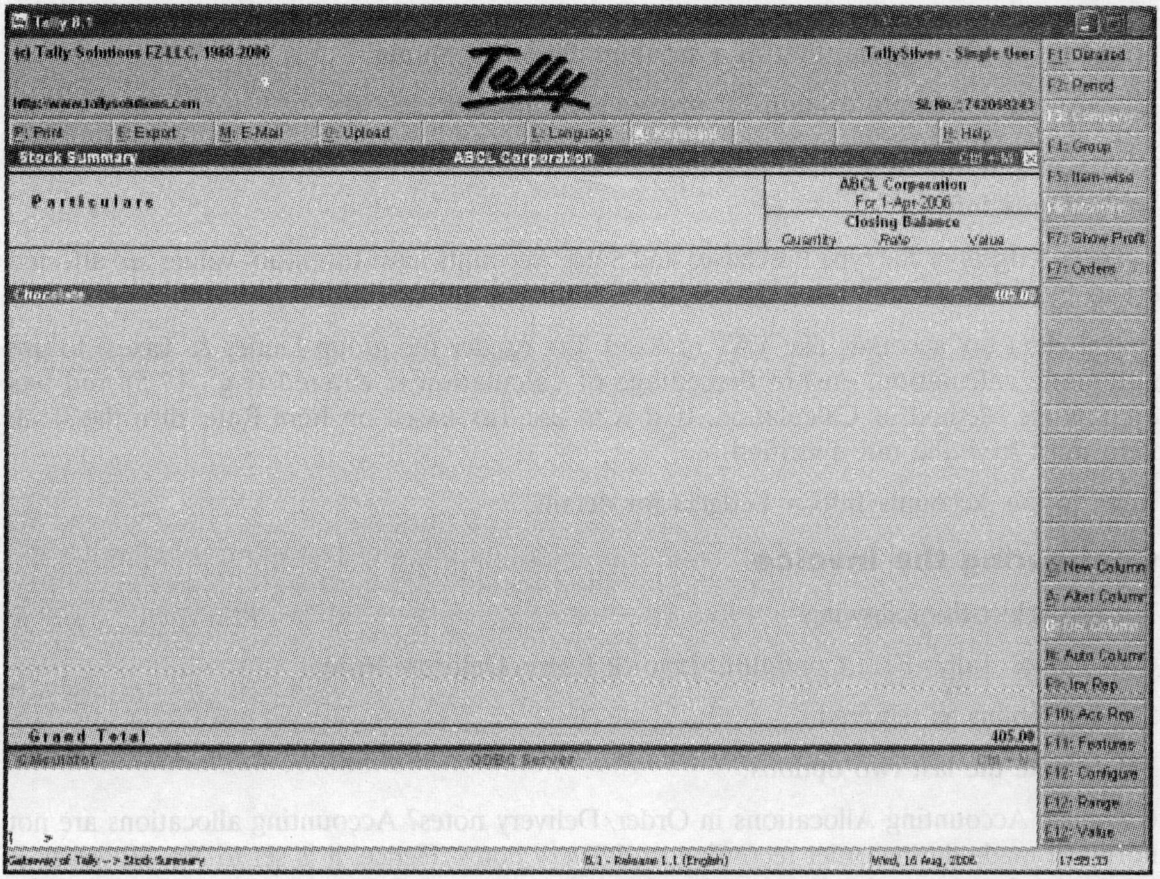

However, you can print the purchase voucher as a Purchase Invoice or even a Purchase Order. The advantage of using the invoice format for sales invoice entry is that it enable automatic calculations of taxes and duties accounts (those falling under the group Duties and Taxes or those groups for which the field Used for calculation is enabled.) In reordering both sales and purchase invoice details, you can adjust accounting and inventory balances and accounts for VAT, all at the same time. The default invoice formats have a variety of configuration options. Using them you may print your invoices. You may not need to create new invoice formats. It is recommended that you attempt to configure the default invoice itself. However, should you finally feel that the invoice does not meet the needs, you can design a new invoice using Tally's Definition Language Report Designer. The TDL is quite an advanced language with which you can create new reports and screens. You may even modify existing reports and screens. However, it is specialist's job and would require advanced training.

Ensure that you have activated Invoice Entry capability in F11: Company Features

Ensure that:

In F12: Configure under Gateway of Tally, Voucher Entry, in the Accounting Vouchers section of the screen, Show Inventory Details is set to Yes.

In F11: Features and in the top section of the screen, Allow Invoicing is set to yes. This brings up another option, that of a separate discount column.

If you want a separate column for discounts in invoices, say Yes.

Also ensure that:

In Accounts Info

Ledgers, ledgers of the type Purchases and Sales Accounts have Inventory values are affected set to Yes.

If you want tax accounts like VAT or Sales Tax (under the group Duties & Taxes) to use automatic calculation, ensure Percentage of calculation is entered (e.g., 17.5) and has appropriate Method of Calculation. If it is to use Tax based on Item Rate, then the stock item must have the rate specified.

Refer to the Accounts Info > Ledgers for details.

Configuring the Invoice

For this select the following:

Gateway of Tally>F12: Configure>Invoice Entry/Delivery Note

Set the options as required.

Please note the last two options.

Complete Accounting Allocations in Order/Delivery notes? Accounting allocations are not normally made during order recording or delivery notes. Hence, it is set to No. However, it is permitted and, should you want it, change it to Yes.

Allow modification of ALL fields during entry? Default order/delivery note entries appearing in the invoice can be changed during invoice entry. To permit modification of all fields set it to Yes. Else No.

Further to invoice entry configuration, you can configure its printing.

For this select the following:

Gateway of Tally>F12:Configure>Printing>Sales Transactions>Sales Invoice

Set the print options as desired. As you would see, you can configure the invoice to a great extent. The options depend on the various F11 Company Features and F12: Configure options that have been set for your company either by you or by the administrator. In the above screen, the options are turned to Britain/Europe settings. These would change if you opt for India/Asia in the basic company settings.

Likewise, the details that you give during invoice entry, depend very much on the configuration settings. Let us look at a typical invoice entry screen:

During invoice entry, some of the information will be input in separate pop-up screens. The invoice format is different from the normal sales voucher where the accounting information is the primary information and the stock information is secondary. In the invoice format, the accounting information is secondary and the stock information primary. Hence, you give accounting information, i.e., the sales account to be credited in a pop-up window.

Sales Voucher Number

This number is controlled by the settings in the voucher type masters.

Date

Change date using [F2], when you need to.

Reference

This is an optional field. Give any reference particulars that can be later picked up using the range or filter mechanism. This has, traditionally, been used for tracking missing tax forms.

Party's A/c Name

Select the customer's ledger account. This account will be debited by the total invoice amount. You may select a party ledger (Falling under the group Sundry Debtors or Sundry Creditors) or even Cash or Bank Account (for cash sales.)

Party's other Details

This information is to be filled up in the secondary screen that pops up.
You may have a different consignee name and address than the buyer. (if configured for).

Delivery Note No(s)

Select the delivery note if there was any made for this shipment from the Pop-up List of Tracking numbers. This way you reconcile goods despatched with the invoice and financial records. Select Not Applicable if no separate delivery exists. The choice is required only in case Tracking Numbers are active.

Dispatch Details

Give the dispatch details here. These are printed out on the invoice.

Other Details

The order particulars may be entered here. If a prior order was recorded for the customer, a pop-up list of opening orders appears from which you select the relevant order or orders. You may raise in invoice against a single order or even a multiple orders. Select New Number if no prior orders exists for this invoice but you want to record the order particulars. Select Not Applicable if not applicable. Select End of List to move to the next item.

Buyer's Details

The Buyer's Address as per the master records appear as default, but you may alter it. If you have configured to have the Consignee address as well as Buyer address, its details too appear. Accept or modify them as necessary.

Inventory Allocations

Inventory items that are to be invoiced have to be entered. Once you have selected the first item and the tracking number, if you have multiple locations set up, a secondary screen pops up for accepting the item particulars.

Give the quantity rate and unit particulars. You may select more than one location from where the goods have been despatched. Press [Enter] at the first blank location field to accept the first item's allocation of location and other details. You now have to give the accounting ledger that will be affected for the sale of this item.

The location column appears only if Multiple Location feature has been activated.

Accounting Details

This information is to be given in a secondary screen that pops up after allocation of the each item. Select the relevant sales account to be debited for the first item. Sales of Disks is a ledger account under the group Sales Account. It is the credit entry to the debit effected by the Party A/c name.

Where you have More than One Stock Item

Each item will require item allocation and accounting allocation as above. You must repeat the procedure till you have completed all the items for that invoice. Press [Enter] on blank item or select [end of list] to complete the cycle.

VAT/Tax or other Expenses

These accounts are entered after the total value of stock items. Select relevant ledgers for the list. These are ledger accounts and would affect accounting ledgers. For accounts like VAT/Sales Tax that are under the group Duties & Taxes (or are otherwise specified as Calculate in invoice entry in their masters), the amounts are calculated automatically. Press [enter] on blank item or select [end of list] when you have completed.

Bill Details

After the cursor leaves the total amount field, you must give bill-wise particulars, if the feature is activated for this particular party ledger.

You do this in the bill-wise details screen. After you give the narration, accept the invoice.

Printing Invoices and Vouchers

You can print any voucher or invoice by pressing [ALT]+[P] or clicking on the button [Print]. Do this before saving the voucher. You or administrator may have configured the voucher type to print automatically after saving the voucher. You can always configure the printing options by selecting the appropriate buttons. You can give additional information, change titles, print additional pages, change printer settings, etc. The buttons [Pre-Printed] and [Quick Format] are toggles for [Plain Paper] and [Neat Format] respectively. These are print specifications that you give pre-printed is for pre-printed stationery. Quick Format does not give fonts or other niceties but is ideal for fast printing Select copies and give the number of copies to be printed. 1 is the default. You can set the default number of copies in Invoice Printing Configuration For this select the following:

Gateway of Tally>F12: Configuration>Printing

View Invoice as Voucher and Vice-Versa

Once you create the invoice, you can view it as a voucher by simply displaying it and clicking on the toggle button (As invoice]/[As Voucher] or pressing [CTRL]+[V]. You may do likewise with a sales voucher to be brought up as an invoice.

Display/Alter a Voucher/Invoice

You can display a voucher or alter it (subject to authority) by simply drilling down any display screen. For example, from the Balance Sheet, press [Enter] on the group Sundry Debtors, then on the ledger ABC Corporation Ltd which brings up its monthly summary. Continue the selection process till you see the list of vouchers and the voucher itself. You may opt to alter a voucher by going through the ledger display screen or the Day Book. Since the display interfaces are identical, feel free to use the path most convenient for the circumstance. If you do not have authority to alter a voucher, the voucher would be brought up for display only.

Foreign Exchange Transactions

Entering foreign exchange transaction in Tally vouchers is quite simple once you understand the principles of it. Remember that you must have foreign currency enabled in F11 Company Features. Only genuine bank accounts that are maintained in foreign currencies need to have their currency set up in that foreign currency otherwise all other ledgers should preferably be set to home/base currency only.

Based on the above settings, we shall examine a Purchase voucher entry of an import transaction in foreign exchange and then a payment entry made form a Forex bank account.

Foreign Exchange Transaction of an Import Transaction

In the purchase voucher.

1. Give the date, voucher number and reference as usual.
2. You need to first credit the supplier
3. In the amount field, start with the foreign currency symbol to signal to Tally that it is a Forex transaction. In this case we type Rs (our base currency is remember) and continue with the amount Rs. 150000.
4. A Forex sub-screen now asks for information on the exchange rate. Simply give the rate as quoted by your bank or mentioned on the purchase invoice. (Tally gives the

default exchange rate that you had mentioned in the foreign currency master). You are allowed to change the rate. Alternatively change the amount and the rate will be adjusted automatically. If you want to give only the base currency, clear the forex field and Rate of Exchange file and simply mention the Value in base currency. The exchange rate would then be ineffective.

In inventory item allocation, we show a purchase of 5 copies of Tally software. You may give the rate of the item in the base currency or even in foreign currency. To mention in foreign currency, start the rate entry with the forex symbol. Tally convert it to the base currency at the exchange rate previously mentioned.

The forex entry method is repeated here:

In the amount field, start with the foreign currency symbol to signal to Tally that it is a forex transaction. A forex sub-screen now asks for information on the exchange rate. Simply give the rate as quoted by your bank or newspaper or as recorded in the documents. Tally gives the specified exchange rate by default if it is mentioned in the foreign currency master.

You are allowed to change the rate. Alternatively change the amount and the rate will be adjusted automatically. If you want to give only the base currency, clear the forex field and Rate of Exchange field and simply mention the Value in base currency. The change rate would then be ineffective. Of course, if you do not enter a foreign currency in the amount field, the amount is assumed to be in home/base currency.

Descriptive Type Questions

1. What are the features of an Inventory voucher?
2. How would you create a stock journal?
3. How would you create a manufacturing journal?
4. How would you create a purchase order?
5. What is a purchase order?

6 Value Added Tax (VAT)

WHAT IS VAT?

The essence of VAT is in providing set-off for input tax and this is applied through the concept of input credit/rebate. This input credit in relation to any period means setting off the amount of input tax by a registered dealer against the amount of his output tax. Value Added Tax (VAT) is based on the value addition to the goods, and the related VAT liability of the dealer is calculated by deducting the input credit from the tax collected on sales during the payment period.

This concept is explained with an example, in the Computation of VAT section.

VAT works in two different ways:

If VAT-registered business receives more output tax than the taxes paid as input, they will need to pay the difference to the Commissioner of Taxes (State).

If the input tax paid is more than the output tax collected,

- You can carry forward the Input credit and adjust it against the output tax in the subsequent months.
- You can have the Input Credit refunded to you by the Government at the end of the current or following year.
- You can receive refunds for Input Credit on exports within a period of three months.

GENERAL TERMINOLOGIES USED IN VAT

Term	*Description*
Input tax	This is a tax paid on purchases
Output tax	This is a tax charged on sales
Input Credit	The amount of Input tax that Is permitted to be set off against Output tax.
Composite Dealers	Dealers with annual gross turnover not exceeding a certain threshold (threshold – decided by the respective State Governments) can opt for a composition scheme whereby they will pay tax as a small percentage of their gross turnover. However, retailers opting for this composition scheme will not be entitled to Input Credit. The State Governments fix the periods and the procedures for the payment of the lump sum.

Advantages of VAT

VAT was adopted because the Sales Tax system is complex and induces non-compliance. Moreover, it has been found to be a hindrance in the economic growth of Industry, state and the Country. This cause a huge loss of revenue to the government.

VAT also helps in eliminating the dreaded cascading effect of Tax. For instance, in the existing structure, inputs are taxed before a commodity is produced and the output is taxed after it is produced. This causes an unfair double taxation with cascading effects.

However, in VAT, as a set-off is given for input tax as well as tax paid on previous purchases, overall tax burden will be rationalized and prices in general will fall. VAT thus makes the tax system simple and transparent.

Advantages of VAT over Sales Tax

- As VAT is a multi-point tax with set-off for tax paid on purchases, it prevents repeated taxation of the same product.
- Simple and Transparent: In the Sales tax system the amount of tax levied on the goods at all stages is not known. However, in VAT, the amount of tax would be known at each and every stage of goods sale or purchase.
- VAT has the flexibility to generate large and buoyant revenues, as it levies tax on value additions.
- Zero rating of tax on exports is possible in case of VAT.
- Fair and Equitable: VAT introduces uniform tax rates across the state so that unfair advantage cannot be taken while levying the tax.
- Procedure of simplification: Procedures related to filing of returns, payment of tax, furnishing declaration and assessment are simplified under the VAT system so as to minimize any interface between the tax payer and the tax collector.
- Ability to provide same revenue to the Government with lower rates of tax.
- Tax does not become a cost of doing business.

VAT Rates

According to the White Paper, there are 550 categories of goods under the VAT system. They are classified into the following four groups, depending on the VAT rate:

VAT @ 4%

The largest number of goods (270) comprises of basic necessity items such as drugs and medicines, agricultural and industrial inputs, capital goods and declared goods are under 4% VAT rate.

Exempted from VAT

There are about 46 commodities under the exempted category. This includes a maximum of 10 commodities that each state would be allowed to select, from a broader list for VAT exemption.

The exempted commodities include natural and unprocessed products in unorganized sector as well as items, which are legally barred from taxation.

VAT @ 1%

This is for a specific category of goods like gold, silver, etc.

VAT @ 12.5%

The remaining commodities are under the general VAT rate of 12.5%.

BUSINESS PROCESSES

The effect of VAT in individual business process may be identified as under:

Purchase Process: VAT paid on purchases during a month can be claimed for set off as 'Input VAT'. In case of purchase return, VAT on returns is adjusted against Input VAT and the net amount is treated as Input Vat. Similarly VAT on rate differences etc on purchases are adjusted against Input VAT and the net amount is claimed for set off.

Manufacturing Process: VAT paid on purchase of materials (e.g., raw materials, packing materials etc) is claimed for set off as 'Input VAT'. Additionally, credit for VAT paid on Capital Goods can be claimed in 36 monthly instalments.

Likewise, exporters can get refund for Input VAT paid by them within a period of three months. At the beginning of the year in which VAT is introduced, the Assessing offer will determine the Input Tax component in the opening stock on the first day of the year and the same will be allowed for adjustment as Input Tax in six monthly installments.

Sales Process: VAT charged/payable on Sales during a month becomes the Output VAT for the month. Sales returns or any rate difference allowed are adjusted against Output VAT.

VAT Payable: The net difference between Output VAT and Input VAT, i.e, Output VAT – (minus) Input Vat becomes VAT payable by the dealer. In case Input Tax is higher than Output Vat, the balance is carried forward to the following month or may be refunded in certain cases.

COMPUTATION OF VAT

The essence of VAT is in providing set-off for Input Tax (tax paid on Purchases) against Output Tax (tax payable on Sales). In other words, a registered dealer pays only the differential amount of tax between his tax liabilities on account of sales upon deducting the tax already paid on Purchases during the period.

Example:

'A', a wholesaler, sells a product to 'B', a Dealer, at Rs. 1000 and charges VAT @4%.

'B' sells it ot 'C', a retailer, at a profit of 100 i.e., at Rs. 1100 and charges VAT @4%.

'C', sells it to Consumer at a profit of 100 i.e., at Rs. 1200 and charges VAT @4%.

The implication of VAT can be shown in following table:

Tax implication under Value Added Tax Act

Seller	*Buyer*	*Selling Price Price (Excl. Tax)*	*Tax Rate*	*Invoice Value (Incl. Tax)*	*Tax Payable Rs.*	*Tax Credit Rs.*	*Nett. Tax Outflow*
A	B	1000	4% VAT	1040.00	40.00	0	40.00
B	C	1100	4% VAT	1144.00	44.00	40.00	4.00
C	Consumer	1200	4%VAT	1248.00	48.00	44.00	4.00
Total VAT to Govt.						VAT	48.00

VAT CLASSIFICATION

It is a list of VAT rates, which describes the nature of the Business Activity and type pf transaction. These are in-built in the system and will be updated if and when any statutory changes take place. Some of the classifications are :

- InputVAT@4%
- InputVAT@1 %
- InputVAT@12.5%
- OutputVAT@ 1 %
- OutputVAT@4%
- OutputVAT@12.5%
- Purchases – Capital Goods
- Purchases – Exempt
- Purchases from unregistered dealers

Depending on the type of the business, type of transaction, and the statutory requirements of your State, you will need to select the appropriate classifications from the list during Ledger creations, voucher entries, etc.

The Sales and Purchase transactions are segregated based upon the classification selected during voucher entry and shown in the VAT computation. Thus you can see in the VAT Computation, the classification – wise VAT and Nett values.

VAT DOCUMENTS

A VAT dealer needs to generate VAT compliant Invoice, Credit and Debit Notes and also submit statutory Returns in a prescribed format, as applicable for the state.

The following documents must be generated.

Tax Invoice

A VAT compliant invoice, called Tax Invoice, has to be serially numbered and must have the following details:

- Product is exempt or VAT-able.
- Tax Identification Number (TIN) – registration details along with sellers' name and address.
- Tax point – date of sale.
- Full item list with VAT break-up including VAT totals.

Credit and Debit Notes

Detailed documents of all returns and adjustments have to be maintained since the same will have an impact on the input credit. All Credit and Debit Notes would require the same information as that on TAX Invoice.

VAT RECORDS

The VAT dealer must maintain the following records.

Stock Records

A complete record of purchase and sales must be maintained of each stock item.

Manufacturing Account

Complete records of raw materials and input purchased along with goods manufactured.

VAT Account

As per state specified formats, the VAT Accounts must be properly maintained. The VAT Account is summary of all Input Tax paid for purchase and all Output Tax collected on sales to compute the Net VAT Payable or Input Credit for carry forward.

STATUTORY RETURNS

Monthly Return incorporating beak-up of all types of purchase & sales transactions, input & output taxes computing Net Tax payable or Refundable.

DEALER STATUS

Under VAT Act, a dealer with turnover exceeding the threshold limit must register with VAT authorities. However, a dealer with annual turnover less than the threshold limit need not register under VAT act and as such exempted from the purview of VAT Act.

Dealers Registered Under VAT

A registered retailer falling within the specified limit may opt for composite scheme and thus for registered dealers, the status may be (a) composite Dealer or (b) Registered Dealer.

Registered Dealers

Registered dealers can issue a Tax Invoice and can claim for Input tax credit for VAT paid on purchases within the state. They are required to pay the difference between Output Tax and Input Tax already paid on purchases. They are required to file statutory returns periodically.

Composite Dealers

A dealer may opt to become a composite dealer if his turnover is within a limit set by the state. A composite dealer is required to pay tax on a fixed rate on the turnover of taxable items as set by the state and file a simple return annually. The limitations are that they cannot issue Tax Invoice nor can they claim set-off for Input Tax paid by them.

Ledger Masters

The VAT Classification will be displayed as a drop down list in the ledger Masters. Tally gives the flexibility to the user, to either have the classification selected in the Ledger Master tagged to all transactions, Or, select different classifications each time during voucher entries. This is explained in detail in the Vouchers and Transactions section.

The Ledgers that are affected by VAT are:

- Purchase Ledger
- Sales Ledger
- Duties and Taxes Ledger
- Direct Expenses/Income

Creating Purchase Ledger for VAT

You can enable Tally VAT in the Statutory and Taxation screen shown in Fig. 6.1.

From here you can set your various VAT, Excise, TDS, FBT, etc. options.

We will also create a ledge for the Supplier from when we are buying the VAT exempted item:

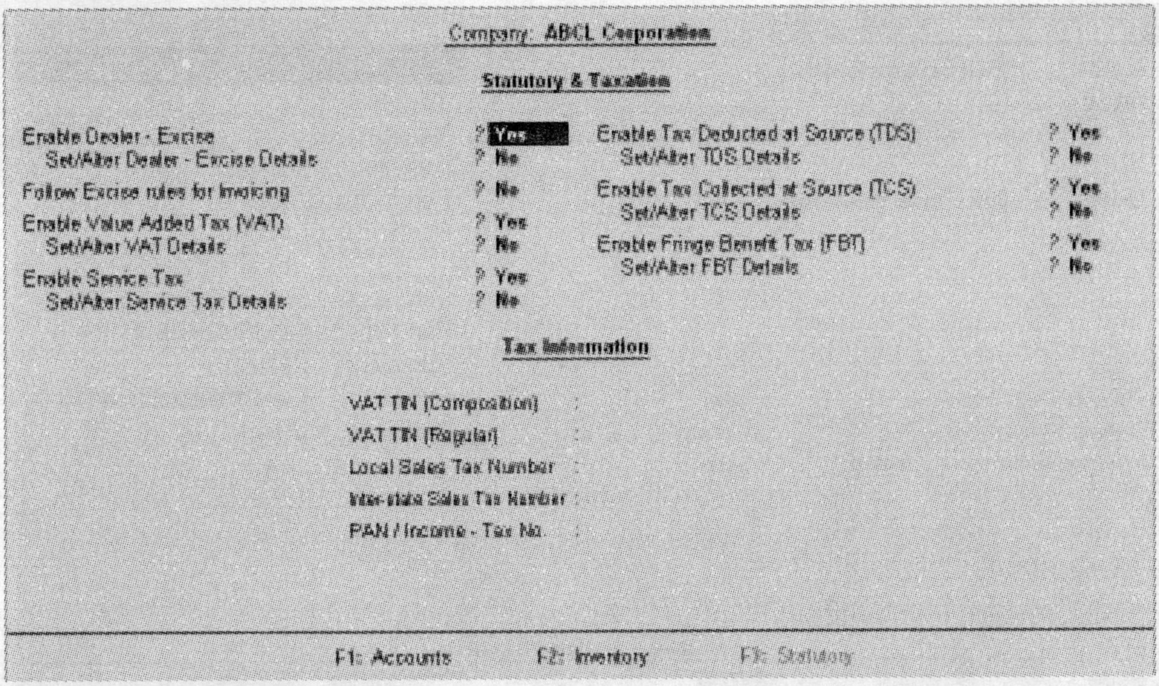

Purchase Ledger

The following additional fields, pertaining to VAT, can now be seen in the Ledger entry screen (Gatewayof Tally > Accounts Info > Ledger>> Create/ Alter).

Used in VAT Return

Set this to Yes if you wish to select VAT classifications for this Ledger. Once you set this to Yes, you will see the Default VAT /Tax Class field.

Default VAT/Tax Class

Select the required classification here from the drop down list as shown above. The drop down list consists of the Purchase classifications pertaining to your state. If you do not wish to select a classification at the Ledger level, you can set this to Not Applicable.

Tally gives the flexibility to the user, to either have the classification selected in the Ledger Master tagged to all transactions, Or, select different classifications each time during voucher entries. This is explained in detail in the Vouchers and Transactions section

The rest of the Ledger creation process is the same as in default Tally

In the above example we have selected a VAT classification of 4%. Let us also take an example of a VAT exempted transaction.

Sales Ledger

Like in the Purchase Ledger screen, select the required VAT/Tax classification in the Sales Ledger too (Gateway of Tally > Accounts Info > Ledger > Create/Alter.)

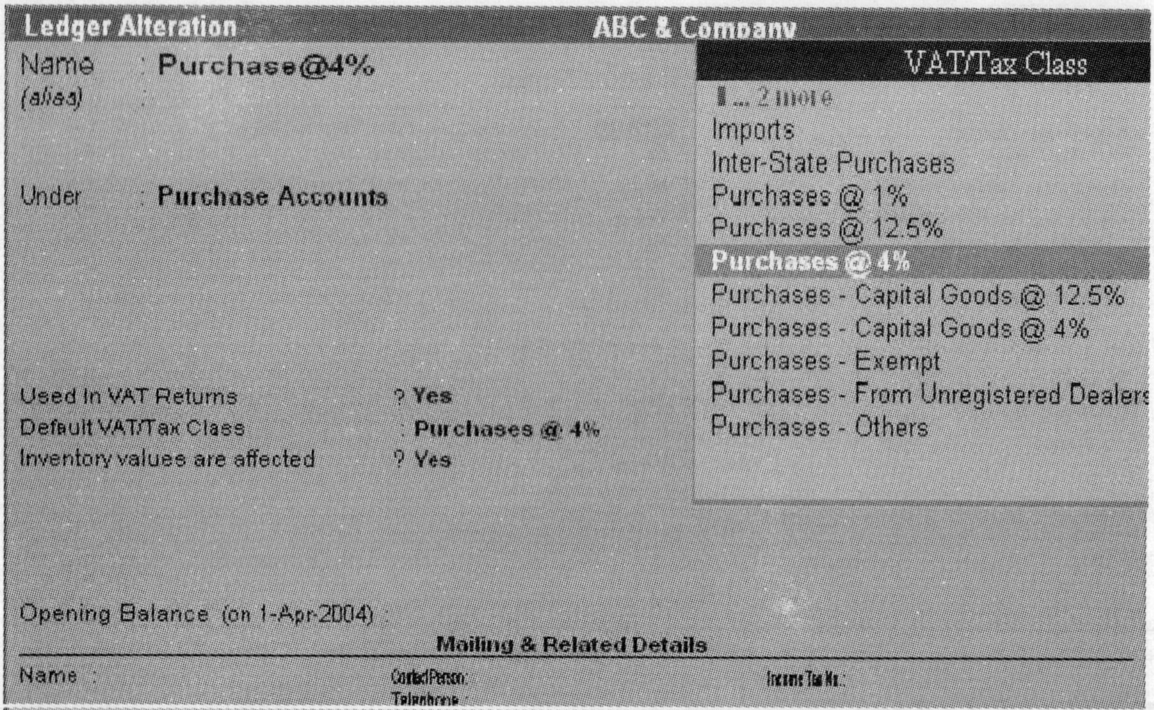
Ledger Alteration
ABC & Company
Name : Purchase@4%
(alias) :
Under : Purchase Accounts
Used In VAT Returns ? Yes
Default VAT/Tax Class : Purchases @ 4%
Inventory values are affected ? Yes
Opening Balance (on 1-Apr-2004) :
Mailing & Related Details
Name :
VAT/Tax Class
... 2 more
Imports
Inter-State Purchases
Purchases @ 1%
Purchases @ 12.5%
Purchases @ 4%
Purchases - Capital Goods @ 12.5%
Purchases - Capital Goods @ 4%
Purchases - Exempt
Purchases - From Unregistered Dealers
Purchases - Others

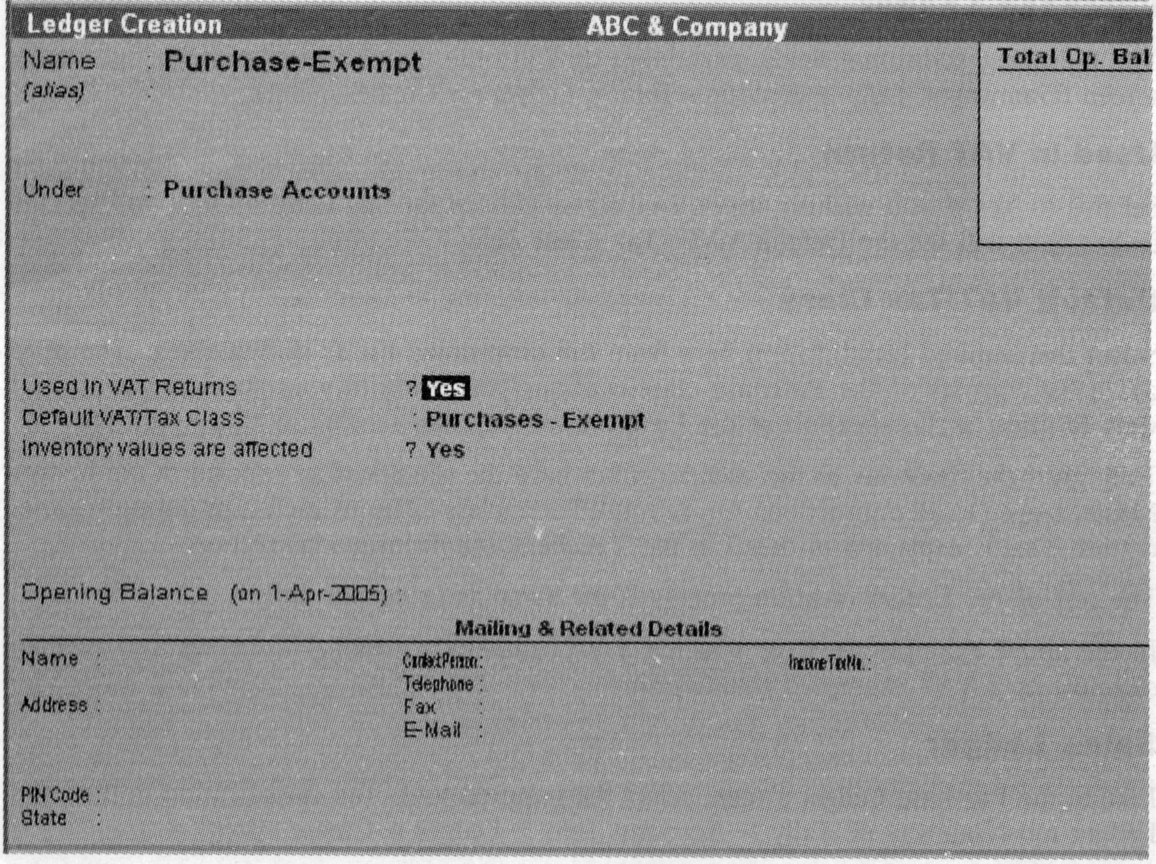
Ledger Creation
ABC & Company
Name : Purchase-Exempt
(alias) :
Total Op. Bal
Under : Purchase Accounts
Used In VAT Returns ? Yes
Default VAT/Tax Class : Purchases - Exempt
Inventory values are affected ? Yes
Opening Balance (on 1-Apr-2005) :
Mailing & Related Details
Name :
Address :
Telephone :
Fax :
E-Mail :
PIN Code :
State :

The rest of the settings are the same as in default Tally.

Duties and Taxes Ledger

The ledger for Input VAT is shown next.

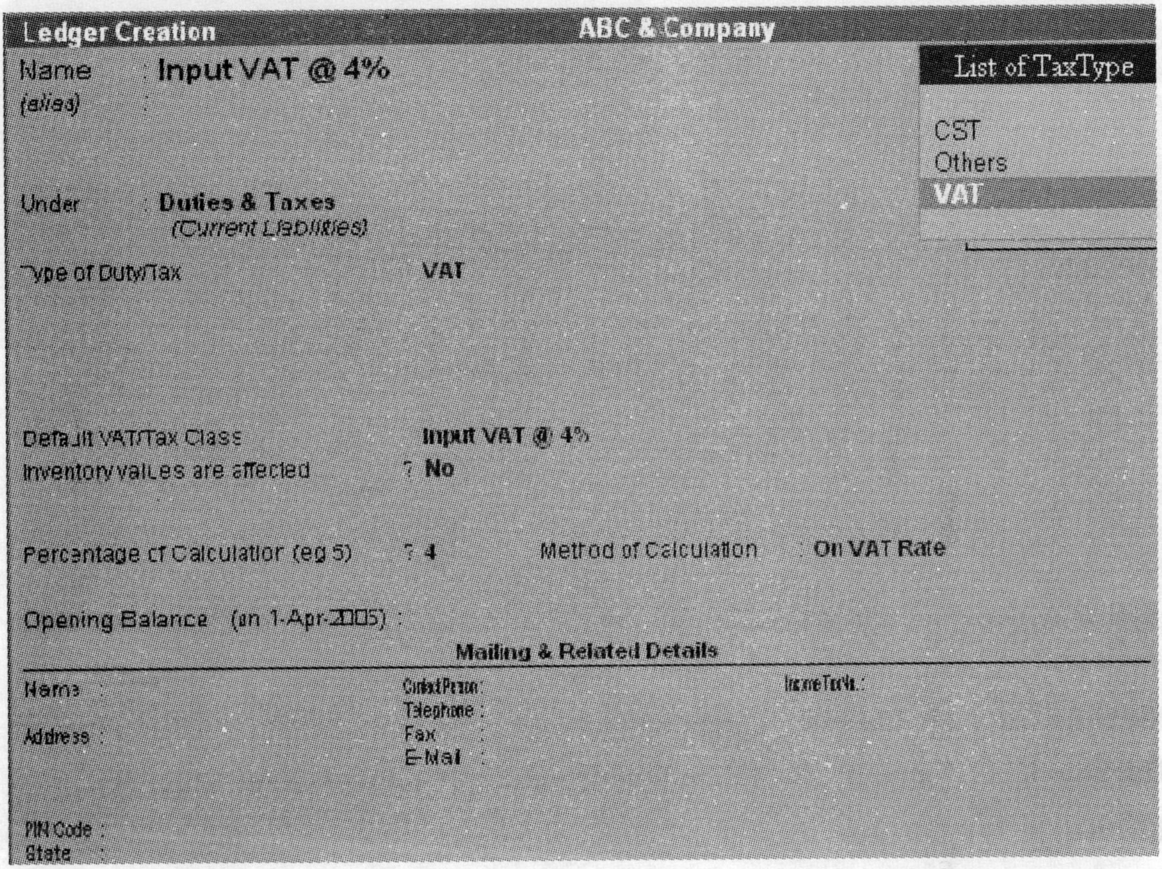

Type of Duty/Tax

On the selection of group Duties and Taxes, the list of Tax Types CST, others and VAT, is displayed. Select VAT for VAT related transactions.

If you have VAT and TDS enabled, the list will also include TDS.

Default VAT/Tax Class

Like in the Purchase and Sales Ledger, this is a drop down list containing the VAT classifications. Select the appropriate classification or select Not Applicable if you wish to select the classifications at the Voucher level, as shown next.

Percentage of Calculation

This will display the VAT rate that you selected in the Default VAT/Tax class field

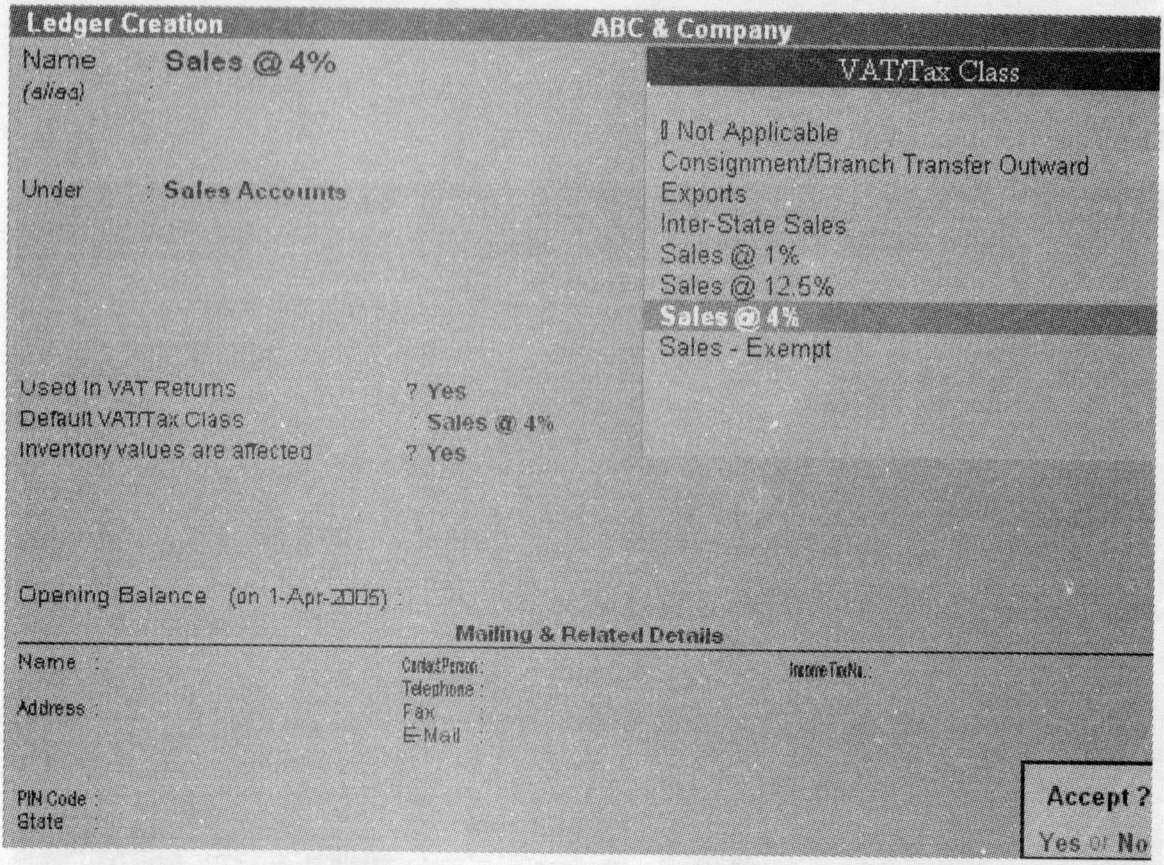

Method of Calculation

This will display On VAT Rate if you have selected VAT under Type of Duty/Tax.

Similarly for Output VAT

On selection of CST, see the result in next figure.

Default VAT/Tax Class

On selection of CST for Type of Duty, you can select either Inter-State Purchases or Inter-State Sales for Tax Class. Once you select this, you need to manually enter the Percentage of Calculation, as shown next.

Method of Calculation

Once you enter the Percentage of calculation, select the Type of Duty from the drop down list. It is shown next.

Direct Expenses/Income Ledger

The VAT related fields in the Direct Expense ledger is the same as for Purchase and Sales Ledgers. This is shown here.

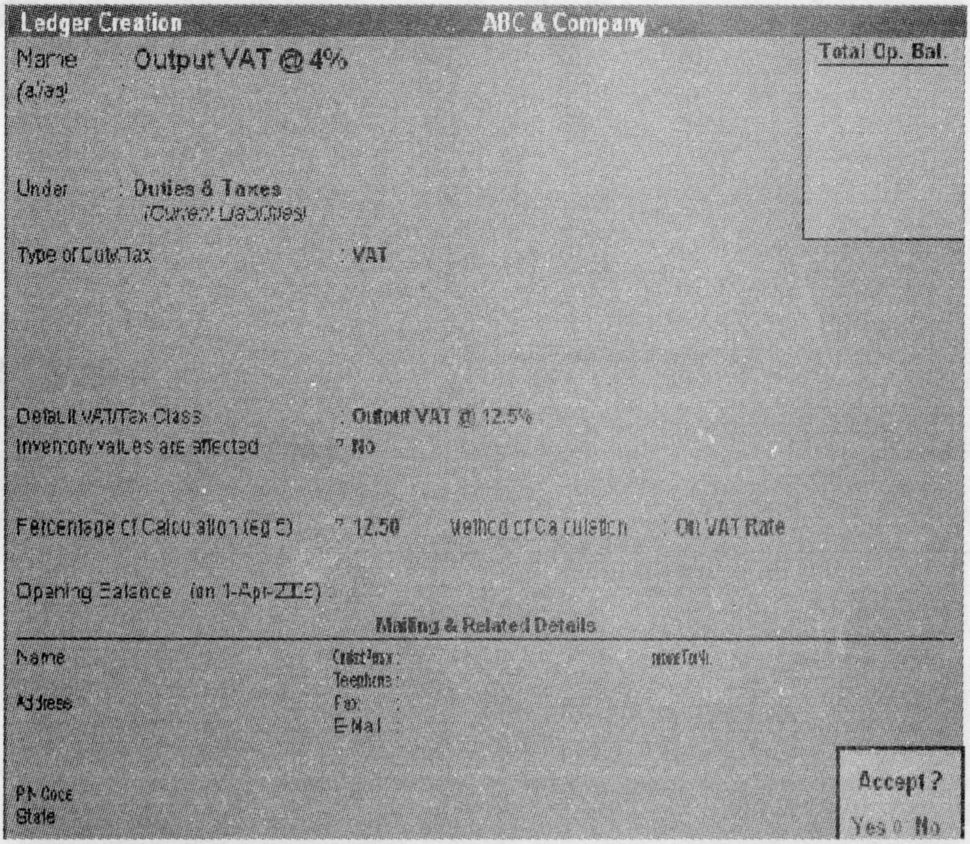
Ledger Creation
ABC & Company
Total Op. Bal.
Name : Output VAT @ 4%
(alias)
Under : Duties & Taxes
(Current Liabilities)
Type of Duty/Tax : VAT
Default VAT/Tax Class : Output VAT @ 12.5%
Inventory values are affected ? No
Percentage of Calculation (eg 5) ? 12.50
Method of Calculation : On VAT Rate
Opening Balance
Mailing & Related Details
Name
Address
Telephone :
Fax :
E-Mail :
PIN Code
State
Accept ?
Yes or No

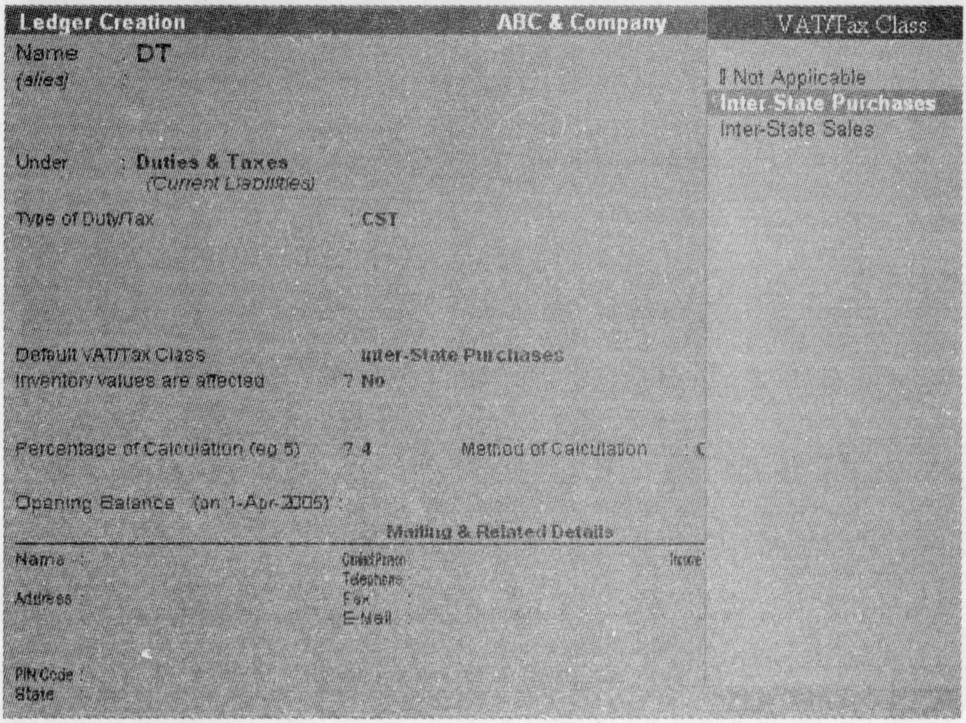
Ledger Creation
ABC & Company
VAT/Tax Class
Name : DT
(alias)
Not Applicable
Inter-State Purchases
Inter-State Sales
Under : Duties & Taxes
(Current Liabilities)
Type of Duty/Tax : CST
Default VAT/Tax Class : Inter-State Purchases
Inventory values are affected ? No
Percentage of Calculation (eg 5) ? 4
Method of Calculation
Opening Balance (on 1-Apr-2005) :
Mailing & Related Details
Name :
Address :
Telephone :
Fax :
E-Mail :
PIN Code :
State

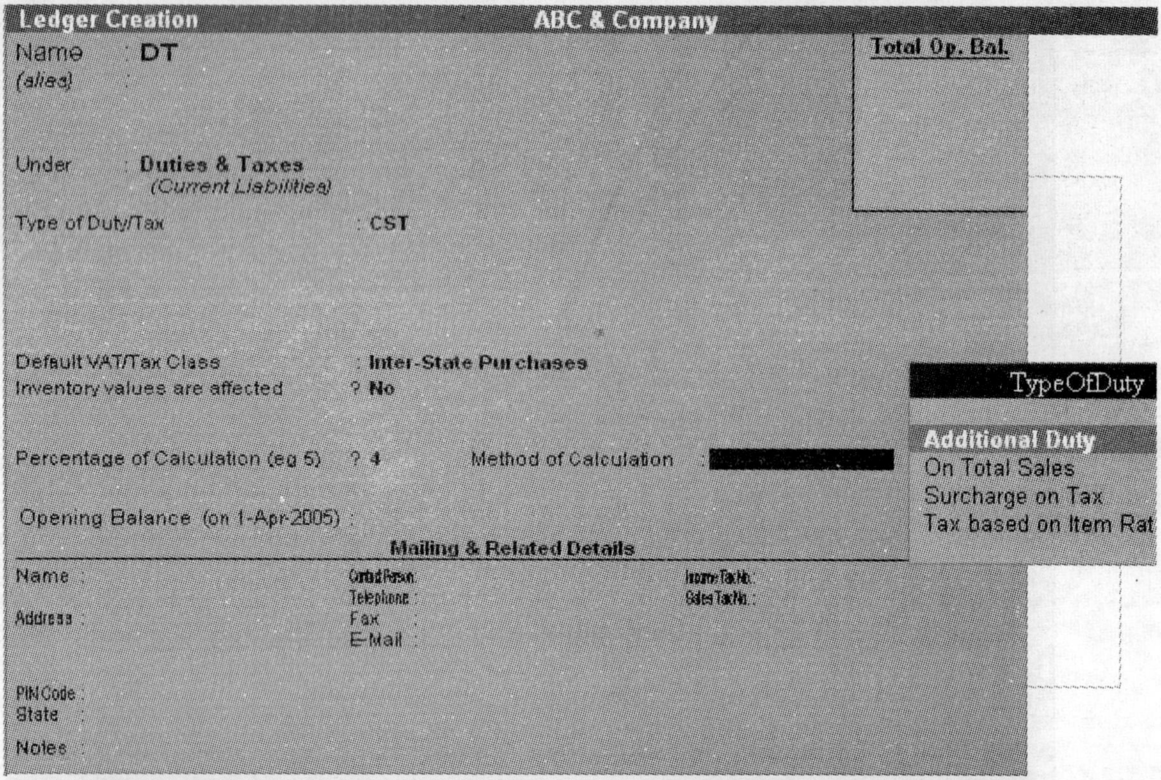
Ledger Creation
ABC & Company
Total Op. Bal.
Name : DT
(alias) :
Under : Duties & Taxes
(Current Liabilities)
Type of Duty/Tax : CST
Default VAT/Tax Class : Inter-State Purchases
Inventory values are affected ? No
Percentage of Calculation (eg 5) ? 4
Method of Calculation :
Opening Balance (on 1-Apr-2005) :
TypeOfDuty
Additional Duty
On Total Sales
Surcharge on Tax
Tax based on Item Rat
Mailing & Related Details
Name :
Address :
Contact Person :
Telephone :
Fax :
E-Mail :
Income Tax No. :
Sales Tax No. :
PIN Code :
State :
Notes :

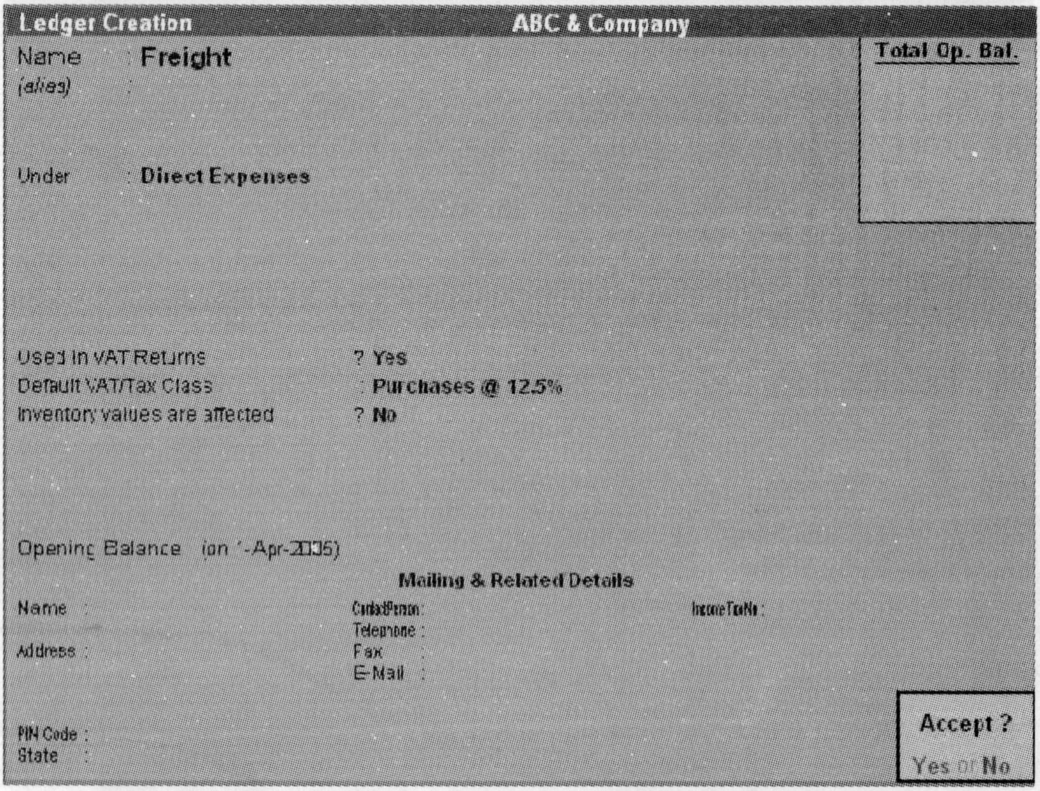
Ledger Creation
ABC & Company
Total Op. Bal.
Name : Freight
(alias) :
Under : Direct Expenses
Used in VAT Returns ? Yes
Default VAT/Tax Class : Purchases @ 12.5%
Inventory values are affected ? No
Opening Balance (on 1-Apr-2005)
Mailing & Related Details
Name :
Address :
Contact Person :
Telephone :
Fax :
E-Mail :
Income Tax No :
PIN Code :
State :
Accept ?
Yes or No

VOUCHERS AND TRANSACTIONS

The entire data entry and Reporting architecture is based upon VAT Classifications selected during Voucher Entry. The Vouchers that are affected by VAT are as follows:

- Purchase
- Sales
- Debit Note
- Credit Note
- Journals

Purchase Voucher (As Invoice)

Invoice can be classified into As Item Invoice and As Accounts Invoice. The VAT functionality though, is the same for both. Given below are examples of transactions in Item Invoice with implementation of VAT.

As Item Invoice

The selection and display of the VAT classifications in the vouchers differ according to the settings in the F12: Configuration screen.

F12: Configuration Screen

The drill down report will thus show as follows:

Use Common Ledger A/c for Item Allocation – NO

When you wish to use more than one ledger during a voucher transaction, you need to set this to No. this way, you need to select a ledger for every item during voucher entry. When you set this to No, you can see the VAT/Tax Class at the header region of the screen if the Allow Selection of VAT/TAX Class during entry? Field is set to Yes.

Allow Selection of VAT/Tax Class During Entry? – YES

Once you select Yes, you have the option to select the VAT classification in the field VAT/ Tax Class which is in header region of the Voucher screen. If it is set to no, the VAT/Tax Class will not be displayed in the voucher screen and the classifications will be taken from the Ledgers.

Consider the following examples

- Example 1: Purchase@4%

The following is the entry for the purchase of item1 when VAT classification is Purchase@4%. Like mentioned before, this classification is selected from a drop down list at the header region of the screen as shown here.

In the VAT/Tax Class field, there is also an option called Not Applicable. You can select

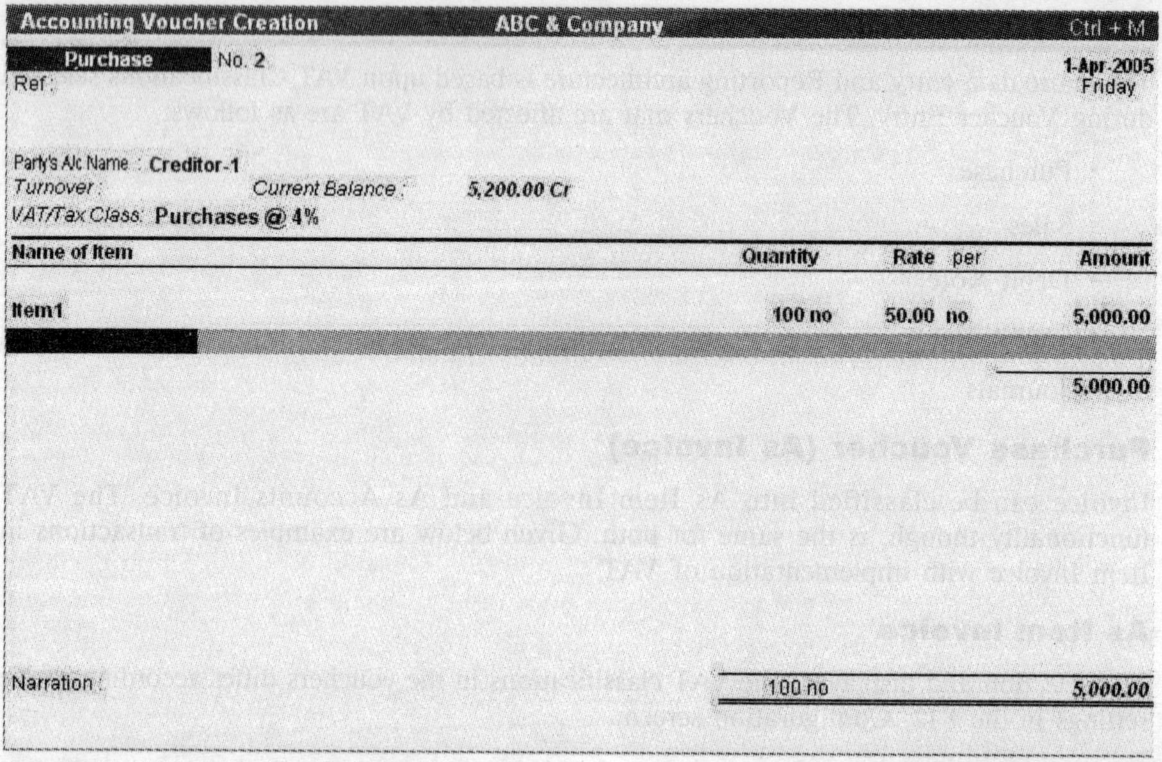

this option if you need different classifications for each item during voucher entry, refer above figure. You will need to select the Duties and Taxes ledger after you are done with the entry of all items.

It will now calculate the VAT amount and add it to the Amount to give you the total. See the new Configuration screen, see next figure.

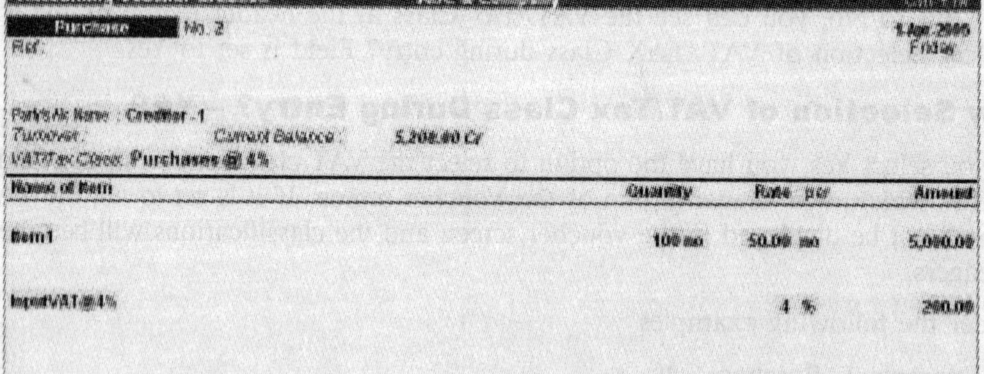

Use Common Leger A/c for Item Allocation – YES

When you wish to use the same Ledger for all items in a transaction, you can set this to Yes. Thus, you need not select a Ledger each time you enter an item during the voucher transaction. The following example to demonstrate the functioning of Assessable Value is shown by setting field to Yes.

Assessable Value: It is the value on which VAT is to be calculated. The value is arrived at after making proper deductions towards Excise/ED Cess payable. It is up to the user to calculate this and enter the Assessable Value column. This manual entry gives flexibility to the user to make the calculations as the the local statutory requirements.

As this example does not include Discount or Excise/ED Cess taxes, the Assessable Value will be Rs. 5200, which is retrieved from the amount column.

Let us assume we have:

- A discount of Rs. 200 on purchases
- Excise tax of Rs. 800 (16% of 5000)
- ED Cess lf Rs. 16 (2% of 800)
  - ➤ Subtracting the discount amount : 5000 – 200 = 4800
  - ➤ Adding the Excise tax amount : 4800 + 800 = 5600
  - ➤ Adding the ED Cess amount : 5600 + 16 = 5616

Therefore, our Assessable Value amount is Rs. 5616.

On the selection of the Duties and Taxes Ledger, you will see the following screen where you need to enter the Assessable value.

VAT is now calculated on this amount automatically on the selection of the tax ledger (Rs. 224) as shown next.

Similarly for Sales Voucher and Credit/Debit notes.

Example 2: Purchase – Exempt

This example is to demonstrate the working of Tally in the VAT exempted transactions and also to show the type and patterns of reports generated for such transactions. We are passing the following entry for the purchase of the VAT exempted item. It is shown in next figure.

As it is exempt from VAT, this particular transaction does not affect the VAT amount in any way. Similarly for Inter-State Sales/Purchases. In the Voucher mode there is no option for selection of the VAT classification at the header region. Therefore, the VAT classification selected in the Ledger will apply always.

Accounting Voucher Creation **ABC & Company** Ctrl + M

Purchase No. 3 — **1-Apr-2005** Friday

Ref :

Party's A/c Name : **Creditor**

Turnover : *Current Balance :*

Purchase Ledger : **Purchase**

VAT/Tax Class: **Purchases @ 4%**

Name of Item	Quantity	Rate	per	Amount
Item2	100 no	50.00	no	5,000.00
Discount				(-)200.00
Excise		16	%	800.00
Ed Cess		2	%	16.00
InputVAT@4%		4	%	224.64

Narration : 100 no **5,840.64**

Accounting Voucher Creation **ABC & Company** Ctrl + M

Purchase No. 1 — **1-Apr-2005** Friday

Ref :

Party's A/c Name : **Supplier**

Turnover : *Current Balance :*

VAT/Tax Class: **Purchases - Exempt**

Name of Item	Quantity	Rate	per	Amount
Item-Exempt	50 no	100.00	no	5,000.00
				5,000.00

Narration : 50 no **5,000.00**

Sales Vouchers (As Invoice)

Implementation is the same as explained in Purchase Voucher. However, in order to understand VAT Computation, let us take the following example of a Sales transaction as follows. Assessable Value: Same as explained in Purchase voucher.

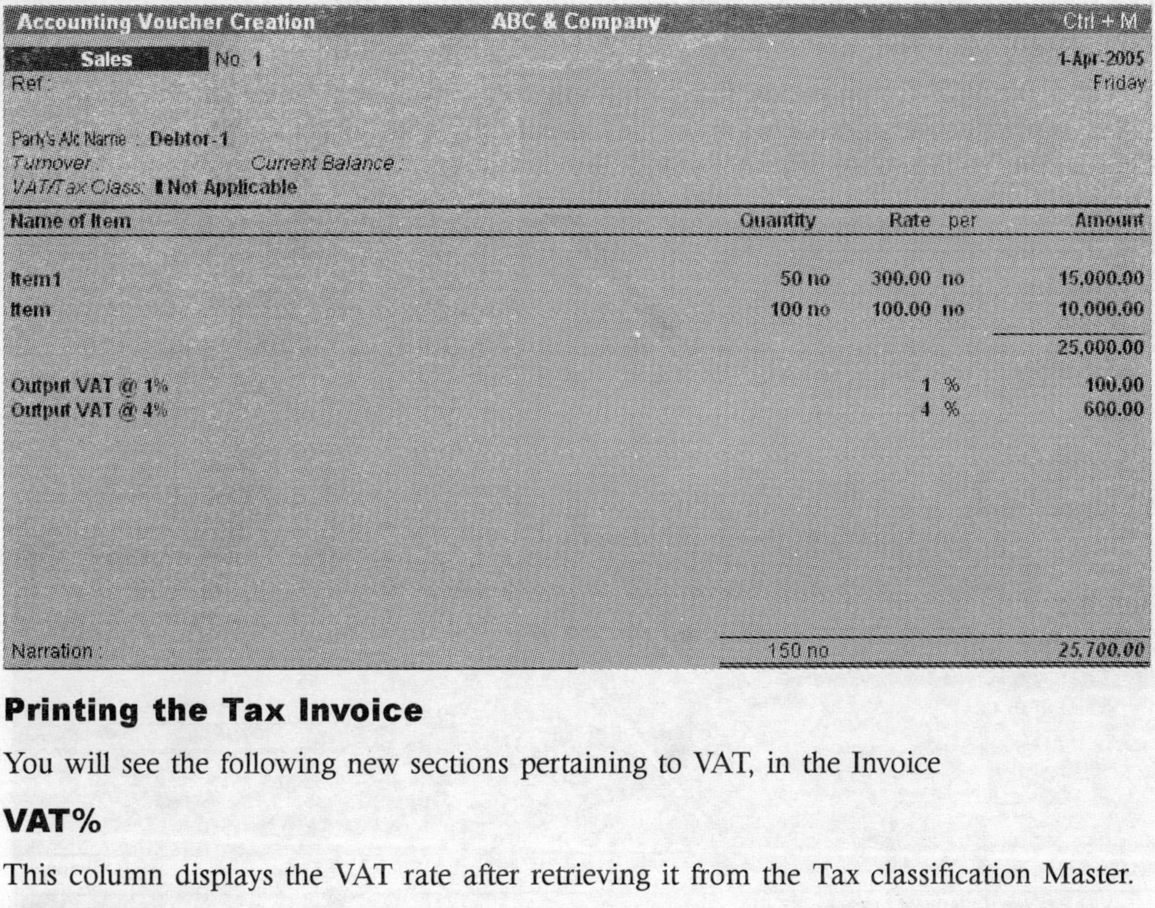

Printing the Tax Invoice

You will see the following new sections pertaining to VAT, in the Invoice

VAT%

This column displays the VAT rate after retrieving it from the Tax classification Master.

VAT Analysis

Displays the VAT amount on the total Net value. If you do not need the VAT details to the printed in the Invoice, you can set the field Print VAT% column in the F12: Configuration screen to No. Similarly, if you do not need the VAT analysis in your Invoice, set the field Print VAT Analysis to No.

VAT Amount (In Words)

Displays the VAT amount in words.

Company's VAT TIN No.

As the name indicates, it displays the Company's VAT TIN number.

Buyer's VAT TIN No.

Displays the Buying Company's VAT TIN number.

Payment of VAT

The following is an example to demonstrate the Journal and Payment Voucher entries for the payment of VAT.

Consider the VAT Computation screen as shown in next figure. (Refer the Purchase and Sales Voucher entries): As shown here, the Output Tax is Rs. 700.00 and Input Tax if Rs. 424.64. The VAT payable is thus Rs. 275.36.

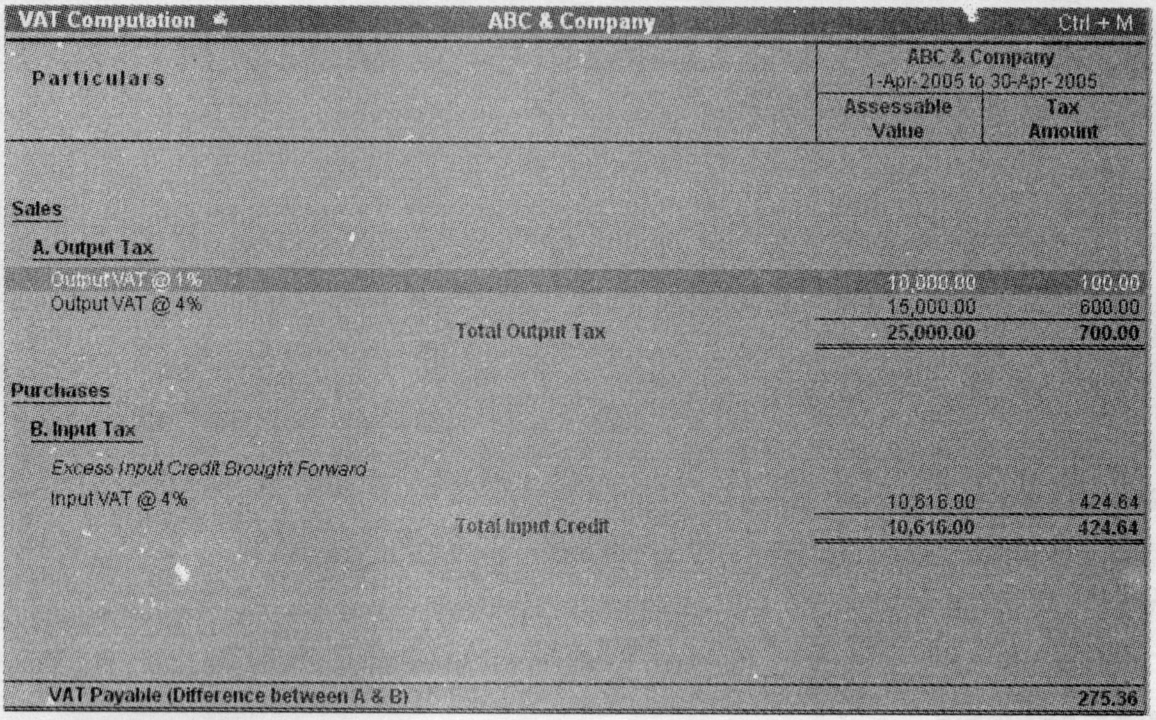

VAT Computation — ABC & Company — Ctrl + M

Particulars	ABC & Company 1-Apr-2005 to 30-Apr-2005 Assessable Value	Tax Amount
Sales		
A. Output Tax		
Output VAT @ 1%	10,000.00	100.00
Output VAT @ 4%	15,000.00	600.00
Total Output Tax	25,000.00	700.00
Purchases		
B. Input Tax		
Excess Input Credit Brought Forward		
Input VAT @ 4%	10,616.00	424.64
Total Input Credit	10,616.00	424.64
VAT Payable (Difference between A & B)		275.36

Journal Entry

Note: The VAT payable Ledger is under the group Duties and Taxes.

Thus the VAT payable, Rs. 275.36 is transferred to the Cash or Bank account, as shown.

Debit Note / Credit Note

Purchase Returns – Debit Note

This is a Purchase Returns entry. Here, you will need to use the Debit Note Voucher.

Sales Returns – Credit Note

Let us now take the example of a Sales Return. Here, you will need to use the Credit Note voucher.

Journal

If you need the Journal transactions for VAT Computation (for example, adjustment of Input credit, output tax, etc) you will need to make the following settings:

Go to Gateway of Tally > Accounts Info > Voucher Type > Create/Alter. You will see the following screen:

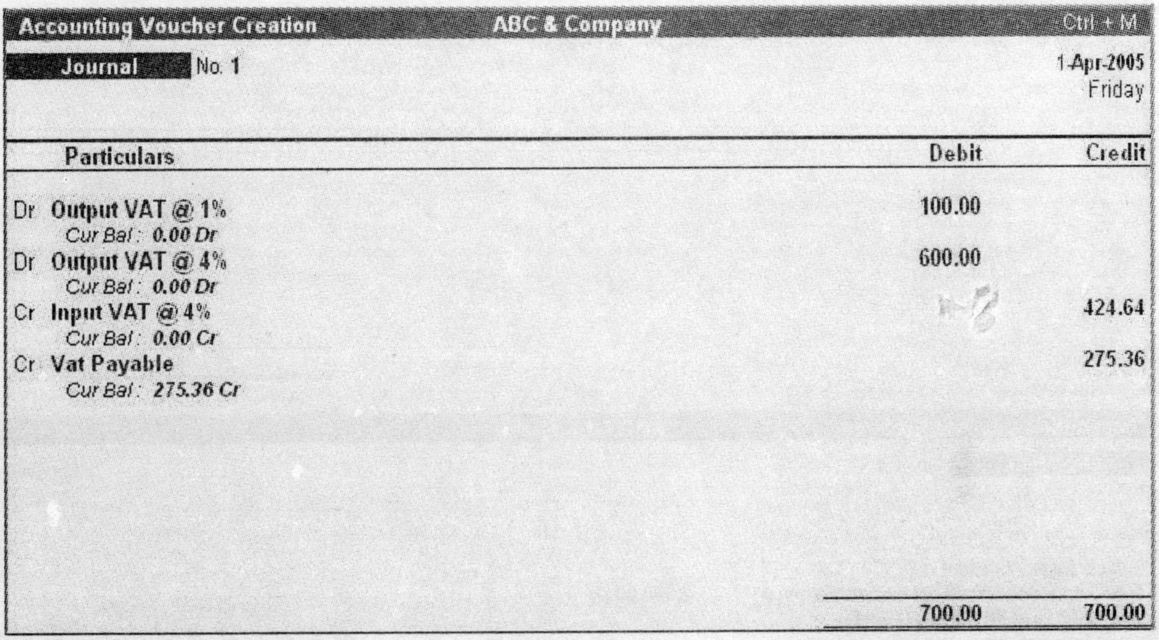

Name of Class

Name the voucher class. In the above example, we have named I as VAT Adjustment Class. Once you hit enter, you will see the figure shown here.

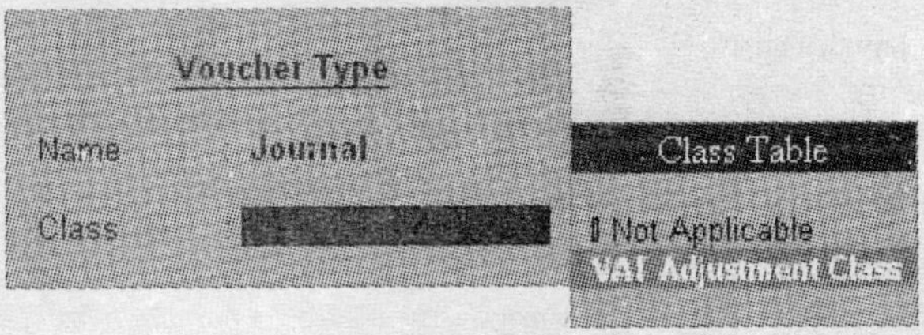

Use Class for VAT Adjustments

As the name implies, you will need to set it to Yes if you want the journal entries to be included in VAT computation, as shown next.

Journal Entries

Let us consider a Purchase transaction and then a reverse entry for adjustment of Input credit.

Typical Purchase Transaction

It is shown next.

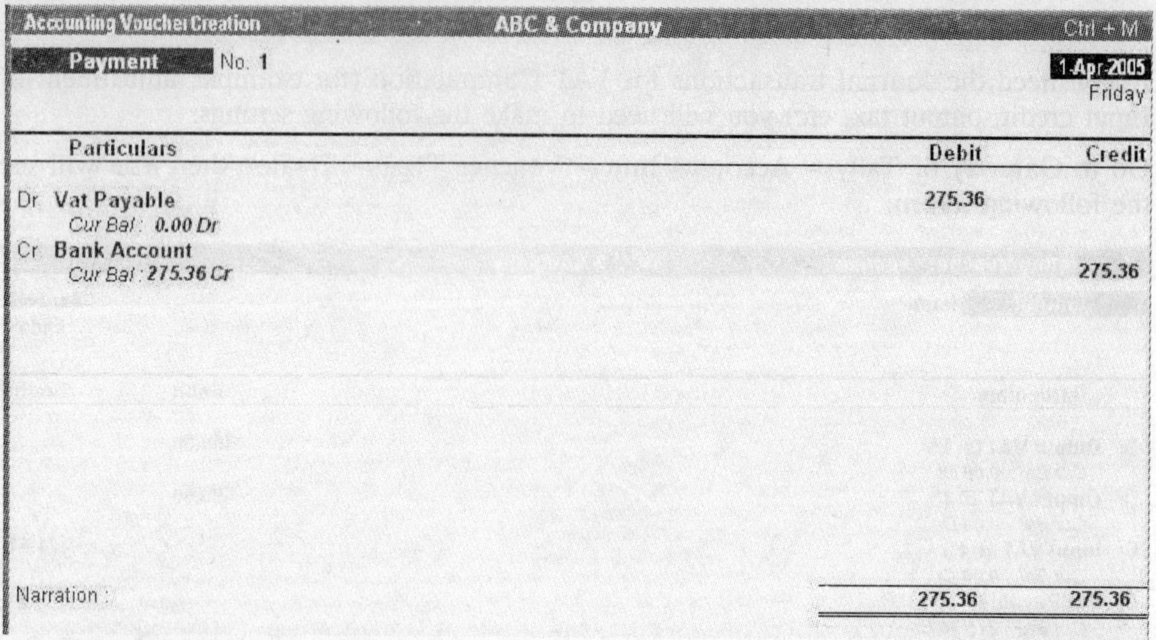
Accounting Voucher Creation ABC & Company Ctrl + M

Payment No. 1 1-Apr-2005 Friday

Particulars	Debit	Credit
Dr Vat Payable *Cur Bal : 0.00 Dr*	275.36	
Cr Bank Account *Cur Bal : 275.36 Cr*		275.36
Narration :	275.36	275.36

Accounting Voucher Creation ABC & Company Ctrl + M

Debit Note No. 1 1-Apr-2005 Friday

Ref :

Party's A/c Name : **Creditor-1**

Turnover : 7,800.00 Dr Current Balance : 2,600.00 Dr

VAT/Tax Class: **Purchases @ 4%**

Name of Item	Quantity	Rate per	Amount
Item1	10 no	50.00 no	500.00
InputVAT@4%		4 %	20.00
Narration :	10 no		*520.00*

Reversal of Input Credit

You can go to the Journal screen by clicking on F7: Journal button on the right side of your screen Or by pressing the F7 key. Firstly, you will see the screen where you need to select the Voucher class created before. Once you have selected this, you can pass the typical reversal entry as shown next.

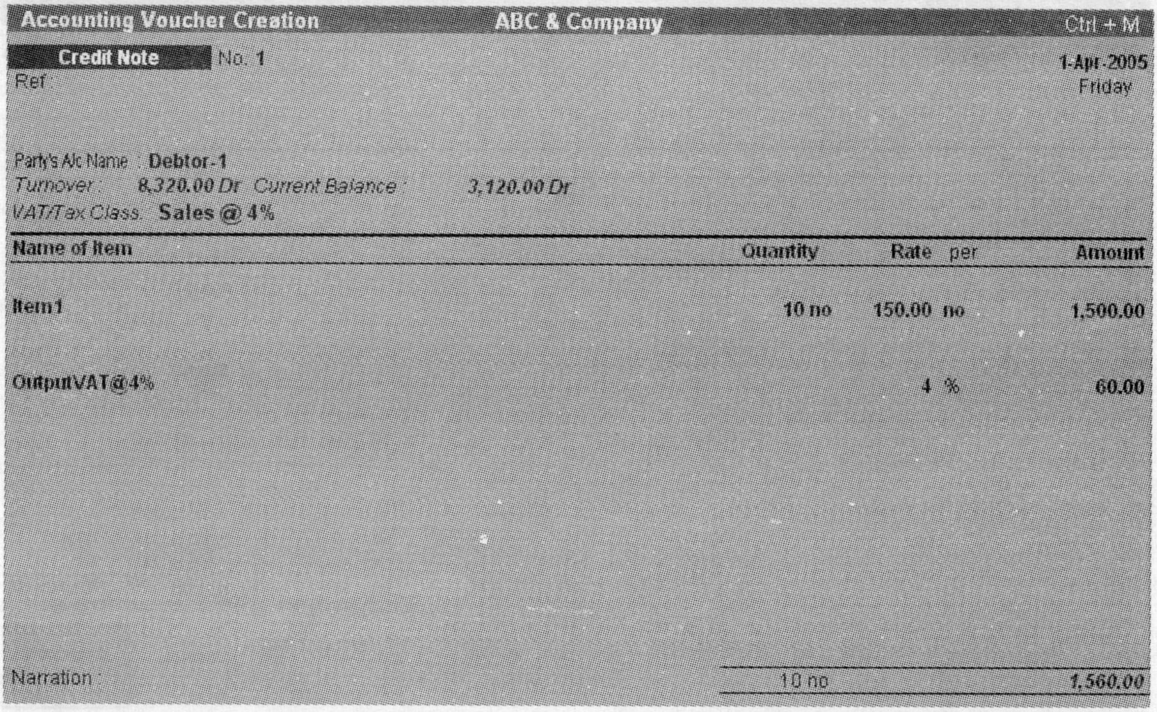

Accounting Voucher Creation | ABC & Company | Ctrl + M

Credit Note No. 1 | 1-Apr-2005
Ref : | Friday

Party's A/c Name : **Debtor-1**
Turnover : 8,320.00 Dr Current Balance : 3,120.00 Dr
VAT/Tax Class : **Sales @ 4%**

Name of Item	Quantity	Rate per	Amount
Item1	10 no	150.00 no	1,500.00
OutputVAT@4%		4 %	60.00
Narration :	10 no		1,560.00

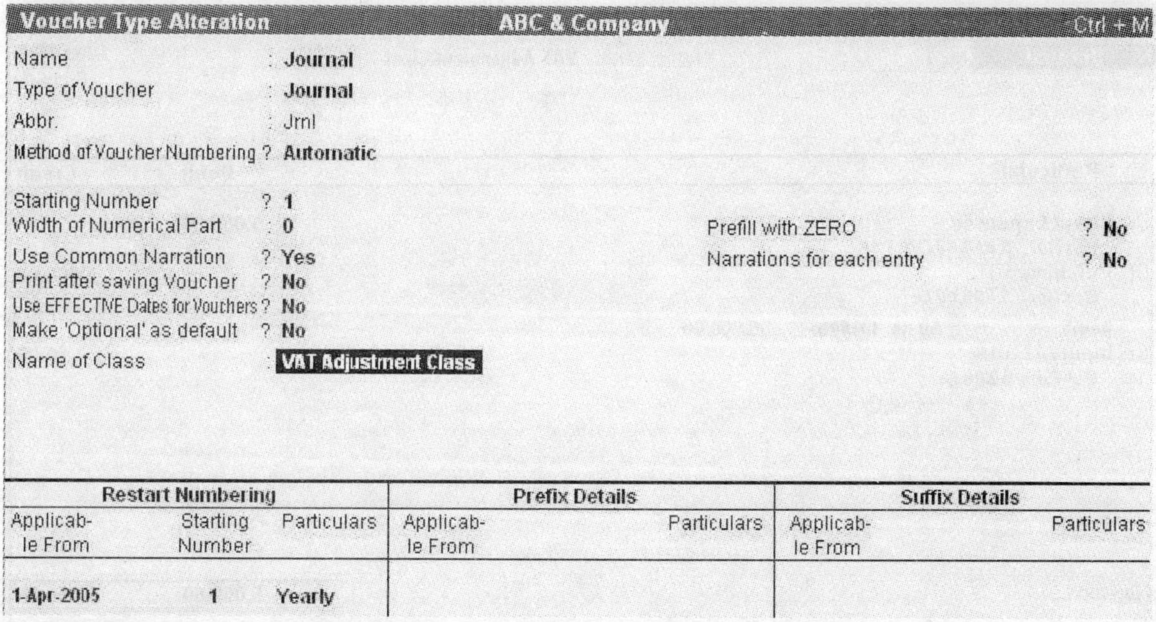

Voucher Type Alteration | ABC & Company | Ctrl + M

Name : **Journal**
Type of Voucher : **Journal**
Abbr. : Jrnl
Method of Voucher Numbering ? **Automatic**
Starting Number ? **1**
Width of Numerical Part : **0** | Prefill with ZERO ? **No**
Use Common Narration ? **Yes** | Narrations for each entry ? **No**
Print after saving Voucher ? **No**
Use EFFECTIVE Dates for Vouchers ? **No**
Make 'Optional' as default ? **No**
Name of Class : **VAT Adjustment Class**

Restart Numbering			Prefix Details		Suffix Details	
Applicable From	Starting Number	Particulars	Applicable From	Particulars	Applicable From	Particulars
1-Apr-2005	1	Yearly				

VAT Computation Report

The VAT Computation report will thus as shown next.

Thus Rs. 50 of the Input Credit is reversed and only the remaining of Rs. 50 can be claimed.

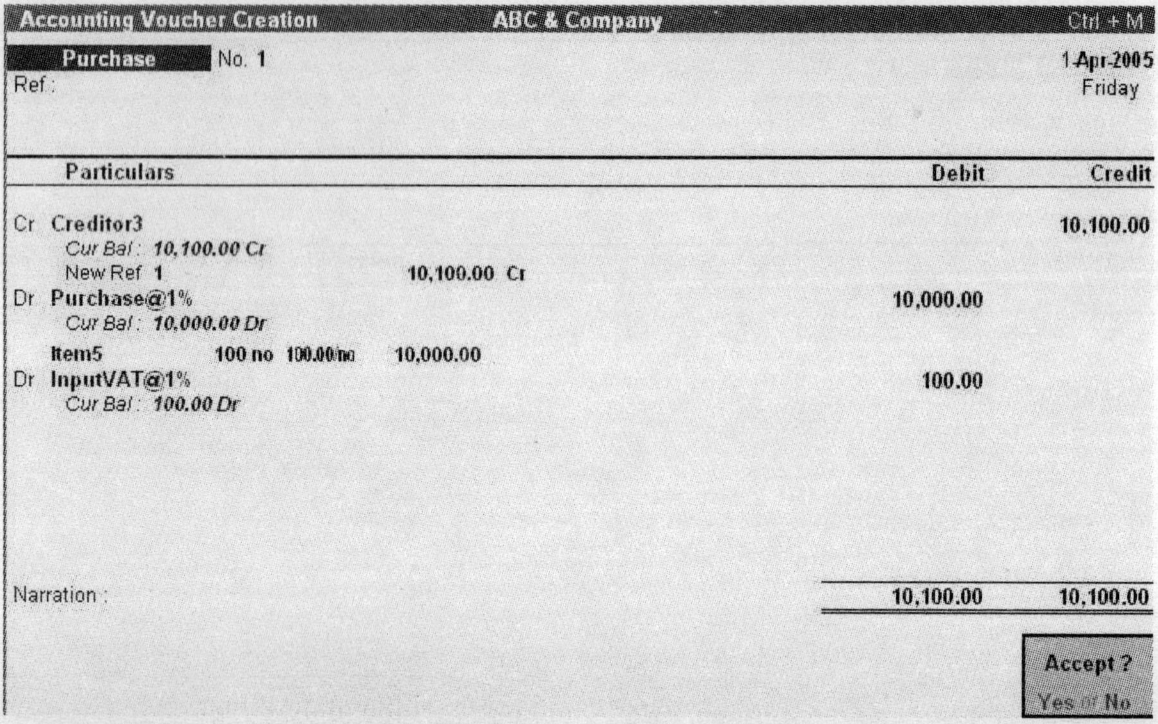

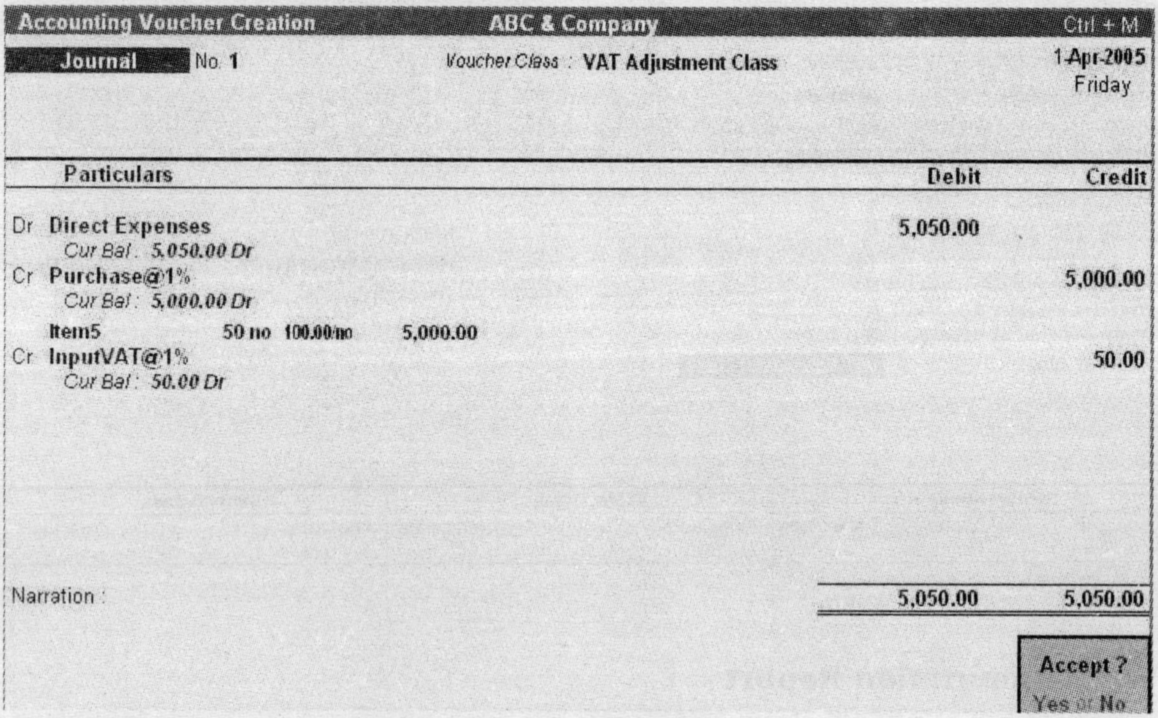

Input Credit Adjustment for Capital Goods

Input Credit for capital goods is available over a maximum period of 36 monthly instalments

VATClassification Voucher — ABC & Company — Ctrl + M

VAT Classification : **Input VAT @ 1%** — 1-Apr-2005 to 30-Apr-2005

Voucher Date	Partys' Name	TIN No.	Voucher Type	Voucher Number	Assessable Value	VAT Amount
1-Apr-2005	Creditor3	86409123342	Purchase	4	10,000.00	100.00
1-Apr-2005	Direct Expenses		Journal	1	(-)5,000.00	(-)50.00
	Grand Total				**5,000.00**	**50.00**

(States have the option to reduce the number of instalments.) Given below is an example for the adjustment of the Input Credit.

The entry for the Purchase of Capital Goods is the same as in default Tally.

Consider the following example:

Purchase of Capital Goods for Rs. 5,00,000.

The Input Credit is Rs. 20,000, which will be available over a period of 36 monthly instalments.

That is (20,000/36) = 555.56

Therefore, Rs. 555.56 can be claimed in the first instalment as Input credit.

We will pass a Journal entry for this as shown in next two figure:

The Drill down report will thus show as shown in next to that.

COMPUTATION OF VAT

You can go to the VAT Computation screen via Gateway of Tally > Display > VAT Reports > VAT Computation.

You will need to go through the following sections before learning Computation screen below:

Purchase Ledger > Sales Ledger > Duties and Taxes > Purchase Voucher > Sales Voucher

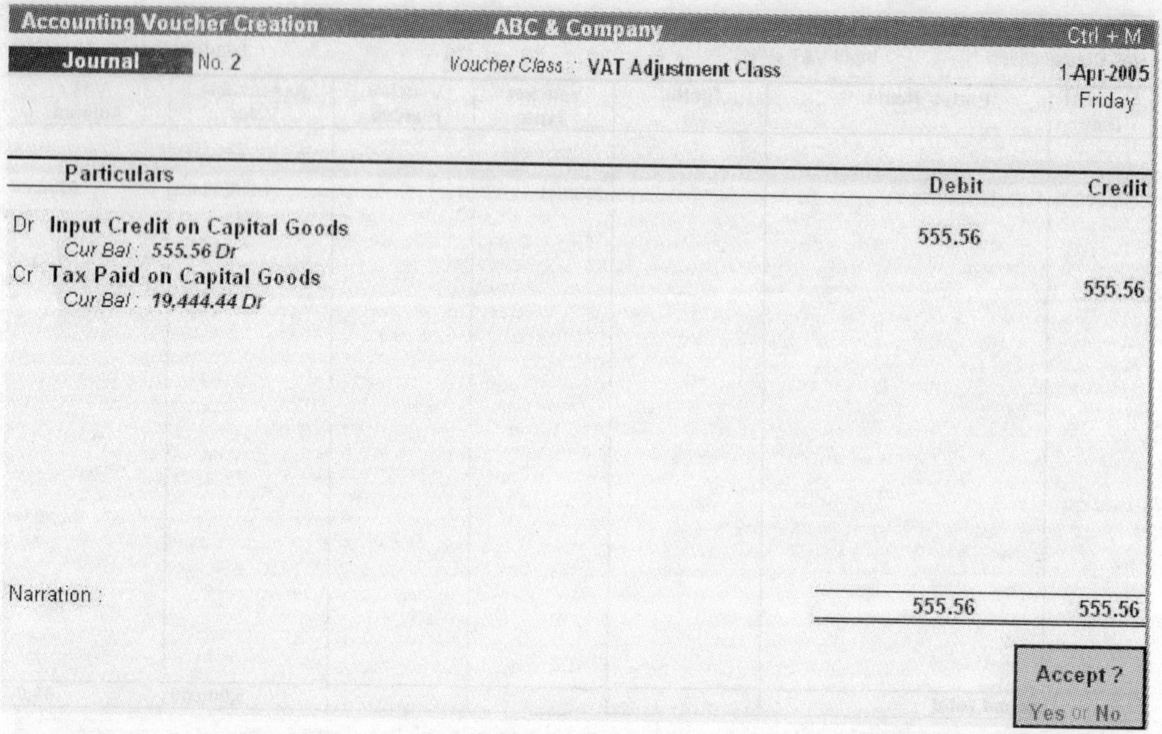

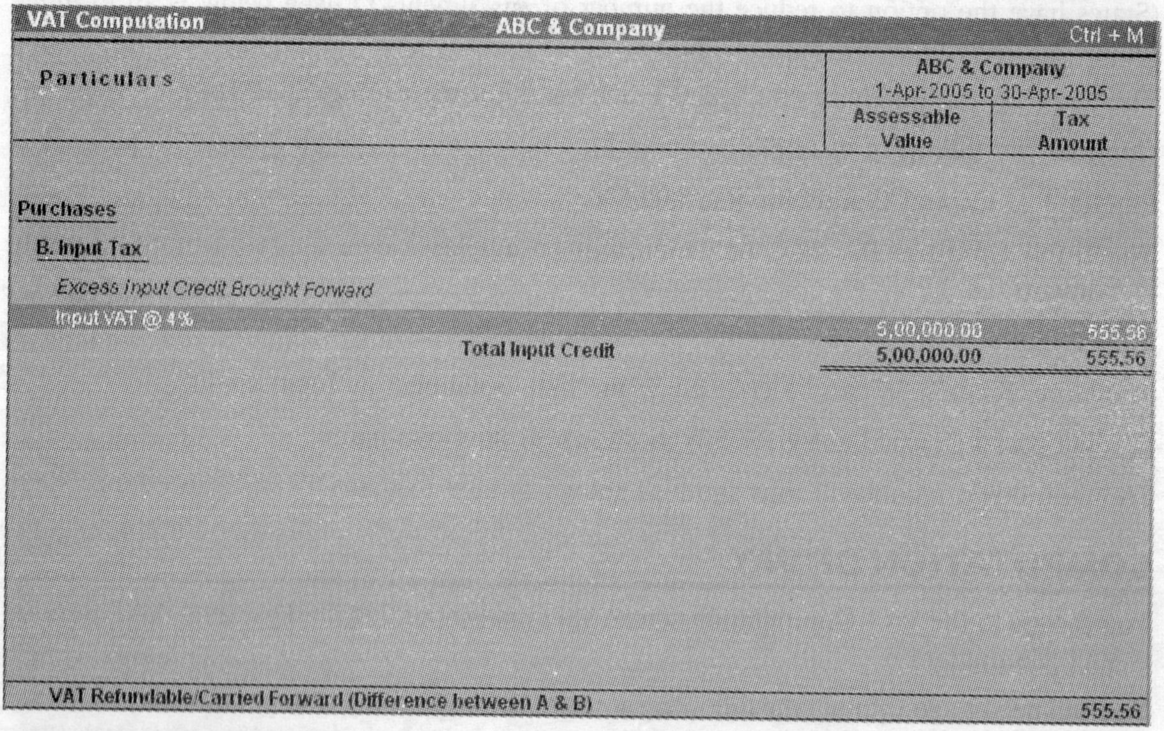

VAT Calculations

The following are the transactions we made:

VATClassification Voucher — ABC & Company — Ctrl + M

VAT Classification : Purchases @ 4% — 1-Apr-2005 to 30-Apr-2005

Voucher Date	Partys' Name	TIN No.	Voucher Type	Voucher Number	Assessable Value	VAT Amount
1-Apr-2005	Input Credit on Capital Goods		Journal	2	5,00,000.00	555.56
	Grand Total				5,00,000.00	555.56

1. Purchased from Creditor – 1, 100 quantities of item1 at the rate of Rs. 50 each.

   The Input VAT@4% for this amount is Rs. 200.

2. Purchased from Creditor, 100 quantities of item2 at the rate of Rs. 50 each. However we applied a discount of Rs. 200 here. Also, Excise tax of Rs. 800 and Educational Cess of Rs. 16 were levied on this.

   Therefore total Input VAT = Rs. 200 + Rs. 224.64 = Rs. 424.64

3. Sale of 50 quantities of item 1@Rs. 300 to Debtor-1.

   OutputVAT@4% = Rs. 600.

4. Sale of 100 quantities of item @ Rs. 100 each.

   Output VAT@1%=100

Therefore total Output VAT = Rs. 600 + Rs. 100 = Rs. 700

Therefore VAT payable -> Output VAT – Input VAT = Rs. 275.36

This is calculated automatically by Tally for you and the VAT Computation screen shown next. The Reports for the two Purchase and One Sales transaction is also shown in next page 3 figures.

For VAT Exempted to Zero Rated Transactions

If you have transactions that are exempted form VAT but however want to have it displayed in the VAT Computation screen, you will need to click on the F12 button and set the Show non VAT classifications also? to Yes.

VAT Computation — ABC & Company — Ctrl + M

Particulars		ABC & Company 1-Apr-2005 to 30-Apr-2005	
		Assessable Value	Tax Amount
Sales			
A. Output Tax			
Output VAT @ 1%		10,000.00	100.00
Output VAT @ 4%		15,000.00	600.00
	Total Output Tax	**25,000.00**	**700.00**
Purchases			
B. Input Tax			
Excess Input Credit Brought Forward			
Input VAT @ 4%		10,616.00	424.64
	Total Input Credit	**10,616.00**	**424.64**
VAT Payable (Difference between A & B)			**275.36**

VAT Classification Vouchers — ABC & Company — Ctrl + M

VAT Classification : **Input VAT @ 4%** — **1-Apr-2005 to 30-Apr-2005**

Voucher Date	Partys' Name	TIN No.	Voucher Type	Voucher Number	Assessable Value	VAT Amount
1-Apr-2005	Creditor-1	08987285763	Purchase	1	**5,000.00**	**200.00**
1-Apr-2005	Creditor	23409465786	Purchase	2	**5,616.00**	**224.64**
	Grand Total				**10,616.00**	**424.64**

Configuration

Show all VAT Classifications ? **yes**

VAT Classification Vouchers ABC & Company Ctrl + M

VAT Classification : **Output VAT @ 1%** 1-Apr-2005 to 30-Apr-2005

Voucher Date	Partys' Name	TIN No.	Voucher Type	Voucher Number	Assessable Value	VAT Amount
1-Apr-2005	Debtor-1	89127649876	Sales	1	10,000.00	100.00
	Grand Total				10,000.00	100.00

VAT Classification Vouchers ABC & Company Ctrl + M

VAT Classification : **Output VAT @ 4%** 1-Apr-2005 to 30-Apr-2005

Voucher Date	Partys' Name	TIN No.	Voucher Type	Voucher Number	Assessable Value	VAT Amount
1-Apr-2005	Debtor-1	89127649876	Sales	1	15,000.00	600.00
	Grand Total				15,000.00	600.00

For example, in the case of Inter-State Sales, the Tax Amount column will shows as NIL in the Computation screen, as shown next.

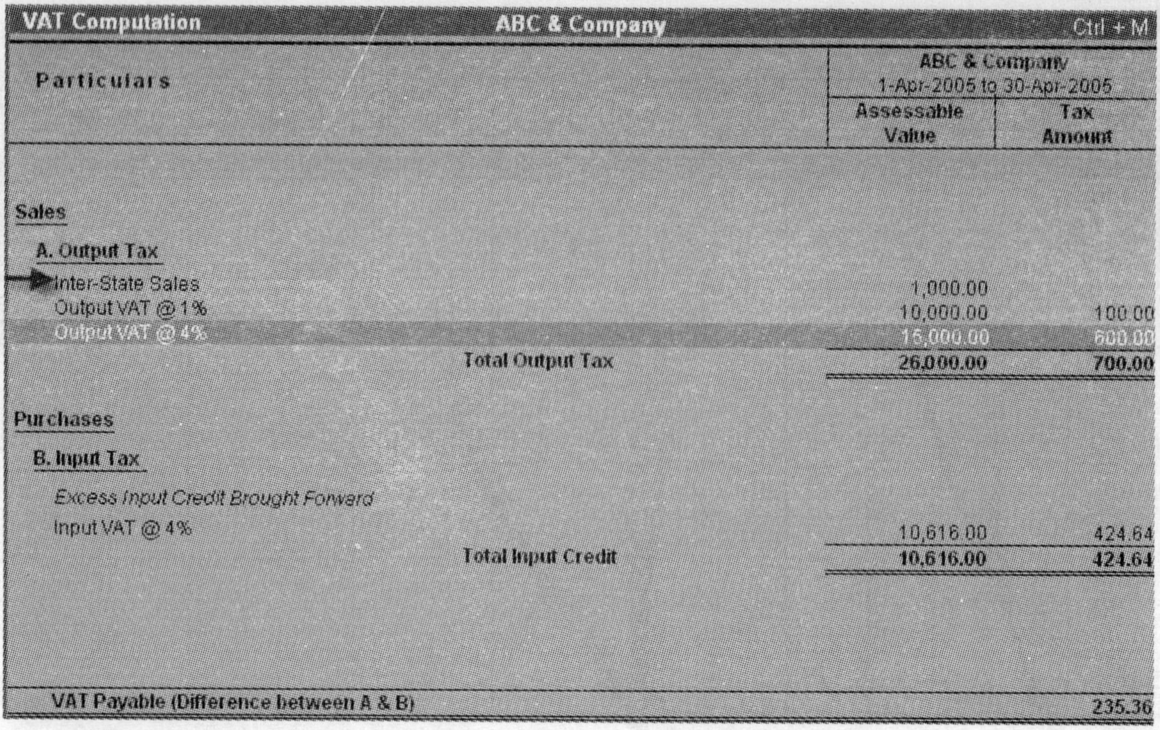

Learn the affect of Purchase and Sales returns transactions in the VAT Computation and VAT Reports Screens.

Computation of VAT after Purchase/Sales Returns

The following example is demonstrated assuming that you have gone through the VAT Computation section.

Purchase Returns – Debit Note

Consider the following Purchase Returns entry (as shown as on next page):

Once this is done, the VAT Computation will show as shown on next page.

That is, in the Purchase section, Rs. 500 is reduced from the Assessable value and Rs. 20 is reduced from the Tax amount (while comparing with the VAT Computation before Purchase Returns). Therefore the VAT payable is now Rs. 295.36

The VAT Computation Report will now show as shown on next page.

Sales Returns – Credit Note

Let us now take the example of a Sales Return.

The VAT Computation Report will now show as shown on next to next page.

The Assessable Value under Sales has reduced from Rs. 25,000 to Rs. 23,500 and the Tax Amount has reduced to Rs. 640.00. This will show in the Reports as shown in next two figures.

Accounting Voucher Creation ABC & Company Ctrl + M

Debit Note No. 1 **1-Apr-2005**

Ref : Friday

Party's A/c Name : **Creditor-1**

Turnover : *Current Balance :* ***5,200.00 Cr***

VAT/Tax Class: **Purchases @ 4%**

Name of Item	Quantity	Rate per	Amount
Item1	10 no	50.00 no	500.00
Input VAT @ 4%		4 %	20.00
Narration :	10 no		***520.00***

VAT Computation ABC & Company Ctrl + M

Particulars	ABC & Company 1-Apr-2005 to 30-Apr-2005 Assessable Value	 Tax Amount
Sales		
A. Output Tax		
Output VAT @ 1%	10,000.00	100.00
Output VAT @ 4%	15,000.00	600.00
Total Output Tax	**25,000.00**	**700.00**
Purchases		
B. Input Tax		
Excess Input Credit Brought Forward		
Input VAT @ 4%	10,116.00	404.64
Total Input Credit	**10,116.00**	**404.64**
VAT Payable (Difference between A & B)		**295.36**

VAT Classification Vouchers ABC & Company Ctrl + M

VAT Classification : **Input VAT @ 4%** **1-Apr-2005 to 30-Apr-2005**

Voucher Date	Partys' Name	TIN No.	Voucher Type	Voucher Number	Assessable Value	VAT Amount
1-Apr-2005	Creditor-1	08987285763	Purchase	1	5,000.00	200.00
1-Apr-2005	Creditor	23409465786	Purchase	2	5,616.00	224.64
1-Apr-2005	Creditor-1	08987285763	Debit Note	1	(-)500.00	(-)20.00
	Grand Total				10,116.00	404.64

VAT Computation ABC & Company Ctrl + M

Particulars	ABC & Company 1-Apr-2005 to 30-Apr-2005	
	Assessable Value	Tax Amount
Sales		
A. Output Tax		
Output VAT @ 1%	10,000.00	100.00
Output VAT @ 4%	13,500.00	540.00
Total Output Tax	23,500.00	640.00
Purchases		
B. Input Tax		
Excess Input Credit Brought Forward		
Input VAT @ 4%	10,116.00	404.64
Total Input Credit	10,116.00	404.64
VAT Payable (Difference between A & B)		235.36

VAT Classification Vouchers — ABC & Company — Ctrl + M

VAT Classification : **Output VAT @ 4%** — 1-Apr-2005 to 30-Apr-2005

Voucher Date	Partys' Name	TIN No.	Voucher Type	Voucher Number	Assessable Value	VAT Amount
1-Apr-2005	Debtor-1	89127649876	Sales	1	15,000.00	600.00
1-Apr-2005	Debtor-1	89127649876	Credit Note	1	(-)1,500.00	(-)60.00
	Grand Total				13,500.00	540.00

VAT Classification Vouchers — ABC & Company — Ctrl + M

VAT Classification : **Output VAT @ 1%** — 1-Apr-2005 to 30-Apr-2005

Voucher Date	Partys' Name	TIN No.	Voucher Type	Voucher Number	Assessable Value	VAT Amount
1-Apr-2005	Debtor-1	89127649876	Sales	1	10,000.00	100.00
	Grand Total				10,000.00	100.00

Therefore the VAT Computation and Reports are updated automatically as you pass the entries.

INTERSTATE SALES AND PURCHASES

In earlier accounting methods, on all purchases, payment was made in the form of Central Sales Tax (CST), but CST paid on purchase is neither set off against 'Output VAT' on sales within the state nor against 'Output CST' on inter-state sales. Therefore, the CST paid on purchase is treated as part of procurement cost and thus, 'CST on purchase' ledger should be placed either under 'Purchases' or 'Direct Expenses' group. The inter-state purchase is reported in the monthly return and thus it appears in the VAT computation.

However, in case of interstate sales, 'Input VAT' can be adjusted against 'Output CST'. Therefore, 'Output CST' ledger need to be placed under 'Duties & Taxes' group and classified as 'CST' for auto-computation.

Let us study this in details

Interstate Purchase

To understand this we will take an example.

Assuming that on 20.4.2004, 20 Nos MSP 245 132 col DM Printers are purchased from Interstate Suppliers @7500 plus CST @ 4%.

Now let us put this in Tally 8.1.

Step 1: Create Ledgers

Name	*Under*	*Used in VAT Returns*	*VAT/Tax Class*	*Percentage of Calculation*	*Method of Calculation*
Inter-state Purchase	Purchases	Yes	Inter-state Purchase	0	

Name	*Under*	*Type of Duty/Tax*	*VAT/Tax Class*	*Percentage of Calculation*	*Method of Calculation*
Input CST	Duties & Taxes	CST	Not Applicable	4	On Total sales

The ledger creation of Input 'CST ledger' is shown in next figure.

Type the Ledger name select 'Duties & Taxes 'Group in under Select 'CST' for 'Type of Duty/Tax 'Select 'Not Applicable' in 'VAT/Tax Class' Type '4' (Four) in 'Percentage of Calculation' In 'Method of calculation' select On Total Sales'.

Step 2: Create Purchase Invoice

Voucher Entry F12: configure

Voucher type: Sales/Purchase

Use common Ledger A/c for Item Allocation No

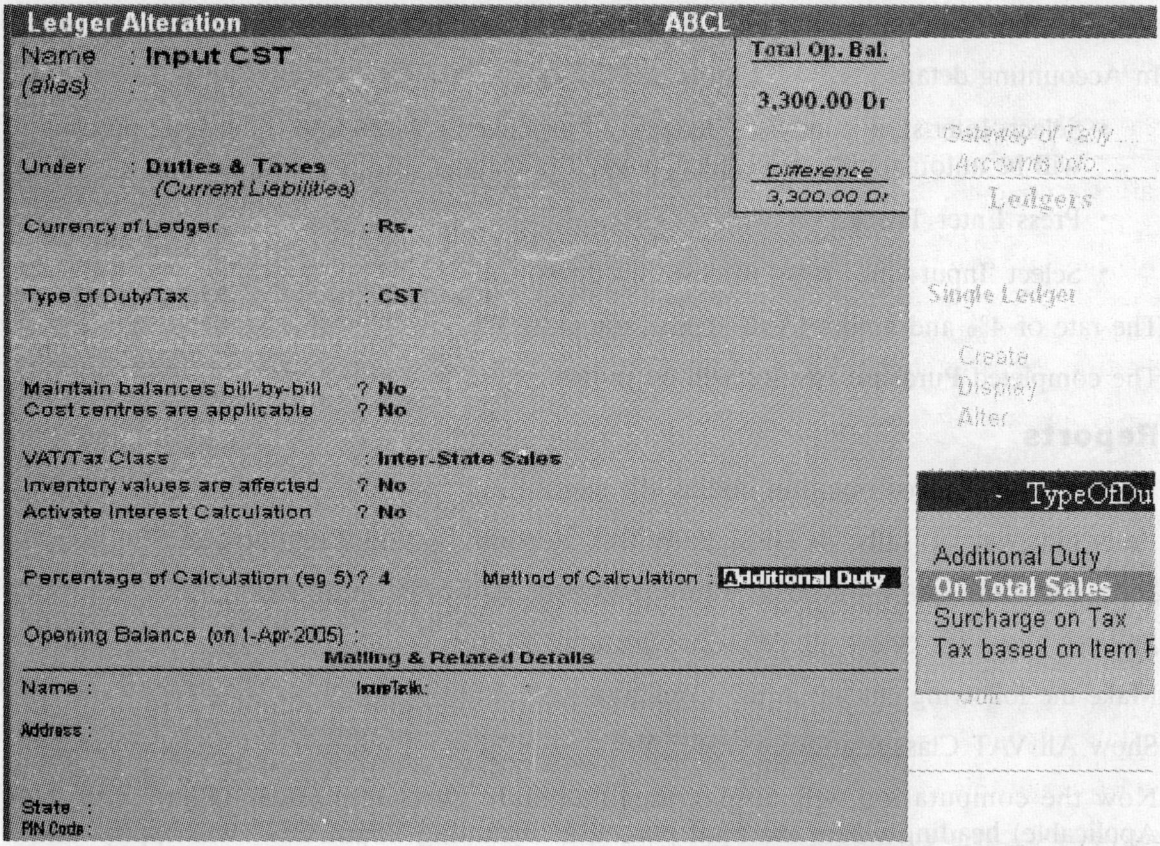

Allow selection of VAT/Tax Class during entry Yes

This is shown here.

Steps

- Select 'Accounting Vouchers' from the Gateway of Tally.
- Press F9 for Purchase Invoice.
- Press F2 and type '20/04/2005' to change the date.
- Select 'Inter-state Supplier' in Party's A/c Name
- Select 'Inter-state Purchases' in 'VAT/Tax Class
- Select 'MSP 245 132 cols DM Printers' in Name of Item

- Type '20' in qty column, '7500' in rate and the amount will appear automatically.

In Accounting details:

- Select 'Inter-state purchases' ledger in Particulars column and 'Inter-state purchases' will be automatically selected in VAT/Tax class.
- Press Enter Twice
- Select 'Input CST' from the list of ledgers.

The rate of 4% and amount will appear automatically.

The completed Purchase Invoice will be shown.

Reports

To view the VAT computation, follow the steps:

From Gateway of Tally –> Display –> VAT Reports –> VAT Computation

Press F12 and type '1-4-2005' in From field and '30-4-2005' in To field.

Press F12 and set 'Show all VAT classifications' to Yes

Make the following change in the Configuration:

Show All VAT Classifications ? **Yes**

Now the computation will display the Inter-state Purchases under Other (VAT Not Applicable) heading where the total purchases including 'Input CST' will appear under Assessable value and Tax Amount column will be blank.

INTER-STATE SALES

This can be shown with the help of the following example:

On 25.4.2005, 3 Nos MSP 245 132 col DM printers are sold to Coimbatore Computers @ 8800 plus CST @ 4%.

To configure Tally 8.1 follow the steps:

Ledger Creation

Name	*Under*	*Type of Duty/Tax*	*Used in VAT Return*	*VAT/Tax Class*	*Percentage of Calculation*	*Method of Calculation*
Inter-state Sale	Sales a/c		Yes	Inter-state Sales	0	
Output CST	Duties & Taxes	CST	Yes	Inter-state Sales	4	On Total Sales

Step 2: Create Sales Invoice

Voucher Entry F12: **Configure**

Voucher Type: **Sales/Purchase**

Use Common Ledger A/c for Item Allocation **No**

Allow section of VAT/Tax Class during entry **Yes**

Steps:

- Select 'Accounting Vouchers' from the Gateway of Tally.
- Press F8 for 'Sales' Invoice.
- Press F2 and type '25-04-2005' to change the date.
- Select 'Coimbatore Computers' in Party's A/c Name
- Select 'Inter-state Purchases' in VAT/Tax Class
- Select 'MSP 245 132 cols DM Printers' in Name of Item
- Type '3' (Three) in qty column, '8800' in rate and the amount will appear automatically.

In Accounting details:

- Select 'Inter-state Sales' ledger in Particulars column and 'Inter-state Sales' will be automatically selected in VAT/Tax class.
- Press Enter Twice
- Select 'Output CST' from the list of ledgers.

The rate of 4% and amount will appear automatically.

Reports

In the VAT computation, the 'Inter-state Sales' appear under 'Output Tax'. The output CST amount will appear in the VAT amount column. The net VAT payable will be computed upon deducting the Input VAT from Output VAT/CST.

Highlight Inter-state Sales and press Enter to drill down to view details of Inter-state Sales and CST amount.

IMPORTS AND EXPORTS

In the age of Globalisation, Import of goods from other countries or export to other countries is a regular feature of the business world. Though VAT is not charged either on Import nor on Export, such transactions need to be properly accounted for and details are reported in the VAT returns. Tally provides special VAT/Tax classifications for Imports and Exports.

Imports

Under VAT laws, Imports are exempted from VAT Levy

For example:

On 25th April 2005, Bangalore Computers imports the following items from SPC Computers and Peripherals, Australia

S.No.	*Item Description*	*Qty*	*Rate*
1.	LG Bed type scanners	20	12,500
2.	Samsung Digital Camera	15	18,500

Ledgers

Create 'Purchase – Imports' under Purchase Accounts, as shown below.

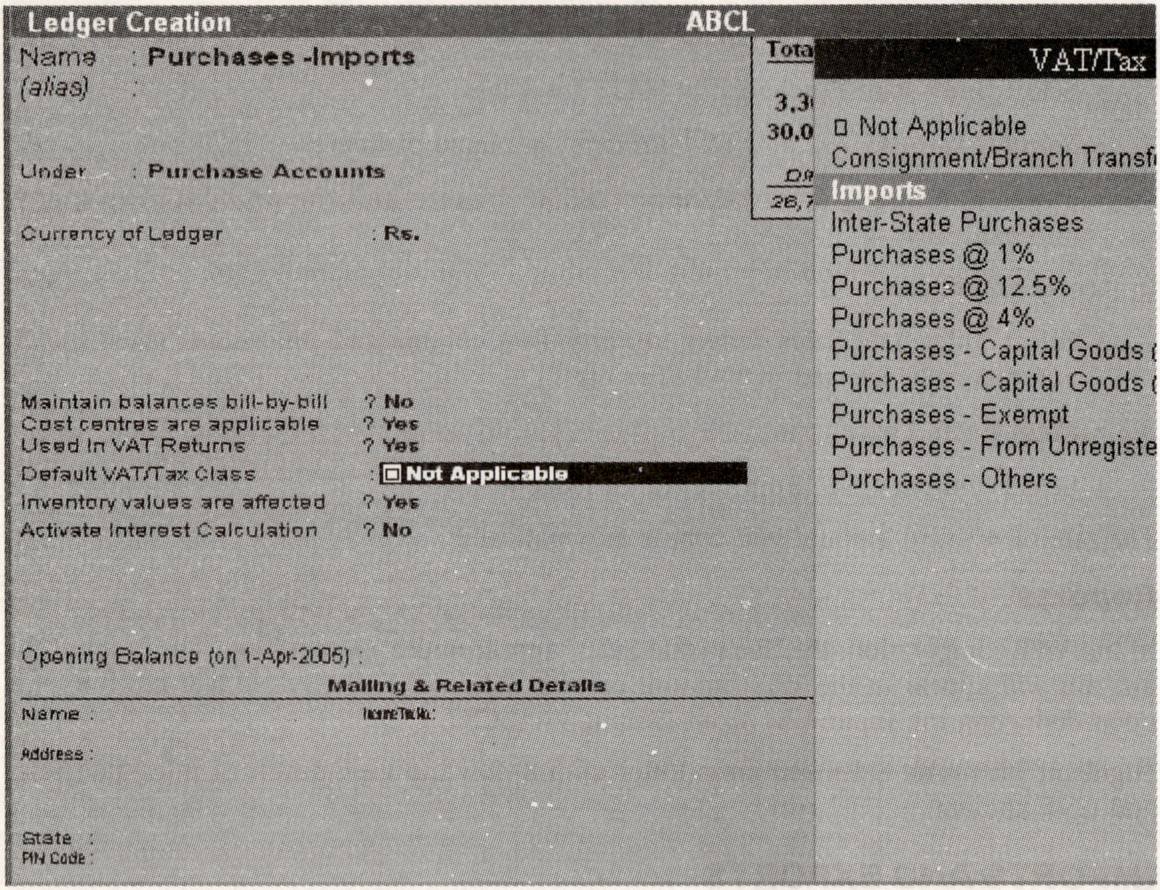

Purchase Invoice

Setup:

Voucher Entry F12: **Configure**

Voucher Type: **Sales/Purchase**

Use Common Ledger A/c for Item Allocation **Yes**

Allow section of VAT/Tax Class during entry **No**

Create Purchase Invoice

- Press 'V' for 'Accounting Vouchers'
- Press F9 for 'Purchase Invoice'.
- Press F2 and change date to '25/04/2005'.
- Select 'SPC Computers & Peripherals' in Party's A/c Name.
- Select 'Purchase – Imports' in 'Purchase Ledger'.
- Select 'LG Bed Type Scanner' in Name of Item.
- Type '20' as Quantity and '12500' in Rate.
- Select 'Samsung Digital Camera' in Name of Item.
- Type '15' as Quantity and '18500' in Rate.
- Type 'Being goods Imported from Australia' in Narration.
- Press Ctrl + A to Accept.

EXPORTS

With zero-rating of exports in VAT i.e, VAT on goods exported are zero yet credit is allowed on input tax paid on raw materials or goods purchased for imports. A special class 'Exports' is available in Tally for classifying Export transactions, as shown next.

For example:

On 26th April 2005, Bangalore computers exports 25 Nos of PIV CPU Cabinets to M/s. Lexmac Pty Ltd., of Newyork, USA @ Rs. 3,500 each.

The Cabinets were purchased from M/s Gajendra & Sons, Bangalore on 24.4.2005 at the rate of Rs. 2,800/- per piece; VAT paid on purchases @ 4% which was allowed to set-off in full after 3 months.

Ledgers

To correlate the Input tax paid on purchase of goods exported (later) and claim refund after 3 months or on the date of approval, the following ledgers are required to be created.

S.No.	*Ledger Name*	*Group*	*Duty/Tax Type*	*VAT Class*
1.	Tax Paid on Exports Goods	Duties & Taxes	Others	Nil
2.	Input VAT on Export Goods	Duties & Taxes	VAT	Input VAT @ 4%

Setup:

Voucher Entry F12: **Configure**

Voucher Type: **Sales/Purchase**

Use Common Ledger A/c for Item Allocation **Yes**

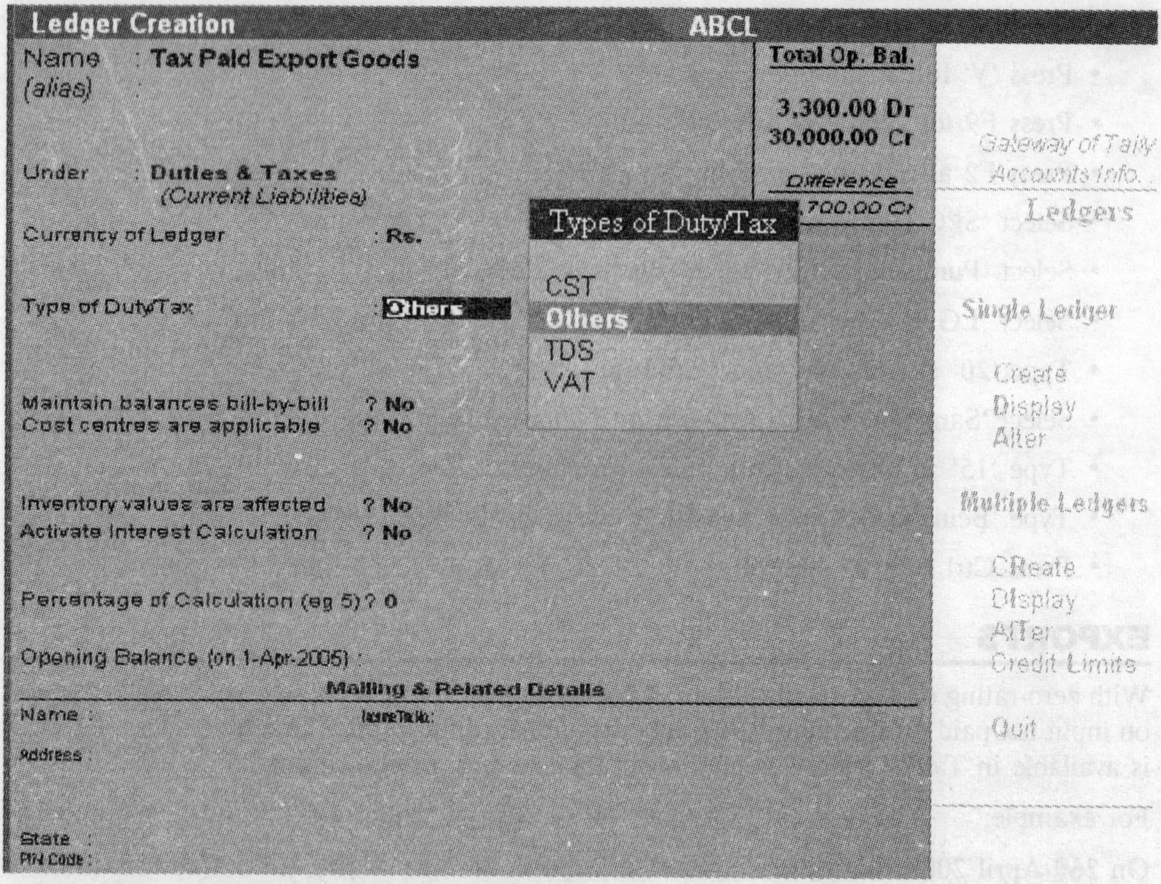

Allow section of VAT/Tax Class during entry **Yes**

Purchase Transaction

The transaction may be entered as listed below:

S.No.	***Entry***	***Occasion***
1.	Purchase Entry	On purchase of Goods meant for Exports
2.	Journal Entry (With Journal Adjustment Class)	At the time of sanction of credit (within 3 months)

Create Purchase Invoice

- Press 'V' for 'Accounting Vouchers'
- Press F9 for 'Purchase Invoice'.
- Press F2 and change date to '24/04/2005'.
- Select 'Gajendra & Sons' in Party's A/c Name.
- Select 'Purchase @ 4%' in 'Purchase Ledger'.

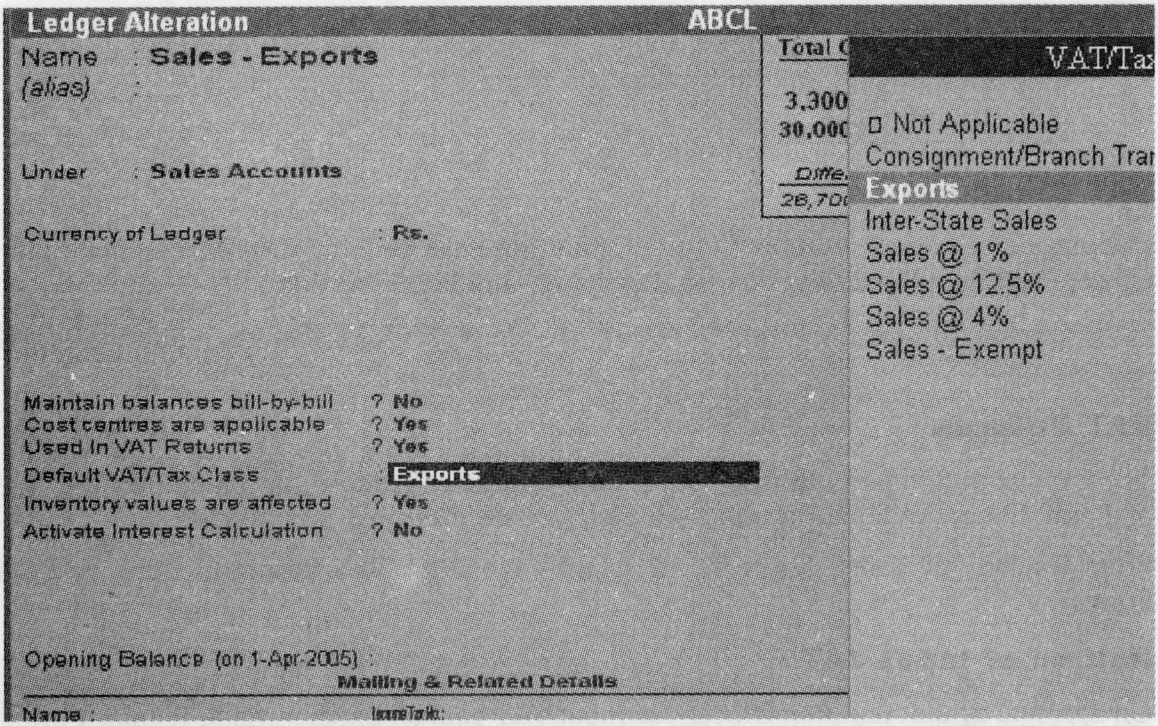

- Select 'Purchase @ 4%' in 'VAT/Tax Class'.
- Select 'PIV CPU Cabinet' in Name of Item.
- Type '25' as Quantity and '2800' in Rate.
- Select 'Tax paid on Exports Goods'
- Type '4' (four) in Rate
- Type 'Being PIV CPU Cabinets Purchased' in Narration.
- Press Enter to Accept.

Sales Invoice

Create sales ledgers for exports and categorize under appropriate 'Exports' class.

Create Sales Invoice:

- Press 'V' for 'Accounting Vouchers'
- Press F5 for 'Sales Invoice'.
- Press F2 and change date to '26/04/2005'.
- Select 'Lexmac Pty Ltd.' in Party's A/c Name.
- Select 'Sales – Exports' in 'Sales Ledger'.
- Select 'PIV CPU Cabinet' in Name of Item.

- Type '25' as Quantity and '3500' as Rate.
- Type 'Being PIV Cabinets exported' in Narration.
- Press Enter to Accept.

VAT Computation

The value of Imports as well as Exports for the particular period is displayed in the heading Others (VAT Not Applicable) under 'Purchases' and 'Sales' sections.

From Gateway of Tally – Press 'D' (Display) – Press 'V' (VAT Reports) – Press 'V' (VAT Computation)

VAT Returns

The Exports and Import turnover for the period specified is shown in column No. 7 and 13 of Form 100 of VAT returns and both turnover are exempted from VAT.

From Gateway of Tally – Press 'D' (Display) – Press 'V' (VAT Reports) – Press 'A' (VAT Forms)

Refund of Input VAT

On approval by the Assessing Officer, the Input VAT paid on Exports will be refunded within 3 months. Therefore the claim for the Input VAT paid on purchase of goods meant for exports will have to be raised.

The entry can be passed through Journal Voucher Class.

Let's first create Journal Voucher Class.

Creation of Journal Voucher Class

From Gateway of Tally – Press 'A' (Accounts Info) – Press 'V' (Voucher Type) – Press 'A' (Alter) – Select 'Journal' from List of Voucher Type – At Name of Class, enter name of Voucher class, e.g., VAT Adjustment Class', as shown in next figure.

In the voucher Class sub-screen, 'Use Class for VAT Adjustments' to yes. Press Ctrl + A to accept and repeat the same to save the modifications in Voucher Type.

Journal Entry

Select Journal Voucher and then 'VAT Adjustment class'. Enter the transaction when the refund is due crediting the tax paid on Exports Goods and debiting Input VAT on export Goods Ledger to claim the refund.

- Press 'V' for 'Accounting Vouchers'
- Press F7 for 'Journal'
- Select the 'VAT Adjustment Class' from 'Class Table'
- Press F2 and change date to 28/07/2005

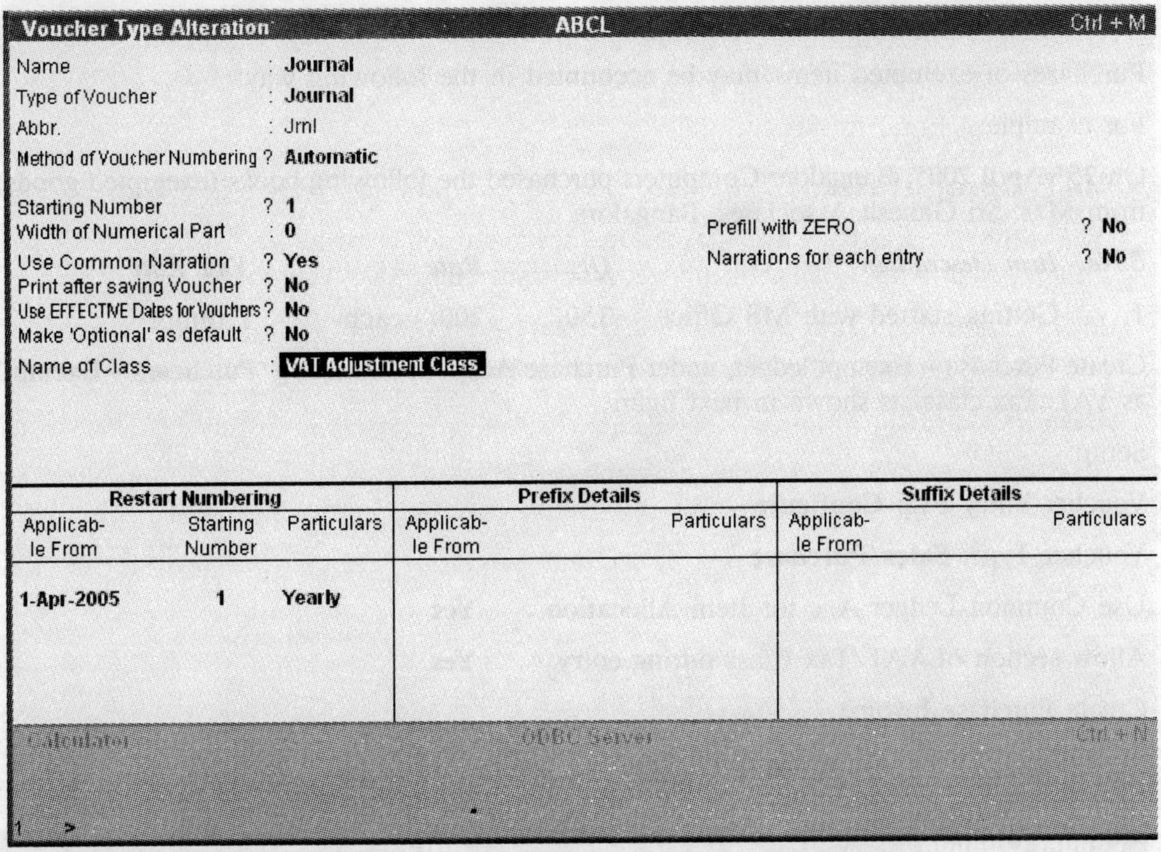

Voucher Type Alteration ABCL Ctrl + M

Name : Journal
Type of Voucher : Journal
Abbr. : Jrnl
Method of Voucher Numbering ? Automatic

Starting Number ? 1
Width of Numerical Part : 0
Prefill with ZERO ? No
Use Common Narration ? Yes
Narrations for each entry ? No
Print after saving Voucher ? No
Use EFFECTIVE Dates for Vouchers ? No
Make 'Optional' as default ? No
Name of Class : VAT Adjustment Class

Restart Numbering			Prefix Details		Suffix Details	
Applicable From	Starting Number	Particulars	Applicable From	Particulars	Applicable From	Particulars
1-Apr-2005	1	Yearly				

Calculator ODBC Server Ctrl + N

1 >

- Select 'Input VAT on Exports Goods' ledger
- Press enter the VAT/Tax class will automatically appear as Input VAT @ 4%
- Type amount as '2800' in Assessable Value'
- Select 'Tax paid on export goods' ledger for credit
- Type 'Being Input Tax credit on exports set-off' in Narration

This reverse the effect on 'tax paid on Export Goods' ledger and Input Tax claim will be stacked for refund.

EXEMPTED PURCHASES AND SALES

Under the VAT Act, about 46 commodities comprising natural and unprocessed products in unorganized sectors and items which are legally barred from taxation (e.g., Books) are placed under Exempted goods list. Besides the common list, from a list of goods, each state has been authorized to choose a maximum of 10 commodities of local social importance; for example Karnataka has chosen Paddy, Rice, Wheat, Pulses, Seeds, Avalakki, Mandakki, Pappad, branded Bread and Bun. Transactions for these items do not carry any VAT charge as per the VAT definitions.

Exempted Purchases

Purchases of exempted items may be accounted in the following way:

For example:

On 25th April 2005, Bangalore Computers purchased the following books (exempted goods) from M/s. Sri Ganesh Associates, Bangalore.

S.No.	*Item Description*	*Qty*	*Rate*	*VAT Rate*
1.	Getting started with MS Office	350	200/- each	Exempt

Create Purchase – Exempt ledger, under Purchase Accounts, selecting 'Purchases – Exempt' as VAT/Tax class, as shown in next figure.

Setup:

Voucher Entry F12: **Configure**

Voucher Type: **Sales/Purchase**

Use Common Ledger A/c for Item Allocation **Yes**

Allow section of VAT/Tax Class during entry **Yes**

Create Purchase Invoice

- Press 'V' for 'Accounting Vouchers'

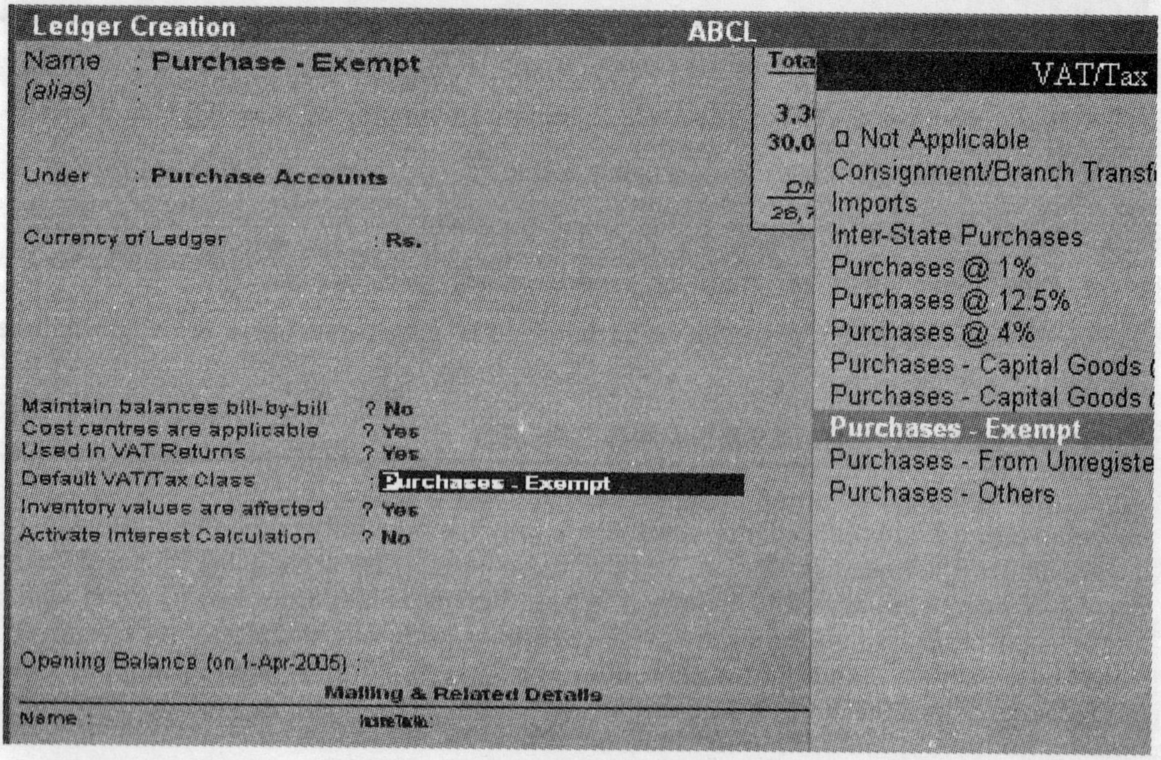

- Press F9 for 'Purchase Invoice'.
- Press F2 and change date to '25/04/2005'.
- Select 'Sri Ganesh Associates' in Party's A/c Name.
- Select 'Purchase – Exempt' in 'Purchase Ledger'.
- 'Purchase – Exempt' in VAT/Tax Class' will appear automatically.
- Select 'Getting Started with MS Office' in Name of Item.
- Type '350' as Quantity and '200' as Rate.
- Type 'Being Computer books purchased' in Narration.
- Press Enter to Accept.

Exempted Sales

Sales of exempt items may be accounted in the following way:

For example,

On 27th April 2005, Bangalore Computers sold 'Getting Started with MS-Office' 80 copies @ Rs. 250/- each to M/s. Ganesh & Co., of Bangalore. The goods transacted are exempt under VAT.

Create Sales – Exempt ledger, under Sales Accounts, select 'Sales – Exempt' as VAT/Tax Class

Create Sales Invoice

- Press 'V' for 'Accounting Vouchers'
- Press F8 for 'Sales Invoice'.
- Press F2 and change date to '27/04/2005'.
- Select 'Ganesh & Co' in Party's A/c Name.
- Select 'Sales – Exempt' in Sales Ledger'.
- 'Sales – Exempt' in VAT/Tax Class' will appear automatically.
- Select 'Getting Started with MS Office' in 'Name of Item'.
- Type '80' as Quantity and '250' as Rate.
- Type 'Being computer books sold' in Narration.
- Press Enter to Accept.

VAT Computation

In VAT computation, the value of exempted Purchases and Sales will appear under Other (VAT not applicable) column and will not form part of taxable turnover in VAT Computation.

From Gateway of Tally – Press 'D' (Display) – Press 'V' (VAT Reports) – Press 'V' (VAT Computation)

Setup

Press F12: **Configuration** and set 'Show All VAT Classifications' to **'Yes'**

VAT Forms

In Statutory returns, the total exempt turnover for the specified period will fall under Box No. 6 and purchases in Box No. 15 of the Statutory Form.

From Gateway of Tally – Press 'D' (Display) – Press 'V' (VAT Reports) – Press 'A' (VAT Forms)

VAT DOCUMENTS

Every registered dealer shall issue a Tax Invoice when he sells. A Tax Invoice shall be consecutively numbered and incorporate details like Date, Name, Address & TIN of the Seller and buyer; full description of the goods, Quantity, Value; rate and amount of VAT charged for taxable goods and the total value of Invoice. The Buyer's copy should be marked as 'Original'.

The Debit or Credit Note will also have similar details and further the reference of Tax Invoice to which it relates should also be mentioned.

Tally 8.1 supports generation of compliant Tax Invoice, Debit Note and Credit Note.

To print the document, on completing the voucher entry

- Press Alt +P
- Press F12 to get Invoice Printing Configuration
- Type 'Tax Invoice' in Title
- Enter Height, Width and space to leave on top for Normal Invoice
- Set 'Print in Simpler Format' to No.
- Set 'Print VAT Analysis of Items' to Yes
- Set 'Print Company's Tax Regn. Numbers' to Yes
- Set 'Print Buyer's Tax Reg. Number, to Yes
- Set 'Print Buyer's Tax Regn. Number' to Yes
- Set 'Print VAT % Column' to Yes

To print multiple copies, in the Voucher printing screen press 'Alt+C' and in the number of copies prompt, enter copies to be printed, e.g.,2. This will mark the first copy as 'Original'.

REPORTS

As per VAT Act, every registered dealer is required to maintain proper Books of Accounts and records for all sale, purchase and production. And also VAT account-containing details of Input and Output tax.

The VAT system is based on self-assessment and transparency at every stage of transaction. Hence, accurate documentation and record keeping is of critical importance.

In Tally 8.1, you can print state specific statutory returns.

VAT CONTROL LEDGER

For the purpose of calculating net tax liability under VAT for the specified period, it is important to create a VAT control ledger in the manner given below:

Create 'VAT Payable' a VAT Control Ledger, under Duties and Taxes group and assign Tax/ Duty type as 'Others', as shown in next figure.

At the end of every month, pass a journal entry to offset Output VAT against Input VAT and transfer the excess/short to the 'VAT Payable' ledger, in order to arrive at the net tax liability for the month. Though in case of Inter-state purchases, the Input Tax paid on Inter-state purchases is not allowed to set-off against the Output VAT on local or Inter-state sales but 'Input VAT' paid on local purchases can be adjusted against 'Out CST' (tax due on account of Inter-state sales).

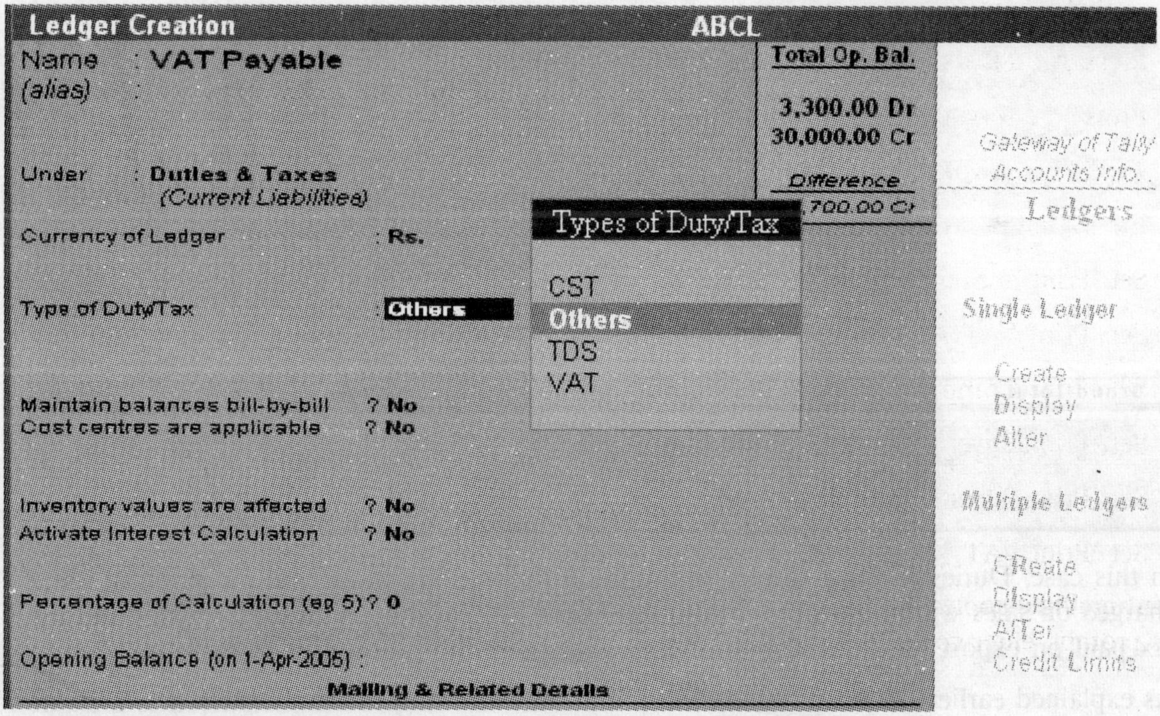

In the course of offsetting, the excess of Input tax credit will be carried forward to the successive month (i.e., brought forward as opening balance in the next month's VAT Computation report) and if vice versa, will be payable for the period.

GROUP SUMMARY

Group summary gives ledger wise break-wise. Displays the closing balances of all sub-group and ledgers falling under the selected group.

Duties & Taxes

From Gateway of Tally – Press 'D' (Display) – Press 'A' (Accounts Books) – Press 'G' (Group Summary) – Select 'Duties & Taxes'.

Press F12 and type 'Yes' to show Opening balance, transactions, closing balance to display, as shown here.

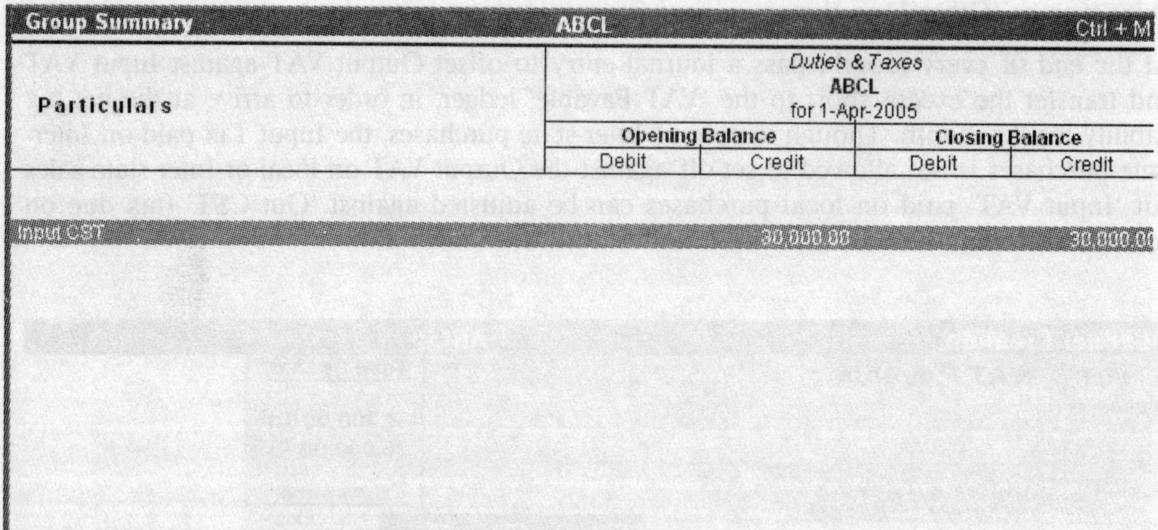

In this case, Duties & Taxes group summarizes the various taxes paid on purchases and charged on sales within the state. It also shows the tax payable on Inter-state sales and the tax paid on export goods available for future credit in the subsequent months.

As explained earlier, all the payable amounts in VAT tax ledgers are transferred to a single control ledger 'VAT payable' account. This ledger shows credit balance denoting the next tax liability for the given period.

The Group Summaries can also be generated for any period, say monthly, quarterly or annually or for any specified period for that matter.

Monthly columnar group summaries can also be generated for comparison and to check the correctness of the entries. Its comprehensive display facilities timely payment of tax dues the helps tax planning.

Sales Account

From Gateway of Tally – Press 'D' (Display) – Press 'A' (Accounts Books) – Press 'G' (Group Summary) – Select 'Sales Accounts' to get the ledger wise break-up, as shown next.

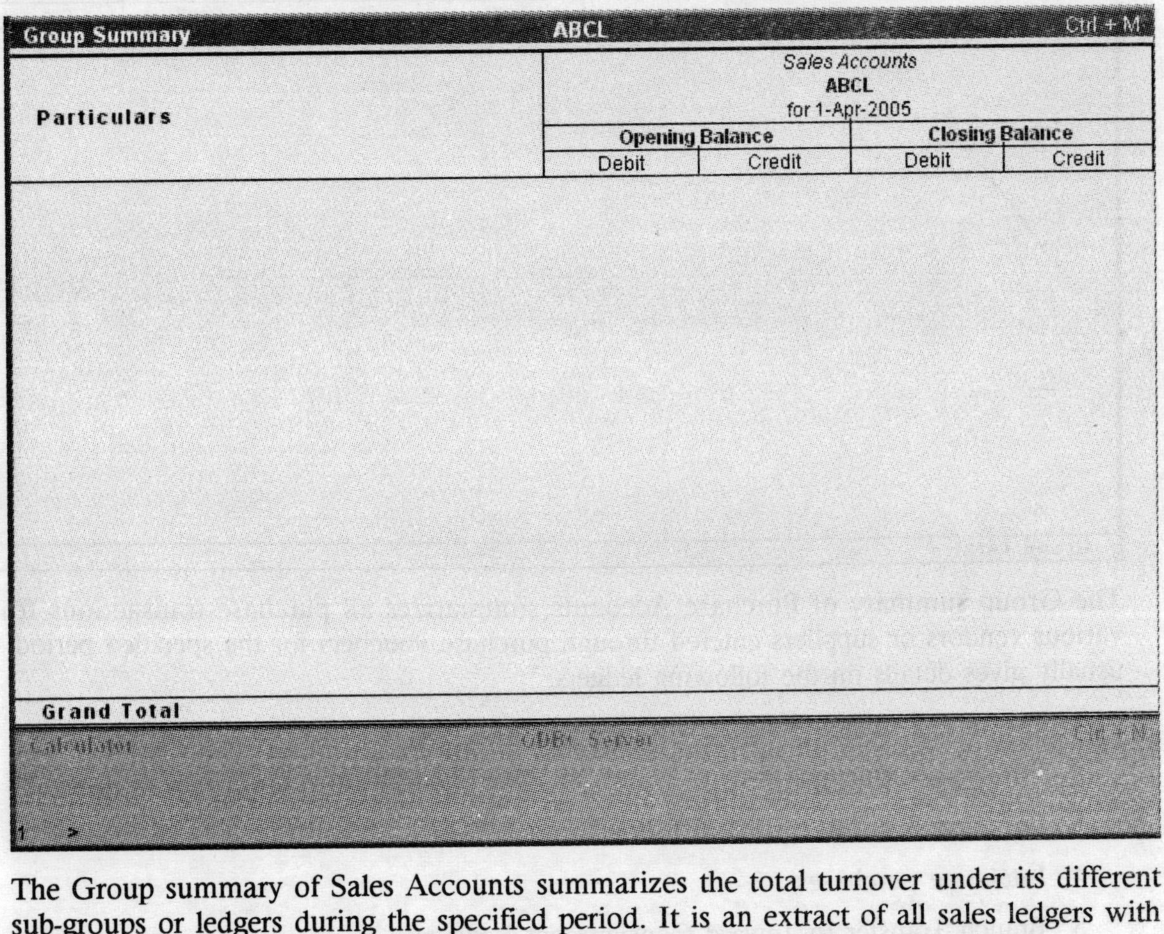

The Group summary of Sales Accounts summarizes the total turnover under its different sub-groups or ledgers during the specified period. It is an extract of all sales ledgers with their proceeds mentioned alongside. It generally gives details on the following:

1. Sales Ledgers (Separate ledgers for different rates)
2. Exempt Sales Ledgers
3. Sales – Export Ledgers

4. Interstate Sales Ledgers
5. Branch Transfer out/Outward Consignment Ledgers

Purchase Account

From Gateway of Tally – Press 'D' (Display) – Press 'A' (Accounts Books) – Press 'G' (Group Summary) – Select 'Purchase Accounts' to get the ledger wise break-up, as shown here.

Group Summary — **ABCL** — Ctrl + M

Particulars	*Purchase Accounts* ABCL for 1-Apr-2005			
	Opening Balance		Closing Balance	
	Debit	Credit	Debit	Credit
Grand Total				

The Group summary of Purchase Accounts summarizes all purchase transactions from various vendors or suppliers entered through purchase vouchers for the specified period. It usually gives details on the following ledgers:

1. Purchase Ledgers (Separate for different VAT rates)
2. Purchase – Exempt
3. Purchase from unregistered dealers
4. Interstate purchases
5. Branch Transfer In/Inward Consignment Ledgers

As explained earlier, configure the report to show the opening balance, transactions, closing balance etc., Data on value of purchase returns is shown against he respective purchase ledger in the credit column, which is very essential to calculate the absolute figures on purchases. The percentage share of each purchase type (depending upon VAT rate) to the gross purchases can also be elucidated.

SALES REGISTER

From Gateway of Tally – Press 'D' (Display) – Press 'A' (Accounts Books) – Press 'S' (Sales Register) to get monthly break-up of sales, as shown next.

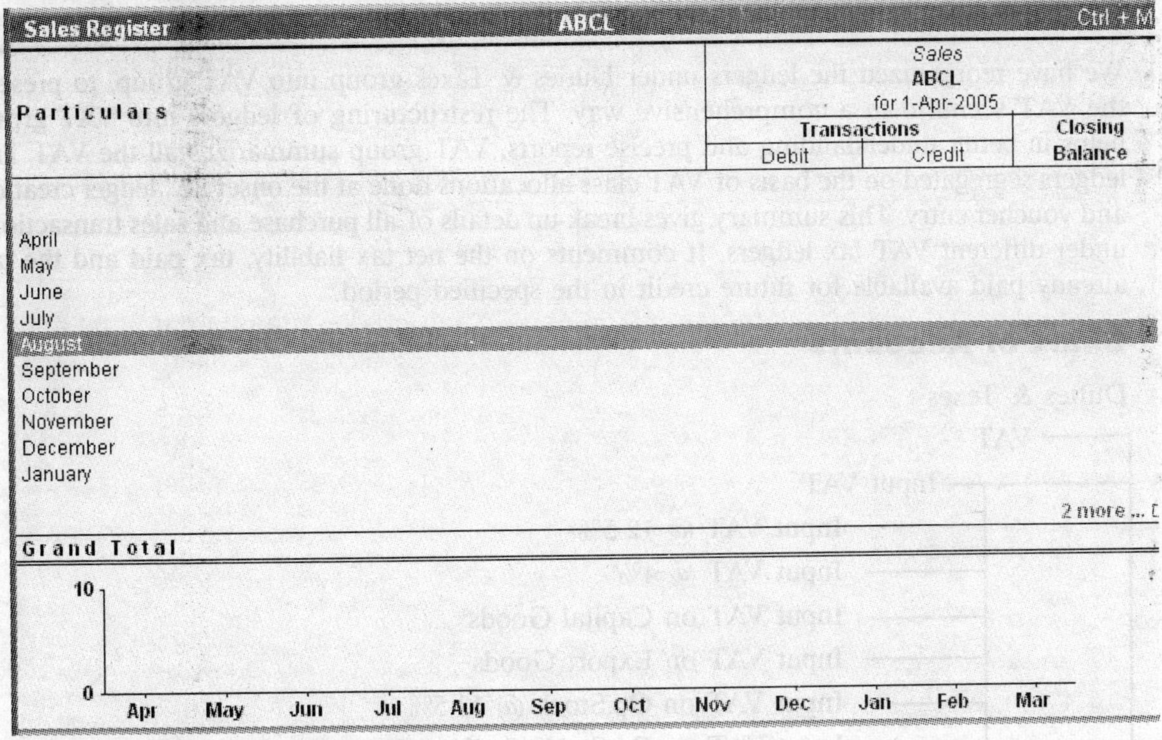

Columnar Sales Register

In the list of Sales Voucher, press F5 and press Ctrl + A to get Column and Sales Register, which reveal complete deal of information on sales turnover achieved during the specified period. It displays detail reading, date of transaction, nature of sales (whether it is exempt, stock transfer, Interstate or exports), customer or party to whom the goods were sold, Voucher number, Voucher reference and even the inventory details are obtainable. It gives entire data on sales made during the month or period under different VAT tax rates. In short, it shows a complete picture on the sales proceeds achieved under different ledgers during the period. This summation reports is self-explanatory and regulates occurrences of errors.

This statement proves advantageous for sales and output VAT reconciliation due to convenience in printing various Sales and VAT ledgers in different columns.

To re-define the columns, press F5 and select the required parameters of reports ledgers or group to be shown in individual or common column.

Extract Sales

In the list of Sales Voucher, press F6 to get Extract Sales that provides information on the list of ledgers that are used or involved in invoicing on sales entry. It displays the origin of such ledgers from their parent groups/sub-groups. It also denotes the total proceeds form each ledger during the specified period. The total of this report shows the total turnover achieved in the current period. In case of sub-groups press Shift + Enter to explore the next level details.

REORGANIZING VAT GROUP

We have reorganized the ledgers under Duties & Taxes group into VAT group, to present the VAT scenario in a comprehensive way. The restructuring of ledgers into VAT group helps in better understanding and precise reports. VAT group summarizes all the VAT Tax ledgers segregated on the basis of VAT class allocations done at the onset i.e., ledger creation and voucher entry. This summary gives break-up details of all purchase and sales transactions under different VAT tax ledgers. It comments on the net tax liability, tax paid and the tax already paid available for future credit in the specified period.

Chart of Accounts

Duties & Texes

- VAT
  - Input VAT
    - Input VAT @ 12.5%
    - Input VAT @ 4%
    - Input VAT on Capital Goods
    - Input VAT on Export Goods
    - Input VAT on Op.Stock @ 12,5%
    - Input VAT on Op.Stock @ 4%
  - Output VAT
    - Output VAT @ 12.5%
    - Output VAT @ 4%
    - Output VAT CST
  - VAT payable
  - Tax paid on others
    - Tax paid on Capital Goods
    - Tax paid on Export Goods
    - Tax paid on Op.Stock

Ledgers:

1. VAT Payable

   i) Input VAT Group: This group contains all input VAT Tax ledgers. It gives details on Input VAT paid on purchases at different rates depending upon this category / Class under VAT definitions viz.,

   a) Input VAT 2 12.5% paid on purchases taxable at the general rate of 12.5%

b) Input VAT @ 4% paid on purchases taxable at the rate of 4%

c) Monthly claim of Input VAT credit allowed on purchase of Capital Goods. (Spread over 36 months)

d) Monthly installment of Input VAT credit permitted on purchase of goods meant for Exports (after 3 months from the date of purchase)

e) Credit allowed on tax suffered stocks at the beginning of the year (extent of relief as ascertained by the Ascending Officer)

ii) Output VAT Group: This group contains all Output VAT Tax Ledgers charged. It gives details on Output VAT on sales at different rates depending upon their Category / Class under VAT Laws viz.,

a) Output VAT 2 12.5% paid on sales taxable at the general rate of 12.5%

b) Output VAT @ 4% paid on sales taxable at the rate of 4%

c) Output CST collected on Interstate sales.

iii) Tax paid on others: This group contains all ledgers, for Input VAT time available for future credit. This sub-group points out the following ledgers:

a) Tax paid on Capital Goods at the time of purchase of such assets.

b) Tax paid on Export Goods at the time of purchase of such goods.

c) Tax suffered by the Stock left unsold in the beginning of the year for which relief granted by Assessmebt officer.

VAT Payble ledger: This ledger specifies the next tax liability of the company for the given period. The credit balance of this ledger shows the amount of tax due.

VAT COMPUTATION

From Gateway of Tally – Press 'D' (Display) – Press 'V' (VAT Reports) – Press 'V' (VAT Computation) to get summary on VAT calculation, as shown in next figure.

VAT Computation report displays various types of Input VAT Tax and Out VAT Tax ledgers employed and transacted during voucher entry. It gives a clear-cut presentation on how VAT is computed for the given period. Basically, there are two categories of tax ledgers, one that are used in sales vouchers and others, which are used in purchase vouchers. As explained earlier, Input tax is paid on Purchases so, all the ledgers of this nature are categorized under input tax and tax ledgers on sales will be classified under Output tax. Similarly, Exempt or zero – rated of either type will fall under relevant groups under 'Others'. This report precisely reveals the system of offsetting input tax credit against output tax. Any excess of credit available is brought forward in the next month's report. In the same way any shortfall is also reported.

STATUTORY VAT RETURNS

The report provides drill down facility for each item that displays relevant at classification listing all vouchers under the classification.

- To Print, Press Alt + P.

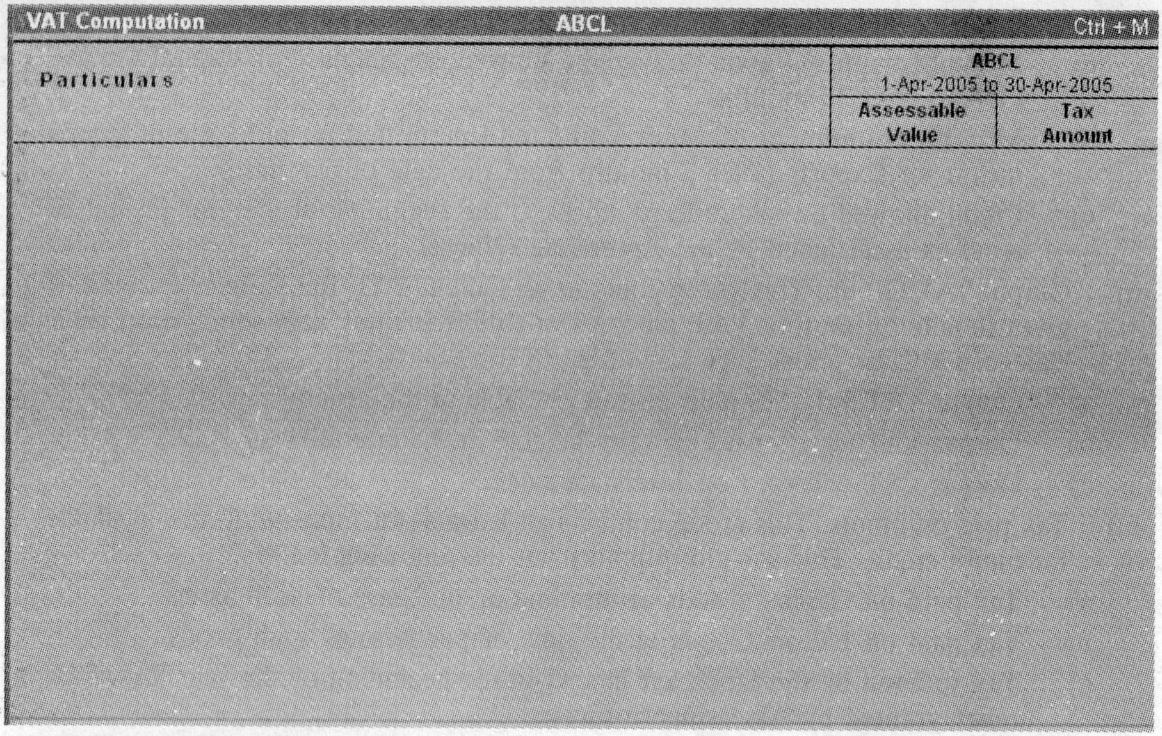

By drilling down any voucher listing, you get the voucher in alteration mode. Thus VAT computations provide a bird's eye view of all transaction related to VAT.

From Gateway of Tally – Press 'D' (Display) – Press 'V' (VAT Reports) – Press 'V' (VAT Forms) to view statutory returns for the state

In Tally 8.1 you can generate and print state specific monthly, quarterly or annual VAT Returns. Under Karnataka VAT laws, Form No. 100 is the statutory form used for filling monthly returns by a registered dealer. Under Form No. 100 the different columns indicate turnover at different rates and the taxes applicable to them as per VAT definitions. Contents of each column are briefed as under:

Box No.	***Contents***
1.	Taxable turnover @ 4%
2.	Taxable turnover at the general rate of 12.5%
3.	Turnover related to other rates like 1%
4.	Turnover on Interstate Sales
5.	Turnover on Consignment/Stock transfers out
6.	Turnover on Exempt sales
7.	Turnover on Exports
8.	Total turnover (Total of Box Nos. 1 to 7)
9.	Purchases from Un-Registered Dealers
10.	Total Purchases @ 4 %
11.	Total Purchases @ standard rate of 12.5 %
12.	Total Purchases @ other rates of tax i.e, 1 %

13. Total Value of Imported goods and Interstate purchases
14. Good received by Stock transfer / Consignment transfer
15. Value of other purchases viz., Exempt or zero rated
16. Total value of Purchases (Total of Box Nos 10 to 15)
17. Net value of Purchase of Capital Goods
18. Output tax collected @ 4% (on Box No. 1)
19. Output tax collected @ 12.5% (on Box No. 2)
20. Output tax collected @ 1% (on Box No. 3)
21. Output CST collected on Interstate Sales (Box No. 4)
22. Total Output tax collected on the taxable turnover (Box No. 18 to 21)
23. Tax paid on Purchases from Unregistered Dealers (On Box No. 9)
24. Input Tax paid @ 4% (On Box. No. 10)
25. Input Tax paid @ 12.5% (On Box. No. 11)
26. Input Tax paid @ 1% (On Box. No. 12)
27. Total value of Input Tax on Purchases (Total of Box Noz 24to 26)
28. Total Tax paid on purchase of Capital Goods (Box No. 17)
29. Allowed monthly installment of Input Credit on capital goods
30. Deductible Input Tax including partial rebating scheme u/s 17 of VAT act (excluding Box No. 29)
31. Deductible Input Tax under special rebating scheme u/s 15.
32. Value of Input tax on purchases made from unregistered dealer under sec. 3(2) of VAT act.
33. Value of refund brought forward
34. Value of net input tax i.e., total of Input tax paid minus the deductible input tax
35. Net Tax payable or refundable (i.e., it is the sum of Column 22 + 23) minus (Column 29 + 30 + 31 + 32 + 33) or (22 + 24 + 24) minus (27 + 29 + 33).

INVENTORY RECORDS

The VAT Act requires each registered dealer to maintain accounts and records of each commodity sold, purchased or manufactured. Tally 8.1 assists maintenance of Inventory accounting of materials. Though Tally generates numerous reports for Inventory, the most important ones in this context are referred here.

Stock Item

This report displays Inward and Outward Summary of selected item.

From Gateway of Tally – Press 'D' (Display) – Press 'I' (Inventory Books) – Press 'S' (Stock Item) – Select a Stock Item to get monthly summary of Inwards, Outwards and closing balance for the selected item.

To view transactions for any month, highlight the month and press Enter to get transactions for the month in columnar break-up of Inwards, Outwards and Closing balance.

Manufacturing Accounts

Summarized reports for Stock Journal Manufacturing Journal are available through following options:

1. Stock Transfer:

   Display List of All Stock Journal vouchers with break-up in Inward and Outwards columns. From Gateway of Tally – Press 'D' (Display) – Press 'I' (Inventory Books) – Press 'T' (Stock Transfer) – Highlight a month and press Enter.

2. Transfer Analysis:

   Displays item-wise break-up of Goods in and Goods Out transactions entered in Stock Journal or Manufacturing Journal vouchers. From Gateway of Tally – Press 'D' (Display) – Press 'I' (Inventory Books) – Press 'M' (Movement Analysis) – Press 'T' (Transfer Analysis) – Select the voucher type and press Enter to list all summary 0 all transactions entered through the selected voucher.

Descriptive Type Questions

1. What is VAT?
2. Describe the various terms used in VAT.
3. What are the advantages of using VAT over Sales Tax?
4. Which VAT records you have to keep?
5. Which VAT documents you have to maintain?
6. How would you create Ledger Masters for VAT?
7. What is VAT TIN No.?
8. How is Output VAT caluculated?
9. How are purchase and sales vouchers entered?
10. How would you print the invoice?
11. Describe the process of generating Journal entries.
12. How are Debit and Credit note prepared?
13. What is VAT Computation Report?
14. What do you understand by Interstate Purchases?
15. How is Interstate Sales entered in Tally?
16. How are Imports and Exports affected in Tally?
17. How are Exmpted Purchases and Sales entered in Tally?
18. For each case compute the VAT.
19. How are VAT Forms created for each?
20. Which are the VAT documents?
21. Which reports have to filed for VAT?
22. How is sales register computed?
23. Describe the various groups of VAT.
24. Which are the Statutory VAT Returns?
25. How does VAT figure in Inventory Reports?

7 Tax Deducted at Source (TDS)

INTRODUCTION TO TDS

Tax deducted at source is one of the modes of collecting income tax from the taxpayers. Such collection of tax is affected at the source when income arises or accrues. Hence where any specified type of income arises or accrues to any one, the Income Tax Act enjoins the prayer of such income to deduct a stipulated percentage of such income by way of income tax and pay only the balance amount to the receiver of such income.

The tax so deducted at source by the payer has to be deposited in the Government treasury to the credit of central government within the specified time. The tax so deducted from the income of the receiver is deemed the payment of Income tax by the receiver at the time of his assessment. Income from several sources is subjected to tax deduction at source.

Presently this concept of TDS is also used as n instrument in enlarging the tax base. Some of such incomes subjected to TDS are salary, interest, dividend, interest on securities, winnings from lottery, horse races, commission and brokerage, rent, fees for processionals and technical services, payments tonon-residents etc.

The deductor files the TDS returns containing the details of the deductee and the bank, where the TDS amount is deposited to the Income Tax Department (ITD). The deductor also provides Form 16A to the deductee.

The Income Tax Department has prescribe the formats for filling these returns electronically, which the deductor has to submit on a CD/floppy. Filling of e-TDS is a must for companies and not for others; however, they can also optionally file the returns electronically.

For additional details, visit the Income Tax Website at http://www.incometaxindia.gov.in

As is the motto of tally, Power of Simplicity, handling TDS related information is easy and with complete flexibility to handle almost all types of TDS related issues.

FEATURES OF TDS IN TALLY IES 8.1

The TDS functionality in Tally ies 8.1 supports the following features:

- Simple and User-friendly
- Quick and Easy to set up and use
- Partial/full payment of Tax deducted
- Auto and Manual calculation of TDS amount
- Generates TDS Challan and Exception reports

- Complete tracking of each transaction from deduction to payment
- Challan management and printing ensures prompt and accurate filing of Tax
- The Auto allocation feature prevents error-prone data entry and helps to track the transactions faster

Flowcharts of TDS

A seller (deductee) provides services to the buyer (Deductor). The buyer deducts the amount towards TDS prior to the services or the bills received. The buyer Form No. 16A to the deductee and deposits the deducted amount to the Authorized Bank (Treasury). The buyer flies annual returns electronically to the Income Tax department.

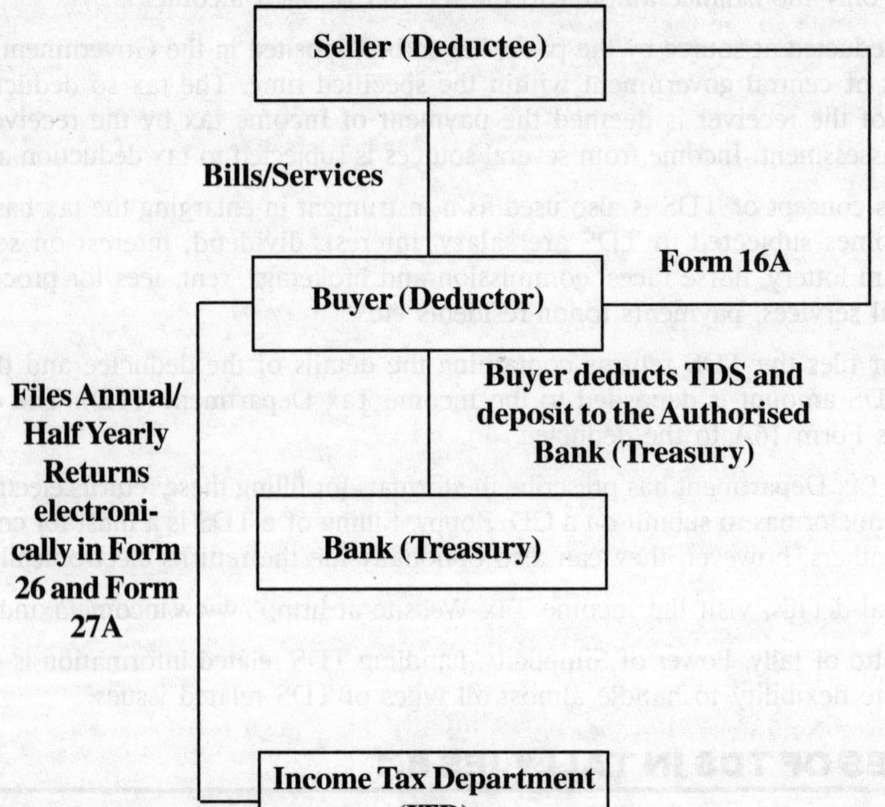

Who is Required to File e-TDS Return?

The Income Tax Department has made it mandatory for all Corporate Companies like private limited and public limited to file their TDS returns in electronic media (i.e. – TDS returns). However, the Non-Corporates like individuals, proprietary firms and partnership firms can furnish their returns in physical form to their respective Income Tax Offices. They can also furnish their returns in electronic form through TIN facilitation centers established by NSDL. Filling of e-TDS return to Non-Corporate deductors is optional.

Filling e-TDS Returns

The Buyer (Deductors) has to furnish the TDS returns in electronic form and Form 27A in physical from along with the e-TDS return CD-floppy.

Form 27A must be furnished separately for each return (Form 24, 26 or 27).

NSDL has developed a utility called File Validation Utility (FVU) to verify whether the e-TDS return file prepared by the Buyer (deductors) conforms to the prescribed format.

TDS ACCOUNTS

Accounts Classification for TDS

Income Tax Department has specified income arising or accruing from the below mentioned types as deductable by the payee.

Nature of Payments

1. Commission on Brokerage.
2. Commission on Sale of Lottery Tickets.
3. Fees for Professional or Technical Services.
4. Income From Foreign Currency Bonds or Shares.
5. Income in Respect of Units of Non-Residents.
6. Income of Foreign Institutional Investors.
7. Income Payable to A Resident Assessee.
8. Insurance Commission.
9. Interest on securities.
10. Interest Other Than Interest on Securities.
11. Other sums payable to A Non-Resident.
12. Payment of Compensation on Acquisition.
13. Payments in Respect of Deposits Under NSS
14. Payments in Respects of Units to an Offshore Fund.
15. Payments on Account of Re-Purchase of Units by....
16. Payments to Contractors (Other Than Advertisement)
17. Payments to Non-Resident Sportsmen/Sports Association.
18. Payment to Contractors. (Advertisement Contractors)
19. Payment to Sub-Contractors.
20. Rent.

21. Winning From Horse Race.
22. Winning From Lotteries and Crossword Puzzles

For the above-mentioned payments a separate 'TDS ledger expense masters' must be created.

For the statutory masters, the following details are preset as per Income Tax Laws.

- Section Number
- Payment Code

From Gateway of Tally – Press 'D' (Display) – Press 'U' (StatUtory Masters) – Press 'S' (TDS Nature of Pymts) – Select any of the 'TDS Nature of Payment' from the 'List of TDS Nature of Payment' (e.g. Commission on Brokerage).

In addition, for each of the deductee type, following details are also preset.

- Date of Applicability
- Exemption Limit
- Rate of Tax

Type of Deductees

The above-mentioned TDS has to be deducted from the deductee. The various types of deductees are as follows:

1. Association of Persons
2. Body of Individuals
3. Company – Non Resident
4. Company – Resident
5. Co-operative Society
6. Individual / HUF – Non Resident
7. Individual / HUF – Resident
8. Local Authority
9. Partnership Firm

For the deductee type the following details are preset as per Income Tax Laws.

- Residential Status
- Deductee Status
- Periodic details
- Applicable from
  - ➢ Surcharge Exempt Limit

- Surcharge Percentage
- Addl Surcharge (Cess) percentage

TDS TRANSACTIONS

Purchase Voucher

Purchase voucher can be used to book the expenses. However, the TDS should not be deducted at this point.

Journal Voucher

Journal voucher is used to deduct the TDS applicable on the expenses incurred. Journal voucher can also be used to book the expenses. The TDS so deducted is payable to the Government Treasury.

Payment Voucher

Payment voucher can be used to make advance payments to the parties towards expenses. The deduction of TDS is possible at this point. Payment voucher has to be used for making payments to the Government Treasury. The challan is generated with the help of the details stored in the payment voucher.

CONFIGURING TALLY FOR TDS

Through Tally ies 8.1 you can calculate the tax amount that is payable to the government treasury while entering the transaction. You can also view various TDS reports, Challans & Outstanding statements when required.

To Enable TDS in Tally

Press F11: Features.

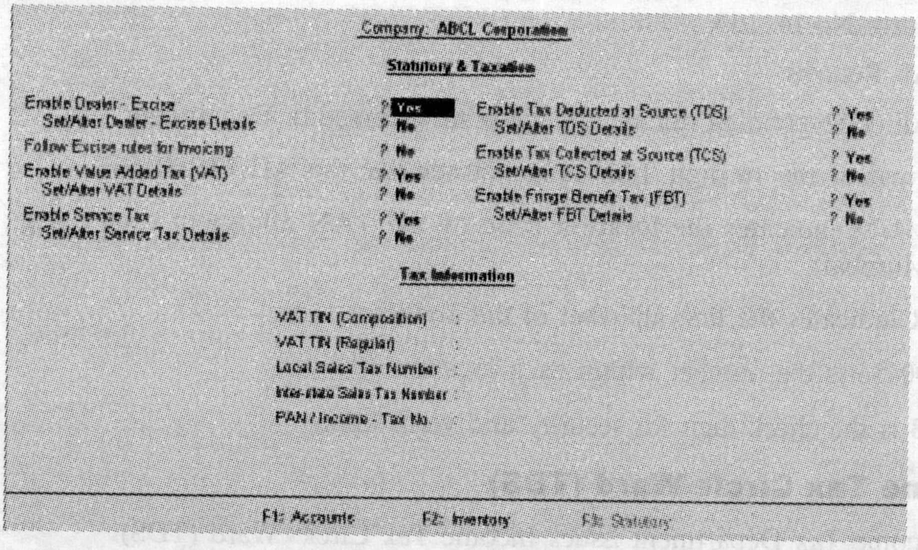

Company Deductor/Collector Details

Tax Assessment Number : [redacted]

Income Tax Circle/Ward (TDS/TCS) :
Deductor/Collector Type : **Government**
Name of person responsible :
Designation :

Click at Statutory and Taxation to get the screen.

- Set 'Enable TDS' to Yes.
- Set 'Set/Alter TDS Details' to yes to get the following screen.
- Fill the details asked for or leave blank.

Tax Assessment Number

The Tax Assessment Number (TAN) is a ten-digit alphanumeric number, issued to the deductors by the Income Tax Department (ITD). Only one TAN is required for different types of deductions.

TAN must be quoted properly on

- Challans
- Payment for TDS
- Returns
- All Certificates
- Form No.16/16A
- All Returns
- All corresponding documents given to Income-tax Department.

The format of the 10 digit TAN is something like this MUMR00456B

- MUM indicates the location code of the TAN allotment center (e.g., MUM for Mumbai)
- R indicates the first alphabet of the deductor name
- 00456 is the number within each location
- B is the check digit for security and verification

Income Tax Circle/Ward (TDS)

The Income Tax Department issues Income Tax Circle/Ward (TDS).

Deductor Type

Select the Deductor Type (Company or Non-Company) depending on whether your organization is a Company or a Non-Company.

Name of the Person Responsible

Enter the name of the authorized person responsible to file the TDS returns of your company.

Designation

Enter the designation of the authorized person filing the TDS returns.

CREATION OF MASTERS

Masters that must be created on Tally for TDS are of three types

- Expense Ledgers
  - Professional Fees
  - Rent A/c
  - Insurance Commission
  - Contractor Fee
- TDS Tax Ledgers
  - TDS on Rent
  - Contractor Fees
  - Professional Fess etc
- Party Ledgers classified in different deductee types.

Check whether following features from F11 Company Operations Screen are enabled, if not enable them.

Setup:

- Press F11 Feature and set 'Enable TDS?', 'Maintain Bill-wise details' to Yes
- F12 Configuration set 'Allow ADVANCED entries in Masters' , 'Use CONTACT DETAILS for Ledger Accounts' to Yes

TDS Expense Ledgers

Expense ledgers must be created for each of the expense account separately.

Create the following expense ledger accounts under 'Indirect Expenses Group'

- Rent A/c

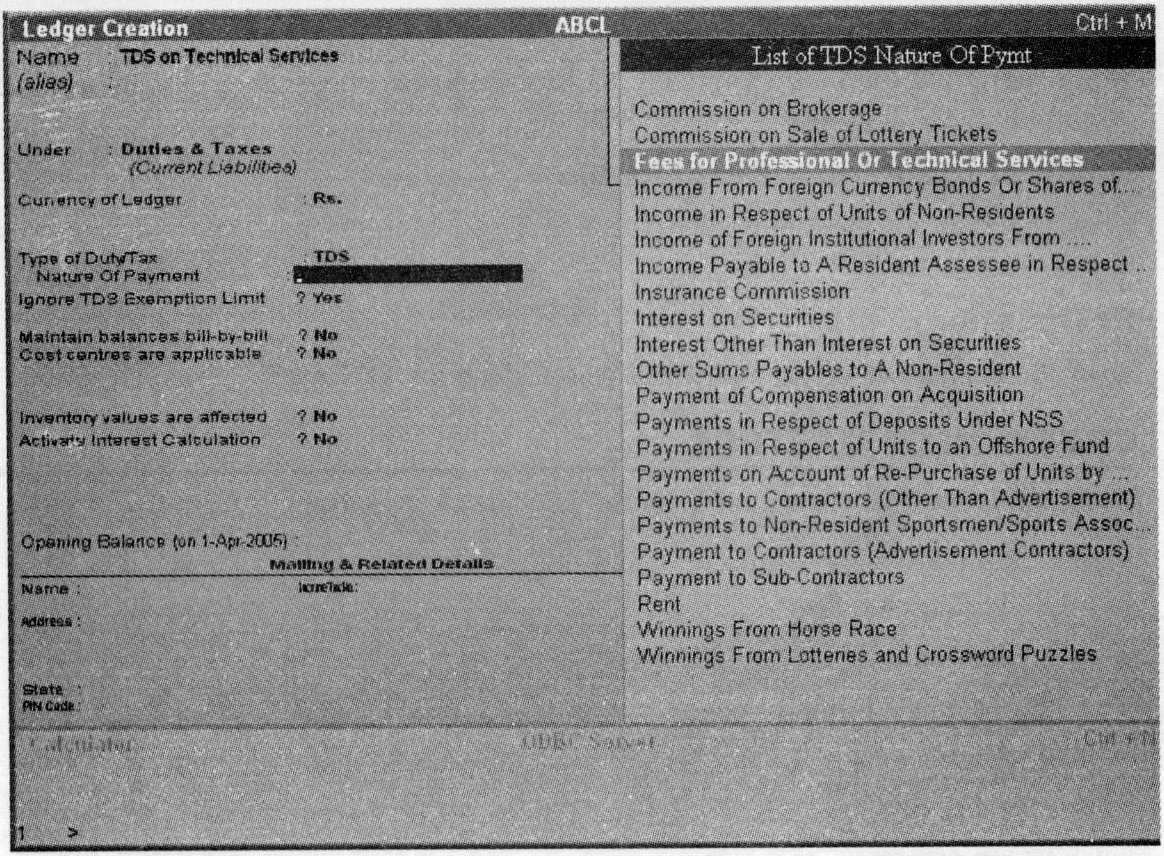

- Professional fees A/c
- Interest Paid A/c

TDS Tax Ledgers

The Tax ledger have to be created under the group Duties and Taxes. The group 'Duties and Taxes' is automatically used for calculation of tax. This Ledger holds the entire automatic calculation for TDS tax deductors at the voucher entry level. It is internally enabled to calculate the Tax.

The option to specify the Tax Type is available only for ledgers under the group 'Duties and Taxes'.

The Tax ledger master screen can be reached by following the menu path:

Gateway of Tally > Accounts Info > Ledgers > Create

Enter the following information on the screen.

Name

Enter the name of the Tax Ledger:

Under

Select the group as Duties and Taxes from the list. On the selection of group Duties and Taxes, you will get the option to select type of Duty/Tax.

Type of Duty/Tax

Select TDS tax type from the list

Nature of Payment

Select the appropriate TDS Nature of Payment as statutorily applicable, given/.desired by the Govt. e.g. Fees for Professional Or Technical Services. By default, Tally provides you with a List of TDS Nature of Payment. You need to select the appropriate TDS Nature of Payment from the list.

Ignore TDS Exemption Limit

If the total transaction limit exceeds the actual limit you need to set the Ignore TDS Exemption Limit field to Yes then the tax is not calculated up to exemption.

VOUCHER ENTRY FOR TDS

TDS affects expenses entered in books of accounts. The expenses can be booked through either a Journal Voucher or a Purchase Voucher. In some cases, Advance Payments are made before a Journal or a Purchase voucher is passed, and hance TDS needs to be deducted at the time of advance payment itself.

Further, over and above the TDS to be deducted, there is Surcharge & Cess that are applicable, of which for sucharge there are separate exemption limits based on the deductee type & nature of payment. During computation of TDS, the exemptions can eb overlooked or can be taken into consideration on case-to-case basis.

Tally also allows you to start deducting TDS only when the exemption limit is crossed.

All these scenarios can be handled in Tally to take care of tax to be deducted at source.

Journal Voucher

Booking of Expense

For example, on 12.10.2004, Mega Consulting submitted bill for Rs.22,500.00 towards professional services rendered by them towards marketing survey.

Create Journal Voucher:

- Press 'V' for' Accounting Vouchers'.
- Press 'F7' for Journal Voucher'.
- Press F2 and change date to '12/10/2004'.

In Particular:

- Select 'Professional Fees A/ c' as Dr.
- Type '22,500' as Amount.
- Select 'Mega Consulting' as Cr.
- Type '22,500' as Amount.

In Bill-wise Details:

- Select 'New Ref' in 'Type of Ref'.
- Select 'TDS on Professional Fees' from 'List of TDS Ledgers' in 'TDS Ledger' field.
- Type '22,500' as Amount.
- Press Ctrl + A to Accept.
- Press Enter to Accept.

TDS Deduction Voucher

Since TDS has to be deducted on the same day the credit was booked, a Journal voucher is passed to account for the same. Tally allows automatic TDS computation.

Create Journal Voucher:

- Create Journal Voucher.
- Press 'V' for' Accounting Vouchers'.
- Press 'F7' for Journal Voucher'.
- Press' Alt+S' for 'TDS Deduction'.
- Press F2 and change date to '12/10/2004'.

In Particular:

- Select 'Mega Consulting' as Dr.

In TDS Details for:

- Select 'TDS on Professional Fees' in TDS Ledger.
- The 'Total Amount Paid/Payable' will appear automatically.
- Select '1 12-Oct-2004 22,500.00Cr TDS on Professional Fees' in TDS field.

In Particulars:

- * The Amount'1,176' will appear automatically.
- * Select 'TDS on Professional Fees' as Cr.
- Press Enter to Accept.

Payment Against Bills Pending

For example, on 30.10.2004 payments was made to Mega Consulting in full. The entry does not attract any TDS implication; hence this is a normal payment entry.

Setup:

Press F12: Configuration and set 'Use Single Entry mode for Pymt/Rcpt/Contra' to No.

Create Payment Voucher:

- Press 'V' for' Accounting Vouchers'.
- Press F5 for 'Payment Voucher',
- Press F2 and change date to '30/10/2004'.

In Particulars:

- Select 'Mega Consulting' as Dr,
- Type '21324' as Amount.

In Bill-wise Details:

- Select 'Agst Ref' in 'Type of Ref'.
- Select '1 12-Oct-2004 21,324.00Cr' from 'List of Pending Bills' in 'Name'.
- Type '21324' as Amount.
- Press Ctrl+A to Accept.

In Particulars:

- Select 'HDFC Bank' as Cr.
- Press Enter to Acept.

TDS Payment to Govt. Treasury

TDS deducted in any month should be deposited to the government latest by 7th of next month. So on 5th November 2004, for TDS deducted in October 2004, a cheque is issued for Rs.1176.00 towards TDS on Professional Fees.

Along with the cheque, a challan mentioning the computation needs to be submitted to the treasury, Tally prints the challan based on the inputs provided while entering the TDS payment.

Setup:

Press F12: Configuration and set 'Pre-Allocate Bills for Payment/Receipt' to Yes.

Create Payment Voucher:

- Press 'V' for' Accounting Vouchers'.
- Press 'F5' for 'Payment Voucher'.
- Press F2 and change date to '05/11/2004'.
- Select 'HDFC Bank' in Account'.

In Particulars

- Select 'TDS on Professional Fees'.
- Type '1176' as Amount.

Tax Details for:

- Select' Agst Ref' in 'Type of Ref'.

- Select '2 12-Oct-2004 1,176.00 Cr' from 'List of TDS Payable' in 'Name'.
- The Due Date or Credit Days and Amount will appear automatically.
- Press Ctrl + A to Accept.
- Press Enter to Accept.

Printing of TDS Challan

Select the payment voucher that was entered earlier.

Setup:

Press Alt + P 'Print' and set 'Print as TDS Challan?' to Yes.

PURCHASE VOUCHER

The alternate way of booking expense voucher can be a purchase voucher. We will consider the different steps required from booking of expenses to payment to the party & treasury, including the printing of statutory challan.

Booking of Expense

For xxample, on 3.11.2004, rent of Rs. 66000.00 was paid to Shankar Krishnan on account of rent from April to September 2004.

Create Purchase Voucher:

- Press 'V' for' Accounting Vouchers'
- Press F9 for 'Purchase Invoice
- Press Alt + I to enter in Acct Invoice format
- Press F2 and change date to '03/11/2004'
- Select 'Shankar Krishnan' in 'Party's A/ c Name'
- Select 'Rent A/ c' in 'Particulars
- Type' 66000' as Amount

In Bill -wise Details:

- Select 'New Ref' in 'Type of Ref'
- Type '1(one)' as Name
- Select 'TDS on Rent' from List of TDS Ledger' in TDS Ledger
- Press Ctrl + A to Accept.
- Press Enter to Accept

For example, on 27.10.04 Interest of Rs. 14000.00 was credited to Naresh Shah (Unsecured Loans) on account of Interest due for 7 months April to October 2004 for Rs. 2000.00 per month on an unsecured loan taken for Rs. 200000.00 @12.00% per annum.

Create Journal Voucher:

- Press 'V' for' Accounting Vouchers'
- Press F7 for 'Journal Voucher'
- Press F2 and change date to '27/10/2004'

In Particulars:

- Select 'Interest Paid A/c' as Dr
- Type '14000' as Amount
- Select 'Naresh Shah' as Cr
- Type '14000' as Amount

In Bill-wise Details:

- Select 'New Ref' in 'Type of Ref'
- Type '3' in Name
- Select 'TDS on Interest paid' in TDS Ledger
- Press Ctrl + A to Accept.
- Press Enter to Accept

TDS Deduction Entry

Since the TDS has to be accounted the same day the credit has been allotted, pass journal entries for TDS to be deducted to Rent A/c and Interest Paid a/c respectively.

Step 1: Create Journal Voucher

- Create Journal Voucher
- Press 'V' for' Accounting Vouchers'
- Press 'F7' for Journal Voucher
- Press 'Alt+S' for Deduction'
- Press F2 and change date to 03/11/2004'

In Particular:

- Select 'Shankar as Dr.

In Details for

- Select on Rent' in TDS Ledger
- The 'Total Amount Paid/Payable' will appear automatically
- Select '1 3-Nov-2004 55,902.00Cr' from TDS Applicable Bills' in TDS
- Press Ctrl + A to Accept

In Particulars:

- The Amount '10098' will appear automatically

- Select 'Tds on Rent' as Cr
- Press Enter to Accept

Step 2: Create Journal Voucher

- Press 'V' for' Accounting Vouchers'
- Press 'F7' for Journal Voucher'
- Press' Alt + S' for 'TDS Deduction'
- Press F2 and change date to '04/11/2004'

In Particulars:

- Select 'Naresh Shah' as Dr .

In TDS Details for:

- Select 'TDS on Interest Paid' in TDS Ledger
- Press Ctrl + A to Accept

In Particulars:

- The Amount '1428' will appear automatically
- Select 'TDS on Rent' as Cr
- Press Ctrl + A to Accept

Payment Against Bills

For xxample, the Balance rent payable is paid on 8.11.2004 and Interest payable is paid on 14.11.2004 through HDFC Bank.

Step 1: Create Payment Voucher

- Press 'V' for' Accounting Vouchers'
- Press 'F5' for Journal Voucher'
- Press F2 and change the date to '08/11/2004'
- Select 'HDFC Bank in Acount'

In Particulars:

- Select 'Shankar Krishnan'
- Type '55902' as Amount

In Bill-wise Details:

- Select 'Agst Ref' in 'Type of Ref'
- Select '1 3-Nov-2004 55,902.00 Cr' from 'List of Pending Bills' in 'Name'
- Press Ctrl + A to Accept

In Narration:

- Type 'Ch. Noo. 590045'

Press Enter to Accept.

Step 2: Create Payment Voucher

- Press 'V' for' Accounting Vouchers'
- Press 'F5 'for' Payment Voucher'
- Press F2 and change date to '14/11/2004'
- Select HDFC Bank' in Account'

In Particulars:

- Select 'Naresh Shah'
- type '12572' as Amount

In Bill-wise details:

- Select 'Agst Ref' in 'Type of Ref'
- Select '3 27-Oct-2004 12,572.00Cr 'List of Pending Bills' in 'Name'
- Press Ctrl + A to Accept

In Narration:

- Type 'Ch. No. 590046'
- Press Enter to Accept.

TDS Payment with Auto–Fill

TDS payment due towards Rent A/c was made on 3rd December 2004

Tally provides TDS helper facility while making TDS payments to the treasury that makes the data entry easier. We will make use of this facility to enter the two transactions described above.

Step 1: Create Payment Voucher

- Press 'V' for' Accounting Vouchers'
- Press 'F5 'for' Payment Voucher'
- Press F2 and change date to '03/12/2004'
- Press Alt + S for 'TDS Helper'

In TDS Filters:

- Select 'TDS on Rent' from List of TDS Ledgers' in 'TDS Ledger'
- Select 'Non Company' from 'Deductee Status'
- Type '30/11/2004' in 'To Date'
- Select HDFC Bank' in Account'
- The Details will appear automatically.
- Press Enter to Accept.

For example, TDS payment towards Interest was made on 13th December 2004. Since the due date of the TDS was on 7th December 2004, an interest @2.00 percent per month was also paid to the treasury. Since we need to take care of Interest factor, we will not consider the TDS helper for this transaction.

Step 2: Create Payment Voucher

- Press 'V' for' Accounting Vouchers'
- Press 'F5' for 'PaymentVoucher'
- Press F2 and change date to '13/12/2004'

In Particulars:

- Select TDS on Interest Paid' as Dr.
- Type '1428' as Amount

Tax Details for:

- Select 'Agst Ref' in 'Type of Ref'
- Select '5 4-Nov-2004 1,428.00 Cr' from List of TDS Payable' in 'Name'
- The Due Date or Credit Days and Amount will appear automatically
- Press Ctrl + A to Accept

In Particulars:

- Select 'Interest Paid on TDS' as Dr
- Type '5 (five)' as Amount
- Select 'HDFC bank' as Cr .
- Press Enter to Accept.

TDS Challan Printing

Select the TDS payment vouchers that were entered on 3.12.2004 & 13.12.2004.

Setup: Press F12: Configuration and set 'Print as TDS Challan?' to Yes

ADVANCE PAYMENT

Accounting of Bill with TDS against Advance

For example, on 15th December 2004 an advance payment of Rs. 50000.00 is made to Advait & Co. towards Technical know-how fees through HDFC Bank, TDS is deducted while making the payment.

Step 1: Create Payment Voucher

- Press 'V' for' Accounting Vouchers'.
- Press 'F5' for 'Payment Voucher'.
- Press F2 and change date to '15/12/2004'.
- Select 'HDFC Bank' in Account'.

In Particulars:

- Select 'Advait & Co'
- Type '50000' as Amount.

In Bill-wise Details:

- Select 'Advance' in 'Type of Ref'
- Select '7' in 'Name'
- Select 'TDS on Professional Fees' in TDS ledger
- Press Ctrl + A to Accept
- Press Enter to accept 'TDS on Professional Fees'

In Detials for:

- Type '7' in Name
- Press Ctrl + A to Accept
- Press Enter to Accept.

Booking of the Expense

For example, on receipt of the advance, Advait & Co. sent a bill of Rs.80,000.00 on 21st December 2004. The Expenses were booked the same day.

Create Journal Voucher:

- Press 'V' for' Accounting Vouchers'
- Press F7 for 'Journal Voucher'
- Press F2 and change date to '21/12/2004'

In Particulars:

- Select 'Professional Fees A/ c ' as Dr
- Type '80000' as Amount
- Select Advait & Co' as Cr
- Type '80000' as Amount

In Bill-wise Details:

- Select' Agst Ref' in 'Type of Ref'
- Select '7' in Name
- Type '50000' as Amount
- Select 'New Ref' in 'Type of Ref'
- Type '6' in Name
- Select 'TDS on Professional Fees' in TDS Ledger
- Type '30000' in Amount
- Press Ctrl + A to Accept

- Press Enter to Accept.

TDS Deduction for Balance Amount

Since the TDS is to be deducted on the same day, create a journal voucher to pass the TDS.

Step 1: Create Journal Voucher

- Create Journal Voucher
- Press 'V' for' Accounting Vouchers'
- Press 'F7' for Journal Voucher'
- Press' Alt+S' for 'TDS Deduction'
- Press F2 and change date to '21/12/2004'

In Particular:

- Select' Advait & Co' as Dr.

In TDS Details for:

- Select 'TDS on Professional Fees' in TDS Ledger
- The 'Total Amount Paid/Payable' will appear automatically
- Select '6 21-Dec-2004 30,000.00 Cr TDS on Professional Fees' in TDS
- Press Ctrl + A to Accept

In Particulars:

- The Amount '1568' will appear automatically
- Select 'TDS on Professional Fees' as Cr
- Press Enter to Accept.

TDS REPORTS

TDS Challan Reconciliation

The TDS challan printed to deposit the TDS in the Government treasury needs further data to be stored into it. The reconciliation is made available in the respective ledgers of TDS.

The details to be fed in are

Bank Challan number	145
Challan Date	3-12-2004
BSR Code (Bank Branch Code)	3214504 (7 digit code)

To view the TDS Challan Reconciliation:

From Gateway of Tally – Press 'D' (Display) – Press' A' (Account Books) – Press 'L' (Ledger) – Select 'TDS on Rent' from List of Ledgers – Press Alt+F5 for Challan Reconciliation

Enter the Bank Challan No, Date and BSR Code

TDS COMPUTATION REPORT

This report shows all the ledgers wherein TDS is applicable. In addition, each ledger will further have multiple TDS ledgers, if that party has had more than one type of services rendered to the company.

To view he TDS Computation report:

From Gateway of Tally – Press 'D' (Display) – Press' S' (Statement of Accounts Books) – Press 'T' (TDS Outstandings) – Press 'T' (TDS Computations) – Press Alt + F12 and change date to 1/4/2004 till date.

Press Alt + P to print the TDS Computation report.

Note:

1. Particulars column provides you with a list of Party and the TDS ledger names associated with the Party Ledger.
2. Amount Paid/Payable Till Date column gives the total amount that has to be paid to the party not taking into consideration the amount paid.
3. Tax Rate displays the rate specified by the Income Tax department for the services provided by the party.
4. Tax gives the total income tax amount calculated at the rate specified in the Tax Rate column.
5. Surcharge Rate displays the rate of additional levey on Income Tax.
6. Surcharge provides the total surcharge value calculated at the rate specified in the Surcharge Rate column.
7. Addl. Surcharge (Cess) Rate displays the rate of additional levy on the Income Tax and Surcharge.
8. Addl. Surcharge displays the additional surcharge value at the rate specified.
9. Total TDS Amount displays the total TDS amount.
10. Less: TDS Deducted Till Date provides the TDS amount deducted till date.
11. Net TDS to Deduct provides the TDS amount that is not pais.

TDS Pending Statement (All Ledgers)

TDS Payables report provies you with the information on the status of TDS payable (pending) transactions for all TDS ledgers created under the Group Duties & Taxes.

The items displayed in the report are the references of pending bills created while enering the vouchers.

To view TDS Pending Statement (All Ledgers):

From Gateway of Tally – Press 'D' (Display) – Press' S' (Statement of Accounts Books) – Press 'T' (TDS Outstanding) – Press 'D' (TDS Payables) – Press Alt + F1 and get detailed format.

TDS Pending Statement – (Single Ledger)

The pending statement for a single ledger shows all the pending references for that ledger.

As in the case of all ledgers, ageing analysis can also be performed for the TDS ledger.

To view TDS Pending Statement (Single Ledger):

From Gateway of Tally – Press 'D' (Display) – Press' S' (Statement of Accounts Books) – Press 'T' (TDS Outstanding) – Press 'L' (Ledger) – Select 'TDS on Professional Fees' from List of TDS Ledgers – Press Alt + F1 to get detailed format.

Descriptive Type Questions

1. What is TDS?
2. Who is required to file TDS returns?
3. What are the various types of deductions and payments in TDS?
4. What sort of vouchers would you pass for TDS?
5. How would you configure TDS for Tally?
6. How would you create masters for TDS?
7. What sort of challans are printed for TDS?
8. Describe all the TDS reports printed.

8 Service Tax in Tally

SERVICE TAX

It is different than Sales Tax. As Sales Tax is an indirect Tax on goods sold, Service Tax is indirect Tax on Services provided. Service tax is paid by buyer of service to seller of service, who in turn, deposits the tax with government.

Setting up for Service Tax

Click F11: Features & set Yes at Enable Service Tax at Company Operations screen to activate Service Tax features for the company.

Company Service Tax Particulars Entry

At Company Operations screen, set Yes at Set/Modify other Company Features (the last field) to get Company Advanced Operations screen.

At Company Advanced Operations screen, set Yes at Enter Service Tax Details to get Company Service Tax Details entry screen.

Company Service Tax Details

Enter the general information of the Company, relating to Service Tax, as below:

- *Service Tax Regn #*: At Service Tax Registration Number, enter the Service Tax Registration Number, allotted to the organization on registering under Service Tax rules.
- *Date of Service Tax Registration*: At Assessee Code: At Assessee Code, enter the Service Tax Assessee code allotted to the organization.
- *Organization Type*: At Type of Organization, select the appropriate Organization Type (like Company – Resident) from the list of Organization Type, according to the constitutional organization nature of the Company.-
- *Service Category Name*: At Major Service Category Name, select the appropriate Service Category (like Architect) of the Company, from the list. You may select Not Applicable, if the organization does not fall in any of the Category listed.
- *Credit Adjustment (%)*: Enter the Credit Adjustment %. Normally it is 20% (where the expenses relating to Tax Credit are not solely attributed to service income) or 100% (where the expenses relating to Tax Credit solely attributed to service income).

Company Operations Alteration

Company : **ABCL**

Integrate Accounts and Inventory	? **Yes**	Maintain Budgets and Controls	? **Yes**
Allow Multi-Currency	? **Yes**	Allow 0 valued entries in Vouchers	? **Yes**
Allow Invoicing	? **Yes**	Allow Purchase Order Processing	? **Yes**
Enter Purchases in Invoice Format?	**Yes**	Allow Sales Order Processing	? **Yes**
Separate Discount column on Invoices	? **Yes**	Enable TDS	? **Yes**
Enable Service Tax	**Yes**		

Accounting Features		**Inventory Features**	
Maintain Billwise Details	? **Yes**	Maintain Stock Categories	? **Yes**
(for Non-Trading A/cs also)	? **Yes**	Maintain Batch-wise Details	? **Yes**
Maintain Cost Centres	? **Yes**	(set Expiry Dates for Batches)	? **Yes**
(more than ONE Cost Category)	? **Yes**	Maintain Multiple Godowns	? **Yes**
Use Rev. Journals & Optional Vouchers	? **Yes**	Use Tracking Numbers	? **Yes**
Use Debit/Credit Notes	? **Yes**	Use Rejection Notes	? **Yes**
Use Invoice mode for Credit Notes?	**Yes**	Use different Actual & Billed Qty	? **Yes**
Use Invoice mode for Debit Notes?	**Yes**	Track additional costs of Purchase	? **Yes**
Activate Interest Calculation	? **Yes**		
(use advanced parameters)	? **No**		
Income/Expense Stmt instead of P & L?	**No**		

Set/Modify other Company Features ? **Yes**

Advanced Company Operations

Company : **ABCL**

Use Multiple Price Levels for Invoicing	? **No**
	? **No**
Follow Excise rules for Invoicing	? **No**
	? **Yes**

Service Tax Authority Particulars

Enter the particulars of the Jurisdictional Service Tax administering authority.

- *Service Tax Division Code*: Enter the Code of the Service Tax Division to which the organization falls.
- *Service Tax Division Name*: Enter the Name of the Service Tax Division to which the organization falls.
- *Service Tax Range Code*: Enter the Code of the Service Tax Range to which the organization falls.

Division		
	Code	: MY/9
	Name	: Bank of India
Range		
	Code	: 10
	Name	: North
Commissionerate		
	Code	: 4
	Name	: NW

- *Service Tax Range Name*: Enter the Name of the Service Tax Range to which the organization falls.
- *Service Tax Commissionerate Code*: Enter the Code of the Service Tax Commissionerate Division to which the organization falls.
- *Service Tax Commissionerate Name*: Enter the Name of the Service Tax Commissionerate Division to which the organization falls.

Bank Details

Banks here are the nominated banks to receive Service Tax for a specified area. Each such Bank is allotted a Bank Code (This code is available with the Commissionerate of Service Tax).

Enter the following particulars relating to the Focal bank into which the Service Tax of the Company would be deposited.

- *Focal Bank Code*: Enter the code of the Focal Bank
- *Focal Bank* Name: Enter the name of the Focal Bank
- *Focal Bank Address*: Enter the Address of the Focal Bank

Service Category Profile

From time to time, Government notifies the specific categories of Service which are subject to Service Tax rules. It can be different from State to State. Tally provides an updated profile of such Service Categories, their applicability date, rates of Service Tax and Surcharge etc. This profile may be uploaded from the website of Tally.

Select Display > Statutory Masters to get Statutory Masters menu.

At Statutory Masters Menu, select Service Categories.

Select the Service Category for which you like to view the Service Category Profile.

CREATION OF PARTY LEDGER

At creation of Party Ledgers, enter the following details relating to Service Tax Ledger. If the Company Provides services of multiple Category types, you should create a Ledger Account for each major category of Service. Service Tax Applicability: At Is Service Tax Applicable filled in the Service Tax Ledger Account, set

- Yes for Customers whom you charge Service Tax in your bills.
- Yes for Suppliers who charges you service tax that you claim for credit.
- No for other ledger accounts.

Service Tax Exemption Details

For parties for which Service Tax is applicable, you get another subscreen to specify the Exemption details.

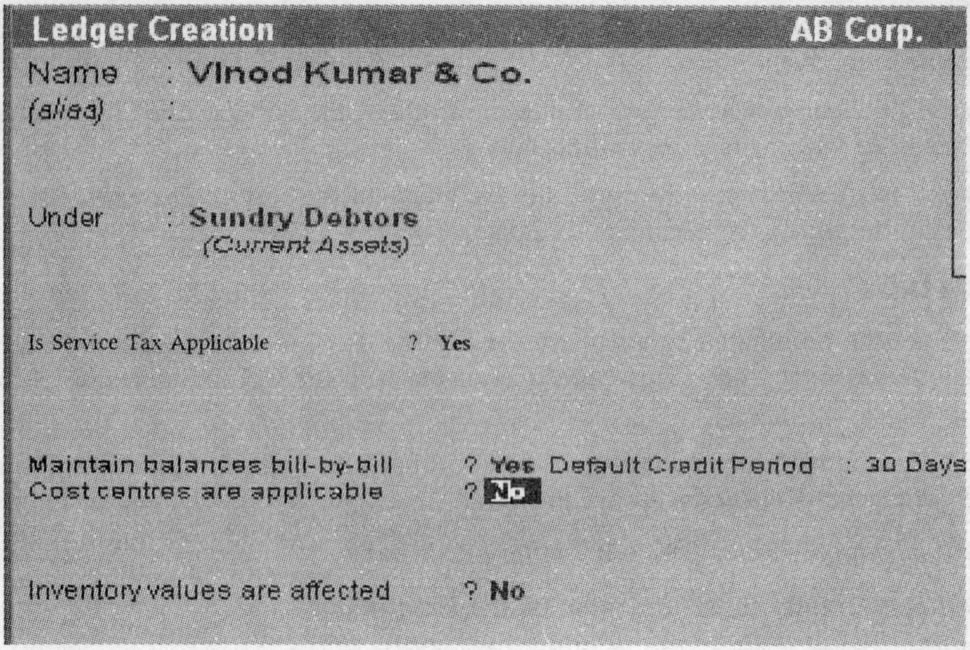

- *Exemption Status*: At Is Exempted, set Yes if the Party is Exempted from Service Tax by any government notification, else set No.
- *Exemption Notification Reference*: If exempted, at Notification Details, enter the Exemption Notification Reference.

Party Service Tax Registration Particulars

Further, specify the Service Tax registration particulars of the party.

- *Service Tax Regn Number of the Party*: Enter the Service Tax Registration Number of the Party.
- *Service Tax Regn Date of the Party*: Enter the Service Tax Registration Date of the party.

SERVICE INCOME/EXPENSES LEDGER A/C CREATION

At Service Income Ledger Creation for each Service Income on which Service Tax is chargeable, enter the following details relating to Service Tax.

Service Tax Applicability: At Is Service Tax Applicable field in the Service Tax Ledger Account, set

- Yes for Income Accounts on which Service Tax is charged.
- Yes for Expenses Account on which you claim Service Charge Credit.
- No for other ledger accounts.

The Service Income Ledger account may be placed under Sales Group or under Direct

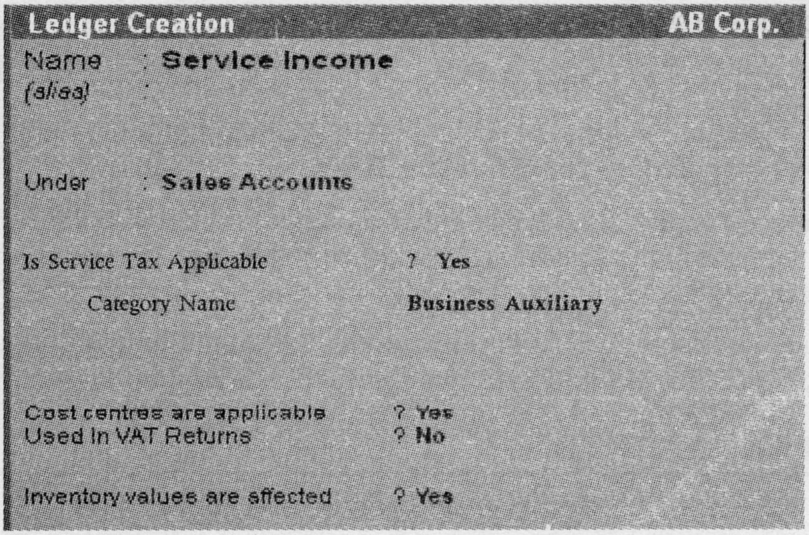

Income. Set Yes at Inventory Values are affected to get the Service Tax & Cess computed by Tally (otherwise you will have to enter the Service Tax Cess Amount) in Sales Voucher.

Service Tax Ledgers Creation

At creation of Duties & Taxes Ledger, enter the following details relating to Service Tax.

- *Duty Type*: At Type of Duty field, select Service Tax form the drop down list.
- *Service Category*: At Category Name field, select the Major Service Category relating to the business, from the list.

Sales Voucher Entry

In the Service Tax details are already computed, you may enter in Voucher mode. To get the Service Tax computed, enter the Sales Voucher in Invoice Mode.

Sales Voucher Entry in Voucher Mode

In first line of Sales Voucher entry, select the Party and enter the Total Amount of the voucher in the Bill Allocation window. Select the Service Tax Ledger in the Bill Allocation window. In the 2nd line, select the Service Income Account. In the 3rd line, select the Service Tax ledger. Enter the details of Service Tax and Cess amount.

Sales Voucher Entry in Invoice Mode

Normally, you will enter Sales Voucher in Invoice Mode. First Select the Party Ledger. Next, select the Service Income Account at Sales Ledger. At table area, select the Service Income Ledger and enter the Service Charge Amount. Next, select the Service Tax ledger and enter the Service Details. Enter the Service Tax Rate & Cess Rate. The Total Service Tax is posted against the Bill Reference number.

Computation of Service Tax

On selection of Service Tax Ledger Account, you get a subscreen to enter the details to compute Service Tax.

Receipt Voucher Entry for Service Bills

On receipt of money against service bill, create a receipt voucher. After selection of Party Ledger, select the Sales Bill reference against which the money is received and enter the amount. You may select several bill reference in one voucher, if applicable.

Select the Service Tax ledger account for the list. The screen will show Bill allocation screen after entry of Service Tax ledger and amount received against the Bill Reference.

SERVICE TAX REPORTS

Select Display > Service Tax Reports to get Service Tax Reports Menu.

Service Tax Reports Menu

Service Tax Payables Report having received payment against the Service Bill, Service Tax is now payable. If full payment is received, the full amount of Service Tax becomes payable. In case of part payment, the proportionate amount is payable.

At Service Tax Reports menu, select Service Tax Payable to get Service Tax Payable Report. It shows the details of Service Tax for the entire bill and the proportionate service tax on the amount received.

Deposit of Service Tax

To deposit the Service Tax payable as per Service Tax Payables Report, create a payment voucher. Select Service Tax Account. The bill allocation screen appears. Select Agnst Ref to get the list of Bills for which Tax is payable. The amount payable appears as default. This way select all the Bills for which Service Tax to be paid.

TR – 6 Challan Printing

At the Payment Voucher entry screen, click Print button to get voucher printing dialogue and set Yes at Print TR – 6 Challan.

INPUT SERVICE TAX

We have discussed Service Tax in sales voucher for services provided and deposit of proportionate tax on receipt of payment against service bills.

Some organization also buys services paying service tax. If the service is bought to render the service sold, then the Service Tax paid on serviced purchased (called Input Credit) may be adjusted from the Service Tax payable on services rendered.

Input Credit Rate

At Company Service Tax details, at Credit Adjustment Rate, enter the Rate of Service Tax credit.

Credit Adjustment (%)

Enter the Credit Adjustment %. Normally it is 20% (where the expenses relating to Tax Credit are not solely attributed to service income) or 100% (where the expenses relating to Tax Credit solely attributed to service income). The Purchase Service Tax may be adjusted to the extent of Credit Adjustment %. For example, if the Rate is 20%, then only 20% of the Input Credit may be adjusted.

We now discuss about Service Purchase entry, payment of Service Charges, Adjustment of Input Credit, payment of balance service tax after adjustment, printing to TR – 6 Challan & ST – 3 Form showing adjustment of input credit.

Service Purchase Ledger Account

Like Service Sales Ledger account, create Service Purchase Ledger Account.

Purchase Voucher Entry

In the 1st Ledger account of Purchase Voucher, enter the Service Supplier Account and enter total amount including Service Tax. Now enter the details in Bill Allocation screen. In the 2nd Ledger Account, select the Service Purchase Account and enter the amount. In the 3rd Ledger account, select the Service Tax Account. You will get the Service Tax details entry screen to enter the computation details for Service Tax.

Payment of Service Purchase Bill

At Payment Voucher entry, select the party Ledger Account and select the Bill for which Payment is being made, in Bill Allocation screen.

Select the Service Tax account and the amount paid against the Service Bill.

Input Credit Form

Having paid for Purchase Service Bill, print the Input Credit Form. At Service Tax Reports menu, select Input Credit Form to print Input Credit Form, showing the amount of Input Credit that you may avail to adjust against the Service Tax payable.

Adjustment of Input Credit

Now, while making payment for Service Tax, you may adjust the Input Credit. In the Payment Voucher, select the Service Tax Payable account (Debit) and select the References for which you are making the payments.

Next select the Input Credit Tax Account (Credit) and select the References of Service Tax which you like to adjust.

Now select the Bank Account and enter the net amount paid.

Challan For Balance Tax Deposit

After adjustment of Input Tax, print the TR – 6 Challan to deposit the Tax with the authority.

Creation of Service Expenses Ledger Accounts

Sometimes expenses are incurred exclusively for providing of Services. Such expenses may be deducted to compute the Assessable value in the Service Tax details.

Abatement

In some cases where materials are also supplied in the service and sold as a composite item, an abatement is allowed (e.g. 30%) to compute the Assessable value. The Abatement rate is fixed by government according to Service Category as shown in the Service Category Profile.

In Service Tax computation details, enter the Abatement %. The Assessable value is computed after deducting for Abatement.

Descriptive Type Questions

1. What is Service Tax?
2. What changes you would have to make in the ledger for Service Tax?
3. How would you compute Service Tax?
4. What sort of vouchers are made for Service Tax?
5. Which report is created for filing up of Service Tax?
6. How would you fill up the challan for Service Tax?

9 Display/Reports in Tally

OUTPUT REPORTS

Tally's Display of information has been designed to give you maximum benefit of the data that has been entered through Vouchers. You would have found that voucher entry itself is so much like your through process. Display of information and the amazing variety of it all, puts you in charge of your business information.

The best way to extract utmost from Displays is to experiment with the different options. It is not possible to cover the almost infinite options and ways in which you can present your data in a single manual. It is through Displays that Tally users get money saving ideas!

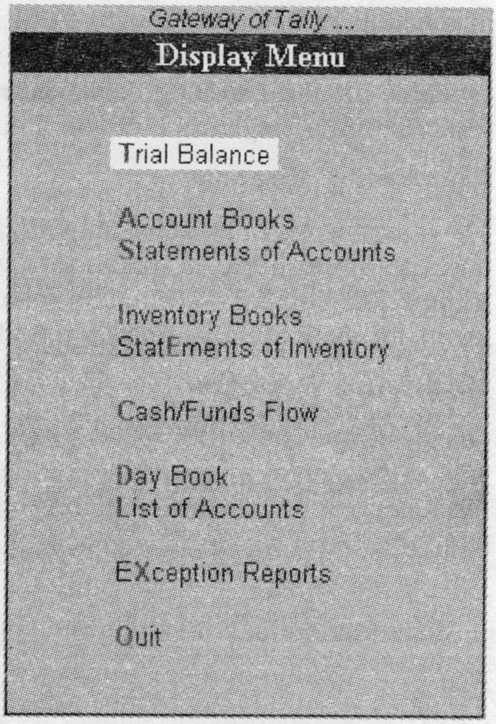

Fig. 9.1

Display screens take advantage of your monitor's capabilities. They are dynamic and interactive and are not merely print files. The purpose of putting in all your data is, after all, to present them in the form of comprehensible accounting reports. Tally far exceeds these expectations. By way of entry, all you do is to enter your vouchers. You do that, any way for your accounting purposes. Tally uses the same data and gives you management control reports in addition to all books and statements. Tally is real-time all reports are up-to-date at all times. They are displayed as at the last voucher entered.

All reports are very pleasing to the eye and obtained instantaneously. They are not spooled print files thankfully, but are specially designed for the screen. However, whatever you see on the screen, you can print as well – but using the printer's capabilities. Only the Balance Sheet and Profit and Loss Account are displayed directly from the Gateway of Tally. Tally accords these statements the highest importance. As you can see from the menu, displays are roughly organized into Accounts information displays and Inventory information displays – conforming to the two major areas of operations. Each area is grouped separately into books and statements. Confirming to showing the main financial statements separately, the Cash and Funds Flows are not grouped under Statement of Accounts. The day Book contains all the vouchers for the day, including inventory vouchers. Its purpose is to show you a day's transactions. However, you can display any report for any period by using the change period option.

The list of Accounts gives the tree structure of all your masters, namely, Groups, Ledgers, Stock items, Cost Centres, Currencies, etc. Exception Reports are reports that track unusual transactions or balances.

Basic Features of Displaying Reports

Tally prepares the books of accounts and financial statements based on the vouchers you have entered to date. You can then vary the appearance of reports according to your needs, for example, to make comparisons between different companies, periods of the financial year, groups and ledgers.

In each case, when you display a report, you can step-down to the next level of detail by highlighting he item and pressing Enter and you can keep going until you reach an individual voucher. Similarly, you can step back to higher levels by pressing [Esc]. The special features available for the currently displayed report are indicated on the button bar and can be selected with a single click of the mouse.

Accessing Reports

The Gateway of Tally menus provide access to all the financial reports, as in the diagram opposite. For example, if you want to view the Sales Register then, in the Gateway of Tally menu select Display, Account Books and Sales Register in turn and Tally will display the report for the currently selected period.

Modifying Reports

Once you have selected a report and its screen appears, you can modify the display to suit your requirements using the appropriate buttons on the button bar. You will get to know the functions of the various buttons as you become more familiar with Tally but some buttons perform similar functions in all reports, providing they are appropriate to the screen you are viewing.

If you select the buttons using the keyboard, the conventions are:

Fn:

just press the Fn key.

Fn:

Press [Alt]+Fn.

F1: Detailed/Condensed

Adds a further level of detail to the report or condenses the report to a higher level of detail.

F2: Period

Enables you to change the period of the report by specifying new form/to dates.

F3: Company

If you have more than one company selected, this button enables you to change companies to display the new company data in the current screen format.

F4: to F10

The functions performed by these buttons vary from report to report.

F11: Company Features

This button is not related to displaying reports but to selecting options that affect voucher entry. The screen it displays must not be changed during training.

F12: Configure

This button is very relevant to displaying and enables you to define the report-specific options you wish to use. For example, depending on the report you are in, you can specify whether it should be horizontal or vertical format, show percentages, show gross profit, show opening and/or closing balances, change the periodicity, change the sorting method and so on. If you select F12: Configure while in the Gateway of Tally screen, this takes you to a Configuration menu. If you select General, it brings up an option screen which. amongst other things, enables you to specify that you wish to see graphs with monthly reports.

F12: Range

This button enables you to filter the information you see displayed based on monetary value. For example, you can specify you only want closing balances greater than 5,000.

F12: Value

This button enables you to filter which vouchers you wish to be used in the calculations. For example, you can specify you only want vouchers having a narration containing the expression XYZ Project.

New Column

This button enables you to add another column to the report to display comparable information for another company or for a different period for the same company, all on the same screen.

Alter Column

This button enables you to alter the details of a new column you have previously created, for example, the data range. You select the column to alter by positioning the cursor in it prior to selecting the button.

Del Column

You use this button to delete columns which you no longer wish to see in the report.

Auto Column

You use this button to add multiple columns to a report, for example, columns for each month or to accommodate several companies. You can also have a total column for the total of each item across all columns.

Report Specific Options

If there are report specific options available for the report, they are displayed in the bottom half of the screen and can be amended according to your requirements.

Printing Reports

You can obtain a printed version of the screen you are currently displaying by selecting Print from the top of the button bar menu. This brings up new button bar options and the Print Configuration screen for the report, which asks Print? Yes or No. If you select Yes, the report will be printed using the options specified on the screen. If you select No, you can change the options before printing.

Tally's neat printing is just too neat! Print out an invoice and you would not consider using preprinted stationery at all.

There are two types of print configuration options:

1. As a print button or [ALT]+[P] key combination is all display screens. Remember, it is not a print screen – it is special printing and printed reports would differ form displays. Tally takes advantage of a printer's capability and uses to maximize aesthetics in printed output
2. As a printing menu option through the Gateway of Tally. You can print multiple reports at a time through this option.

If you select to print a displayed document or report, the Print Dialog Box expects you to view the output before printing. It defaults to With Preview. You can however, change it to No Preview by clicking the appropriate Button. The Preview screen allows you to view the document and even scrolls if it is multi-page; print from there or even E-mail the document as an attachment. Hence, if you want to see how a document that you originally wanted to E-mail, would appear at the destination, use Print Preview.

Common Printing Options

Common printing options affect the printing of current selected reports. They are changed by selecting the appropriate button form the button bar.

Auto Column

If the screen version of the report supports Auto Column, this button will be available and performs a similar function.

Titling

To change the title of the report.

Page Numbers

To specify the starring page number and page number range.

Pre-Printed/Plain Paper

Toggle to make the selection.

Quick Format / Neat Format

Toggle between quick (draft) and neat (standard) formats.

With Colour

This option is only relevant if you have a colour printer.

Copies

To specify the number of pages to be printed.

Printer

To change the printer settings. This also displays the default paper size that you have set for the printer.

Other Printing options

Multi-Account Printing

For this select the following:

Gateway of Tally>Multi- Accounting Printing

Principally geared towards printing the Primary Books of Accounts, like the Cash and Bank Books, Account Ledgers, Sales and Purchase Registers etc., without needing to select the accounts one at a time and pressing Alt+P. The facilities provide the printing of One Account at a time, All Accounts or All Accounts in a selected Group. Before printing, the date range and other selections may also be set up. The current mechanism of printing used by Tally, will require that for large company accounts, you choose to print each ledger account on separate pages – otherwise the memory requirements of the system become so large as to bring must systems to their knees.

Draft Mode Printing (Quick Format)

Almost every report can also be printed in Draft Mode (except for Cheques!). The default behavior of Tally is to print in Neat Format – and you may alter this by pressing Alt+F just before printing. All subsequent reports will be printed in Quick Format, until Alt+F is pressed again at the Printing Screen. (The button equivalent for this is marked Quick Format). Draft mode necessarily brings in additional restrictions in the printing, which you will quickly learn by experimentation. It also enables Printing to a File, which may be selected pressing Alt+E (to Select the Printer whose dimensions are to be used and the name of the File to output to.)

Display Account Books and Statements

Books of account record the individual transactions details you have entered. Although you may post items to many different ledgers, Tally brings all the transactions of one category together into a book of accounts for viewing and printing. For example, the cash book records all the transactions affecting cash, the Sales Book records all the sales transactions.

Statement of Accounts pertain to cost centres and Outstanding analysis. These are derived from individual transactions but are not statutory requirements.

Financial statements on the other hand are still derived from individual transactions but tend to show summary totals, ratios and statistics, analyzing a company's financial data in a wide variety of ways. Typical financial statements include the Balance sheet, Profit and Loss Account and Cash Flow Analysis. Financial statements are usually statutory requirements in most countries.

1. All books are displayed first as a monthly summary with opening and closing balances.
2. Select a month and press [enter] to display all transactions for the month. The opening and closing balances as well as transaction totals are also displayed.
3. Select a transaction to bring up the voucher. This voucher comes up either in display or in alteration mode depending upon the access rights available to you.
4. This is a typical display method and is available from most places, including

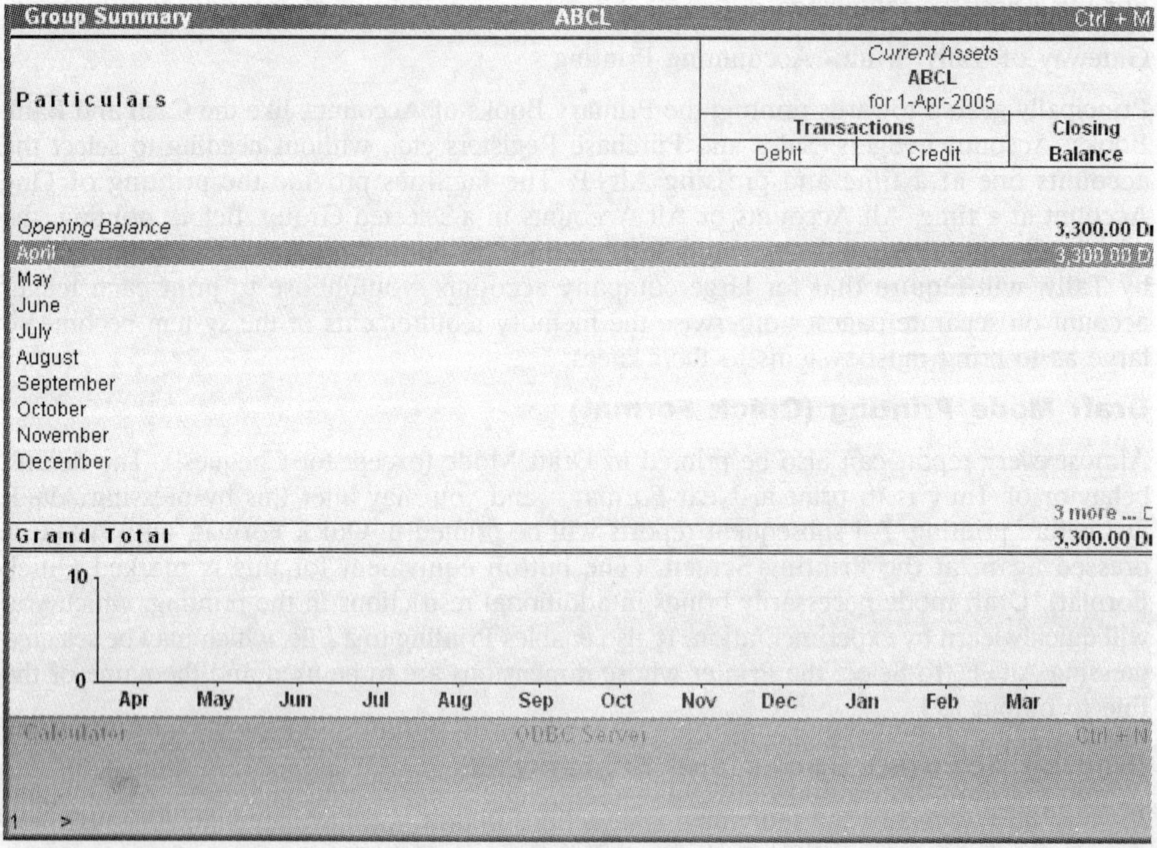

Fig. 9.2

statements. For example, even from a Balance Sheet, you would first display the group summary, then the ledger monthly summary and finally the transaction voucher itself.

Let us see some typical examples of how to display the books of account and financial statements. You will then be able to experiment with other statements for yourself.

Viewing Cash/Bank Books

For this select the following:

Gateway of Tally>Display>Account Books>Cash/Bank Books

This displays the Cash/Bank Summary:

1. Select a bank account if there are more than one. Press Enter to display the Ledger Monthly Summary.
2. Select F12: Configure to bring up the Configuration/Graphs option menu.
3. Use the Tab key to tab down to Show with graph? and type and press Enter. Select Bar and press Enter to return to the Ledger Monthly Summary, now displaying a graph of the figures.
4. With the highlight bar over the one month's, say July's figures, press Enter to display the Ledger Vouchers screen. Note that all the vouchers for July are listed. Press [Esc] to return to the Ledger Monthly Summary screen.
5. Select F12: Value to bring up the Value to Calculate in Report screen. From the Particulars menu, select Voucher Type. from the next Particulars menu, select name (the only option). From the Range of Info. menu select equal to. Then type Contra and Press Enter. From the Condition menu select End of List and press Enter twice.
6. Notice in the Ledger Monthly Summary that the figures are now reduced as they only show Contra vouchers. To check this, position the highlight bar over the July figures and press Enter to display the details.
7. Keep pressing [Esc] until you return to the Gateway of Tally menu.

Display Balance Sheet

The Balance Sheet gives the state of financial affairs of a company on a given date. It lists out the Assets and Liabilities based on the Primary Groups of Tally. The Balance Sheet in tally in updated instantly with every transaction voucher that is entered and saved. No special processing is required to produce a Balance Sheet.

For this select the following:

Gateway of Tally>Balance Sheet

The Balance Sheet is displayed in the form, set up for it in F12: Configure

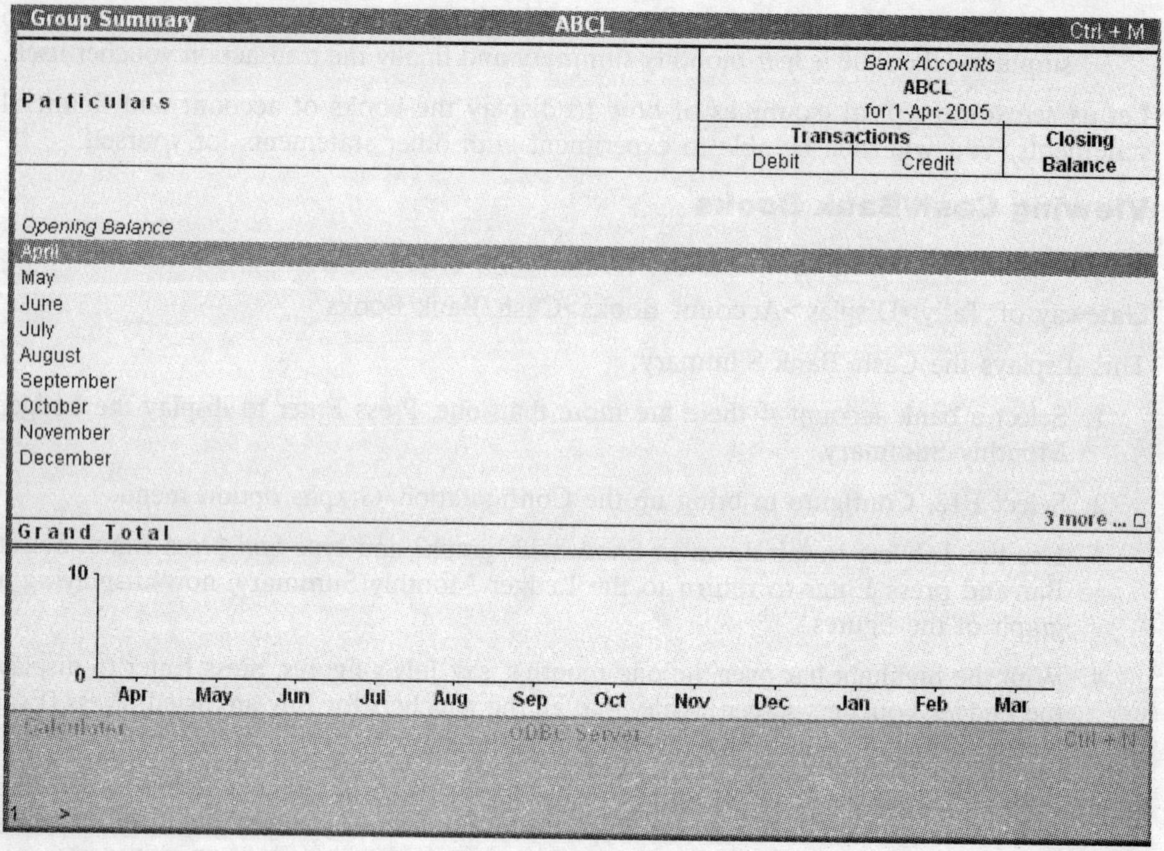

Fig. 9.3

Horizontal Form of Balance Sheet

The above example, Fig. 9.3 is of the horizontal form. It could be up to appear in the vertical form. You can extract different information by using the various options in the Button Bar.

Select Detailed to explode the summarized information. Change the date of the Balance Sheet using F2: Period.

Bring up new columns and Select a Balance Sheet for a different date to compare alongside the present date or Select a column to give the Balance Sheet in a different currency or Select a column with Budget figures and analyse variances or Select a column and see the effect of different Stock Valuations on the Profit/Loss.

Configure the Balance Sheet?

Select F12:Configure when you have the Balance Sheet on the screen to have the dialog box, as shown here. Various options are:

Show Vertical Balance Sheet?

No will display Horizontal form. Yes will display Vertical form. In the British/Europe configuration the Vertical Balance Sheet will have the titles Liabilities and Assets whereas the Indian/Asian configuration will have Sources of Funds and Application of Funds as titles.

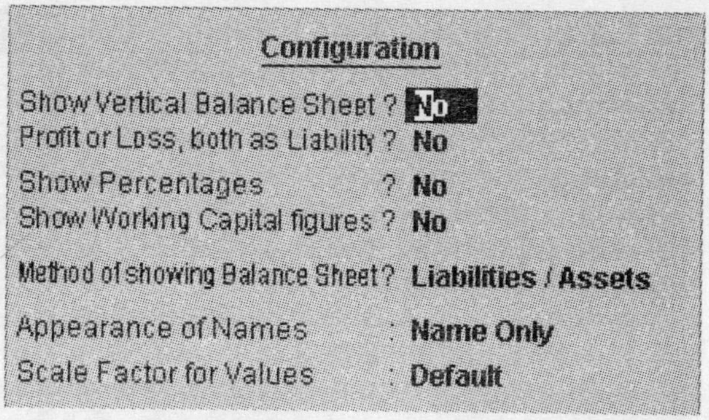

Profit or Loss, Both as Liability?

(Applicable only in the horizontal form)

If no, then Loss moves the Profit and Loss Account to the Assets side of the Balance Sheet.

Show Percentages?

Each line will be expressed as a percentage of the total.

Show Working Capital Figures?

To show Current Assets-Current Liabilities.

Method of Showing the Balance Sheet

The options are: Liabilities/Assets and Assets/Liabilities. This is simply the order in which the Balance Sheet is shown. Both the options are shown on the next page, i.e. Fig. 9.4 shows liabilities/assets and Fig. 9.5 shows assets/liabilities.

For Horizontal Balance Sheet it is in the format: Left Hand Side/right Hand Side

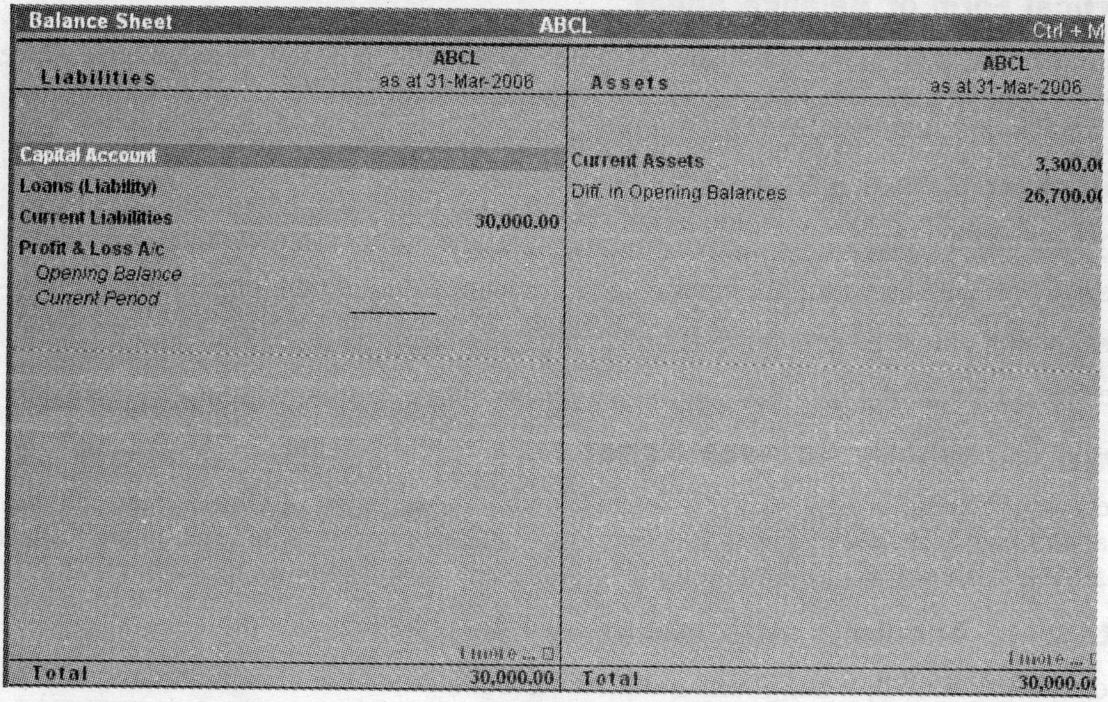

Fig. 9.4

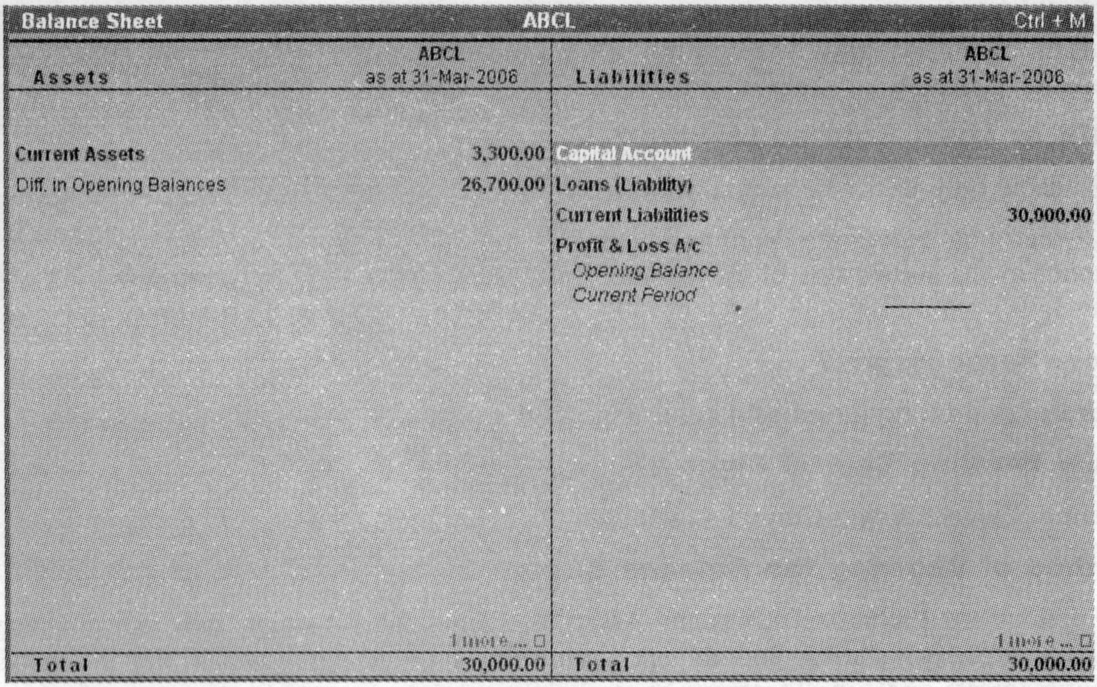

Fig. 9.5

For Vertical Balance Sheet it is in the format: Top/Bottom.

Vertical Form of Balance Sheet

Select the Format using F12: Configure. This Balance Sheet is in the UK/Europe Style where Assets are given first. The default order is, however, Liabilities/Assets. In India/Asia Style, the Vertical Balance Sheet will be:

Columnar Balance Sheets

Some examples:

Select a Balance Sheet for a different date to compare alongside the present date:

Select New Column or keys ALT+C and change only the period.

The Balance Sheet in Fig. 9.6 are converted at this rate.

Show Fortnightly Balance Sheet

Select Auto-column or keys ALT+N. Select Monthly form the list of periods. The monthly balance sheet is shown in Fig. 9.7. Similarly, you can choose to see the balance sheet Quarterly, as shown in Fig. 9.8.

Integrate Accounts with Inventory

Effect on Balance Sheet and Profit and Loss Account

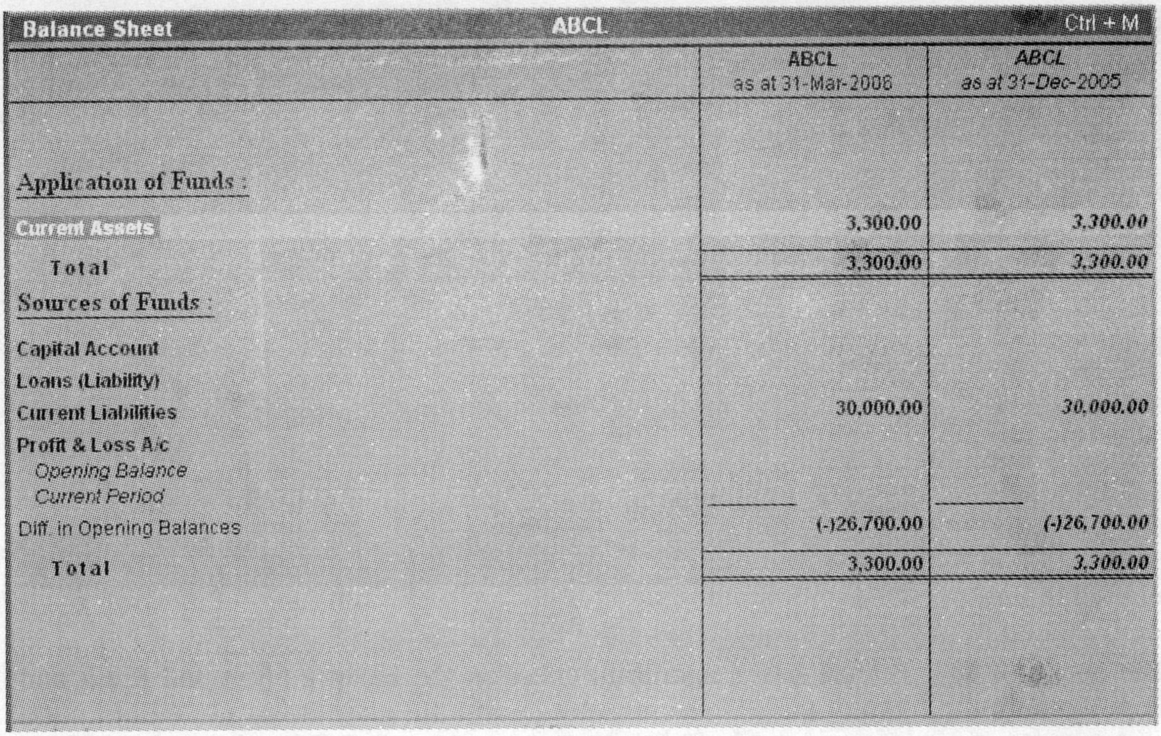

Balance Sheet	ABCL as at 31-Mar-2006	ABCL as at 31-Dec-2005
Application of Funds :		
Current Assets	3,300.00	3,300.00
Total	3,300.00	3,300.00
Sources of Funds :		
Capital Account		
Loans (Liability)		
Current Liabilities	30,000.00	30,000.00
Profit & Loss A/c		
Opening Balance		
Current Period		
Diff. in Opening Balances	(-)26,700.00	(-)26,700.00
Total	3,300.00	3,300.00

Fig. 9.6

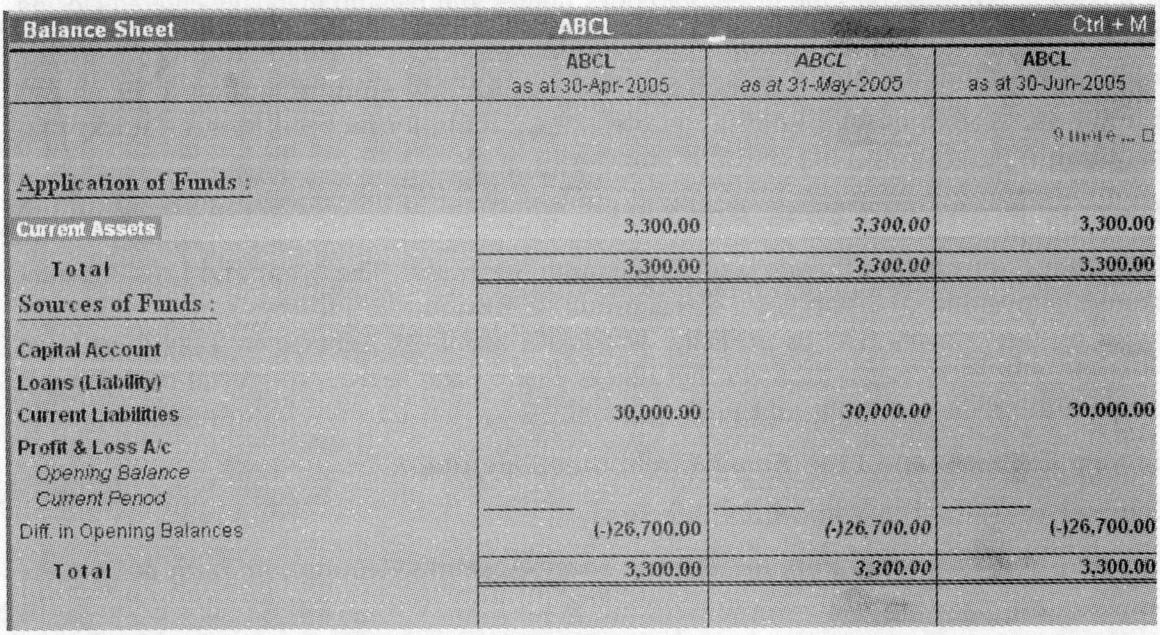

Balance Sheet	ABCL as at 30-Apr-2005	ABCL as at 31-May-2005	ABCL as at 30-Jun-2005
			9 more ...
Application of Funds :			
Current Assets	3,300.00	3,300.00	3,300.00
Total	3,300.00	3,300.00	3,300.00
Sources of Funds :			
Capital Account			
Loans (Liability)			
Current Liabilities	30,000.00	30,000.00	30,000.00
Profit & Loss A/c			
Opening Balance			
Current Period			
Diff. in Opening Balances	(-)26,700.00	(-)26,700.00	(-)26,700.00
Total	3,300.00	3,300.00	3,300.00

Fig. 9.7

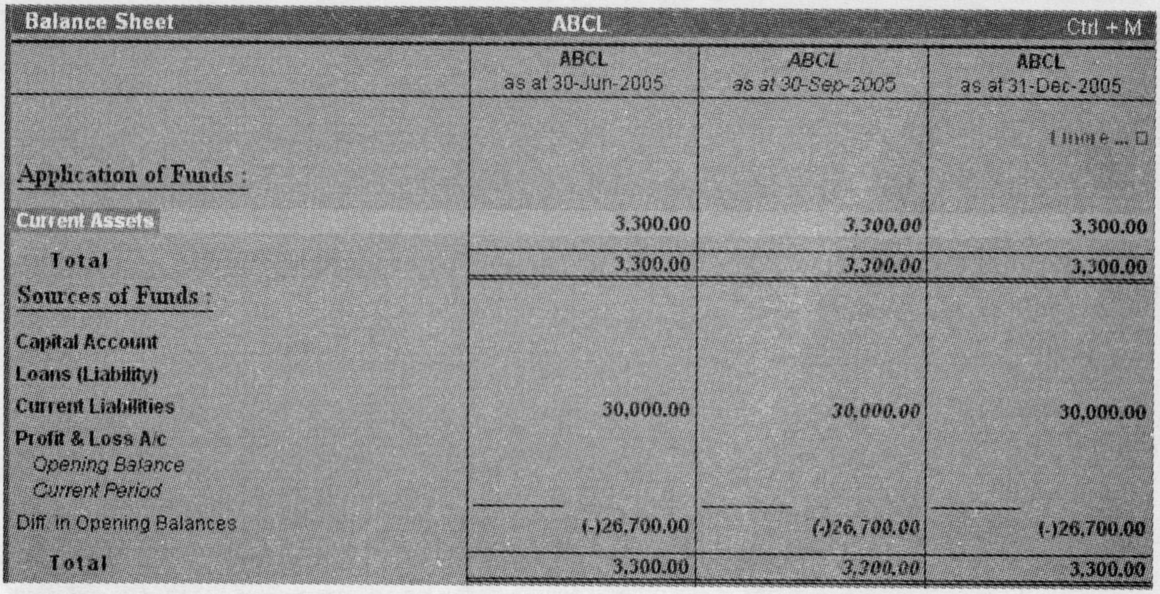

Balance Sheet	ABCL		Ctrl + M
	ABCL as at 30-Jun-2005	ABCL as at 30-Sep-2005	ABCL as at 31-Dec-2005
			1 more ...
Application of Funds :			
Current Assets	3,300.00	3,300.00	3,300.00
Total	3,300.00	3,300.00	3,300.00
Sources of Funds :			
Capital Account			
Loans (Liability)			
Current Liabilities	30,000.00	30,000.00	30,000.00
Profit & Loss A/c			
Opening Balance			
Current Period			
Diff. in Opening Balances	(-)26,700.00	(-)26,700.00	(-)26,700.00
Total	3,300.00	3,300.00	3,300.00

Fig. 9.8

The option in F11: Feature has a significant effect on the Balance Sheet and Profit and Loss Account.

If set to Yes, it brings the stock/inventory balance figures from the inventory figures from the inventory records and provides a drill down to the Stock registers from the Balance Sheet.

If it is set to No, it ignores the inventory books figures and pick up manually entered closing stock balances.

Stock records often contain compensating errors caused by wrong allocation to items and the like. the feature enables finalization of books waiting for reconciliation of stocks that may take time.

Display Profit and Loss Account

It has beeen renamed as Income and Expenditure Statement. The Profit and Loss Account shows the operational results for a given period. It lists out the Incomes and Expenditures based on the Primary Groups of Tally. The Profit and Loss Account in Tally is updated instantly with every transaction voucher that is entered and saved. No special processing is required to produce a Profit and Loss Account.

To view the Profit and Loss Account, select the following:

Gateway of Tally>Profit and Loss Account

You may even drill down from the Balance Sheet, Accounts Reports and Profit & Loss A/C.

The Profit and Loss Account is displayed according to the configuration set up for it in F12: Configure

Horizontal Form of Profit and Loss Account

The above example, as shown in Fig. 9.9, is of the horizontal form. It could be set up to appear in the vertical form.

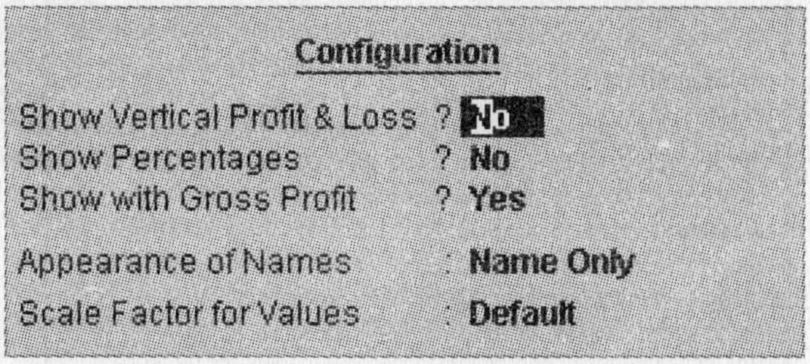

You can extract different information by using the various options in the Button Bar.

Select Detailed to explode to summarized information.

Change the date of the Profit and Loss Account using F2: Period.

Bring up new columns and:

Select a Profit and Loss Account for a different period to compare alongside the present period or Select a column to give the Profit and Loss Account in a different currency or Select a column with Budget figures and analyse variances or Select a column and see the effect of different Stock Valuations on the Profit/Loss.

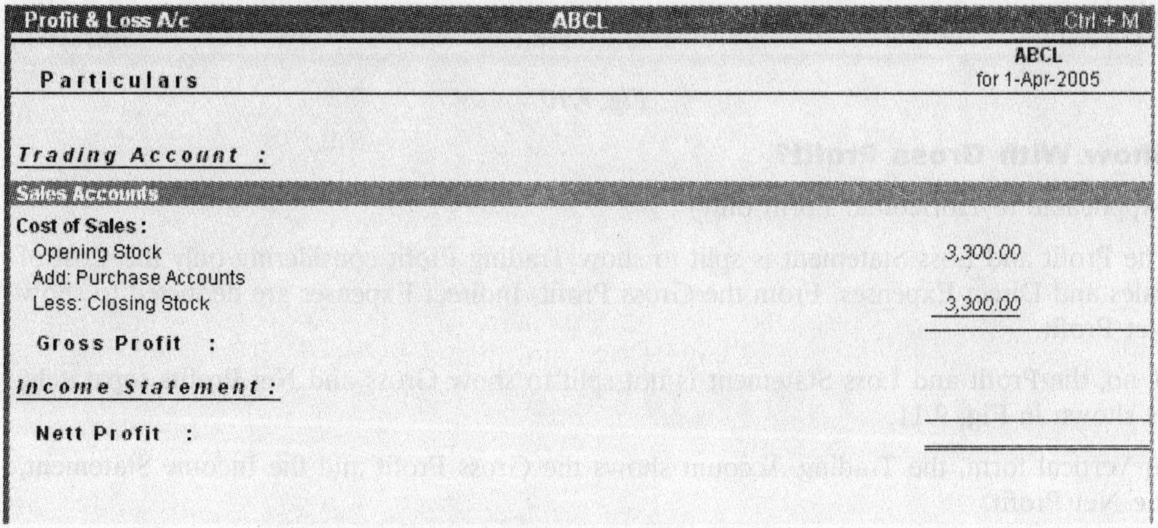

Fig. 9.9

Show Vertical Profit and Loss Account?

No will display Horizontal form. Yes will display Vertical form. A horizontal form of Profit and Loss is shown below in Fig. 9.10.

The vertical form always shows the Trading Account and the Income Statements separately.

Show Percentages?

Each time will be expressed as a percentage of Sales Accounts, i.e. Sales Accounts will be 100% and the rest of the lines will be a percentage of Sales Accounts.

Profit & Loss A/c | ABCL | Ctrl + M

Particulars		ABCL 1-Apr-2005 to 31-Dec -2005	Particulars		ABCL 1-Apr-2005 to 31-Dec -2005
Opening Stock		**3,300.00**	**Sales Accounts**		
Juices	3,300.00		*Sales Bills to Make*		
Purchase Accounts			**Closing Stock**		**3,300.00**
Purchase Bills to Come			Juices	3,300.00	
Nett Profit					
Total		**3,300.00**	**Total**		**3,300.00**

Fig. 9.10

Show With Gross Profit?

(Applicable to Horizontal Form only)

The Profit and Loss Statement is split to show Trading Profit considering only the Cost of Sales and Direct Expenses. From the Gross Profit, Indirect Expenses are deducted to show Net Profit.

If no, the Profit and Loss Statement is not split to show Gross and Net Profits separately, as shown in Fig. 9.11.

In Vertical form, the Trading Account shows the Gross Profit and the Income Statement, the Net Profit.

Columnar Profit & Loss Accounts: Some Examples

Select a Profit & Loss Account for a different period to compare alongside the present period.

Select New Column or keys ALT + C and change only the period, as shown in Fig. 9.12.

Select a column to give the Profit and Loss Account in a different currency.

Select New Column or keys ALT+C and change only the Currency and give the closing Exchange Rate.

The Profit and Loss Account figures are converted at this rate.

Select a column to give the Profit and Loss Account in a different stock valuation method.

Profit & Loss A/c — ABCL — Ctrl + M

Particulars		ABCL 1-Apr-2005 to 31-Dec -2005	Particulars		ABCL 1-Apr-2005 to 31-Dec -2005
Opening Stock		**3,300.00**	**Sales Accounts**		
Juices	*3,300.00*		***Sales Bills to Make***		
Purchase Accounts			**Closing Stock**		**3,300.00**
Purchase Bills to Come			Juices	*3,300.00*	
Gross Profit c/o					
		3,300.00			**3,300.00**
Nett Profit			***Gross Profit b/f***		
Total			**Total**		

Fig. 9.11

Profit & Loss A/c — ABCL — Ctrl + M

Particulars	ABCL 1-Apr-2005 to 31-Dec -2005	*ABCL 1-Apr-2005 to 31-Dec -2005*
Trading Account :		
Sales Accounts		
Sales Bills to Make		
Cost of Sales :		
Opening Stock	*3,300.00*	3,300.00
Add: Purchase Accounts		
Less: Closing Stock	*3,300.00*	3,300.00
Gross Profit :		
Income Statement :		
Nett Profit :		

Fig. 9.12

Select New Column or keys ALT+C and change only the Stock Valuation Method to Last Purchase Cost.

Show Quarterly Profit and Loss Account

Select Auto-column or keys ALT+N. Select Quarterly from the list of periods.

Income/Expenses Statement Instead of P&L?

For Non-Trading accounts like accounts for Charitable Organizations, the Trading and Profit and Loss Statement are irrelevant. They need an Income and Expenditure Account. They should activate the feature in F11: Features and set the option Income/Expense Stmt instead of P&L to Yes.

The Profit and Loss Account is now displayed as Income and Expenditure Statement.

Display Trial Balance

For this select the following options:

Gateway of Tally>Display>Trail Balance

The Trial Balance Report provides account balance listing for all accounts for the company sorted according to groups, i.e., the Trial Balance is displayed in grouped form with main groups and their closing balances. The fact that the debit and credit balances match proves the arithmetic accuracy of the entries. In Tally, the matching of the Trial Balance is a foregone conclusion as all voucher entries are in the debit and credit format and must balance at the entry point. Note that as per accounting principles, the Trial Balance does not list Closing Stock.

You can drill down a Group for further details of that particular group. or Select Detailed to break down the grouped information to another level. or Select Led-wise to take an alphabetic listing of all ledgers and their closing balances. Select Columns to bring up the closing balances for another date, as shown in Fig. 9.13, Fig. 9.14 and Fig. 9.15.

Account Reconciliation Statement

Take a single report that shows the flow of the accounts from Opening Balance to the effect of transactions on Closing Balance.

Select F12: Configure

The Trial Balance Reconciliation Statement is produced.

Similarly, the Trial Balance can be configured to show only Opening and Closing Balances.

Day Book

Gateway of Tally>Display>Day Book

The Day Book is a list of all transactions for a particular day, by default the current date. It can also list all the transactions for a period. Transactions include all financial vouchers, reversing and memorandum journals as well as inventory vouchers.

Trial Balance — ABCL — Ctrl + M

Particulars	ABCL for 1-Apr-2005 Closing Balance	
	Debit	Credit
Current Liabilities		**30,000.00**
Current Assets	**3,300.00**	
Diff. in Opening Balances	26,700.00	
Grand Total	**30,000.00**	**30,000.00**

Fig. 9.13

Trial Balance — ABCL — Ctrl + M

Particulars	ABCL for 1-Apr-2005 Closing Balance		*ABCL for 1-Apr-2005* Closing Balance	
	Debit	Credit	Debit	Credit
Current Liabilities		**30,000.00**		***30,000.00***
Current Assets	**3,300.00**		***3,300.00***	
Diff. in Opening Balances	26,700.00		*26,700.00*	
Grand Total	**30,000.00**	**30,000.00**	***30,000.00***	***30,000.00***

Fig. 9.14

Trial Balance ABCL Ctrl + M

Particulars	ABCL for 1-Apr-2005 Closing Balance		ABCL for 1-Apr-2005 Closing Balance		ABCL for 1-Apr-2005 Closing Balance	
	Debit	Credit	Debit	Credit	Debit	Credit
Current Liabilities		30,000.00		30,000.00		30,000.00
Current Assets	3,300.00		3,300.00		3,300.00	
Diff. in Opening Balances	26,700.00		26,700.00		26,700.00	
Grand Total	30,000.00	30,000.00	30,000.00	30,000.00	30,000.00	30,000.00

Fig. 9.15

For example:

Day Book for the current date:

Day Book for a period:

The list can be filtered to show transactions of a particular voucher type, as shown in Fig. 9.16. Use Chg Vch button.

When a specific voucher, e.g., Delivery Notes, options like Extract and Columnar become available.

Books and Registers

All transactions are posted to different books and registers. The purpose of the books and registers is to compile similar entries in one place so that they are meaningful, e.g. all cash entries in the Cash Book, all sales entries in the Sales Day Book (called Sales Register in tally). A Tally voucher may contain many lines of debit and credit entries. Each line is a Ledger Account and has to be ultimately reflected in the Ledger.

The Tally Transaction Flow

Apart from the subsidiary books, entries are also filled under each Voucher Type Registers. Therefore, there will be as many registers as there are voucher types.

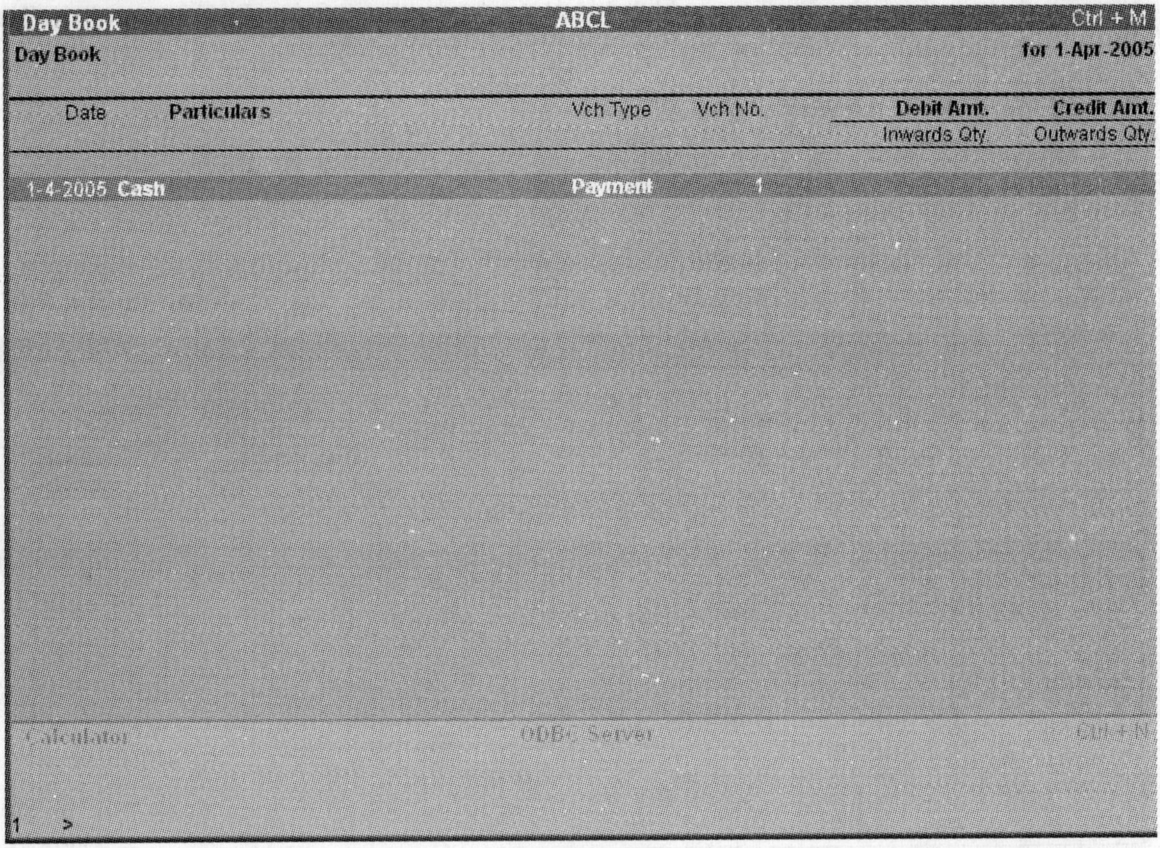

Fig. 9.16

Journals, Day Books and Registers

Journal, Sales Register, Purchase Register, Debit Note Register, Credit Note Register, Payment Register, Receipts Registers, etc.

There are three ways to see different registers:

1. From the display menu
2. By changing the Voucher type from within a Register
3. From the Statistics Page

We will discuss the Sales Register, which has the most options, Other Registers are similar. Please use the same explanation (except for Invoice Profitability) for other Registers.

Sales Register (Sales Day Book)

This explanation should be used for all Day Books and Voucher Registers.

Gateway of Tally>Display>Account Books>Sales Register

All registers first display the Monthly Summary with Transactions and Closing Balance for Balance Sheet Accounts, Opening Balance will be given at the top, as shown in Fig. 9.17.

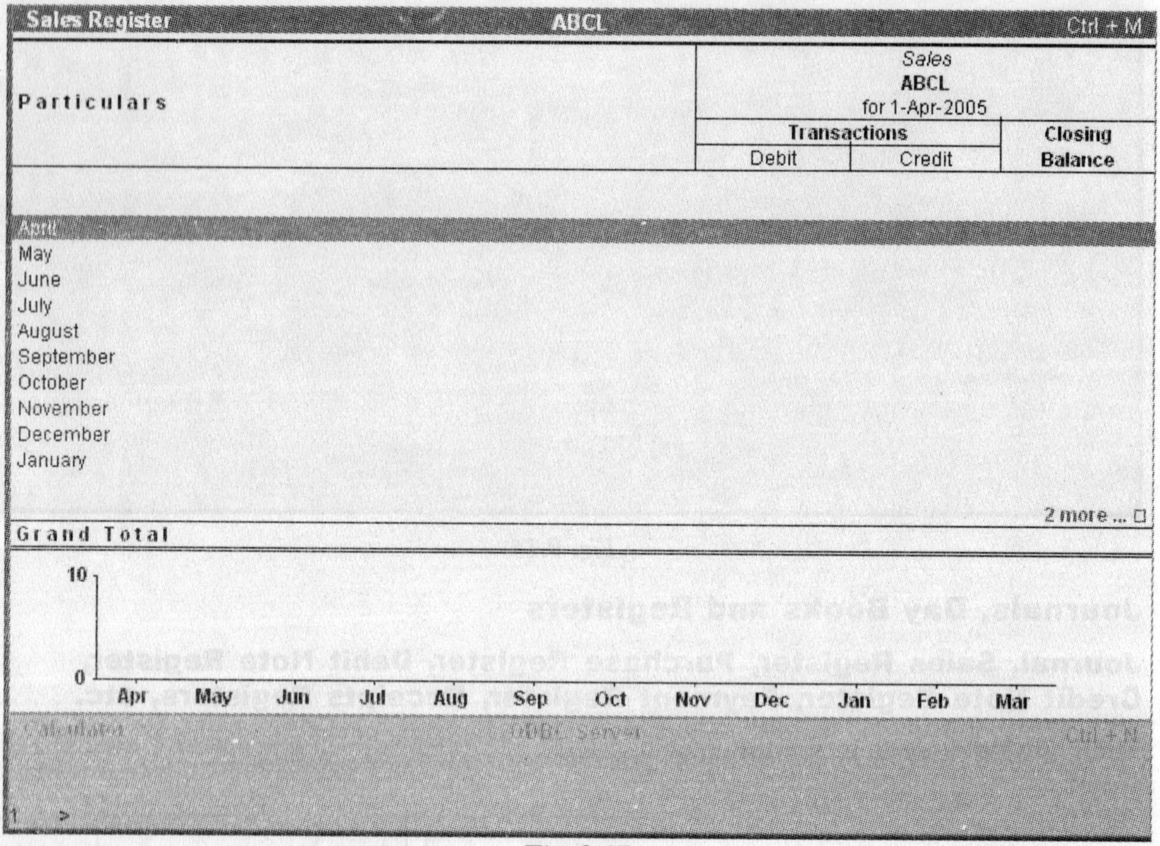

Fig. 9.17

Select a month and press enter to see the Sales Voucher Register. This is a list of all sales vouchers for that month. Use the options in the button bar to change the details. You can change the period of the report as well as the depth of information.

F12: Configure to see the report with some or all of the following details:

Narrations, Bill-wise details, Cost Centre details and Inventory details. Click on Detailed to see all the details selected.

Invoice Profitability

Display the Sales Voucher Register for a period by drill down a month and change to the period required.

Select F7: Gross Profit (or select from F12: Configure)

The report now shows each invoice with:

Transaction Value

It is the Invoice Value including taxes.

Gross Revenue

This is the actual sale value minus taxes.

Cost

This is the book cost of the product

Gross Profit

Amount of profit or loss on the sale.

Sales Register Extract

While in the Sales Voucher Register.

Select/click on **Extract**.

The Extract gives a break-down of the sales vouchers and groups them to provide totals for each group and ledger used in all sales vouchers for the period. The information is useful where you want to know the how much each group of customers bought, what the tax component is or what is the total value of each sales ledger.

Inventory-wise Extract of Sales Register

In the Sales Voucher Register, click on Extract.

F12: Configure

Set Yes to Inventory-wise Extract to take a report of the stock items sold with quantity and value details.

Columnar Sales Register

While in the Sales Voucher Register:

Select/click on Columnar. The different columns can be selected for the report and are retained for future use.

Type of Column

The Type of Column needs to be explained. Here you select the type you want and if it is a ledger or a group, the selection in shown under. Name of Account.

The options are:

All Item (Automatic Columns)

Every ledger account used in any voucher in the period of display takes a column.

All Item (In One Column)

All the ledger accounts are shown in one column

Group

Select a group of ledger accounts to be shown together in one column, e.g. All sales accounts. For other columns you can now have further options viz, Related accounts in automatic columns or related accounts in one column, in addition to available options.

Ledger

Select a specific ledger account for which you want the sales register, e.g., VAT/Sales Tax. All other accounts can be put in one or more columns.

Related Items (Automatic Columns)

Related items means the ledger accounts used in a voucher. Hence, the report will be similar to All Items (automatic columns) if only this option is selected. However, the option is useful if selected in conjunction with a Group or a specific ledger account in the first column.

Related Items (In One Column)

Related items means the ledger accounts used in a voucher. Hence, the report will be similar to All Items (in one col.) if only this option is selected. However, the option is useful if selected in conjunction with a Group or a specific ledger account in the first column.

Change Vch

Use this button option to see a different Register from within an existing register. E.g. change to Payment Register from a Sales Register by pressing the button Change Vch.

Payment Register

You can select Payment vouchers to have Payment Voucher Register.

Registers from Statistics

Voucher registers can be accessed from the Statistics page:

Gateway of Tally>Display>Statements of Accounts>Statistics

Drill down a specific Voucher Type to view the Register as shown in Fig. 9.18.

Monthly Summary

When drilling down from a statement into any Group, Ledger, Stock item or cost centre or any such object, the first screen is the Monthly summary. Monthly Summary is also available from a Voucher level screen by using the button Monthly.

The monthly summary shows the Opening Balance for the year, then lists each month's total transactions both debit (inwards for stocks) and credit (outwards for stocks) and finally each month's closing balance.

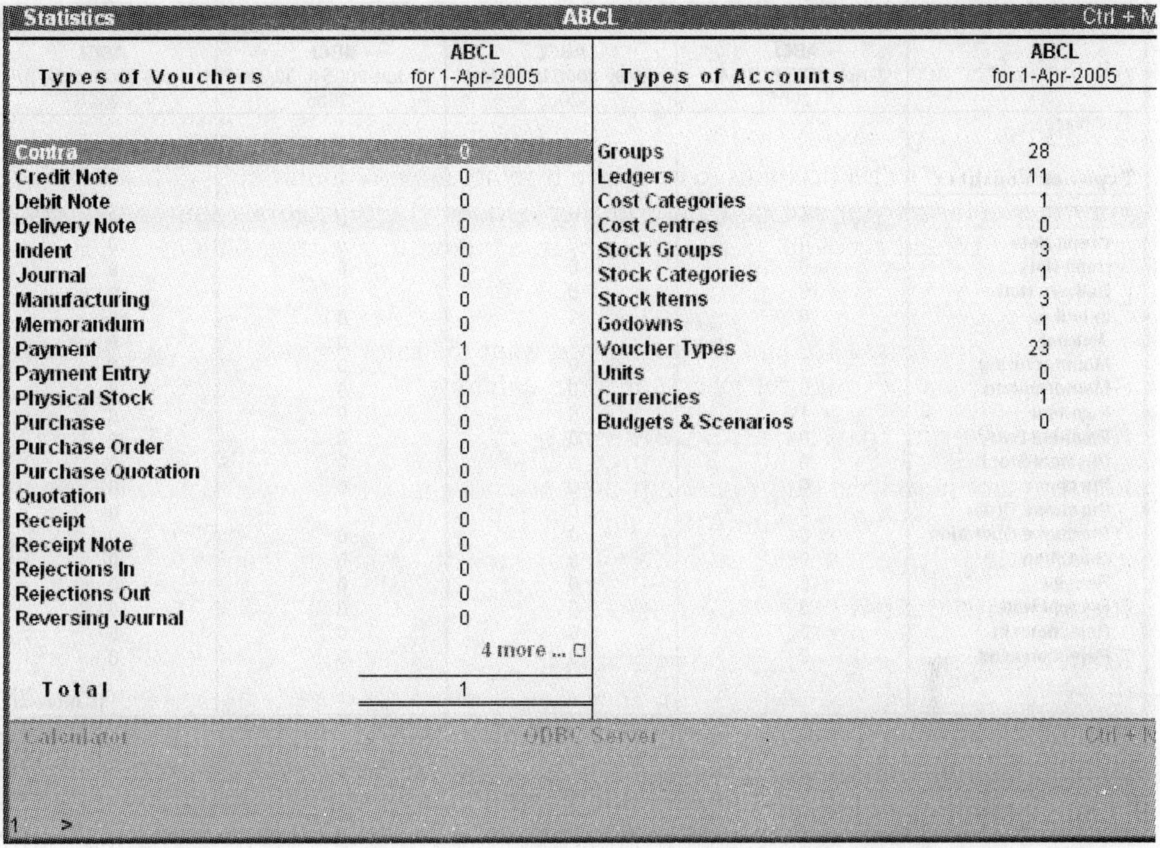

Statistics — ABCL — Ctrl + M

Types of Vouchers	ABCL for 1-Apr-2005	Types of Accounts	ABCL for 1-Apr-2005
Contra	0	Groups	28
Credit Note	0	Ledgers	11
Debit Note	0	Cost Categories	1
Delivery Note	0	Cost Centres	0
Indent	0	Stock Groups	3
Journal	0	Stock Categories	1
Manufacturing	0	Stock Items	3
Memorandum	0	Godowns	1
Payment	1	Voucher Types	23
Payment Entry	0	Units	0
Physical Stock	0	Currencies	1
Purchase	0	Budgets & Scenarios	0
Purchase Order	0		
Purchase Quotation	0		
Quotation	0		
Receipt	0		
Receipt Note	0		
Rejections In	0		
Rejections Out	0		
Reversing Journal	0		
	4 more ...		
Total	1		

Calculator — ODBC Server — Ctrl + N

1 >

Fig. 9.18

Below the monthly summary, is a bar chart showing the movement of transactions. Use F12: configure to see more or less details including the graph.

For example, the different options under the button bar are very useful for managerial reports. For example, use the New Columns option to bring up the Monthly summary of another ledger or object or the same object in another company. Quarterly shows summarized quarterly figures.

F12: Configure provides options to see percentages, average details as well high/low information.

Ledger Monthly Summary

This is shown next., Fig. 9.19.

Group Summary

For this select the following:

Gateway of Tally>Display>Accounts Books>Group summary

Statistics	ABCL			Ctrl + M
	ABCL 1-Apr-2005 to 30-Apr-2005	ABCL *1-May-2005 to 31-May-2005*	ABCL 1-Jun-2005 to 30-Jun-2005	ABCL *1-Jul-2005 to 31-Jul-2005*
				8 more ...
Types of Vouchers :				
Contra	0	0	0	0
Credit Note	0	0	0	0
Debit Note	0	0	0	0
Delivery Note	0	0	0	0
Indent	0	0	0	0
Journal	0	0	0	0
Manufacturing	0	0	0	0
Memorandum	0	0	0	0
Payment	1	0	0	0
Payment Entry	0	0	0	0
Physical Stock	0	0	0	0
Purchase	0	0	0	0
Purchase Order	0	0	0	0
Purchase Quotation	0	0	0	0
Quotation	0	0	0	0
Receipt	0	0	0	0
Receipt Note	0	0	0	0
Rejections In	0	0	0	0
Rejections Out	0	0	0	0
				18 more ...

Fig. 9.19

Select a Group, e.g. Current Assets

It is shown in Fig. 9.20.

The Group Summary Statement shows the Closing Balances of the accounts falling under the selected group for the period up to the current date. The standard view is that of sub-groups in the group. Using the different options provided in the buttons bar, you can change the view to:

Detailed, Individual Ledger account listing under the selected group, monthly summary as well as bringing up new columns of information for comparison and analysis.

List of Vouchers

Vouchers or transactions of a similar nature or type are collated and listed together for a period to give meaningful information. There are different types of Voucher Lists, e.g., Group Vouchers, Ledger Vouchers, Stock Vouchers, Godown/Location Vouchers, etc. The main feature of such statement is that they belong to a particular entity from which they were accessed and provide the lowest level of detail after which the only detail possible is the voucher itself.

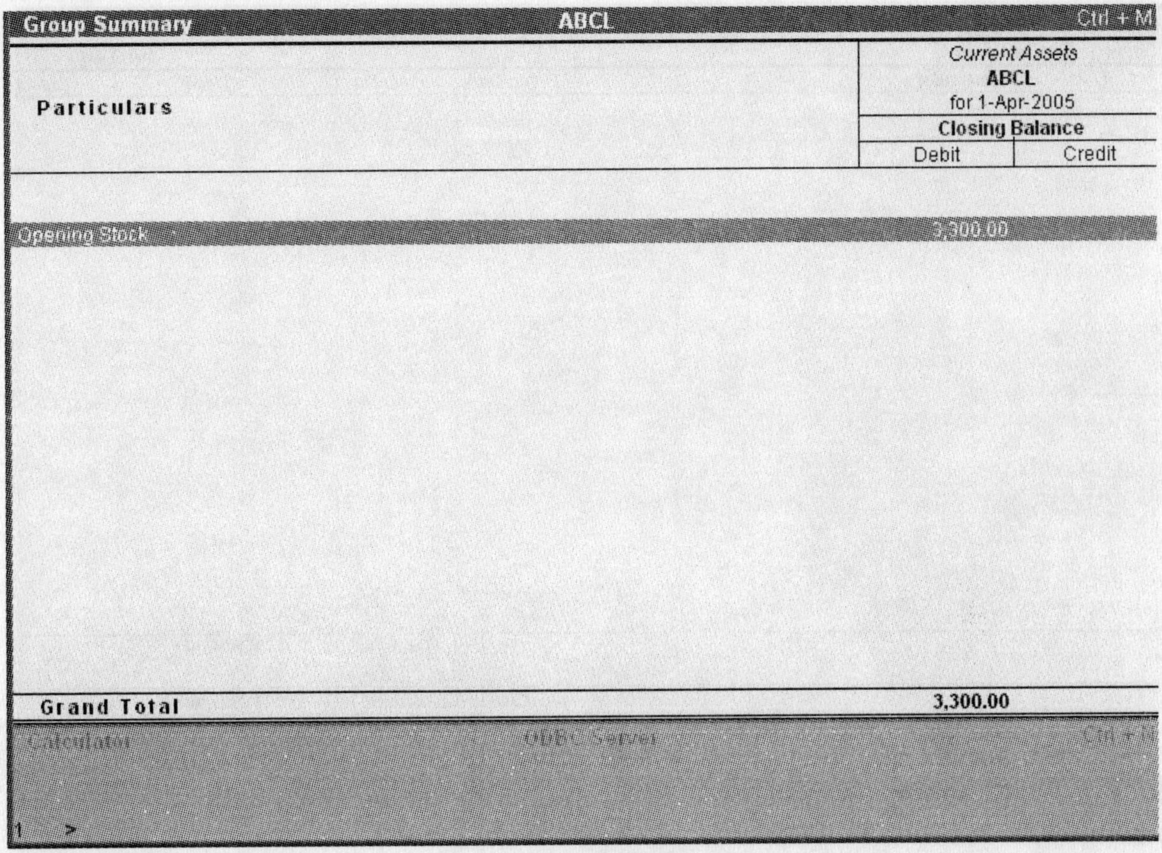

Fig. 9.20

Group Vouchers

Gateway of Tally>Display>Accounts Books>Group Vouchers

Select a Group, e.g. Current Assets

Group Vouchers is a list of all vouchers that have at least one ledger account entry belonging to the selected group during the period of display. This statement is useful when you want to list all transactions for a particular group.

Ledger Vouchers

For this select the following:

Gateway of Tally>Display>Accounts Books>Ledgers

Select Ledger Account. The list of vouchers for the current month is displayed. This list of vouchers for a ledger is the lowest level of collated data drilling down after which is the actual voucher. You may also access Ledger Vouchers by drilling down from different statements, like, Group Summary and Monthly Summary, as shown in Figs. 9.21 and 9.22.

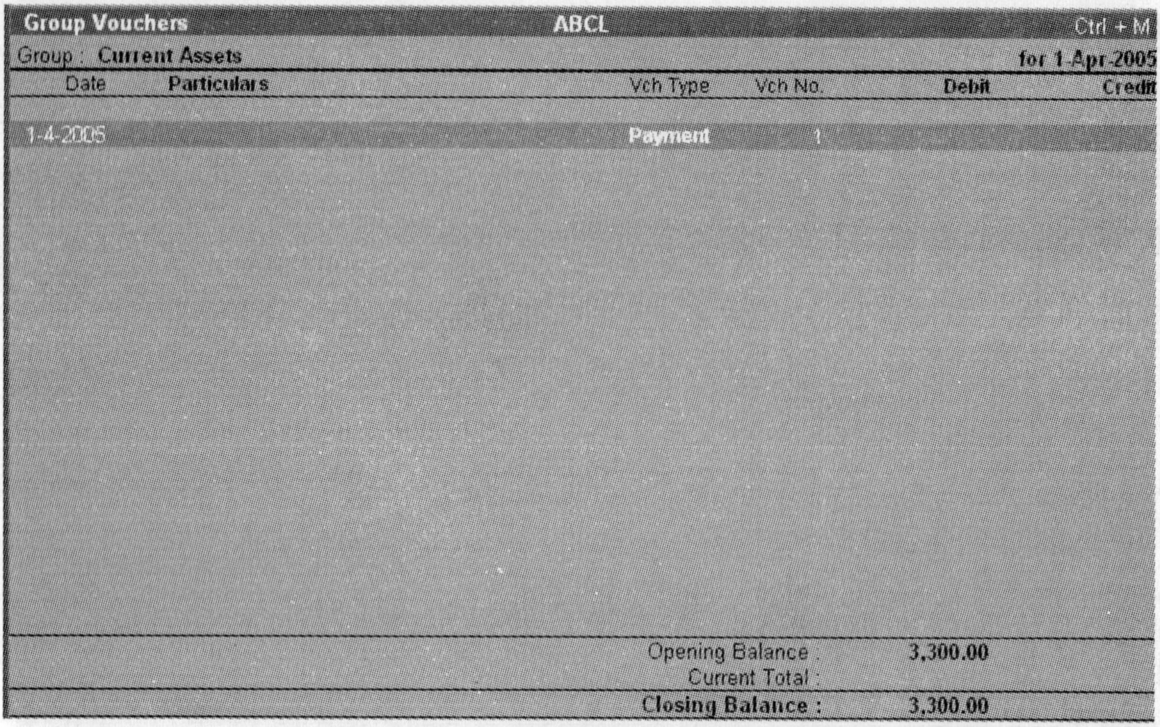

Fig. 9.21

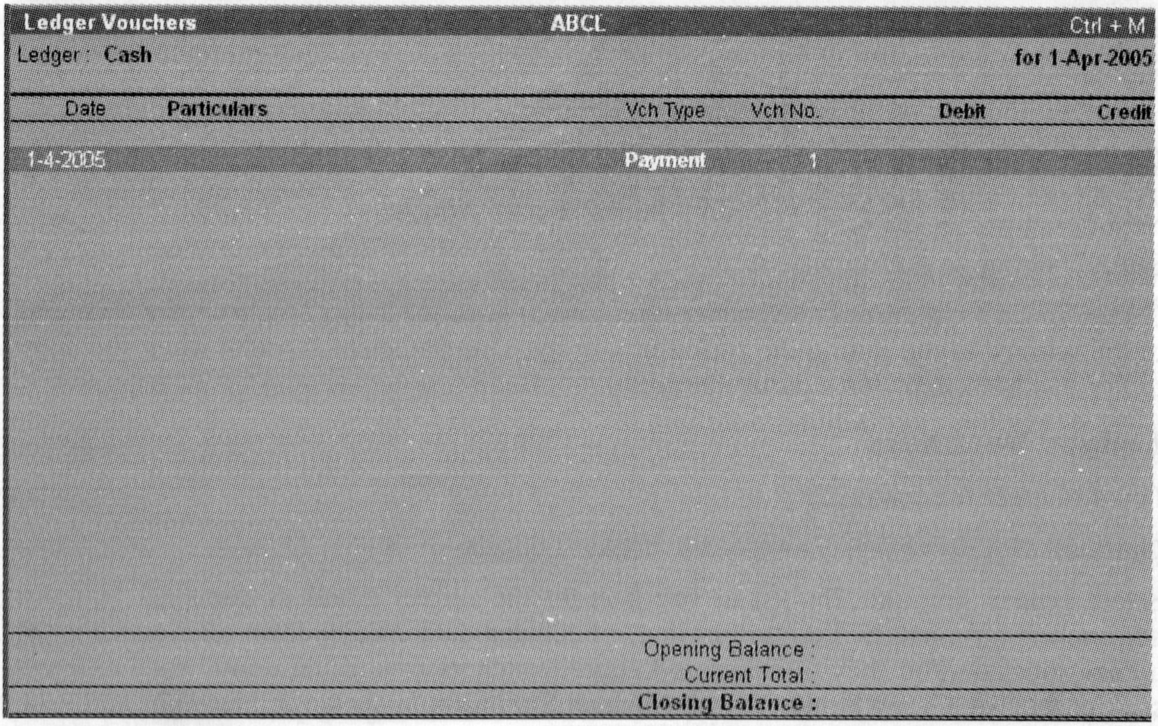

Fig. 9.22

Ratio Analysis

Gateway of Tally>Ratio Analysis

The Ratio Analysis Statement is a Single Sheet Performance Report for a selected period. It gives important values and key performance indicators for the company. It is one report that top management need to look at to know the state of the company's financial health and where it is going in the short term. The Ratio analysis Screen is divided into two parts: Principal Groups and Principal Ratios. The Principal Groups are the absolute key figures that give perspective to the ratios. Principal Ratios relate two pieces of financial data to get a comparison that is more meaningful when compared with ratios of other companies.

Working Capital

Tally allows the Accountants' definition and has the Net Working Capital calculated as Current Assets less Current Liabilities. Financial Analysts often mean total Current Assets as Working Capital. This is measure of the extent the firm is protected from liquidity problems. This is shown in Fig. 9.23.

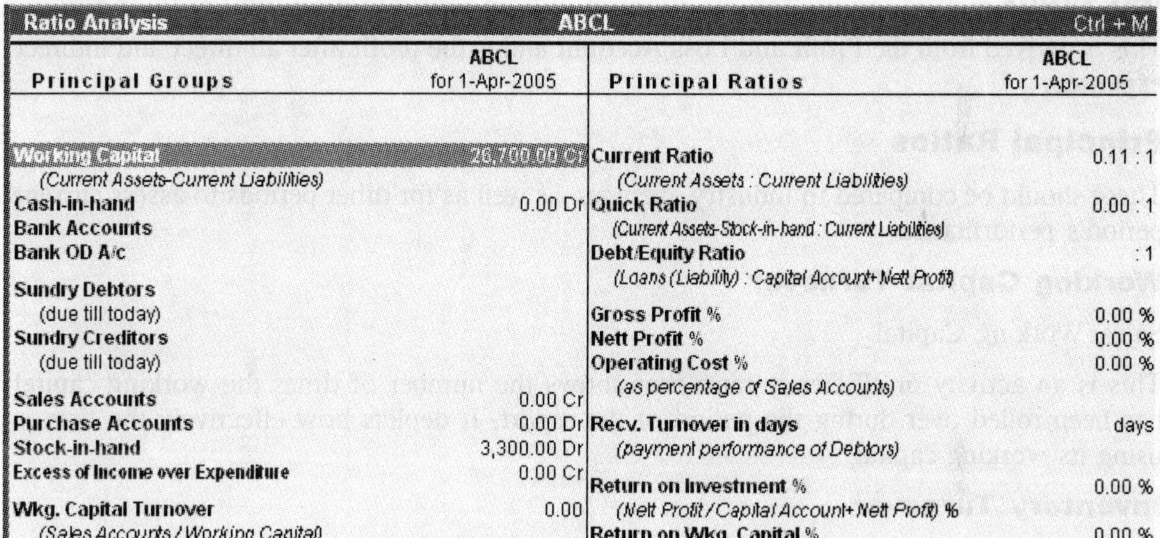

Fig. 9.23

Cash in Hand and Bank Balances

These are indicated in the Ratio analysis screen to give the liquidity perspective.

Sundry Debtors

(Due till today)

These are two figures, total debtors and debtors that are due on the date of the Statement.

Sundry Creditor

(Due till today)

These are figures for total creditors and those that are due as on the date of the Statement.

Sales and Purchase Accounts

These show the trading activity for the period

Stock in Hand

This is the stock in hand as on the date of the report. Together with cash and Bank Balances and Debtors, Stocks complete the Current Assets aspect of Working Capital.

Net Profit

This is derived from the Profit and Loss Account and is the profit after all direct and indirect expenses.

Principal Ratios

These should be compared to industry averages, as well as for other periods to assess current period's performance.

Working Capital Turnover

Sales/Working Capital

This is an activity or efficiency ratio that shows the number of times the working capital has been rolled over during the period of the report. It depicts how effectively the firm is using its working capital.

Inventory Turnover

Sales/Closing Stock

This is an activity or efficiency ratio that shows the number of times stocks has been rolled over during the period of the report. It depicts how effectively the firm is using its inventories.

Current Ratio

Current Assets: Current Liabilities

This is a liquidity or solvency ration and is the most off-used ratio for assessing the capability of a firm to meet its short-term obligations. It specifically shows a firm's ability to cover its current assets with current liabilities.

Quick Ratio

Current Assets-Stock in Hand: Current Liabilities

This liquidity or solvency ratio is called Acid-Test Ratio that concentrates on more liquidity of the current assets to measure a firm's ability to meet its current obligations. It is through that stocks and inventories are the least liquid if all current assets and hence a firm might become insolvent if its current assets comprise a high proportion of inventories.

Debt-Equity Ratio

Loans (Liability: Capital+Net Profit)

This is a gearing ratio that shows the extent to which long-term debt is used to finance the firm. It shows the proportion borrowed funds to Owners' Equity. The lower the ration, the higher the amount of funds invested by the owners. If the ration is high, it indicates that borrowed funds are more than own funds and the firm, which makes the firm lower credit-worthiness.

Gross Profit %

This is the trading profit before indirect expenses and taxes expressed as a percentage of total sales. It measures the efficiency of a firm's operations as well as indicates how products are priced.

Net Profit %

This is the profit after all expenses including direct and indirect expenses but before taxes expressed as a percentage of total sales. It is a more specific measure of the efficiency of a firm's operations. By considering both Gross Profit % and Net Profit % together, we are able to gain considerable insight into a firm's operations and the part played by the direct and indirect expenses.

Operating Cost %

As percentage of Sales Accounts

This is total cost including direct and indirect expenses but before taxes expressed as a percentage of sales. A high ratio shows that even a slight rise in costs would be risky and might necessitate increase in price.

Return on Investment %

(Net Profit/Capital + Net Profit) %

Net Profit here is Profit after all expenses but before taxes. This is a profitability ration that an investor is most interested in. The investor needs to know how much is earned on each dollar invested. If the investor finds other avenues that gives better returns, he will move his money from the firm.

Return on Working Capital %

(Net Profit/Working Capital) %

This is another profitability ration that ignores costs in Fixed Assets and assesses how profitably a firm uses its net current assets.

Receivable Turnover in Days

Payment Performance of Debtors

It is an efficiency ratio that measures the quality of a firm's receivables and how successfully it collects its debts Receivable Turnover in days is a figure that tells us the average number of days that receivables are outstanding before being collected. It should be compared with the average credit policy of the firm.

It is arrived at using the formula (Closing Balance of debtors/Total Sales)*Number of Days.

Payment Performance of Sundry Debtors

Payment Performance of Debtors is the average of the time customers take to actually pay their bills irrespective of the outstanding balance on the statement date. It is possible that the receivable turnover is low but payment performance ration is high indicating that though the customer(s) cleared their outstandings, they look a long time doing it. To get group level and customer level performance reports, drill down. Drill Down into the ration to get a more detailed position of debt collection. It is possible to take a customer's statement that shows both the receivable turnover in days and the customer's actual payment performance.

The Ledger Payment Performance statement shows at the top, the receivable turnover in days as 322.83 days, which is the balance outstanding in relation to total sales to the customer multiplied by total number of days in the period. However, even if the outstanding balance is only a few days old, the ration will still be the same. Therefore, the ratio should be read with the Average Performance of actual payments and the payment history of the customer to assess how long it might take to pay the outstanding balance. The Actual payment history is given in the table for each invoice that was paid by the customer. It shows when the invoice was paid, when it was due and what was the delay in payment. At the bottom, the customer's average performance is given for all cleared invoices.

Cost Centre Reports

For conceptual information on Cost Centres and Cost Categories, please look up the relevant chapters under Accounts Information. Cost Centre Reports are primarily performance reports that give different views of transactions and their relation to cost centres.

To access Cost Centre Reports:

Gateway of Tally>Display>Statements of Accounts>Cost Centres

Cost Category Summary

For this select the following:

Gateway of Tally>Display>Statements of Accounts>Cost Centres>Category Summary

The information on all Cost Categories to which voucher transaction have been allocated is accessed here as in Fig. 9.24.

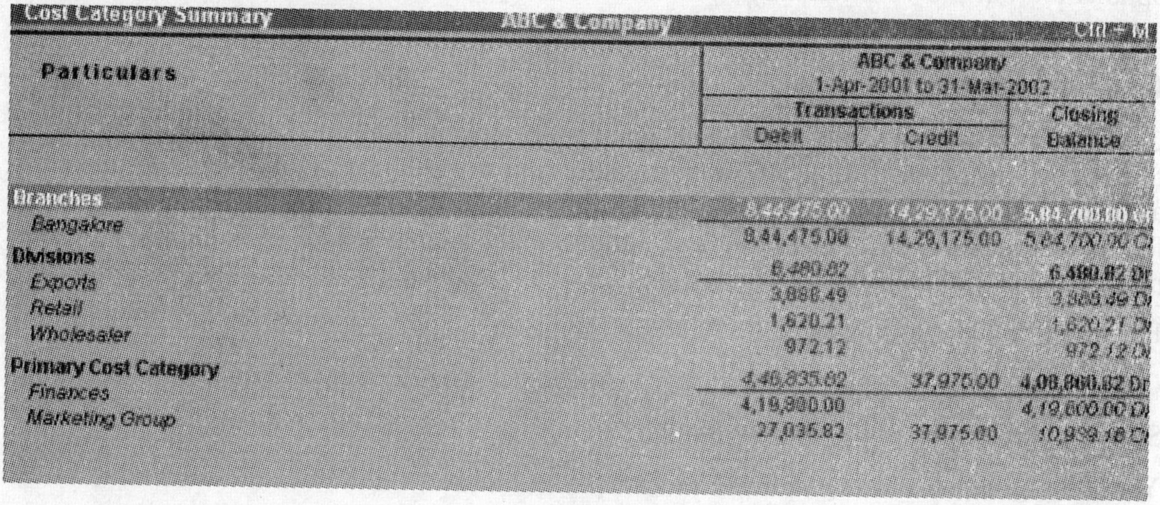

Cost Category Summary — ABC & Company — Ctrl + M

Particulars	ABC & Company 1-Apr-2001 to 31-Mar-2002		
	Transactions		Closing Balance
	Debit	Credit	
Branches	8,44,475.00	14,29,175.00	5,84,700.00 Cr
Bangalore	8,44,475.00	14,29,175.00	5,84,700.00 Cr
Divisions	6,480.82		6,480.82 Dr
Exports	3,888.49		3,888.49 Dr
Retail	1,620.21		1,620.21 Dr
Wholesaler	972.12		972.12 Dr
Primary Cost Category	4,46,835.82	37,975.00	4,08,860.82 Dr
Finances	4,19,800.00		4,19,800.00 Dr
Marketing Group	27,035.82	37,975.00	10,939.18 Cr

Fig. 9.24

Here two cost categories are created apart from the default Primary Cost Category. These are Executives and Projects. Each Category has some cost centres under it. Executives compromises of a Cost Centre Group – Managers, which has cost centres under it.

Note that the names in italics are cost centres that do not have any sub-cost centre. Names that are in normal font, e.g., Managers, are of cost centres that have sub-cost centres under them. General Overheads is a cost centre under primary Cost Category. The debit and credit transaction totals and the closing balance for each cost category are displayed together with their breakdown consisting of cost centres summaries.

Cost Centre Vouchers

From the Cost Category Summary, drill down into a cost centre for monthly break-up of the figures.

Select a month to display the Cost Centre Vouchers for that month. Use F2: Period to expand the date range if required. Use Detailed option, drill down to access the original voucher or use F12: Configure to display more details, as shown in Fig. 9.25.

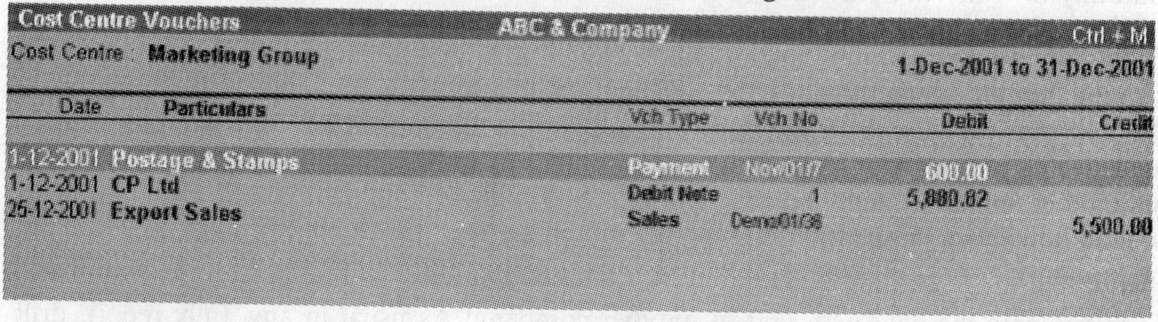

Cost Centre Vouchers — ABC & Company — Ctrl + M

Cost Centre **Marketing Group** — 1-Dec-2001 to 31-Dec-2001

Date	Particulars	Vch Type	Vch No	Debit	Credit
1-12-2001	Postage & Stamps	Payment	Nov01/7	600.00	
1-12-2001	CP Ltd	Debit Note	1	5,880.82	
25-12-2001	Export Sales	Sales	Demo01/38		5,500.00

Fig. 9.25

The Cost Centre Voucher's screen is accessible from all other Cost Centre Reports menu options too but the vouchers displayed are those that relate to the cost centre and relevant to the report.

Cost Centre Break-up

Cost centre Break up shows the ledger accounts that were used in vouchers and allocated to the cost centre, their total transaction values and the balance. If only revenue accounts are considered, the Cost Centre break up becomes the Profit or Loss statement of activities for the cost centre, ignoring only the Opening and Closing Stocks. It is then a powerful performance statement.

For this select the following:

Gateway of Tally>Display>Statement of Accounts>Cost Centres>Cost Centre Break-up

Select a cost centre, e.g., Andrew (which belongs to the Category Executives):

You get a grouped summary of the break up.

Select (click) Detailed to see the ledgers.

The report will resemble this:

Use the buttons to see the report in alphabetic order of ledger accounts. A useful report is the columnar Cost Centre break-up that allows comparison of two or more cost centres and assessment of their relative performance. Use New Column to bring up another cost centre and compare.

Drill down for further details.

Ledger Break-up of a Cost Centre

This is another view of a cost centre report. It enables you to analyse the distribution of a ledger account amongst different cost centres. If you want know how much Conveyance Expenses were incurred by different cost centres, this is the report that you should look at, see Fig. 9.26.

For this select the following:

Gateway of Tally>Display>Statement of Accounts.Cost Centres>Ledger Break-up

Select a ledger account.

Use the buttons to see the report in alphabetic order of ledger accounts. A useful report is the columnar Cost-Break up of Ledger that allows you to compare how different cost centres used two or more ledgers (e.g. expense accounts) For example Use New Column to bring up another ledger account, say, Sales. The report will give you how much each executive sold ad how much he spent on running the motorcar. You will be able to judge their relative performance.

Even compare the data with that of another company! As usual in any Tally report, drill down for more details.

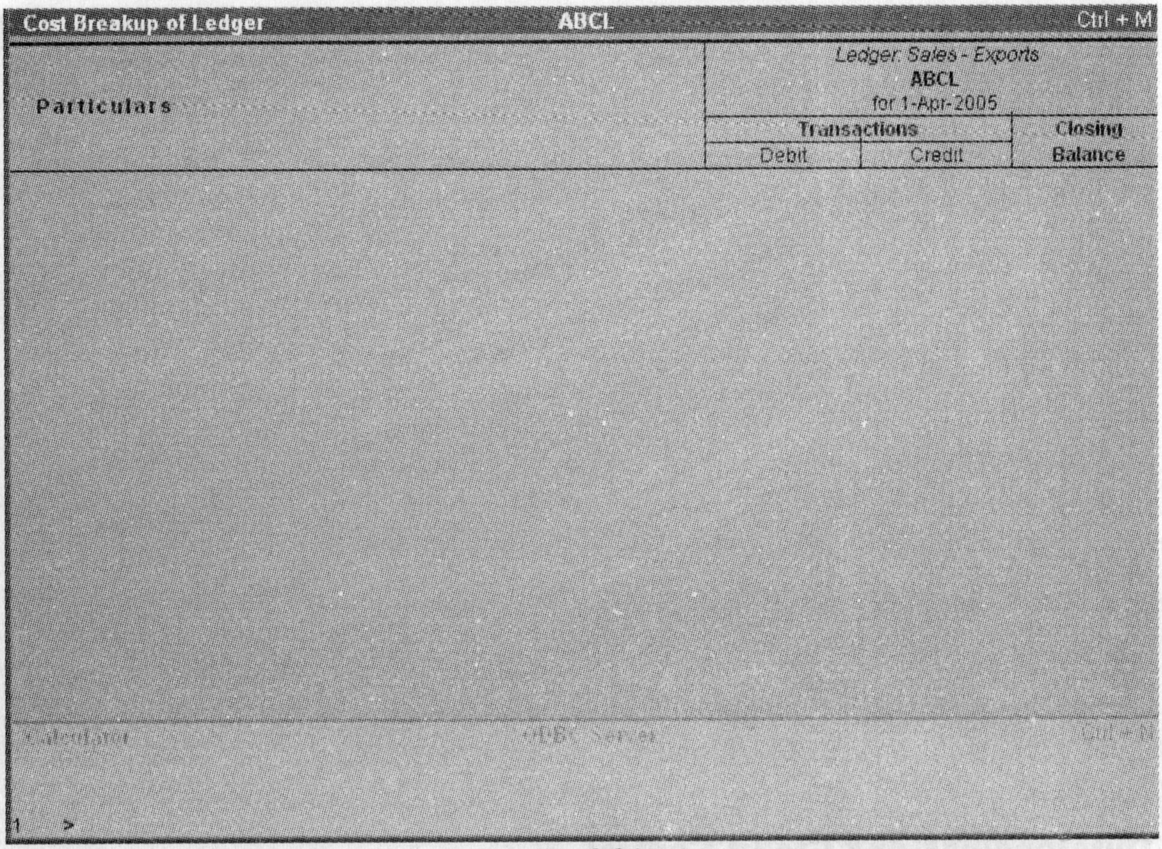

Fig. 9.26

Group Break-up of a Cost Centre

This is another view of a cost centre report. It enables you to analyse the distribution of a group (of total accounts) amongst different cost centres. If you want to know how and what Indirect Expenses were incurred by different cost centres, this is the report that you should look at, see Fig. 9.27.

For this select the following:

Gateway of Tally>Display>Statement of Accounts>Cost Centres>Group Break-up

Select a Group account, e.g., Indirect Expenses. Use the buttons to see the report in alphabetic order of ledger accounts.

A useful report is the columnar Cost-Break up of Groups that allows you to compare how different cost centres used two or more Groups. For example, use New Column to bring up another Group, say, Sales Accounts.

The report will give you how much each executive (cost centres) sold and how much he spent. You will be able to judge their relative performance. Even compare the date with the total of another company!

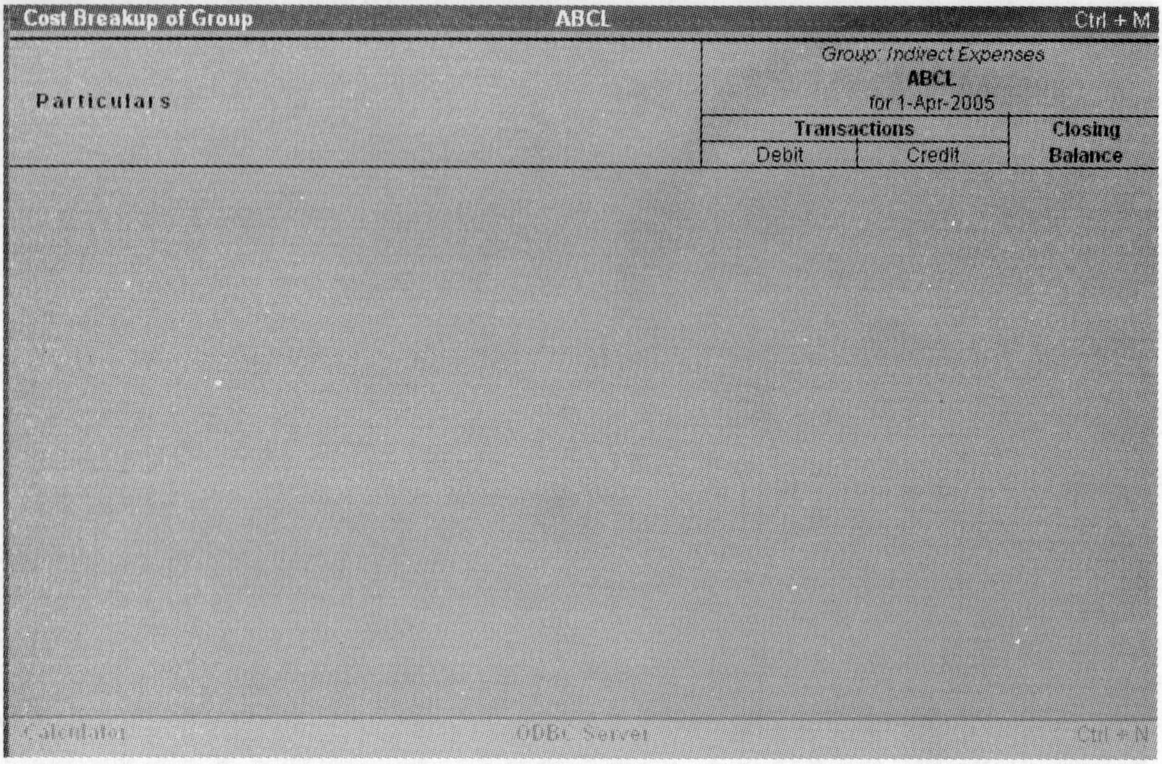

Fig. 9.27

Outstandings and Credit Control

Receivables and Payables

Receivables and Payables are two important components of any firm's working capital and indeed its business activity. Receivables are a part of current assets whereas payables are of current liabilities. Each influences the short-term liquidity and financing of the company. Effective control of both types of Outstandings is necessary for the financial health of the firm. Tally provides many reports and analysis to aid credit control.

For this select the following:

Gateway of Tally > Display > Statement of Accounts > Outstandings

Receivable (Bills Receivable)

The discussion is based on Receivables. Payables are exactly the same and hence not discussed separately.

For this select the following:

Gateway of Tally > Display > Statement of Accounts > Outstandings > Receivables

This report is for all receivable invoice outstanding on the current date. Remember that this report only takes into consideration those accounts that have Bill-by-Bill option activated. (To verify display the account master through Accounts Info). This is shown in Fig. 9.28.

This report has the following information.

Date

This is the EFFECTIVE date of invoice. It is not the actual invoice date. Hence, if your invoice date is 15 November but the effective date is 30 November, 30-Nov-98 will be shown here Credit Period is calculated from effective date.

Ref No

This is the Bill reference number that was entered in the Bill-wise Details

Party's Name

The ledger name appears here.

Pending Amount

This is the outstanding balance on the particular invoice. To see the break-up, press SHIFT+ENTER. To see the break-up of all the bills, select the Detailed button.

Due on

The due date of the bill as entered during voucher entry. It is with reference to the Effective date.

Overdue by Days

It is the period in days from due date to the end date of the report, in the above example, see Fig. 9.28, the end date is 1-Apr-05.

Drill-down

Drill down any invoice for further details.

Buttons

Print or e-mail the report to your bills collector. Use other buttons to configure, query or change the report.

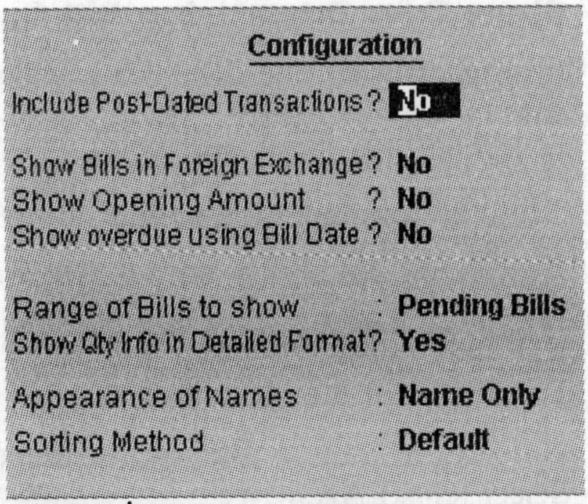

F12: Configure Bill-wise Outstandings Report

This has the following options.

Include Past-Dated Transactions?

Post-dated transactions are those whose voucher dates are after the date of display. These can be included in the Outstandings report if you set this to Yes if you want to see the effect of post-dated transactions.

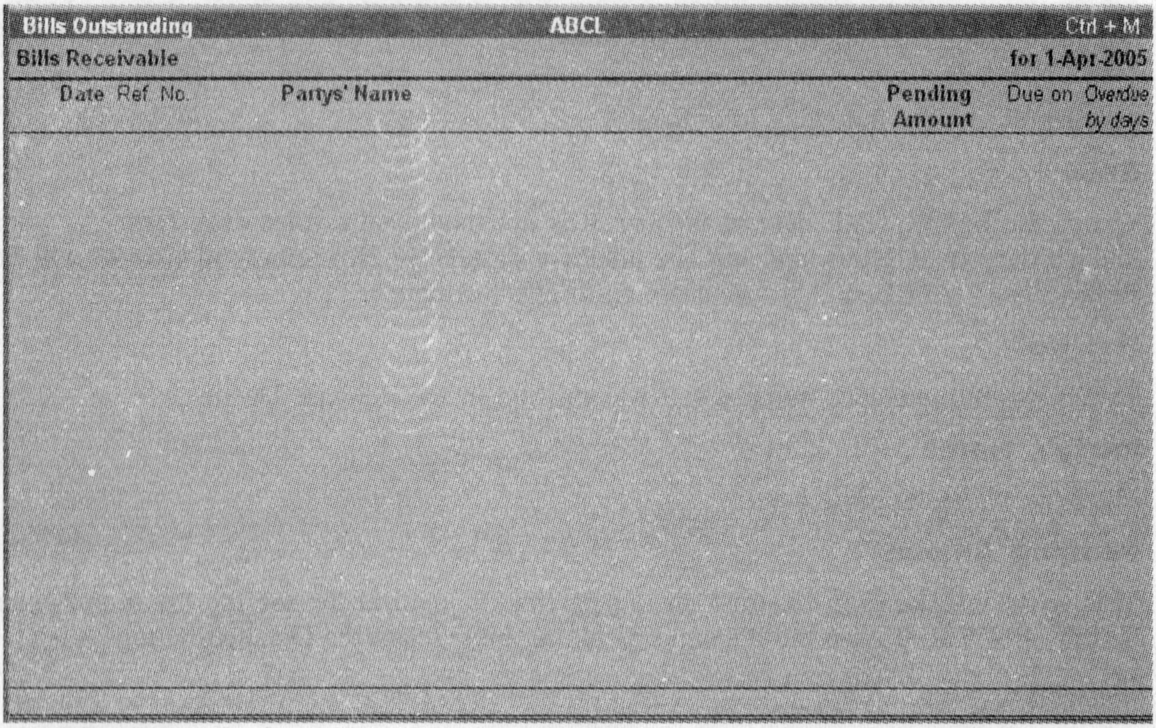

Fig. 9.28

In the above example, note the change in the columns. The payment for the first bill was received by way of a post-dated cheque – (31-12-98). The receipt entry was made on 31-12-98 and marked 'Post-dated'. In the date range 1-1-98, the invoice, which is still outstanding, will be cleared on 31-12-98 and such the Final Balance will be nil.

Show Bills in Foreign Exchange?

The Bills Outstanding report will show only those bills raised in foreign currency. Remember, bills raised in base currency will be excluded if this is set to 'Yes'.

Show Over Dues Using Bill Dates?

Instead of using due dates for calculating overdue days, do you want to sue the invoice date for the calculation? Yes or No. The Overdue column is recalculated to show the age of the invoices in number of days.

The other configuration options are self-explanatory

Age-wise Analysis of all Receivables

If you are not already in the receivables screen.

For this select the following:

Gateway of Tally > Display > Statement of Accounts > Outstandings > Receivables > Select (click) Age-wise

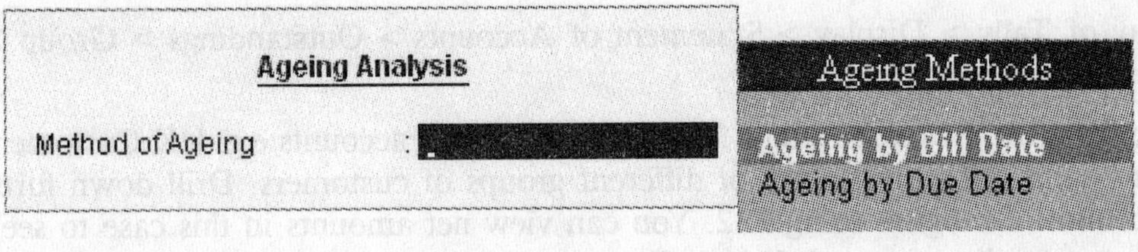

Select one of the two Methods of Ageing: By Bill Date or By Due Date. Set the age periods required for the report. An earlier setting is given and can be accepted as it is or modified. The aged bills report is produced accordingly. You can drill down to query the individual invoices. Age-wise analysis for a ledger account or group of accounts are discussed separately.

Payables (Bills Payable)

For this select the following:

Gateway of Tally > Display > Statement of Accounts > Outstandings > Payables

The button F4: Payable in the Receivable screen switches to Bills Payable report. Likewise, when in Payable Screen, F4: Receivable button is available to switch to Bills Receivable report.

Outstandings Report of a Single Ledger Account

All receivables or all payables serve to give you a total picture of the bills received and issued. If you want to know the outstandings status of the bills of a particular party account, those reports are not suitable. You should use the Ledger Outstandings report.

For this select the following:

Gateway of Tally > Display > Statement of Accounts > Outstandings > Ledger

Detailed functionality available in this report, including F12: Configure and Age-wise Analysis is the same as in All Receivables and has been discussed in detail there. You can however produce Reminder Letters from the ledger Outstandings report. Use the Contact button to view address and other contact details.

Age-wise Analysis of a Single Ledger Account

If you are not already in the receivables screen:

Select the following:
Gateway of Tally > Display > Statement of Accounts > Outstandings > Ledger

Select the ledger account. Select (click) Age-wise. Select one of the two Methods of Ageing. By Bill Date or By Due Date. Set the age periods required for the report. An earlier setting is given and can be accepted as it is or modified. The aged bills report is produced accordingly. You can drill down to query the individual invoices.

Outstanding Report for a Group

For this select the following:

Gateway of Tally > Display > Statement of Accounts > Outstandings > Group > Select a Group

This report gives the outstandings for a group of ledger accounts e.g. UK Customers and is useful to hand out to managers of different groups of customers. Drill down further into each account. Configure using F12. You can view net amounts in this case to see the net balance outstanding for each ledger. For a group that contains sub-groups, e.g., African Customers, the button F5: Ledger-wise is useful. It also toggles to Group-wise.

Age-wise Analysis for a Group

If you are not already there:

Gateway of Tally > Display > Statement of Accounts > Outstandings > Group > Select a Group > Select (click) Detailed > Select (click) Age-wise > Select one of the two Methods of Ageing:

By Bill Date or By Due Date. Set the age periods required for the report.

An earlier setting is given and can be accepted as it is or modified. The aged bills report is produced accordingly. You can drill down to query the individual invoices. You can see Net Balances by configuring it using F12. You cannot print Reminder letters to a group from here but from Multi-Account Printing in the Gateway of Tally.

Reminder Letters

If you are not already there:

Gateway of Tally > Display > Statement of Accounts > Outstandings > Ledger > Select (click) Print (or e-mail)

If the Print (Y or N) box appears, select No.

Tab down to:

Print Reminder Letter:

Change to Yes

Set, accept or modify, as the case may be, the ageing period.

Show Bills in Foreign Exchange

Type Yes or No according to what you need and accept. In this case, we selected No. The text of the reminder letters can be changed through F12: Configure while in the Print option. If you want to print Reminder Letters to a group of customers' ledgers, you should use the Multi-account printing option.

Reminder Letters to a Group of Ledgers

For this select the following:

Gateway of Tally > Display > Statement of Accounts > Outstandings > Ledgers > Group of Accounts

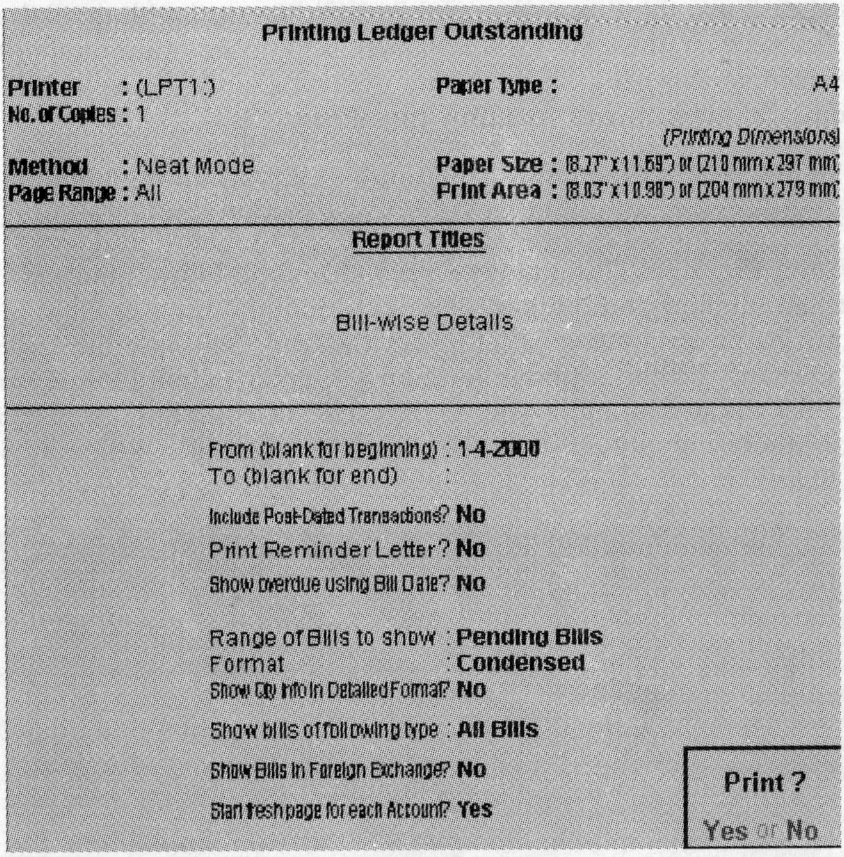

Fig. 9.29

Select the group for which reminder letters are required e.g. Sundry Debtors, as shown in Fig. 9.29.

Select No to Print?

The report by default is a Bill-wise details these are reports that lists the outstanding bills for each ledger in the group. Tab down to Print Reminder Letter. Set it to Yes. Set the age periods. Set other options as necessary. Reminder letters for each account in the group will be printed.

CASH AND FUND FLOWS

Cash management is essential for any business. Many companies continue to project profits even as they go into liquidation because of insolvency. Businesses close down because of lack of cash despite being profitable. Cash and Flow Statements aid in cash management and are an important components of management accounts.

Cash Flow

Tally's Cash Flow Statement is a historical statement of cash (including those with the Bank) moving in and out of the business. It explains changes in cash by listing those activities that increased cash and those that decreased cash. When used with the Balance Sheet and Profit and Loss Account, the Cash Flow Statement helps to assess the reasons for differences between net income and net cash flow from operating activities as well as the effect of cash and non-cash investing and financing transactions.

For this select the following:

Gateway of Tally>Display>Cash/fund Flow>Cash Flow

This is shown in Fig. 9.30. This produces a Monthly Cash Flow Summary that shows the Cash Movement – inflow and outflow for each month and the Net Flow. Select a month and drill down by pressing enter. Select (click) Detailed. You have the cash flow for that month. For Quarterly (or for any other period e.g. Monthly) Cash Flow: Change Period by pressing F2: Set the period e.g. 1-1-98 to 31-12-98. Select (click) Auto Column. Select Quarterly (or Monthly or any other period). You have your columnar cash flow: Columnar Cash Flow Statement

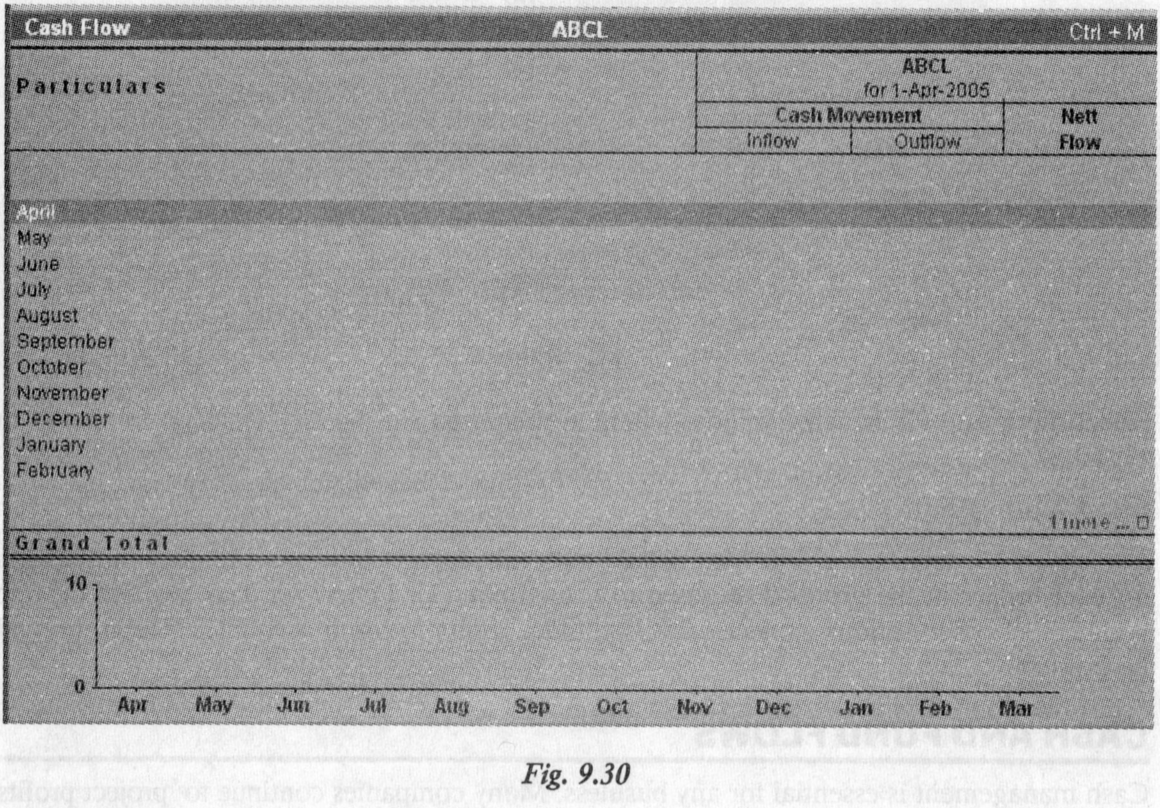

Fig. 9.30

Funds Flow

While Cash Flow Statement is concerned only with cash, Funds Flow takes into account the movement of the entire working capital. It includes increases and decreases in inventories, creditors and debtors apart from cash and bank. The statement, as shown in Fig. 9.31, reveals the Source of Funds and how they were applied.

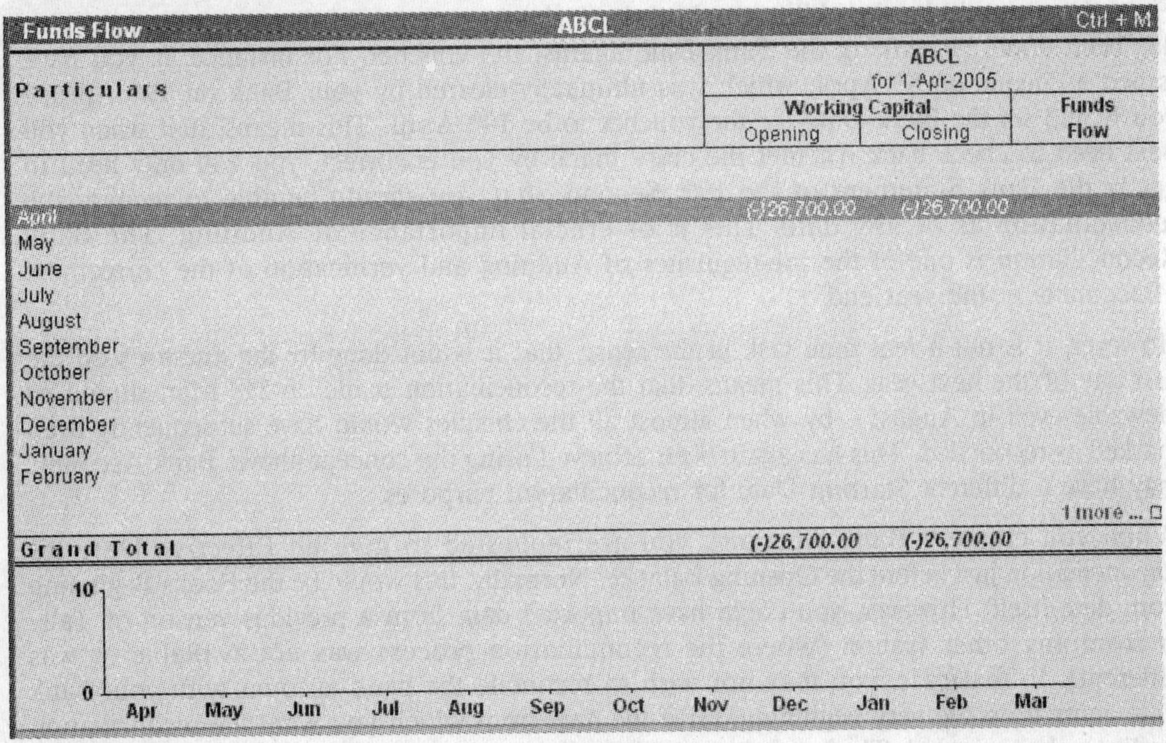

Fig. 9.31

For this select the following:

Gateway of Tally>Display>Cash/Fund Flow>Funds Flow

This produces a Monthly Funds Flow Summary with movement of working capital for each month. It takes a slightly different approach to Cash Flow Summary is that it gives Opening and Closing Balances of each month with the Flow as the extension. Select a month and drill down by pressing enter. Select (click) Detailed. You have the funds flow for that month. The screen is divided into two portions:

1. Application of funds for Long Term Assets
2. Current Assets and Liabilities, i.e. Working Capital movement – note the bottom portion where movement in Working Capital is shown.

You can drill down any line for further details. For Quarterly (or for any other period e.g., Monthly) funds Flow: Change Period by pressing F2: Set the period e.g. 1-4-2000 to 30-6-2000. Select (click) Auto Column. Select Quarterly (or Monthly or any other period). You have your columnar Funds Flow.

Reconciliation of Bank Accounts

Reconciling the Company's Bank Accounts with the Banker's Statement is a fundamental and regular task of Accounting. Our first presentation of this facility aims to tackle two issues.

First, there should be the ability to check back the correctness of the reconciliation. This has been done, by making the Bank Date against the voucher. For instance, if you have issued a cheque on 8th April, which was ultimately cleared by your Bank on 19th April, - you would set the Bank Date for the voucher to be 19th April. This means, that when you next need to check back whether the entry made by you is correct, you will only need to verify the Bank Statement of the 19th. Second, that you should be able to recover the reconciliation as of any date. This is of crucial importance of Auditing. The Bank Reconciliation is one of the pre-requisites of Auditing and verification of the correctness of accounts at the year end.

However, it is not a real time task in the sense, that it is not done by the auditor's on the first day of the next year. This means, that the reconciliation made on 31st Mar, should be viewable even in August – by when almost all the cheques would have subsequently been marked as reconciled. This has again been achieved using the concept above. Bank Accounts may have a different Starting Date for reconciliation purposes.

When you create a Bank Account, you are requested to give an Effective Date for Reconciliation just before the Opening Balance. Normally, this would be the Books Beginning from date itself. However, you could have imported data from a previous version of Tally or from any other system (where the reconciliation process was not available or was different). In that case, you may not wish to reconcile the bank account with your bank statements from the very beginning. Give the date from which you want the reconciliation facility to be activated. Then, previous entries will not appear for reconciliation, but will be taken as a reconciled Opening Balance.

A quick experiment with Reconciliation will show you what is meant. Here is how you go about it:

1. Bring up the monthly summary of any Bank Book (You could do this from the Balance Sheet, Trial Balance or Display/Account Books/Bank Books and selecting a Bank).
2. Bring your cursor to the first month (typically April) and press Enter. This brings up the Reconcile button will be visible on the right. Press F5.
3. The display now becomes an Edit screen in Reconciliation mode. The primary components are: A column for the Bankers Date
4. The Reconciliation at the bottom of the screen, showing:
   - Balance as per Company Books
   - Amounts not reflected in Bank
   - Balance as per Bank

The Balance as per Company Books reflects your Balances as on the last date.

The Balance as per Bank is the Nett effect of your Book Balance offset by the amounts not reflected in the Bank which should equal the balance in the Bank Statement. (Of course, some variation may persist due to entries made in the Bank Statement which you have not yet entered in your Books – but since you WILL definitely enter them and only then print your reconciliation, it will ultimately reflect the correct balance).

You will find, as you mark off the individual vouchers by setting the Bank Date, that the Reconciliation at the bottom of screen keeps reflecting those changes instantly. When you are finished, press Ctrl+A (or press Enter as many times as necessary to skip over the unmarked vouchers) and accept the screen. (If your screen has a largish number of vouchers it may take some time to complete the acceptance – be patient).

The next time you come for reconciliation, you will be presented only with those vouchers which remain unreconciled. Thus, the task keeps becoming simpler. (It may be possible, that due to an error of entry made earlier, you wish to see those vouchers which are already marked as reconciled – so that you may modify their marking.

To do this, press F12: Configure. In case you have already pressed a few keys BEFORE pressing F12, Tally will query whether you wish to discard changes made so far, if any, by asking Quit Y/N. Simply press Y – and the configuration screen will appear. Here, specify whether you wish to see the reconciled vouchers also).

Remember, to print your Reconciliation, just press Alt+P!

Display Inventory Reports and Statements

Tally prepares the inventory reports based on the vouchers you have entered to date. You can than vary the appearance of reports according to your needs, for example, to make comparisons between different companies, periods of the financial year and so on. In each case, when you display a report, you can step-down to the next level of detail by highlighting the item and pressing Enter and you can keep going until you reach an individual vouchers. Similarly, you can step back to higher levels by pressing [Esc].

The special features available for the currently displayed report are indicated on the button bar and can be selected with a single click of the mouse. In other words, inventory operates in exactly the same way as accounting regarding displaying modifying and printing the reports and so you can use the knowledge gained during the accounting module to good effect with inventory.

Because it is very similar in operation, the function of the buttons on the button bar and the various printing options are not repeated here. Instead, this unit concentrates on highlighting some of he special inventory screens, before giving you he opportunity to practice:

Viewing Stock Summary

Stock Summary is a statement of stock in hand on a particular date. The statement is updated with every transaction so that it provides current stock position at any time. The statement can be drilled down as with all Tally reports, and configured to view different details. Indeed, it is possible to see the total flow of stock on a single report. Experiment with the different buttons for this purpose. Tally treats Stock Summary as one of the Primary statements and makes it accessible directly from the Gateway of Tally.

To view the Stock Summary, select the following:

Gateway of Tally>Stock Summary

The default display, as shown in Fig. 9.32 is that of stock group balances. Select detailed to show another level of detail. This could be sub-groups or directly stock items in cases where there are not sub-groups.

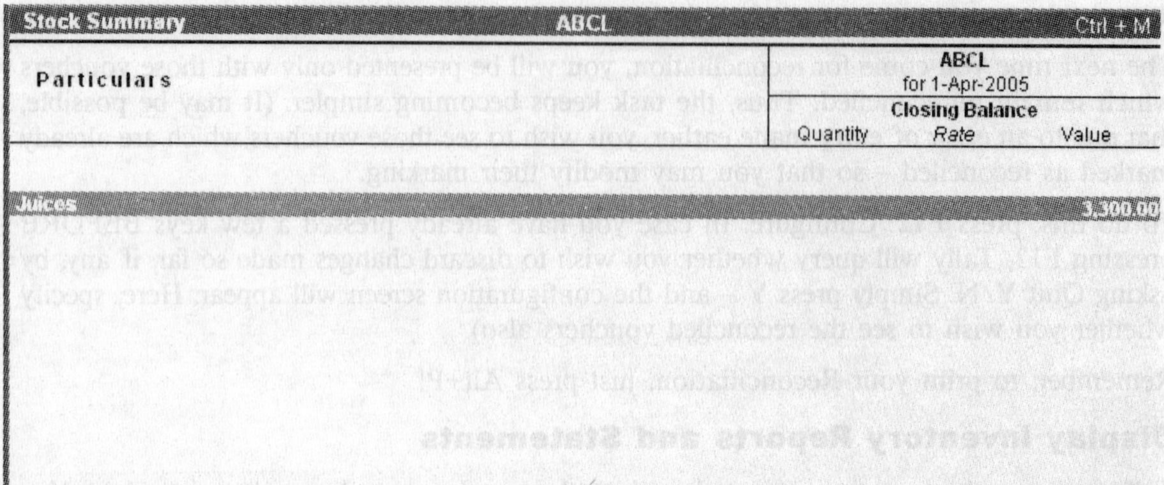

Fig. 9.32

In the above example, note the stock groups with stock items below them. Here, there are two stock groups, viz, Hardware and Software that have closing balances. The Stock groups show total quantities. This is because the unit of measure is the same for all the stock items that have been set up to have quantities of items added. The stock group Services, does not have any balance. This is because of the original set-up of the Services items, where stock is valued at Zero Cost and all sales are treated as Manufactured. Note that there is a grand total too because of a single unit of measure for all addable items. If there were different units of measure, then there would not be grand total.

Stock Flow (reconciliation)

The Stock Summary Statement can be configured to display the flow of goods.

Select F12: Configure while in the Stock Summary Screen. Set the configuration as shown here in Fig. 9.33.

This statement shown in Fig. 9.34 shows the flow of stock: Opening Stock, Goods Inwards,

Configuration

Show Quantities	?	Yes
Show Rates	?	Yes
Show Values	?	Yes
Show Opening Balance	?	Yes
Show goods inwards	?	Yes
Show goods outwards	?	Yes
Show Closing Balance	?	Yes
Show Consumption & Gross Profits	?	No
Show using Alternate Units	?	No
Show Tail Units of Compound Units	?	No
Appearance of Stock Item Names	:	Name Only
Appearance of Names	:	Name Only
Scale Factor for Values	:	Default
Sorting Method	:	Default
Expand all levels in Detailed Format	?	No

Fig. 9.33

Stock Summary — ABC & Company — Ctrl + M

Particulars	ABC & Company 1-Apr-2001 to 30-Jun-2001							
	Opening Balance		Inwards		Outwards		Closing Balance	
	Quantity	Value	Quantity	Value	Quantity	Value	Quantity	Value
Software		**75,000.00**		**2,26,300.00**		**2,03,560.00**		**1,33,722.70**
Tally Ees 6.3-Multiuser			*20 pcs*	*39,800.00*			*20 pcs*	*39,800.00*
Tally Ees 6.3-Singleuser			*185 pcs*	*1,86,500.00*	*160 pcs*	*1,82,500.00*	*25 pcs*	*25,202.70*
Windows 2000	*150 pcs*	*75,000.00*			*42 pcs*	*21,060.00*	*108 pcs*	*68,720.00*
Sony								
Cables	50 Nos	12,500.00			41 Nos	7,485.00	9 Nos	12,500.00
Tally Server			5 Nos	8,304.15			5 Nos	8,304.15
Grand Total	**50 Nos**	**87,500.00**	**5 Nos**	**2,34,604.15**	**41 Nos**	**2,11,045.00**	**14 Nos**	**1,54,526.85**

Fig. 9.34

Goods Outward and Closing Stock. The statement is quantitatively reconciled but not monetarily. What that means is that: Opening quantity + Inward Quantity – Outward

Quantity = Closing Stock Quantity. However, this is not true of values and you should not be disturbed because values do not add up this way. This is because the Outwards value shows Sale Values and not Cost. The Closing Stock Value is however based on cost and the Cost Method adopted for each item.

Value reconciliation is possible using Consumption figures instead of Outwards.

Gross Profits – (Items and Stock Group Profitability)

The Stock Summary can be expanded to show consumption and gross profits for each stock item.

F7: Show Profits or F12: Configure while in the Stock Summary

Activate Show Consumption and Gross Profits. The statement will now be (quantities have been set to No in this example). This is shown in Fig. 9.35.

Stock Summary ABC & Company Ctrl + M

ABC & Company
1-Apr-2001 to 30-Jun-2001

Particulars	Opening Balance		Inwards		Outwards					Closing Balance	
	Quantity	Value	Quantity	Value	Quantity	Value	Consumption	Gross Profit	Perc %	Quantity	Value
Software		**75,000.00**		**2,26,300.00**		**2,03,560.00**	**1,67,577.30**	**35,982.70**	**17.68 %**		**1,33,722.70**
Tally Eos 6.3 Multiuser			*20 pcs*	*39,800.0*						*20 pcs*	*39,800.0*
Tally Eos 6.3 Singleuser			*185 pcs*	*1,86,300.0*	*160 pcs*	*1,82,500.00*	*1,61,297.30*	*21,202.70*	*11.62%*	*25 pcs*	*25,202.7*
Windows 2000	*150 pcs*	*75,000.00*			*42 pcs*	*21,060.00*	*6,280.00*	*14,780.00*	*70.18%*	*108 pcs*	*68,720.0*
Sony											
Cables	50 Nos	12,500.00			41 Nos	7,485.00		7,485.00	100.00 %	9 Nos	12,500.00
[illegible]			5 Nos	9,304.15						5 Nos	9,304.15
Grand Total	50 Nos	87,500.00	5 Nos	2,34,604.15	41 Nos	2,11,045.00	1,67,577.30	43,467.70	20.60 %	14 Nos	1,54,526.85

Fig. 9.35

The Outward Column is expanded to show cost of Goods Outwards termed Consumption and Gross Profit value and percentage. This statement is useful for two purposes: Profitability Analysis of Sales (Outwards) and Value Reconciliation of Stock

Stock Valuation Methods

Stock Summary with different stock valuations serve to show the effect of different methods on the value of stock, as shown in Fig. 9.36. Most popular methods are available. Each

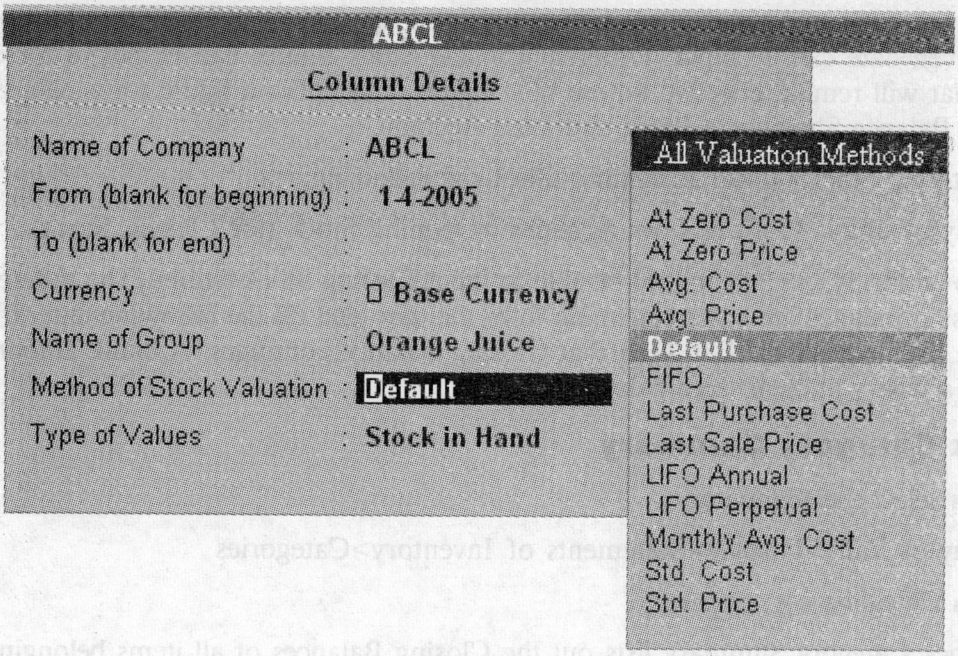

Fig. 9.36

stock item could be set up to have a different stock valuation method as default. However, there are occasions when another method of valuation is needed, for example to asses the replacement value or the scalable value of stock. Tally shows the stocks in any or all the valuation methods dynamically and simultaneously without going through complicated procedures.

Last Purchase Cost method can be used to assess the replacement value whereas Last Sale Price for realizable (sealable) value. While in the Stock Summary, select New Column

Select defaults for all except Stock Valuation Method. Select another method e.g. Last Sale Price

For the following statement:

The prices having fallen, the value that can be realized if all the stocks were sold in actually less than the look values! For Balance Sheet purposes, the lower of cost or releasable value is preferable. The Balance Sheet can be configured to take that value.

Stock Group Summary

This report is available only if the option in Company Features: Integrate Accounts and Inventory is set to **No**.

The statement shows the Opening Closing figures that have been input in the ledger account master rather than picked up from the Stock Summary. Hence, the Stock Summary figures and the Stock Group Summary will show different figures. The Ledger account belongs to the Stock-In-Hand Group.

Drill down the Stock Group Summary to reach the Ledger account where the closing balance for a given date can be input. Different Closing Stock figures can be put in for different dates that will remain effective till the next figure. The relevant figure for a date is picked up into Balance Sheet and Profit and Loss Account.

To get to the Stock Group Summary, select the following:

Gateway of Tally>Profit & Loss Accounts>Opening Stock (for Closing Stock)

Drill down the Stocks Account to be able to input Closing Stock figures. The different dates for Closing Balance are dates beginning from the date and till the following date. If there is no date that follows the last, then that Closing Balance continues. A blank amount figure against a date will mean zero balance.

Stock Category Summary

For this select the following:

Gateway of Tally>Display>Statements of Inventory>Categories

Select a Category, e.g., Software.

The Stock Category Summary lists out the Closing Balances of all items belonging to the selected category. Drill down an item for Item Monthly Summary and for the Stock Voucher list. Use Show Profit for profitability analysis for the Items in the Category, as shown in Fig. 9.37.

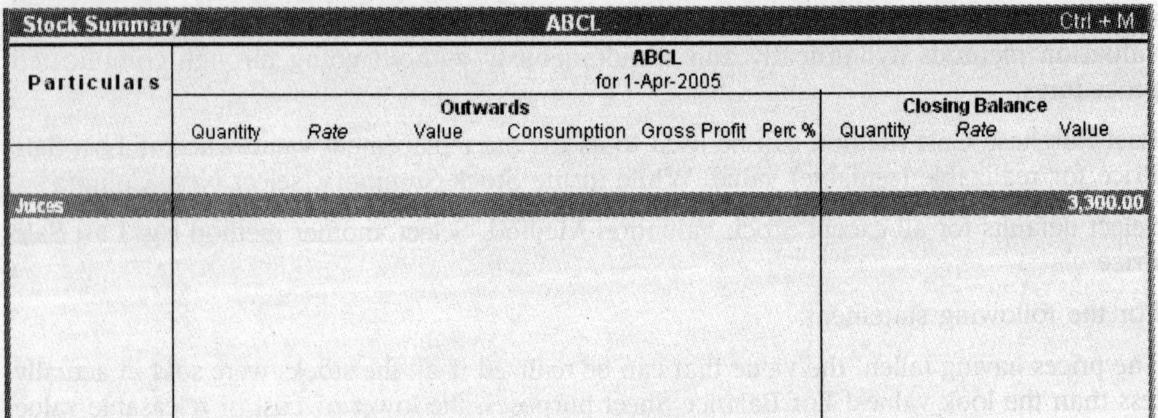

Fig. 9.37

Viewing Stock Items

For this select the following:

Gateway of Tally>Display>Inventory Books>Stock Item.

You may go through the Stock Summary as well. Simply place the cursor on the item and press [enter]

Select an item from the List of Items. Select F12: Configure. Tab down the Configuration menu to Show with Graph? And type y and press Enter. Select Bar and No. You should now see the particulars displayed with a graph of goods inwards and outwards (red for inwards and blue for outwards).

Stock Vouchers

For this select the following:

Gateway of Tally>Display>Inventory Books>Stock Items

Select Item. Select and drill down a month.

The list of stock vouchers for the current month is displayed, as shown in Fig. 9.38. This list of vouchers for a stock item is the lowest level of collated data drilling down after which is the actual voucher. You may also access Vouchers by drilling down from different statements, like Stock Summary.

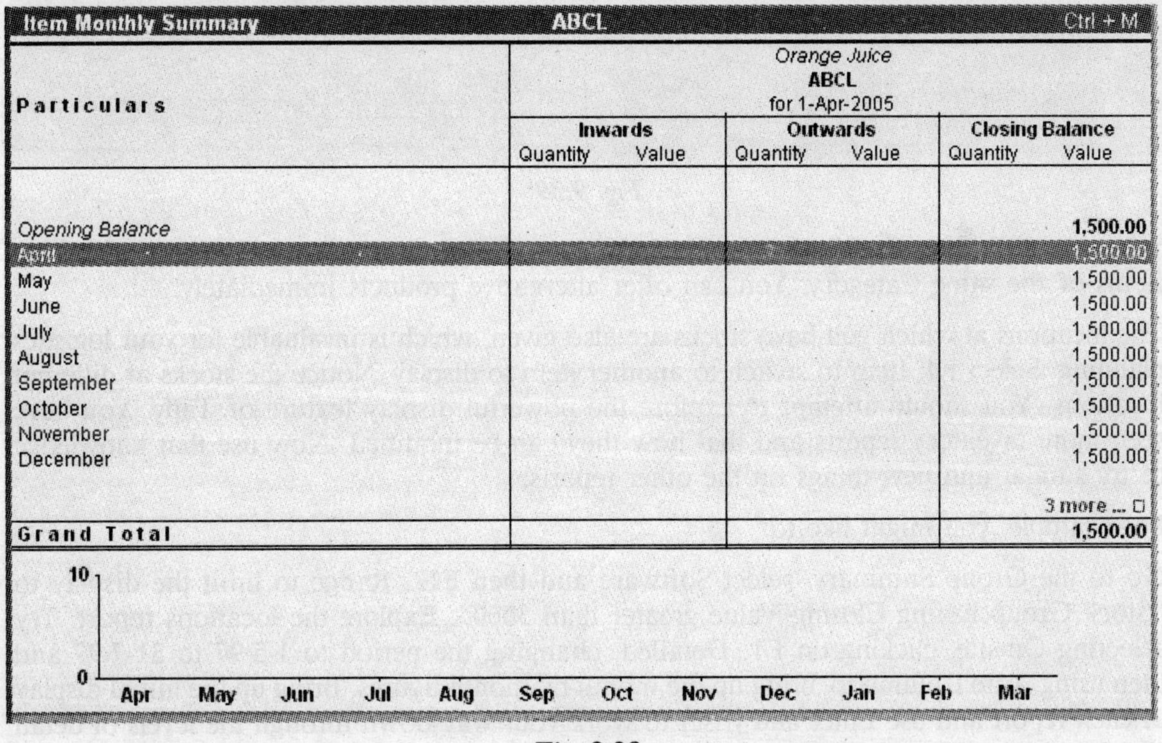

Item Monthly Summary — ABCL — Ctrl + M

Particulars	Orange Juice ABCL for 1-Apr-2005					
	Inwards		Outwards		Closing Balance	
	Quantity	Value	Quantity	Value	Quantity	Value
Opening Balance						1,500.00
April						1,500.00
May						1,500.00
June						1,500.00
July						1,500.00
August						1,500.00
September						1,500.00
October						1,500.00
November						1,500.00
December						1,500.00
						3 more ...
Grand Total						1,500.00

Fig. 9.38

Making a Stock Query

Stock query — the one place for all information on an item, as shown in Fig. 9.39.

For this select the following:

Gateway of Tally>Display>Statement of Inventory>Stock Query

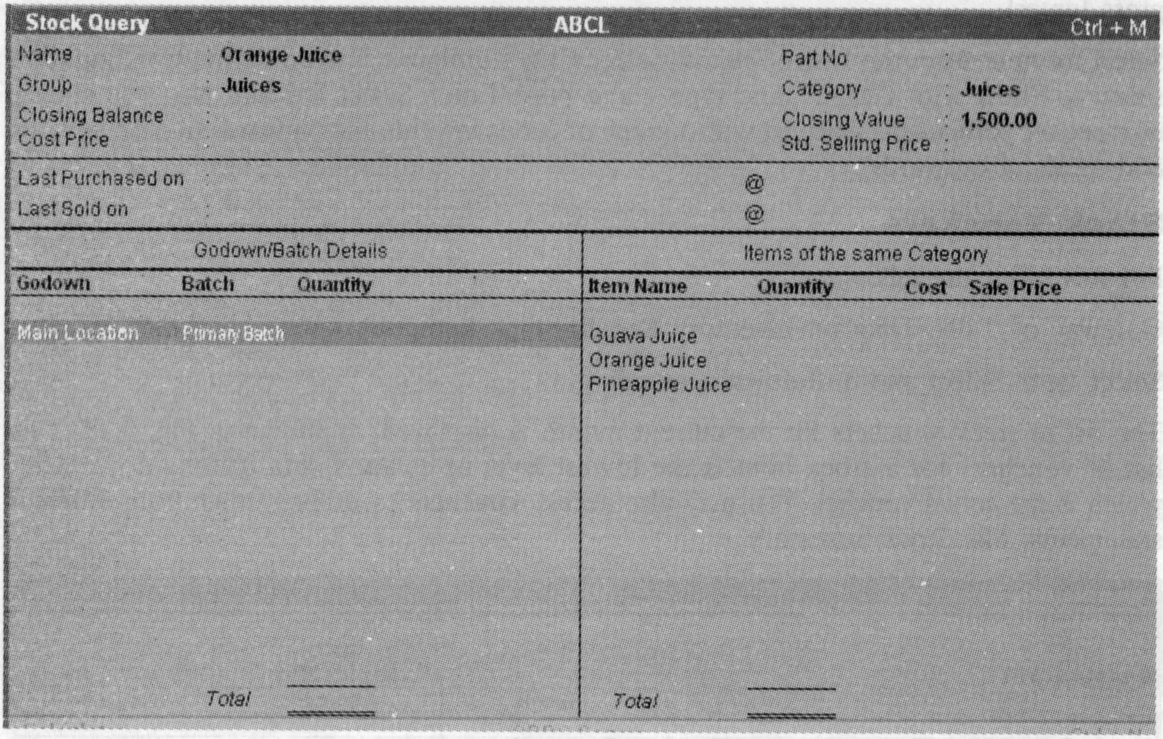

Fig. 9.39

Select an item, from the List of Items. Notice how Tally uses the Stock Category to display Items of the same Category. You can offer alternative products immediately.

The locations at which you have stocks are also given, which is invaluable for your logistics planning. Select F4: Item to switch to another item to display. Notice the stocks at different locations. You should attempt to explore the powerful display feature of Tally. You have seen more inventory reports and that how they can be modified. Now use that knowledge to try similar and new things on the other reports.

For example, you might like to:

Go to the Group Summary, select Software and then F12: Range to limit the display to "Stock Group having Closing Value greater than 3000". Explore the locations report. Try selecting On-site, clicking on F1: Detailed, changing the period to 1-5-97 to 31-7-97 and then using Auto Column to bring up the month-by-month figures. Bring up the initial display of each report and use Enter and [Esc] to work your way down through the levels of detail and back up again.

Analysis of Inventory Movements

The Analysis of Inventory Movements are done for Accounted Transactions only. This is in contrast to the details given through the Stock Summaries and other statements, where Goods Received but Bills not Received and Goods Dispatched but Bills not Raised are also considered. This difference may lead to slightly different figures and values in the Analysis statements. The purpose of these Statements are for comparative study and they should NOT be constructed as authentic Accounts or Inventory Statements.

For this select the following:

Gateway of Tally>Display – Inventory Books>Movement Analysis

You can analyse stock movements by stock groups or categories or even by financial group or ledger.

Movement Analysis (Stock Group Analysis)

Movement Analysis of a selected stock group brings up the Total Inward and Outward movement of all the items in the selected Stock Group. The Quantities shown are Actual Quantities of movement (which in some cases, may be different from the Billed Qty in the transactions). The Inward detail shows the Effective Rate or Final Landed Cost of the materials, after considering all overhead costs (see Valuation of Purchases). In case the Effective Rate is different from the basic Invoice rate of the materials, it is shown in Bold – to highlight a possible candidate for further study. The Outward detail shown the Basic Invoice Rate and Value of Goods sold/transferred out, as shown in Fig. 9.40.

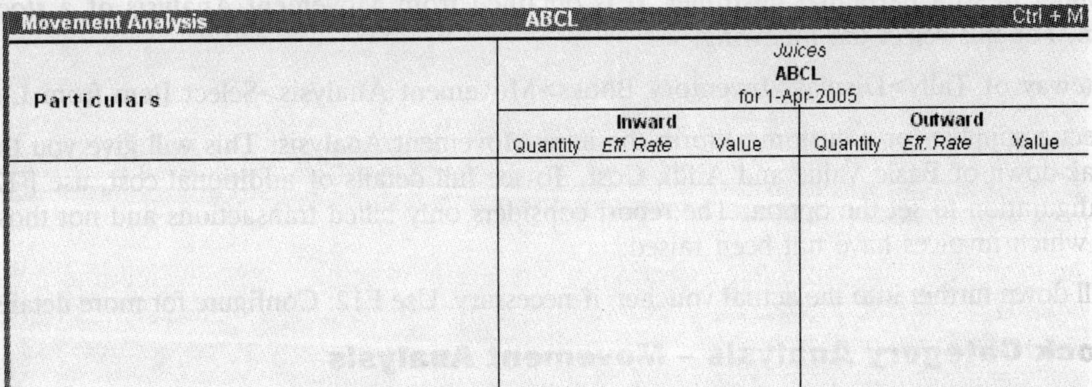

Fig. 9.40

Item Movement Analysis

Item Movement Analysis is the next level of information (press Enter on the stock Item or Display Inventory-Books Stock Item Analysis). This brings up the Party-wise/Transfer-wise detail of Movement In and Out. The Inward details show the Basic Invoice Rate as well as the Effective Rate.

This is a great comparative report to view the effect of Purchase costs from different suppliers. For example, Supplier A may have a loser Basic Invoice Rate as compared to Supplier B, but the Effective Rate may be higher – (perhaps due to differences in Taxes, Packing Costs, Freight Costs etc.) Similarly, in context where a material is both manufactured in-house, as well as purchased – the difference in Purchase Costs and In-house Costs can be compared. Lastly, by selecting multiple columns for different periods, you would get to see the changes in Effective Rate for your purchases. The next level of information (press Enter on the Party Name or Stock Journal Name), gives the transaction level detail of information. Here, the Date of goods received/sold, the Quantities, Basic Rates, Addl. Costs and Effective Rate for each transaction may be viewed Pressing Enter expands into the Date, Type and Number of the Vouchers which have contributed to this transaction. The default screen shows the Addl Costs (if any), put together in a single column. To view the spread of costs, press F12: Configure and select to view A: Addl Costs. This brings up the bifurcation of all Additional Costs entered (see Valuation of Purchases).

Item Voucher Analysis

This report gives value details of all transactions for a selected stock item from a particular supplier or to a particular customer. It is obtained from Movement Analysis of a stock item. For this select the following:

Gateway of Tally>Display>Inventory Books>Movement Analysis>Select Item from List

Select a supplier (or a customer) form the item Movement Analysis. This will give you the break-down of Basic Value and Addl. Cost. To see full details of additional cost, use F12: configuration to set the option. The report considers only billed transactions and not those for which invoices have not been raised.

Drill down further into the actual voucher, if necessary. Use F12: Configure for more details.

Stock Category Analysis – Movement Analysis

For this select the following:

Gateway of Tally>Display>Inventory Books>Movement Analysis>Category Analysis.

Select a category e.g. Primary. Change period, if necessary.

The Stock Category Analysis statement, as shown in Fig. 9.41, shows the movement of stock items of a particular selected stock category. In the example on the next page, the stock items, Lotus 1-2-3 and MS Excel belong to the Category Spreadsheets (though they are grouped under Software). The Inward and Outward movement of these two items are

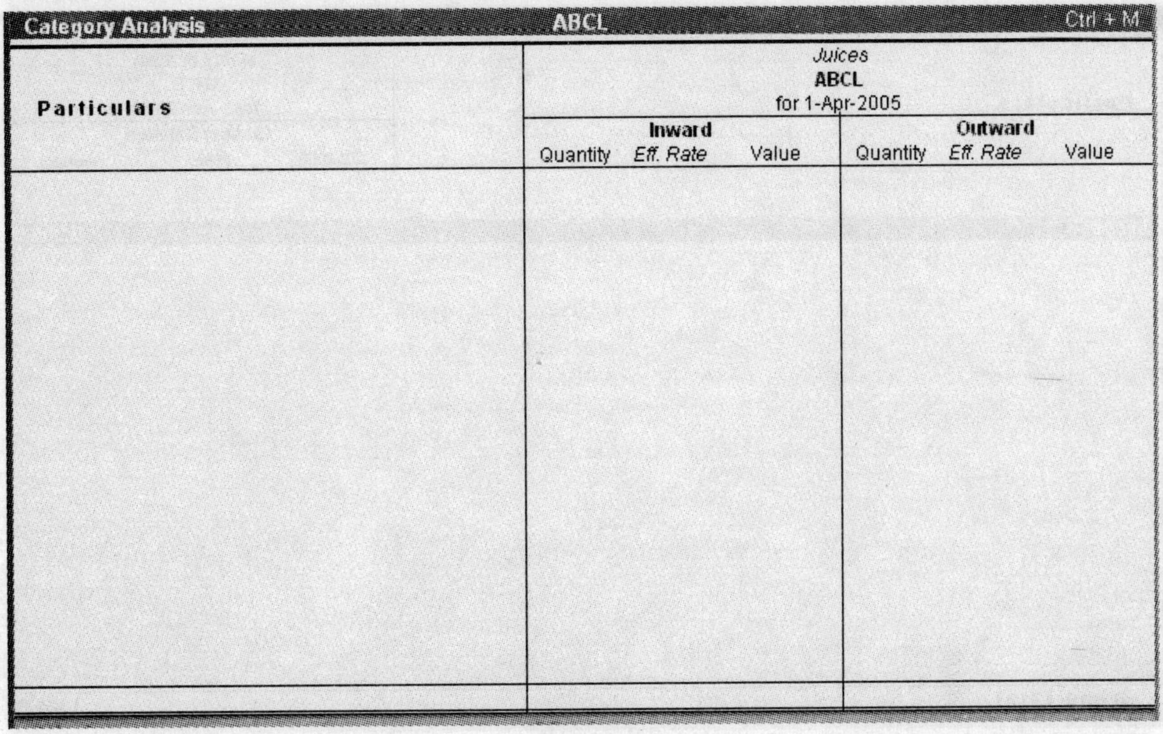

Fig. 9.41

summarized in the Summary. Drilling down will bring up the Item Movement Analysis for the selected item.

Ledger Analysis

Ledger Analysis is similar to Movement Analysis, except for bringing up the movements of the items for the selected Ledger (Party). Thus, you get an analysis of all purchases made from a supplier or all items sold to a customer. The next level of information brings up the transaction level detail.

Transfer Analysis

Transfer Analysis gives the movement details of each type of Stock Journal. This can be used powerfully by following a simple discipline of using different Stock Journal types for each nature of transaction. For example, Item A Prod Item B can be used for the production of Items A and B respectively. In this scenario, the report then represents the total of Item A produced, as well as the Raw Materials used for its production, with overhead costs (as entered). This becomes a very useful costing and waste analysis too. In non-manufacturing segments, but with Multiple Godown, this report becomes a quick check to verify that all transfer have been entered correctly – since the Total Movement In and Out must watch.

Godown Summary (Location Summary)

The Godown/Location Summary statement, as shown in Fig. 9.42, shows the Stock

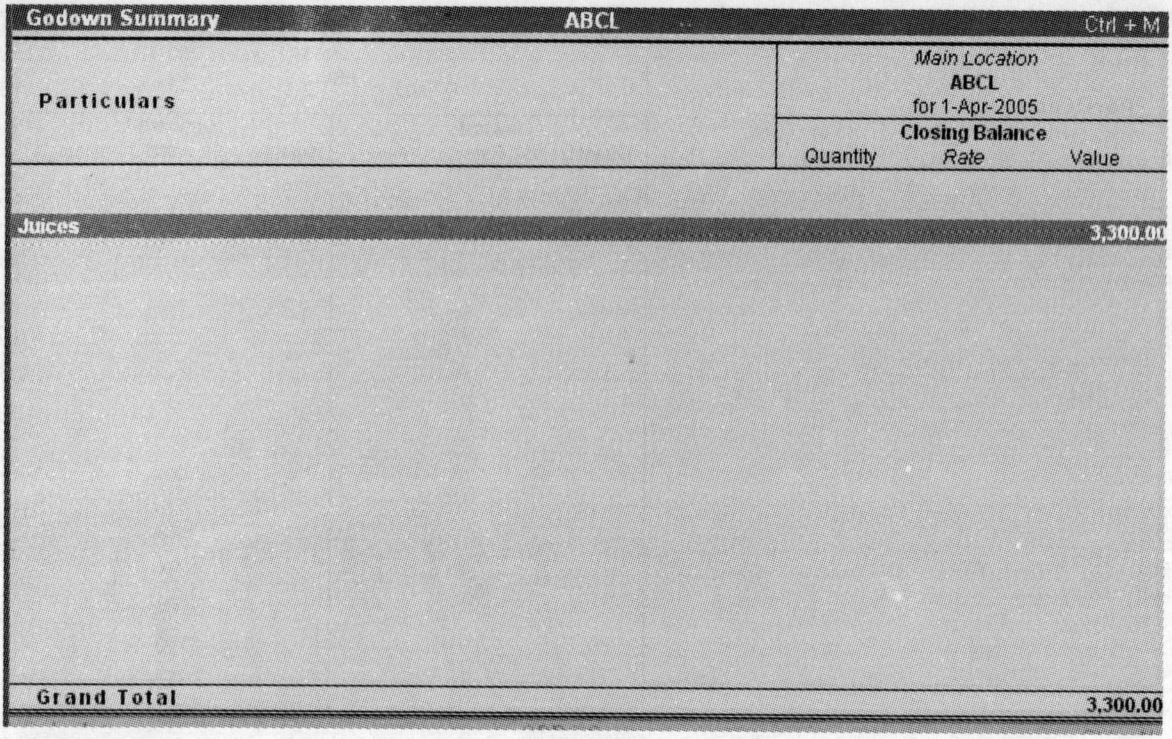

Fig. 9.42

Summary for different Godown/Locations. While the main Stock Summary shows the stock position for the entire company on a given date, the Godown/Location Summary is a statement of stock in hand at each location on a particular date. As with all Tally statements, it is updated with every transaction so that it provides current stock position for any godown/location at any time.

The statement can be drilled down as with all Tally reports and configured to view different details. It is also possible to see the total flow of stock for each location in a single report. Experiment with the different buttons for this purpose.

For this select the following:

Gateway of Tally>Display>Statement of Inventory>Godown/Location

Select Main Location. To view the summary for all Godowns/Locations.
Alternatively

Select a specific Godown/Location to limit information to that location/godown. The default display is that of Godown/Location to limit information to that location/godown. The default display is that of Godown/Location Group balances. Yes, you might have sub-groups of godowns/locations quite like sub-groups of stock items or any other Tally Master entity.

Select Detailed for second level of detail.

This could be a sub-group of godown/location or directly the stock groups under the godown/locations in cases where there are no godown/location sub-groups. In the above example, note the two godowns/locations with stock groups below them. Here, there are two stock groups, viz, Hardware and Software that have closing balances. The Godowns/Locations as well as Stock groups show total quantities. This is because the unit of measure is the same for all the stock items and they have been set up to enable aggregation of item quantities. The stock group Services, does not have any balances. This is because of the original set-up of the Services items, where stock is valued at Zero Cost and all sales are treated as Manufactured. Note that there is a grand total too because of a single unit of measure of all addable items. If there were different units of measure, then there would not be a grand total. In fact, there would not be a total quantity for the Godown/Location too. Two different units cannot be added.

Views of Godown/Location Summary Statement

Use options in the button bar to set up different information views. The buttons are similar to those available in Stock Summary. If there is negative balance, further investigation is possible by expanding the groups and zeroing down on the stock items at both the locations. Perhaps, there was an error in transfer of goods? Bring the cursor on Software and press SHIFT+ENTER to expand the group. This summary is shown in Fig. 9.43.

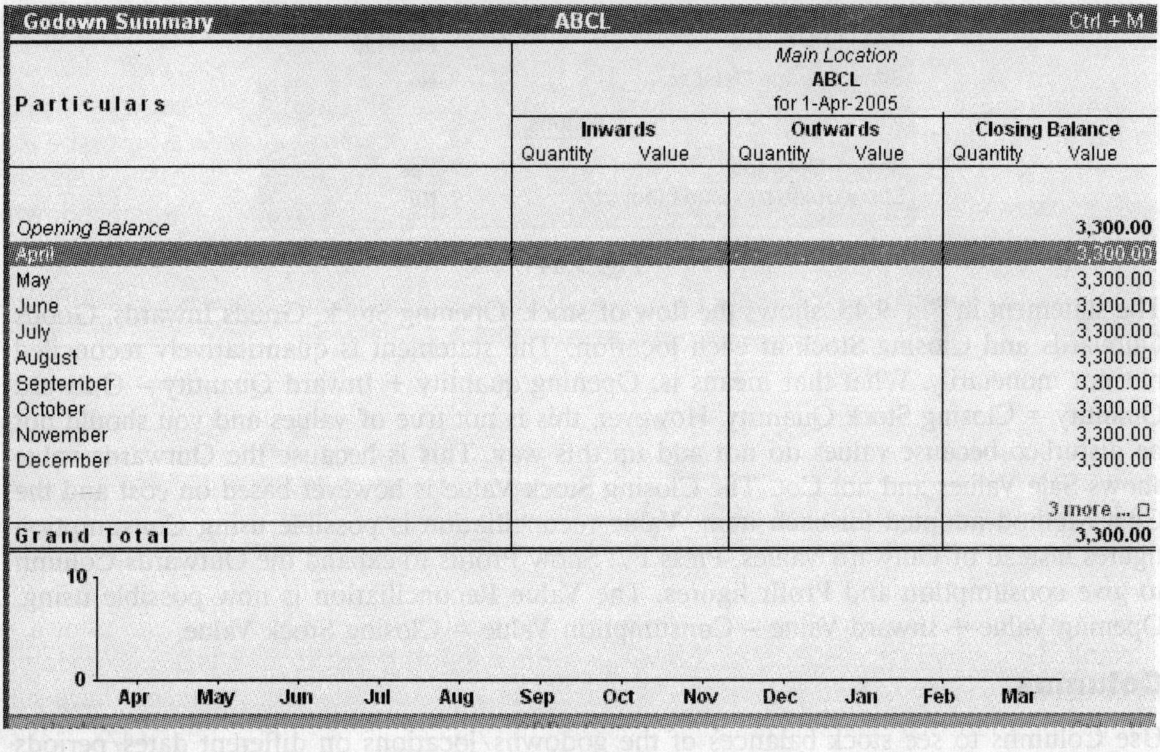

Fig. 9.43

Godown/Location Stock Flow/Reconciliation

The reconciled flow of goods at each location is available.

Select F12: Configure while in the Godown/Location Summary Screen. Set the options, in Fig. 9.44, as above to opt for Opening. Goods Inwards, Goods Outward and Closing Balances.

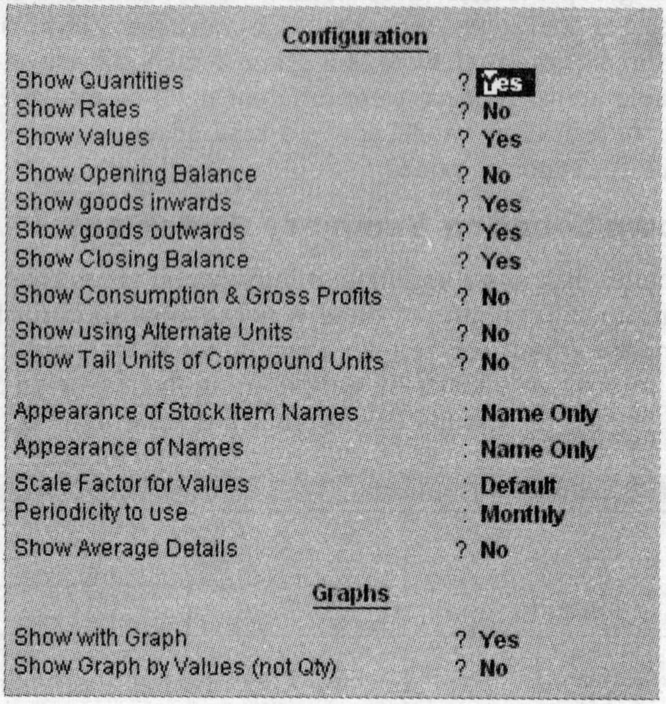

Fig. 9.44

The statement in Fig. 9.45, shows the flow of stock: Opening Stock, Goods Inwards, Goods Outwards and Closing Stock at each location. The statement is quantitatively reconciled but not monetarily. What that means is: Opening quantity + Inward Quantity – Outward Quantity = Closing Stock Quantity. However, this is not true of values and you should not be disturbed because values do not add up this way. This is because the Outwards value shows Sale Values and not Cot. The Closing Stock Value is however based on cost and the Cost Method adopted for each item. Value reconciliation is possible using Consumption figures instead of Outward Values. Press F7: Show Profits to expand the Outwards Column to give consumption and Profit figures. The Value Reconciliation is now possible using. Opening Value + Inward Value – Consumption Value = Closing Stock Value.

Columns

Use Columns to see stock balances of the godowns/locations on different dates/periods or other options. If you have selected a specific Godown/Location on different dates/periods or other options. If you have selected a specific Godown/Location to display, you can still bring up information of the other godown(s)/location(s) in column.

Godown Summary	ABC & Company						Ctrl + M
Particulars	Stores ABC & Company 1-Apr-2001 to 31-Mar-2002						
	Opening Balance		Inwards		Outwards		Closing Balance
	Quantity	Value	Quantity	Value	Quantity	Value	Quantity	Value
Accounting Software	**35 pcs**	**17,500.00**	**405 pcs**	**4,26,300.00**	**380 pcs**	**4,92,500.00**	**60 pcs**	**66,192.68**
Tally Ees 6.3-Multiuser	*10 pcs*	*5,000.00*	*20 pcs*	*39,800.00*	*15 pcs*	*33,750.00*	*15 pcs*	*22,400.00*
Tally Ees 6.3-Singleuser	*25 pcs*	*12,500.00*	*385 pcs*	*3,86,500.00*	*365 pcs*	*4,58,750.00*	*45 pcs*	*43,792.68*
Maxell	**5 pcs**	**18.75**	**600 pcs**	**2,400.00**	**225 pcs**	**1,125.00**	**380 pcs**	**1,519.21**
Maxell Disk Cleaning Kit	*5 pcs*	*18.75*	*600 pcs*	*2,400.00*	*225 pcs*	*1,125.00*	*380 pcs*	*1,519.21*
Maxell Disk 3.5'								
Metal Links	4,500 Nos	40,500.00	57,870 Nos	5,76,675.00	61,076 Nos	10,61,161.00	1,294 Nos	12,804.62
Software		**6,375.00**		**8,975.00**	**167 pcs**	**58,625.00**		**8,615.63**
Microsoft Products		6,375.00		8,975.00	167 pcs	58,625.00		8,615.63
Sony	**10 packs**	**150.00**					**10 packs**	**150.00**
Sony 3.5'	10 packs	150.00					10 packs	150.00
Grand Total		**64,543.75**		**10,14,350.00**		**16,13,411.00**		**89,282.14**

Fig. 9.45

Select New Column or Auto-Column for such displays.

The above statement is obtained by selecting

Auto-Column>Location

And Show Total column

Different reports are available from the Stock Item Monthly Summary including different periodicity and Average stocks. Drill down an item in the Stock or Godown/Location Summary level to the Item Monthly Summary and use F12: Configure options.

Godown/Location Vouchers

For this select the following:

Gateway of Tally>Display>Statement of Inventory>Godowns/Locations

Select a Godown/Location. Select Item.

Godown/Location Vouchers is a list of all vouchers for a selected item that have a relation to the selected Godown/Location during the period of display. The relationship could be a stock in our out of the particular location. This statement is useful when you want to list all transactions for a particular Godown/Location.

Batch Information in Summary Statements

To view the stock of batches of an item:

Gateway of Tally>Stock Summary

This could even be the Godown/Location Summary.

Expand the Stock Group using Detailed or SHIFT + ENTER till it you get the Items displayed. Use SHIFT+ENTER to reveal the Batches and their stock position. Use F12: Configure to use Opening Balances, Goods Inwards and Goods Outwards.

Sales Bills Pending

For this select the following:

Gateway of Tally>Display>Statement of Inventory>Sales Bills Pending

Purchase Bills Pending

For this select the following:

Gateway of Tally>Display>Statement of Inventory>Purchase Bills Pending

AGED STOCK ANALYSIS (AGEING ANALYSIS)

A very important function of Working Capital management is monitoring stocks. Money locked up in stocks can adversely affect the liquidity of company and every company strives or should strive to reduce stock levels to the optimum.

Every business (except perhaps the liquor and antiques dealers) would prefer to dispose of older stocks as they might deteriorate with time, go out of fashion or simply get forgotten. Tally's aged stock analysis or Stock ageing enables you to know the age of stocks in hand according to when they were received and the purchase value.

Ageing Analysis

For this select the following:

Gateway of Tally>Display>Inventory Books>Ageing Analysis

Select the Group of Stock Items to be analysed

Item Inward Details

For this select the following:

Gateway of Tally>Display>Inventory Books>Ageing Analysis

Scenario Management

Scenario management is a management tool that enables different views of your information, both accounts and inventory related, by selectively including certain types of vouchers without affecting the base data. This is useful in reports with provisional figures without

Stock Ageing Analysis | **ABCL** | Ctrl + M

Items Under: **Juices** — **as at 1-Apr-2005**

All Batches (Aged by Date of Purchase) — *Valued based on Actual Purchase*

Particulars	Expiry Date	Total	< 45 days		45 to 90 days		90 to 180 days		> 180 days	
		Quantity	Quantity	Value	Quantity	Value	Quantity	Value	Quantity	Value
Grand Total										

Fig. 9.46

actually putting the entries through the main books. It is also useful for forecasting by entering forecast figures in provisional vouchers and including them to get forecasted figures.

The vouchers that are used in Scenario Management are:

1. Optional Vouchers
2. Memorandum Vouchers
3. Reversing Journals

In this section we will dwell on the way we can use these vouchers in Reports.

You can create a number of scenarios each including and/or excluding one or more types of these voucher entries. Hence, you may have one scenario that is used for reporting monthly figures in which you have to report depreciation provided for the month as well as account for all accruals and outgoings. Obviously, you do not wan to put through your books journal entries for this purely temporary reporting. Of course the entries are available for reference in separate registers. You would decided to include Reversing Journals for Provisional monthly reporting, as shown in Fig. 9.47.

Create a Scenario

Ensure that you have activated the option Use Reversing Journals and Optional Vouchers in F11: Company Features.

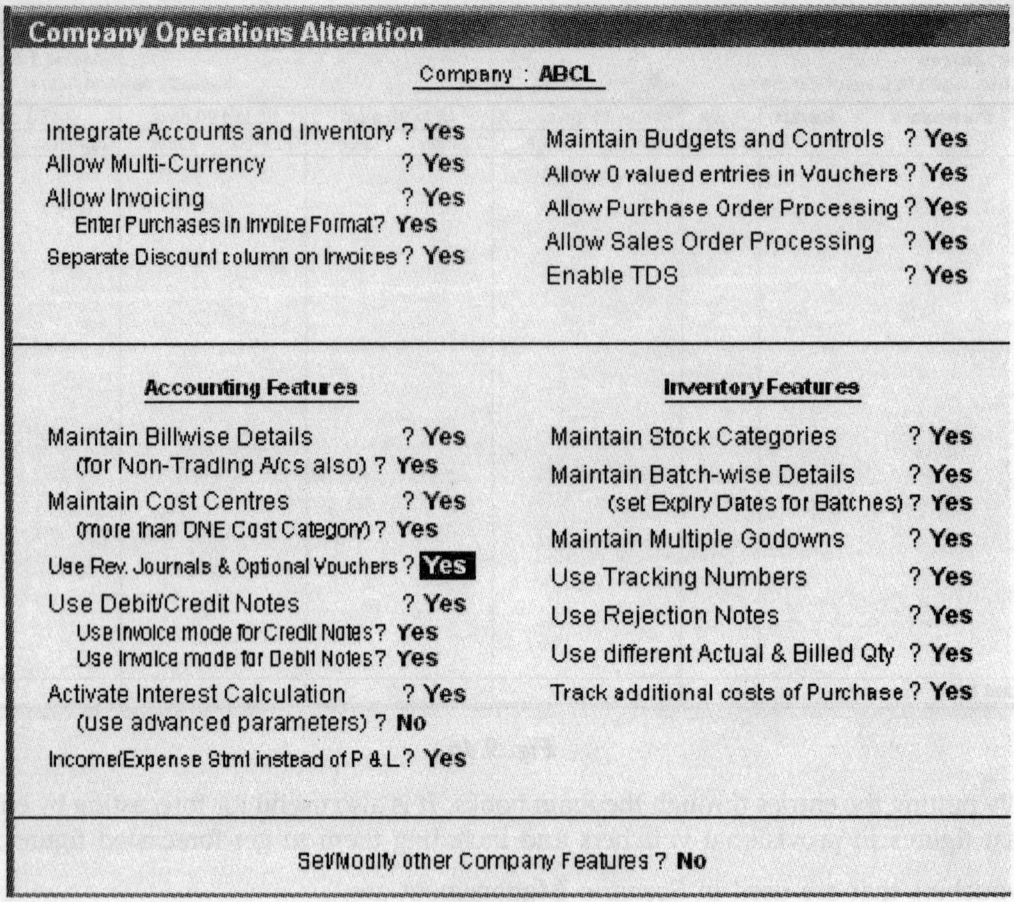

Fig. 9.47

Now select the following.

Gateway of Tally>Accounts Info>Scenario>Create

Here you need to fill up the following information, in the Fig. 9.48.

Name

Give a suitable name to the scenario. In this case, we give Provisional

Include Actuals

Yes, if you want the report to

Exclude Forex Gains/Losses Calculations

Yes, If you do not want the Unadjusted Forex Gain/Loss element to appear in the scenario. No if you want it to appear.

Include

Include from the list of vouchers, the type of vouchers that you want to affect this scenario.

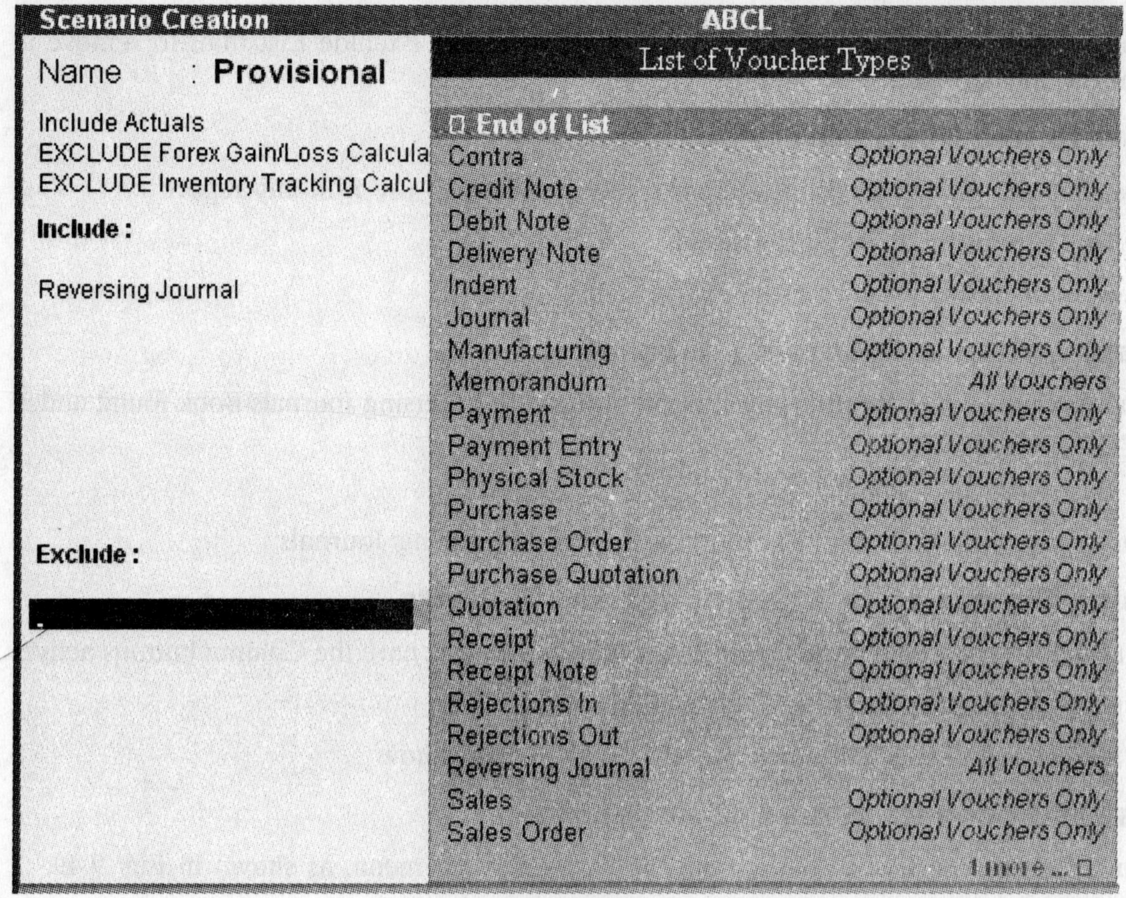

Fig. 9.48

Notice that it picks up the Voucher Types created for this company. Only provisional vouchers are permitted for selection Normal vouchers that are marked Optional are available but not those not marked Optional are available but not those not marked as such. They would affect the books of account.

Exclude

Include from the list of vouchers already included under Include above, the type of vouchers that you DO NOT want to affect this scenario. You would use this typically later in Alter mode and hence is discussed under Alter or Display Scenario Information. Accept to create this scenario.

Alter or Display Scenario Information

For this select the following:

Gateway of Tally>Accounts Info>Scenario>Alter

Exclude

You would use the Alter mode when you do not require a selected included voucher anymore to affect the scenario. It is easier for you put that in the Exclude List than to remove it from the Include List.

How to use Scenarios

Now that you have created one scenario, you are ready to use it in any report.

But first let's create a reversing journal.

Gateway of Tally>Voucher Entry>F10: Memo

Display/Alter a Reversing Journal

You can view or alter the reversing journal through the Reversing Journals Book found under Exceptional Reports.

For this select the following:

Gateway of Tally>Display>Exceptional Reports>Reversing Journals

Using Scenarios in Statements and Reports

You can use scenario in most statements (not registers) that have the Column buttons active.

Display the Balance Sheet. Select New Column

IN the column details, tab down to Types of Values to Show

List of Accounts (Chart of Accounts)

You create the chart of accounts from the Accounts Info menu, as shown in Fig. 9.49.

However, to view an existing chart, select the following:

Gateway of Tally>Display>List of Accounts

List of Groups	List of Cost Categories
List of Cost Centres	List of Budgets
List of Locations	List of Stock Groups
List of Stock Items	List of Currencies
List of Units	List of Voucher Types

Exception Reports

Exception reports are reports that track unusual transactions or balances. The different Exception Reports are:

Gateway of Tally>Display>Exception Reports

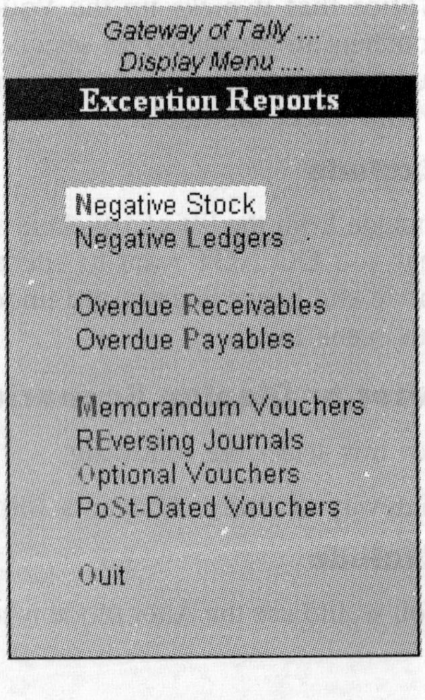

Negative Stock

For this select the following:

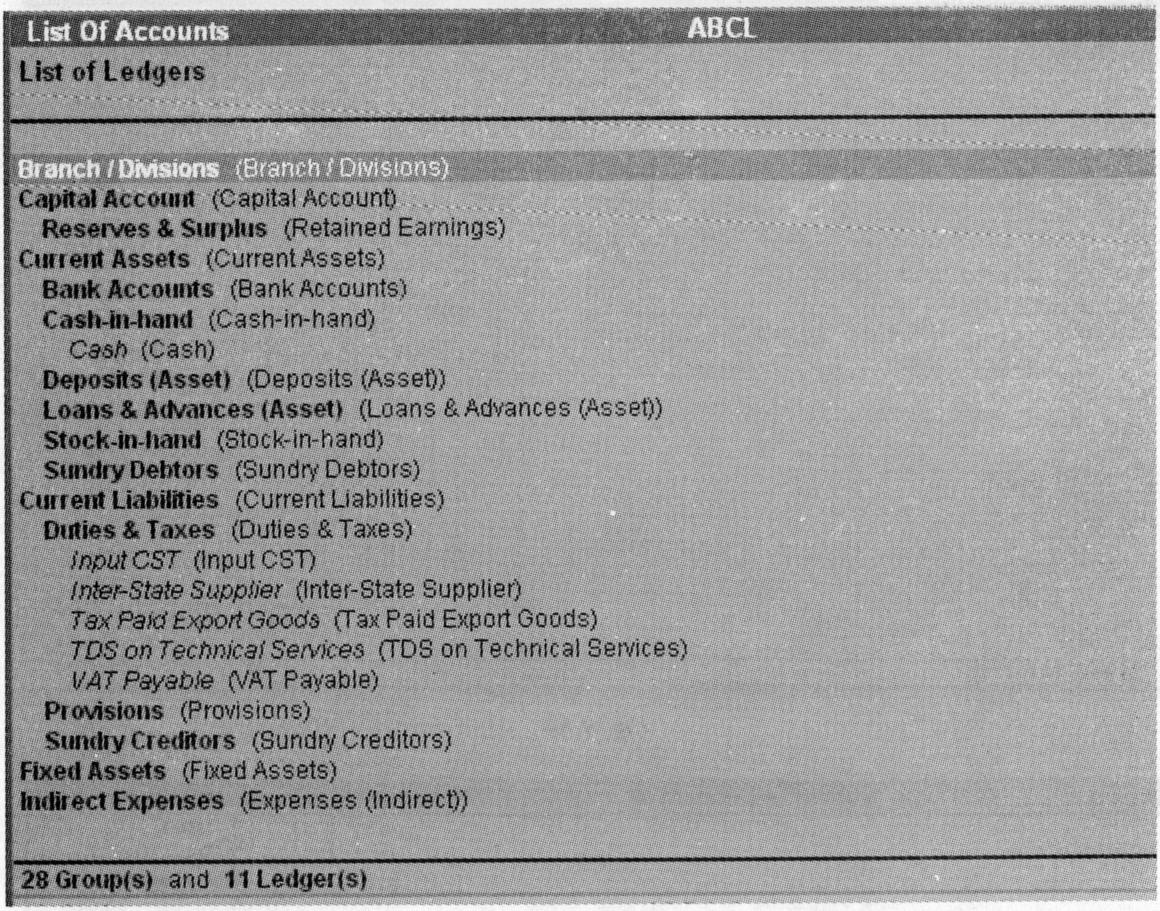

Fig. 9.49

Gateway of Tally>Display>Exception Reports>Negative Stock

This can be seen in Fig. 9.50.

Negative Ledgers

For this select the following:

Gateway of Tally>Display>Exception Reports>Negative Ledgers

This can be seen in Fig. 9.51.

Overdue Receivables

For this select the following:

Gateway of Tally>Display>Exception Reports>Overdue Receivables

This can be seen in Fig. 9.52.

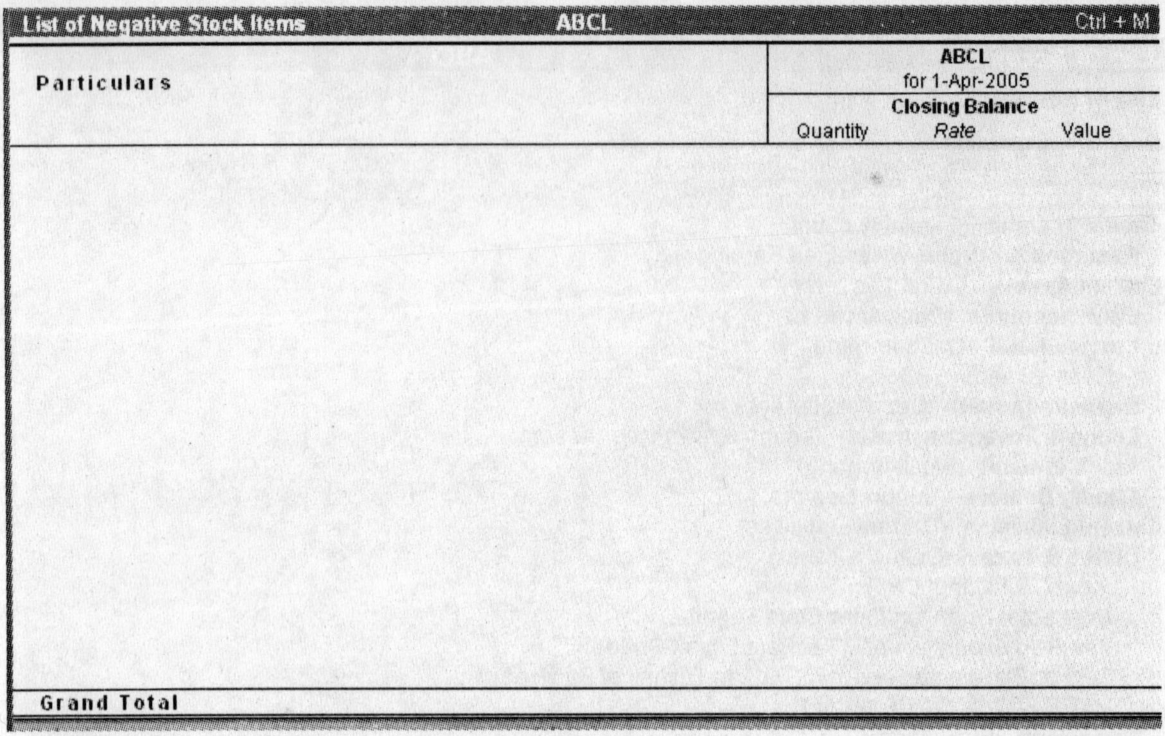

Fig. 9.50

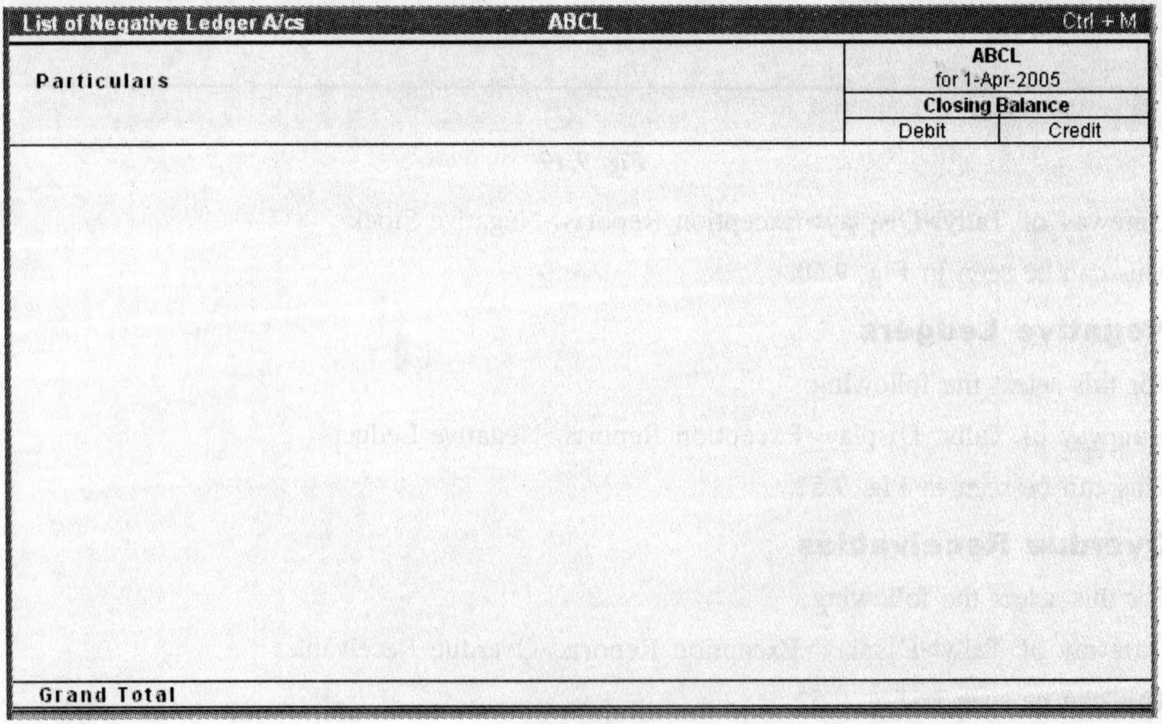

Fig. 9.51

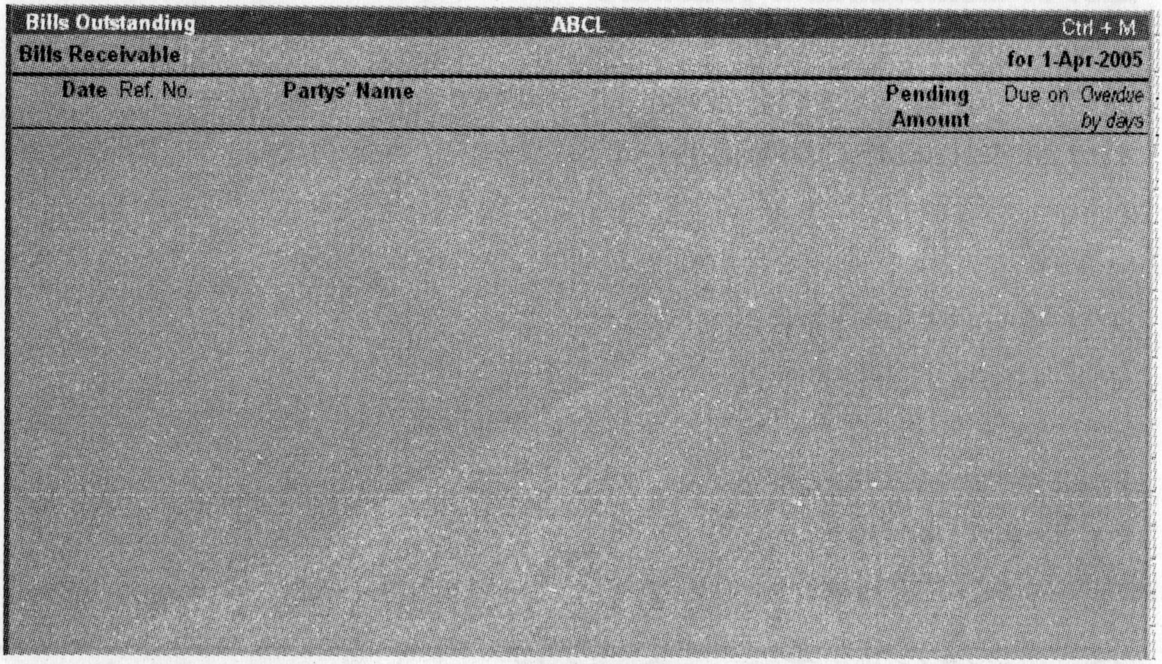

Fig. 9.52

Overdue Payables

For this select the following:

Gateway of Tally>Display>Exception Reports>Overdue Payables

This is shown in Fig. 9.53.

Fig. 9.53

List of Memorandum Vouchers

For this select the following:

Gateway of Tally>Display>Exception Reports>Memorandum Vouchers

List of Reversing Journals

For this select the following:

Gateway of Tally>Display>Exception Reports>Reversing Journal

List of Optional Vouchers

For this select the following:

Gateway of Tally>Display>Exception Reports>Optional Vouchers

Post-dated Vouchers

For this select the following:

Gateway of Tally>Display>Exceptions Reports>Post-dated Vouchers

Descriptive Type Questions

1. Describe the various options of printing reports.
2. Describe the function of various buttons on the print screen.
3. Describe the various options of printing reports.
4. What is Multi-Account printing?
5. Describe the various forms of printing Balance Sheet.
6. How would you configure the Balance Sheet?
7. How would you print Columunar Balance Sheet?
8. How would you show Quarterly Balance Sheet?
9. What are the various options of printing Profit and Loss Account?
10. How would you print Profit and Loss statement in columns?
11. How would you display Trail Balance?
12. Describe the various items of the Day book?
13. What do you understand by Cash flow and Fund flow?
14. How would you reconcile Bank accounts?

10 Fringe Benefit Tax in Tally

FRINGE BENEFIT TAX

Fringe Benefit Tax was introduced as part of Finance Act, 2005 as an additional income-tax and came into force from April 1, 2005.

The term Fringe Benefits means 'any consideration for employment provided by way of any privilege, service, facility or amenity provided by the employer to the employees'.

Fringe Benefit Tax is to be levied on the employer in respect of fringe benefits provided/ deemed to be provided by the employer to his employees during any financial year commencing on or after 1.4.2005

Fringe Benefit Tax is payable at the rate of 30% of the value of fringe benefits computed in the manner prescribed under the Section 115WC.

SALIENT FEATURES OF FBT

Some of the features of FBT are listed as follows:

Fringe Benefit Tax payable by an employer is in respect of perquisites or fringe benefits provided or deemed to have been provided by the employer to his employees in addition to the cash salary or wages paid during the year.

Fringe Benefit Tax is levied in addition to the Income-Tax charged.

Fringe Benefit Tax is payable at the specified rate on the value of fringe benefits provided to the employees. The value of fringe benefits is calculated in accordance with the provisions of Section 115WC of the Income-Tax Act, 1961.

An employer has to pay Fringe Benefit Tax even if no Income-Tax is payable on the total income.

Like any other direct tax, Fringe Benefit Tax is not an allowable expenditure for the purpose of computation of taxable income.

IMPORTANT POINTS RELATING TO FRINGE BENEFIT TAX

Some of the important points to be observed in FBT:

- Rate is calculated on Net Expenses.
- Expenses are not to be segregated between 'Paid to Employees' and 'Paid to Outsiders'.

- Depreciation is calculated on the basis of Income Tax.
- FBT is applicable on Service Tax paid on any of the expenditure chargeable to FBT.
- Payment of FBT in case employers have employees based both in and outside India.
- Medical reimbursement upto Rs. 15,000 per employee is charged to FBT.
- Applicability of FBT in case an employer is engaged in two or more business activities.
- Different rates of tax on the Fringe Benefits provided by different industries.
- FBT is not payable on Advance paid.
- Tax Rate is 30% + Surcharge @10% + Education Cess @ 2%.
- One Ledger may have expenditure relating to different groups under FBT.

CHARACTERISTICS OF FBT

Some of the characteristics of FBT are:

- It is a tax on expenditure, not income.
- It is a tax on employer, not employees.
- It is a surrogate tax on employers.
- It cannot be recovered from the employees.
- It is to tax benefits that are usually enjoyed collectively by the employees and cannot be attributed to individual employees.
- A combination of presumptive and non-presumptive approaches has been adopted.

CLASSIFICATION OF EMPLOYER FOR FBT

Under FBT, an Employer is defined as any of the following:

- Company
- Firm
- Association of Persons or a Body of Individuals (except Fund or Trust or institution eligible for exemption under section 10(23C) or registered under section 12AA)
- Local Authority
- Every Artificial judicial person, not falling within any of the above

CLASSIFICATION OF NOT EMPLOYER FOR FBT

The following are not included as Employer under FBT:

- An Individual (i.e., Proprietorship concern)
- Hindu Undivided Family

- Association of Persons or a Body of Individuals exempt under section 10(23C) or registered under section 12AA
- Central Government
- State Government

DIRECT FRINGE BENEFIT

Direct Fringe Benefit as classified under section 115(WB) (1) means:

- Any privilege, service, facility or amenity, which is directly or indirectly provided by an employer to his employees (including former employee or employees).
- Any free or concessional tickets provided by the employer for private journeys to employees or their family members.
- Any contribution by the employer towards an approved superannuation fund for employees.
- Any reimbursement, which is directly or indirectly made by the employer to employees for any purpose

DEEMED FRINGE BENEFIT

The Fringe Benefits are deemed to have been provided if the employer incurs any expenditure or makes any payment in the course of business or profession. This includes any activity whether or not such activity is carried on with the object of deriving income, profits or gains. Any expenditure incurred or payment made for the following constitutes deemed fringe benefit.

- Entertainment
- Hospitality
- Conference
- Sales promotion including publicity
- Employee welfare
- Conveyance, tours and travel
- Hotel, boarding, lodging
- Repair, running and maintenance of cars
- Repair, running and maintenance of aircraft
- Use of telephone
- Maintenance of any accommodation in the nature of guest house
- Festival celebrations

- Health Club
- Any other club
- Gifts
- Scholarship to employees' children
- Consumption of fuel other than industrial fuel

PAYMENT OF FBT TO THE GOVERNMENT

In accordance with the provisions, the FBT should be paid in advance during any financial year and the regular assessment of fringe benefits is to be made in a later assessment year.

Advance Fringe Benefit Tax

Every assessee who is liable to pay advance tax has to pay tax on the current fringe benefits calculated in the manner laid down.

The amount of advance tax payable in the financial year is 30% of the value of the fringe benefits paid or payable in each quarter. This is payable on or before the 15th day of the month following each quarter except for the quarter ending 31st of March.

For the quarter ending on the 31st of March of the financial year, the amount of advance tax (on an estimated value) is to be paid on or before the 15th of March for the financial year.

If tax is not paid or the tax paid is less than the prescribed rate, the assessee is liable to pay simple interest at the rate of 1% on the amount by which the advance tax paid falls short.

FILING OF FBT RETURN

An employer who has paid or made provision for payment of fringe benefits to his employees during the previous year is required to furnish a return of fringe benefits in the prescribed form and manner to the Assessing Officer before the due date.

For a company as an employer the due date is the 31st of October of the assessment year.

For a person who is an employer but not a company and whose accounts are required to be audited, the due date is the 31st of October of the assessment year.

For any other employer, the due date for filing the return of fringe benefits is the 31st of July of the assessment year.

After the due date, the Assessing Officer may issue a notice to the assessee requiring him to furnish a return in the prescribed form and manner within a period of thirty days.

Failure to furnish a return of fringe benefits or delayed filing of such return will result in the levy of interest at the rate of 1% for each month of delay or till the assessment is made on the amount of tax on the value of fringe benefits.

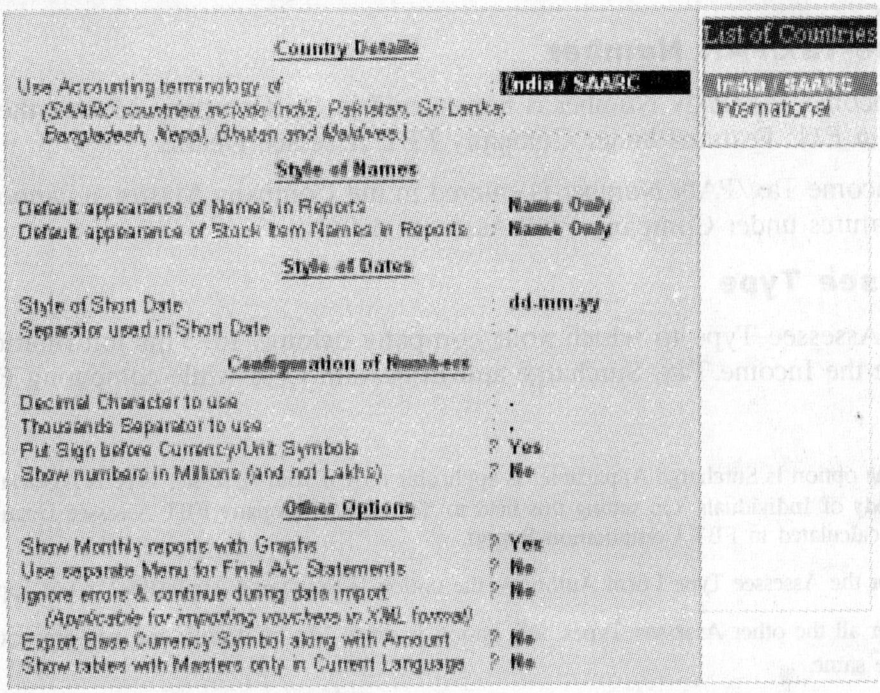

ENABLE FBT IN TALLY

Configuration of FBT

Set the option Use Accounting terminology of as India/SAARC in the F12: Configuration screen.

F11: Features

You can enable Fringe Benefit Tax (FBT) by using the F11: Features screen.

1. Go to Gateway of Tally > F11: Features > Statutory & Taxation
2. Set the option Enable Fringe Benefit Tax (FBT)to Yes
3. Set Set/Alter FBT Details to Yes. The Company FBT Assesse Details sub form appears as shown.

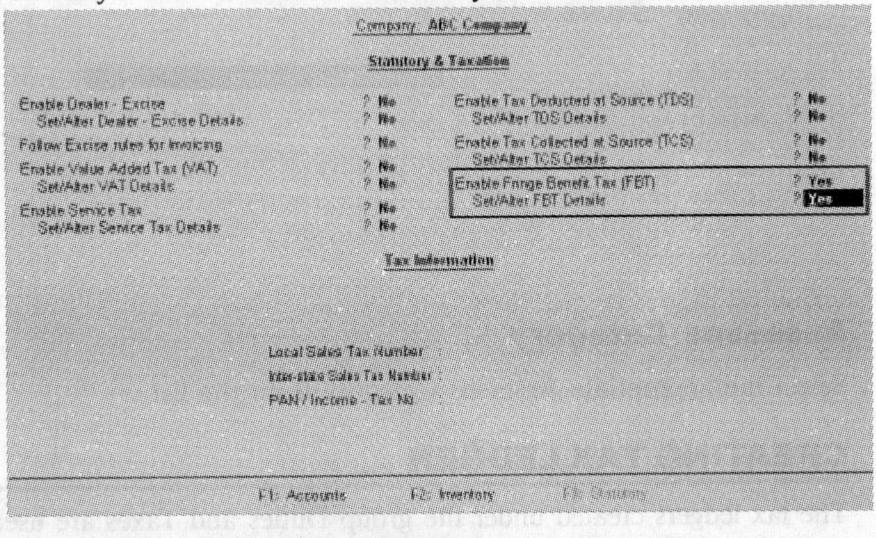

Income-Tax/PAN Number

If the Income Tax/PAN Number is not entered in the Company Master, the same can be entered in F11: Features under Company FBT Assessee Details.

If the Income Tax/PAN Number is entered in the Company Master, it cannot be edited in F11: Features under Company FBT Assessee details.

Assessee Type

Set the Assessee Type to which your company belongs to. This information is used to calculate the Income Tax, Surcharge and Education Cess while computing FBT.

Note:

- The option Is Surcharge Applicable? is applicable only if your Assessee Type is Association of Persons/ Body of Individuals. On setting this field to Yes in the Company FBT Assessee Details, the surcharge is calculated in FBT Computation Report.
- For the Assessee Type Local Authority, the option Is Surcharge Applicable? is not applicable.
- For all the other Assessee Types, this option is set to Yes by default and you are not allowed to edit the same.

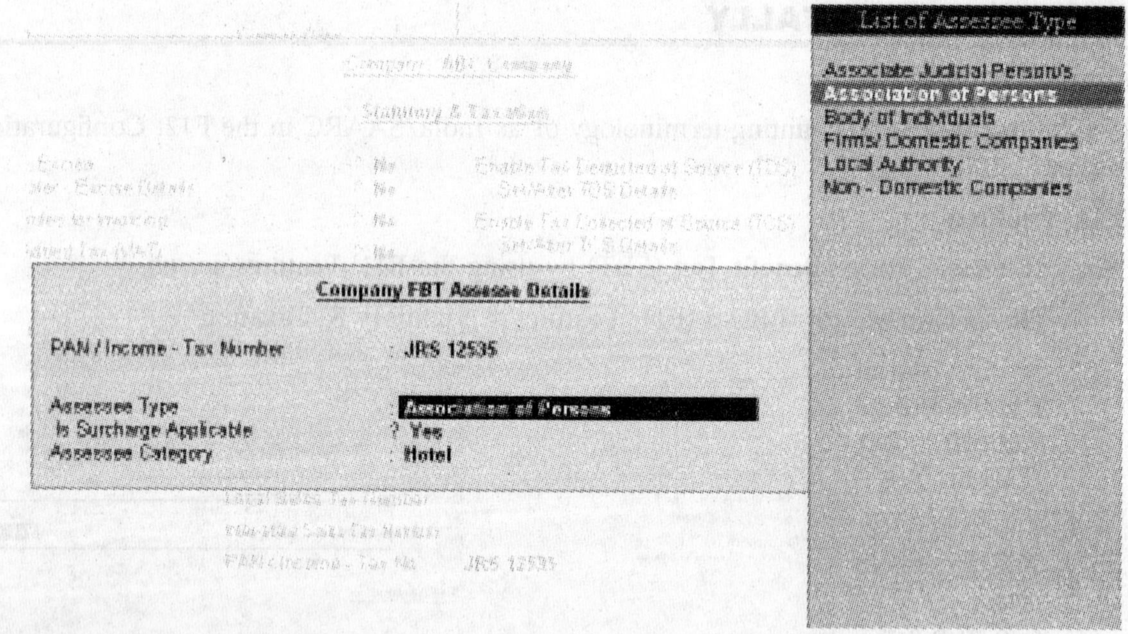

Assessee Category

Select the appropriate Assessee Category from the list.

CREATING TAX LEDGER

The tax ledgers created under the group Duties and Taxes are used for calculation of tax.

Tax Ledger is used in FBT payment.

To create a Tax Ledger,

- Go to Gateway of Tally > Accounts Info. > Ledgers > Create
- Enter the Name of the tax ledger
- Select the group Duties & Taxes from the List of Groups
- Select FBT from the list of Types of Duty/Tax

CREATING A PARTY LEDGER

Create ledgers for Party/Suppliers under the group Sundry Debtors/Sundry Creditors.

To create an FBT Party Ledger,

- Go to Gateway of Tally > Accounts Info. > Ledgers > Create
- In the Ledger Creation screen, enter the name of the party in the Name field
- In the Under field, select Sundry Creditors/Sundry Debtors
- If required, set Maintain balances bill-by-bill? to Yes. Enter details in the Default Credit Period, if applicable. By default, the Inventory Values are affected? field is set to No.
- Accept and Save.

CREATING AN EXPENSE LEDGER

All the expense ledgers are to be created under the group Indirect Expenses. The group Indirect Expenses is used for booking expenses.

To create an FBT Expense ledger,

- Go to Gateway of Tally > Accounts Info. > Ledgers > Create
- Enter the Name of the expense ledger
- Select the group Indirect Expenses from the List of Groups
- When Is FBT Applicable? is set to Yes, the field Default FBT Category? will be displayed. You have to select the appropriate FBT Category from the List of FBT Categories.
- Accept Yes to save the ledger

CREATING/ALTERING FBT VOUCHER TYPE

To create or alter a FBT Voucher type such as Journal

Go to Accounts Info. > Voucher Types > Create/Alter > Journal

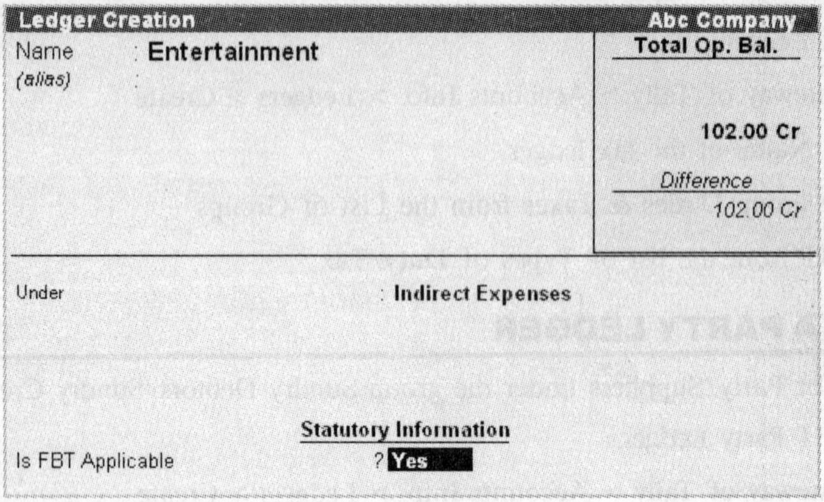

In the Voucher Type Alteration screen, Type the Name of Class. For example, Fringe Benefit Recovery.

The following screen displays.

Set Use Class for FBT Recovery to Yes and Accept the screen.

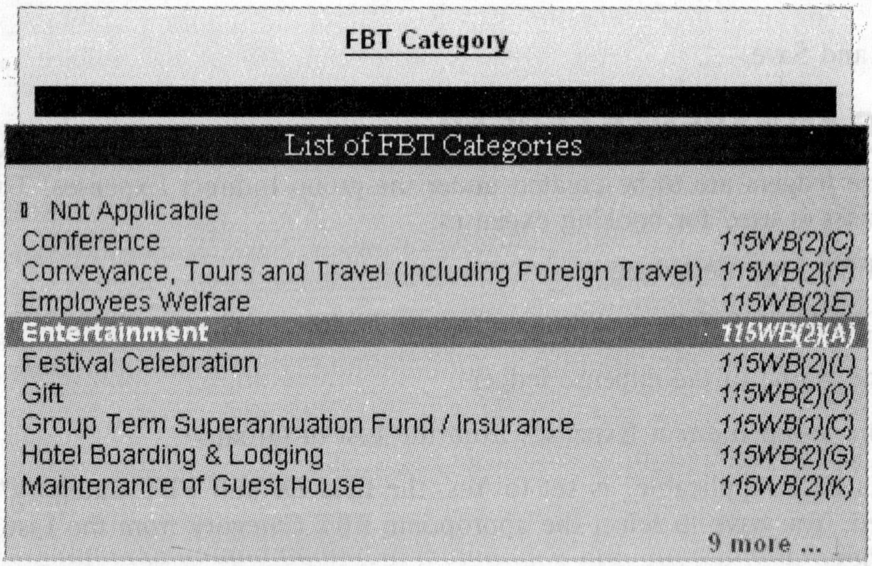

CREATING FBT VOUCHERS

There are various vouchers created for FBT. They are mentioned next.

Creating FBT Journal without a Class

Go to Gateway of Tally > Accounting Vouchers > F7: Journal

Select Entertainment from the list and enter the amount in the debit column

Select the Party (Supplier) from the list. Amount appears automatically in the Credit column

Creating FBT Journal with a Class

To create a Journal Voucher using a Voucher Class,

1. Go to Gateway of Tally > Accounting Vouchers
2. Select F7: Journal button from the button bar or press the F7 key. Select the class as Fringe Benefit Recovery from the list Class Table.
3. The FBT Journal voucher screen displays as shown. This provides the recovery details from an employee and the same appears in the FBT Computation report.
   - Debit the Supplier
   - Credit the Expenses incurred

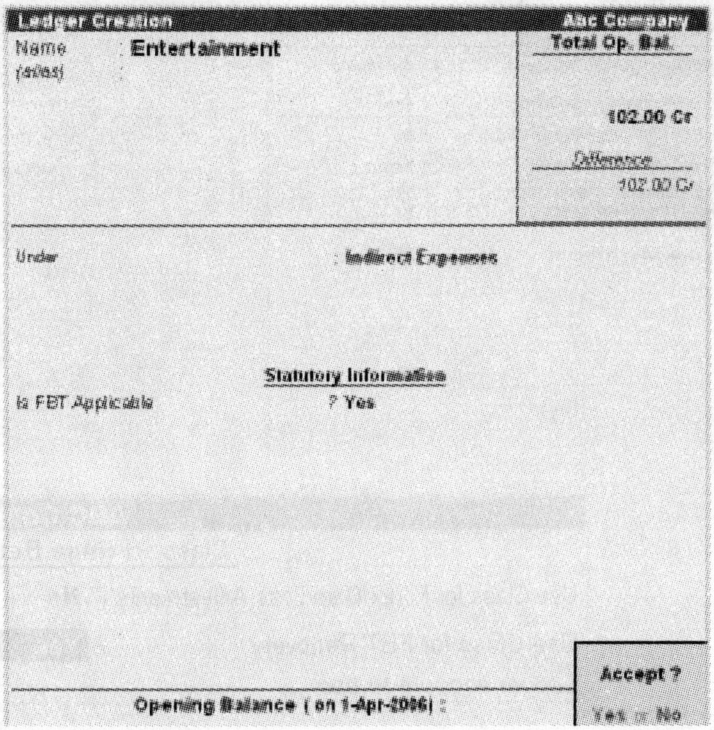

4. Enter the narration, if required
5. Accept the voucher to save

Creating a Payment Voucher to Book Expenses for FBT

To create a FBT Payment voucher,

1. Go to Gateway of Tally > Accounting Vouchers
2. Select F5: Payment from the Accounting Voucher Creation screen
3. Enter the Date
4. Select FBT Ledger in Particulars from the List of Ledger Accounts. The FBT Category sub screen displays. Select the appropriate category from the list of FBT Categories and enter the amount.
5. Credit Bank or Cash through which the payment is to be made against the FBT Ledger.
6. Enter Narration, if required
7. Accept to save

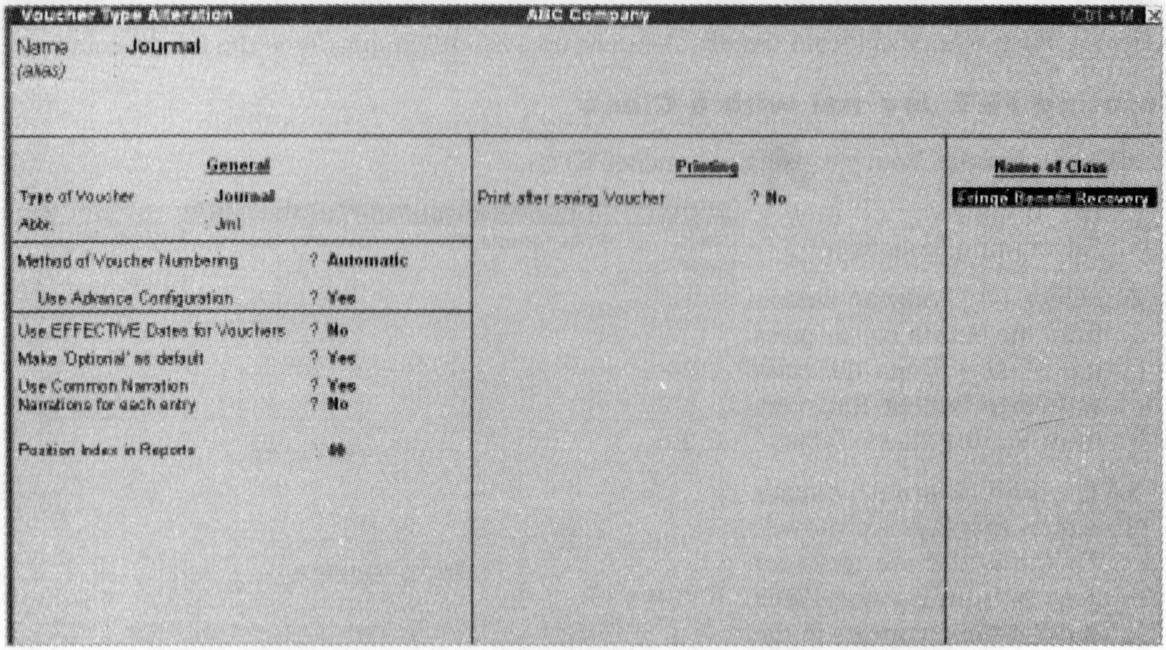

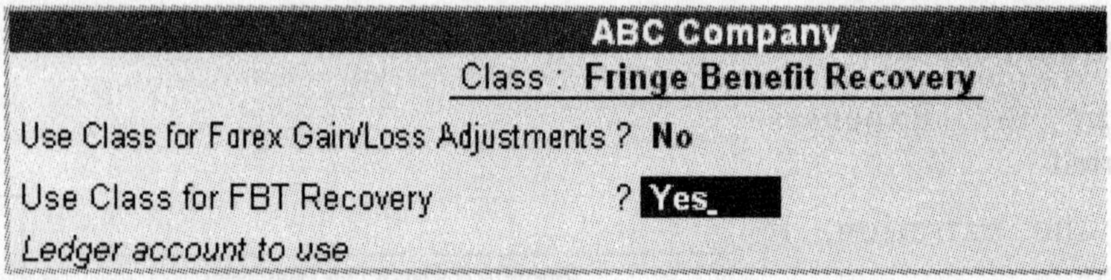

Creating a Payment Voucher without FBT Helper Button

1. Go to Gateway of Tally > Accounting Vouchers
2. Select F5: Payment in the Accounting Voucher Creation screen
3. Select the Bank/Cash from the list
4. Select the FBT Ledger from the list and enter the amount
5. On selecting the FBT Ledger, the field FBT Details displays above the Narration field. Set FBT Details to Yes
6. On setting FBT Details to Yes, the following screen displays
7. Enter the FBT Filter details and Accept to save the payment voucher screen

Creating a Payment Voucher with the FBT Helper Button

Payment of FBT can be made using FBT Helper button. Payment will be calculated only on the vouchers which are between the From Date and To Date.

FBT Helper feature is available only if Use Single Entry mode for Pymt/Rcpt/Contra? in F12: Configure (Voucher Configuration) is set to Yes.

1. Go to Gateway of Tally > Accounting Vouchers
2. Select F5: Payment in the Accounting Voucher Creation screen
3. Press Alt + F or click FBT Helper from the button bar to view the FBT Filters sub screen
4. Select the Type of Payment from the list. The selection will be reflected in the Challan

   For example, if Advance Tax (100) is selected in the payment filter, Advance Tax is automatically marked (x) in the FBT Challan.
5. Select the ledger from the List of FBT Ledgers
6. Enter the From Date and To Date to select the period for computing payment and for the generation of FBT Challan
7. Select the Bank ledger from the List of Ledger Accounts, which is to be credited in the Payment Voucher
8. Enter Narration, if required
9. Click Print button or press Alt+ P to print FBT Challan, if required
10. Accept to save

Printing FBT Challan

You can Print the FBT Challan for a FBT Payment voucher created manually or using the FBT helper button.

To print a FBT Challan,

1. Press Alt + P or click Print from the button bar in the Payment Voucher screen to view the Voucher Printing screen
2. Press Backspace to navigate from Print Yes or No? and move the cursor to Print as FBT Challan?
3. Set Print as FBT Challan to Yes
4. Accept the sub screen to save

Note:

- If the option Print as FBT Challan is set to Yes then Default Payment Challan and Cheque will not be printed.
- Ensure you click With Preview button or press Alt+ I to view the FBT Challan in Print Preview mode

Creating a Purchase Voucher

To create a Purchase Voucher,

- Go to Gateway of Tally > Accounting Vouchers
- Select F9: Purchase from the button bar or press F9
- Select As Voucher/As Invoice
- Enter the Date and Reference
- Credit the party ledger from the List of Ledger Accounts
- Select the expenses from the List of Ledger Accounts and debit the same. The FBT Category sub screen displays. Select the appropriate category from the list of FBT Categories and enter the amount
- Enter Narration, if required
- Accept to save

Creating a Debit Note

A Debit Note for FBT can be entered in Voucher or Invoice mode.

Set the option Use Debit/Credit Notes to Yes in F11: Features.

To create a Debit Note,

- Go to Gateway of Tally > Accounting Vouchers
- Select F9: Debit Note from the button bar or press Ctrl + F9
- Select As Voucher/As Invoice
- Enter the Date and Reference
- Debit Cash from the List of Ledger Accounts
- Select the Party from the List of Ledger Accounts and credit the same
- Enter Narration, if required
- Accept to save

FBT COMPUTATION

FBT Computation lists only those categories for which ledgers are created and transacted.

To view the FBT Computation screen,

Go to Gateway of Tally > Display > Statutory Reports > FBT Reports > FBT Computation

FBT Payment Details

Set the option Show FBT payment Details to Yes in F12: Configure for the payment details to be displayed in the FBT Computation screen.

FBT Computation — ABC Company — Ctrl + M

FBT Computation

1-Apr-2006 to 30-Apr-2006

Particulars	Expenditure Amount	Amount Recovered	Nett Expenditure	Percentage as per Sec 115WC	Value of Fringe Benefit
Conveyance, Tours and Travel (Including Foreign Travel)	2,000.00	20,000.00	22,000.00	20 %	4,400.00
Entertainment	38,400.00	12,500.00	25,900.00	20 %	5,180.00
Festival Celebration	30,000.00	30,000.00	60,000.00	50 %	30,000.00
Gift	50,000.00	40,000.00	90,000.00	50 %	45,000.00
Hotel Boarding & Lodging	55,000.00	45,000.00	10,000.00	20 %	2,000.00
Maintenance of Guest House	10,000.00	8,000.00	2,000.00	20 %	400.00
Use of Telephone	8,000.00	5,000.00	13,000.00	20 %	2,600.00
Total	1,93,400.00	29,500.00	2,22,900.00		89,580.00
Fringe Benefits Tax (User defined Ledger) @ 30 %					26,874.00
Surcharge @ 10 %					2,687.40
Education Cess @ 2 %					591.23
Total Tax Payable					30,152.63

The screen displays as shown above.

Less: Advance Tax Paid

The value in this field is taken from all the Payment vouchers with the FBT Ledger and Type of payment marked as Advance Tax (100) with the appropriate period.

FBT Computation — ABC Company — Ctrl + M

FBT Computation

1-Apr-2006 to 30-Apr-2006

Particulars	Expenditure Amount	Amount Recovered	Nett Expenditure	Percentage as per Sec 115WC	Value of Fringe Benefit
Conveyance, Tours and Travel (Including Foreign Travel)	2,200.00	20,000.00	22,000.00	20 %	4,400.00
Entertainment	38,400.00	12,500.00	25,900.00	20 %	5,180.00
Festival Celebration	30,000.00	30,000.00	60,000.00	50 %	30,000.00
Gift	50,000.00	40,000.00	90,000.00	50 %	45,000.00
Hotel Boarding & Lodging	55,000.00	45,000.00	10,000.00	20 %	2,000.00
Maintenance of Guest House	10,000.00	8,000.00	2,000.00	20 %	400.00
Use of Telephone	8,000.00	5,000.00	13,000.00	20 %	2,600.00
Total	1,93,400.00	29,500.00	2,22,900.00		89,580.00
Fringe Benefits Tax (User defined Ledger) @ 30 %					26,874.00
Surcharge @ 10 %					2,687.00
Education Cess @ 2 %					591.00
Less: Advance Tax Paid					25,000.00
Less: Self Assessment Tax Paid					
Less: Tax Paid on Regular Assessment					
Total Tax Payable					5,152.96

Less: Self Assessment Tax Paid

The value in this field is taken from all the Payment vouchers with the FBT Ledger, Type of payment marked as Self Assessment Tax (300) with the appropriate period.

Less: Tax paid on Regular Assessment

The value in this field is taken from all the Payment vouchers with the FBT Ledger and Type of payment marked as Tax On Regular Assessment (400) with the appropriate period.

Section Code

Set the option Show Section Code to Yes in F12: Configure if the Section code is to be displayed in the FBT Computation screen.

This is shown in the next screen, on the next page.

Expenditure Amount

This field displays the amount that is spent on the FBT marked Indirect Expenses like Entertainment, Conveyance, and so on.

Amount Recovered

The amounts that are recovered from the employees towards the expenses incurred are displayed here.

FBT Computation — ABC Company — Ctrl + M

FBT Computation — 1-Apr-2006 to 30-Apr-2006

Particulars	Section Code	Expenditure Amount	Amount Recovered	Nett Expenditure	Percentage as per Sec 115WC	Value of Fringe Benefit
Conveyance, Tours and Travel (Including Foreign Travel)	115WB(2)(F)	7,020.00	20,000.00	27,020.00	20 %	4,420.00
Entertainment	115WB(2)(A)	38,400.00	12,500.00	25,900.00	20 %	5,180.00
Festival Celebration	115WB(2)(L)	30,000.00	30,000.00	60,000.00	50 %	30,000.00
Gift	115WB(2)(O)	50,000.00	40,000.00	90,000.00	50 %	45,000.00
Hotel Boarding & Lodging	115WB(2)(G)	55,000.00	45,000.00	10,000.00	20 %	2,000.00
Maintenance of Guest House	115WB(2)(K)	10,000.00	8,000.00	2,000.00	20 %	400.00
Use of Telephone	115WB(2)(J)	8,000.00	5,000.00	13,000.00	20 %	2,600.00
Total		1,93,400.00	29,500.00	2,22,900.00		89,580.00
Fringe Benefits Tax (User defined Ledger) @ 30 %						26,874.00
Surcharge @ 10 %						2,687.00
Education Cess @ 2 %						591.00
Less: Advance Tax Paid						25,000.00
Less: Self Assessment Tax Paid						
Less: Tax Paid on Regular Assessment						
Total Tax Payable						5,152.00

Nett Amount

The difference between the amount incurred on the Indirect Expenses and the amount recovered from the Employee is the Nett Amount.

Percentage as Per Sec 115WC

The percentage of Rate of Tax of FBT Category (Enabled in F11: Features) for the respective FBT category is displayed in this field.

Value of Fringe Benefit

The Percentage obtained as per sec 115WC on Nett Amount for the respective category is the value of Fringe Benefit.

FBT LEDGER CATEGORY

From the FBT Computation screen press Enter on any particular FBT Category to drill down to a report that displays all the ledgers marked with respective FBT Category.

Consider the FBT Category Entertainment – under the Section 115WB (2) (A)

Name of the Ledger

Name of the ledger marked with above mentioned FBT Category is displayed here.

Expenditure Amount

The amount spent towards Entertainment - 115WB (2) (A) and accounted for a particular ledger is displayed here.

Amount Recovered

The amount that has been recovered from the employees towards the expenses incurred is displayed here.

Nett Expenditure

The difference between the amount spent on Entertainment and the amount recovered from the Employee is the Nett Amount.

Percentage as Per Sec 115WC

The percentage of the Rate of Tax of Company Assessee Category (enabled in F11: Features) for the respective FBT category is displayed in this field.

Value of Fringe Benefit

The percentage obtained as per sec 115WC on Nett Amount for the respective category is the value of Fringe Benefit.

FBT

Tax is calculated on the value of fringe benefits. Rate of tax is extracted from FBT Assessee Type master for the selected Assessee Type in F11: Features.

For example, if Assessee Type is Association of Persons/Body of Individuals then, Income Tax Rate is 30%, Surcharge is 10 % and Education Cess is 2%.

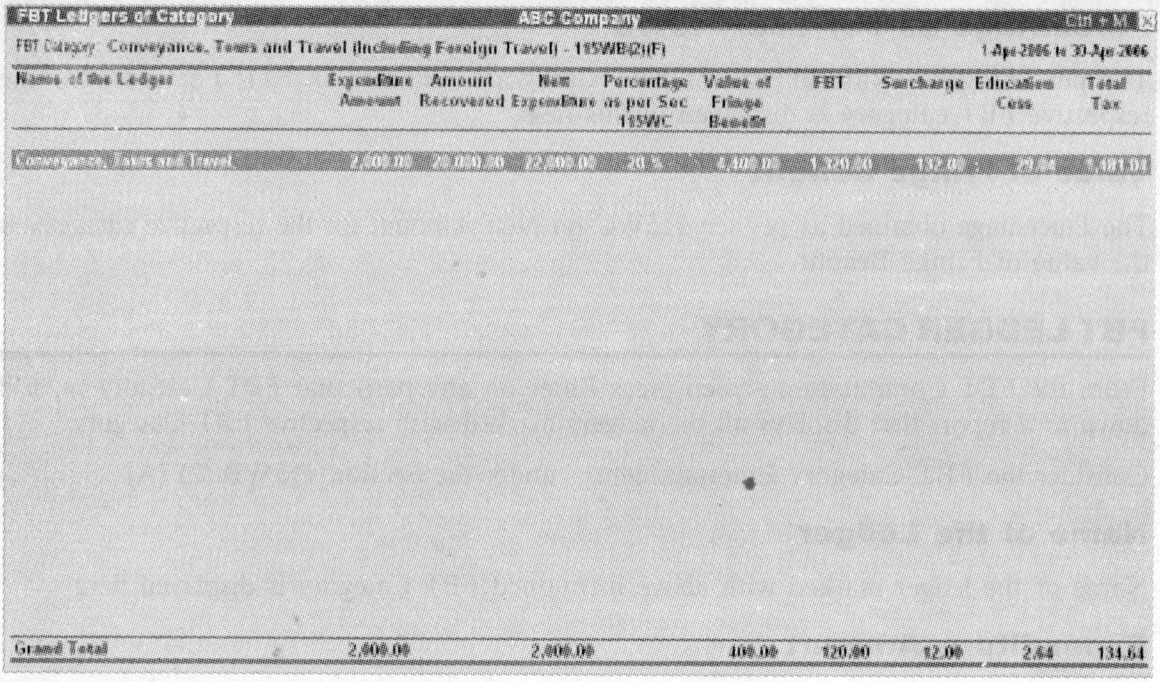

The percentage will vary for different Assessee Types.

Surcharge

Surcharge is calculated on Fringe Benefit Tax Amount and is extracted in the same way as Rate of Tax.

Education Cess

Education Cess is calculated on the sum of value of Income Tax and Surcharge. Additional Surcharge Rate/Cess Rate is also extracted in the same way as Rate of Tax.

Total Tax

This is the total of the Income Tax, Surcharge and Education Cess percentage values.

Descriptive Type Questions

1. What is FBT?
2. How does Tally 8.1 hande it?
3. What are the characteristics of FBT?
4. What do you mean by Direct and Deemed Fringe Benefit?
5. How are Fringe Benefit Ledgers created?
6. How are Fringe Benefit Vouchers created?
7. How is Fringe Benefit Tax computed?

11 The Collaborative Tally

EXPORTING DATE FROM TALLY

Tally has three formats for export of data from E-mail, Export and Upload options:

ASCII (Comma-delimited)

HTML (Web-publishing)

XML (Data-interchange)

ASCII

American Standard Code for Information Interchange (ASCII) is a plain-text format, without any special formatting or fonts, in which data is separated using commas. Commonly used for email and all email programs, ASCII data can also be easily worked upon by other programs.

HTML

Reports in Hyper Text Markup Language (HTML) format retain their formatting and fonts. They can be read using an HTML-enabled mail program, or using browsers such as Microsoft Internet Explorer.

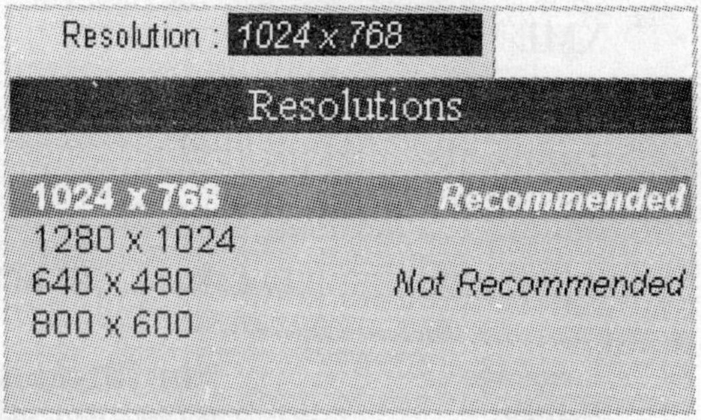

Resolution (Only in HTML format)

Resolution is based on the pixels used to format the report. A higher resolution gives a better quality of output. The Resolution option is available only in HTML format in Tally.

XML

Extensible Markup Language (XML) is an extension of HTML, but the data can be imported by other XML-aware systems. Using XML, Tally allows the user to exchange information even with systems that do not run Tally. An XML file from Tally has an XML envelope and is formatted with XML tags, to enable import into other systems. The destination system requires re-formatting of XML Style Sheets (XSLT), based on the inherent style used in Tally before importing the data. When two systems are running different versions of Tally, XML data can be directly imported using the import menu option, without any re-formatting.

Data from Tally in XML format can be imported by another system with ease in lesser time.

XML is fast emerging as the de facto standard for information exchange all over the world. This format helps the user to collaborate and share information with others.

By default, the exported file will be saved in the Tally folder on your computer. To export to a different folder enter the path of the drive and folder in Output File Name. Another program can be used to import the content from the exported file or used as it is.

EXPORT MASTER DATA

Master Data from Tally can be exported using the export feature to be imported in to another program.

To export Masters from Tally go to Gateway of Tally > Display > List of Accounts

Use Alt+E or click on Export from the button bar. This displays the Report Generation screen. Press Backspace or No to change the default values.

Language

Select the language in which you would like the data exported

Format

Select from the three formats available.

ASCII

HTML

XML

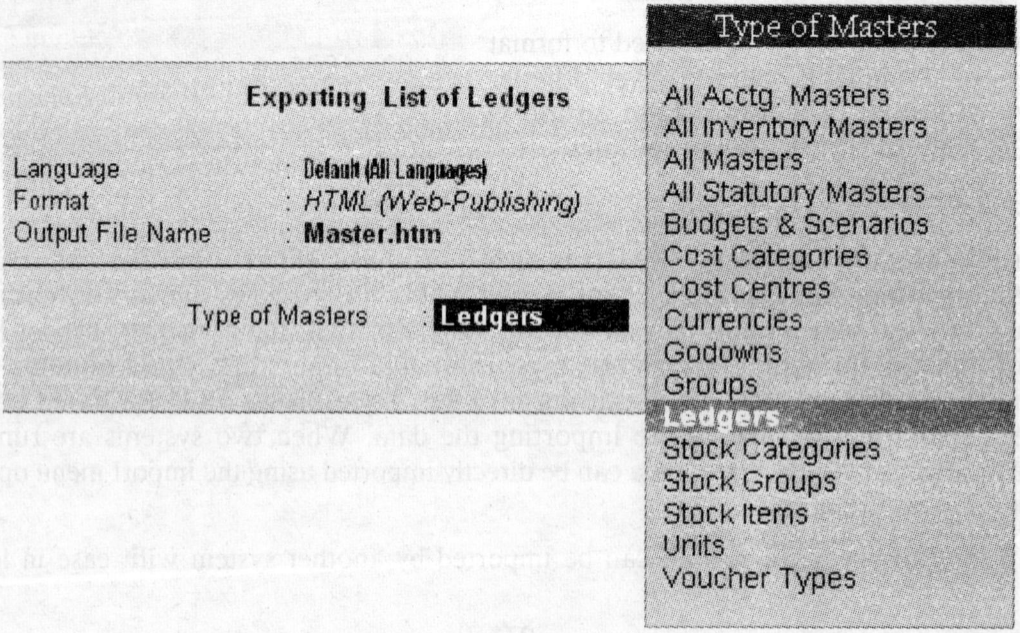

Select HTML to publish or display. If a file is to be exported to be imported into another system select any of the other options.

Output File Name

Enter a name for the file to be exported. By default the file will be saved in the Tally folder in your computer. To export to a different folder enter the path in Output File Name (Example: C:\differentfolder\).

Type of Masters

Select the Masters from the list:

IMPORT OF DATA

Data can be imported to Tally from other users of Tally. Tally can also be programmed to import data from other systems to be used as an integrated system.

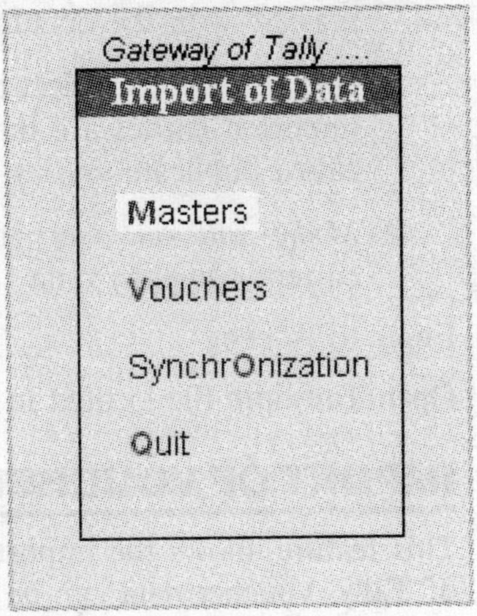

For example, a Customer Contact Management Program, with details such as status of an order and last contact established, can be imported to Tally. This imported data can be merged into a report containing outstanding balances. When data is changed in the other system, the change is also reflected in Tally.

To import data, Go to Gateway of Tally > Import of Data

Import Formats

Only the Tally XML format is supported for import of Data in Tally.

Tally (XML) Format

This option imports data in XML format.

IMPORT OF MASTERS

Masters from another company can be imported to Tally and merged with the data of the current company.

- Load and activate Company before importing data.
- Export the data from another company before importing it.

How to Import Masters:

Go to Gateway of Tally > Import Masters.

The Import of Data screen is displayed.

Enter the full path of the file in the Import File Name field. Example: C:\tallyrel1.11\DayBook.xml.

Select the appropriate option in the Treatment of entries already existing field from the Behaviour menu.

- *Combine Opening Balances:* Select this to combine the opening balance of the imported masters with the opening balance of the current company.
- *Ignore Duplicates:* Select this to ignore duplicate entries from the imported data. When imported entries are the exact replicas of entries in the current company, they are called duplicate entries.
- *Modify with new data:* Select this to add new data from the imported master to the current company data.

Enter to Accept.

Open Tally.imp file located in the Tally folder in Notepad to view log of import activities.

IMPORT OF VOUCHERS

This feature allows the import of vouchers from earlier versions of Tally and other users of Tally. Voucher data can be imported from other programs using XML.

How to Import Vouchers:

Go to Gateway of Tally > Import Transaction > Vouchers.

Only the Tally XML format is supported for import of Vouchers in Tally.

Import File Name – Enter the path of the drive and folder where the file to be imported exists.

TALLY ODBC

Tally use ODBC to connect to other programs and exchange data dynamically.

Outward Connectivity

Pick up data from Tally directly into other programs like Microsoft Excel or Word without any programming! Print labels for greeting cards from the ledger addresses stored in Tally! Even create templates for the likes of Audit Reports and Schedule VI forms and plug in data from Tally. Tally's database is now open for use in most popular programs to give you the unlimited flexibility of creating your own reports using up-to-date data from Tally.

How to Use ODBC?

A brief exercise will explain the process.

We wish to send greeting cards to all our customers. The customer database in Tally already exists. You want to use the names and addresses that you stored there to print out labels for the Greeting Cards. For this job, we will use Tally data in MS Word.

Start Tally. It should keep running.

Ensure that the words ODBC Server is visible in the Gateway of Tally screen

1. Start MS Word > Select Tools > Select Mail Merge
2. Main Document >Create > Mailing Labels
3. Now press the Data Source button
4. Get Data > Create Data Source
5. Click on MS Query (at the bottom of the dialog box beside File Name)

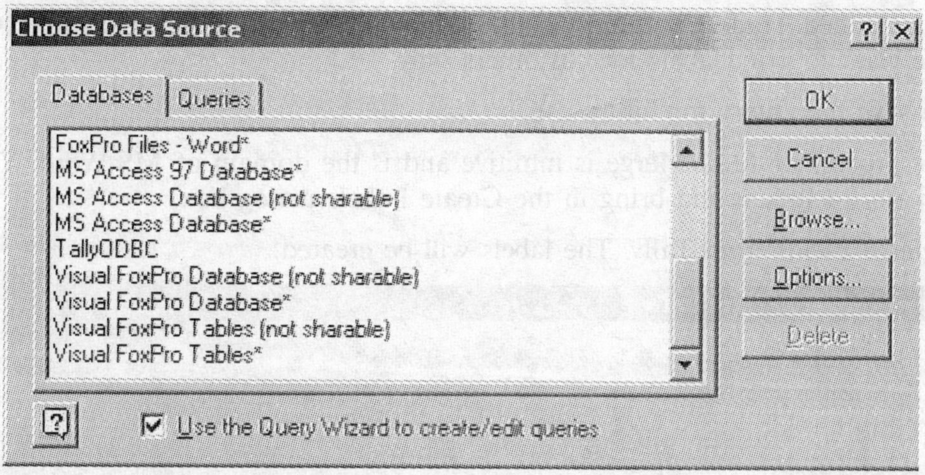

6. Select TallyODBC. (You could use a saved Query by clicking the Tab Queries. Do that after you have saved this query that we are creating)

Let the Use the Query Wizard remain ticked.

The Query Wizard brings the Tally fields that may be selected. You can also give filter conditions to limit the data brought in to only those that match your criteria.

Hence,

Select Ledger and move by click the > button to the right the following fields:

$Name, $Parent, $Address (move all the other address fields as well.

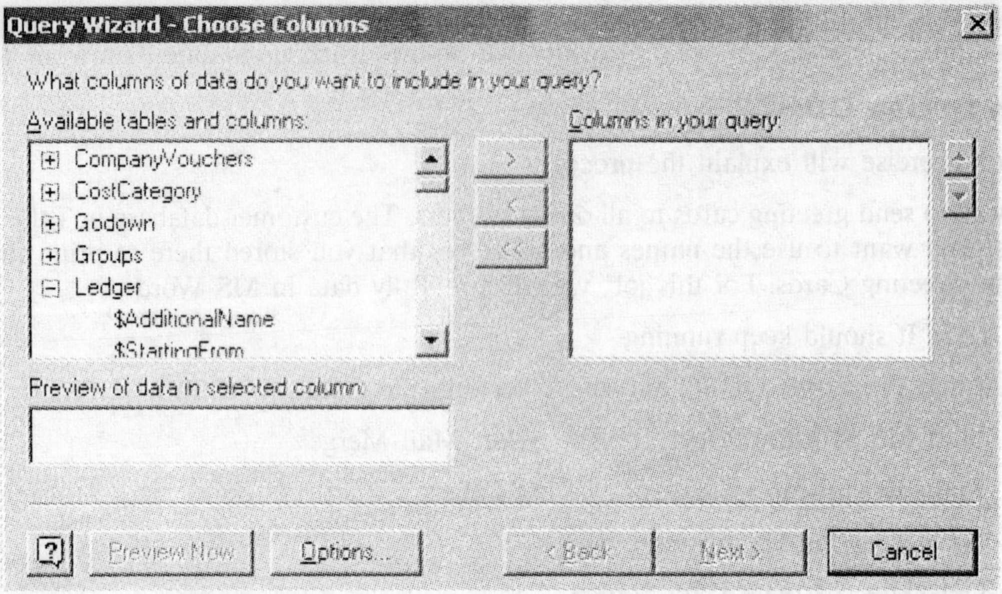

Then in the next Query Wizard Screen – Filter data to limit all ledger accounts belong to the Group that contains the name 'Customer'. (In our Sundry Debtors Group we have created sub-groups called Trade Customers below which we have different Customer Groups as well) We want to print labels for customers only.

You can save the Query for future use.

Then the process of Mail Merge is intuitive and is the domain of MS-Word. You can set up the main document and bring in the Create Labels dialog box,

Insert Merge Fields from Tally. The labels will be created.

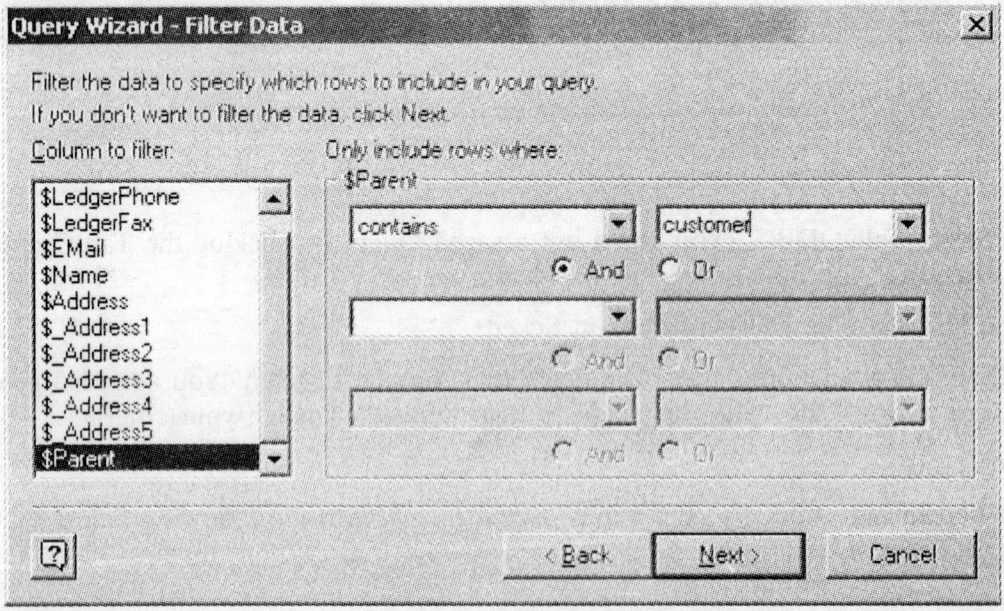

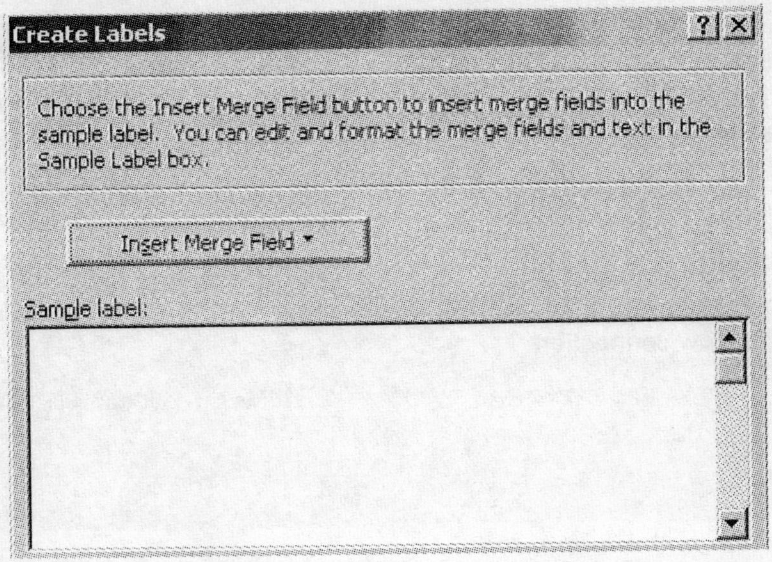

INWARD CONNECTIVITY

On the other hand, Tally ies 8.1 is capable of being programmed by TallyExperts to use data from other systems much more easily. This permits you to continue using other systems and use some of their data in Tally as if they were parts of one integrated system. For example, a customer contact management program may contain various details like status of an order and last contact made. Bring in that data into Tally to merge into a report containing outstanding balances. Any changes in the other data will be immediately reflected in Tally.

CREATING THE CLIENT RULE FOR THE CLIENT MACHINE

At the TallyClient end, load the desired company and create a Client Rule. A client Rule is created by selecting the following option:

Gateway of Tally > Import of Data > Synchronization > Client Rules > Create

Screen items can be explained as:

Name of Rule

Specify any suitable name. Like - "Sync with H O". Rules with same name are not allowed.

Server URL

Specify the IP address / Machine Name followed by the TCP/IP port of the TallyServer. Ex: 192.168.1.1:9000 - where 192.168.1.1 is the IP address of the server and 9000 is the TCP/IP port number.

Secure Server

Specifies whether HTTPS (Secure HTTP) should be used instead of HTTP for synchronization.

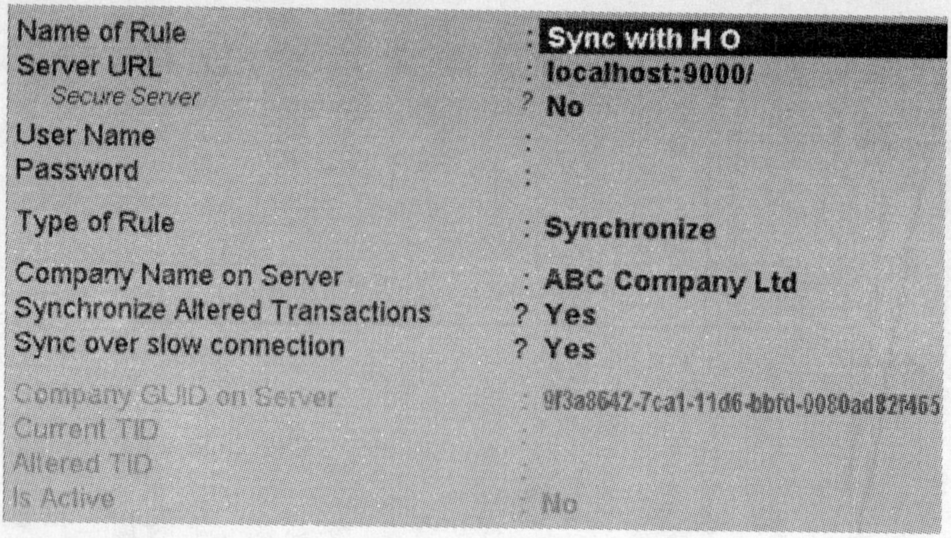

Company Name on the Server

Specify the company name on the server with which you wish to synchronize the data.

Synchronize the Altered Transaction

If any back dated/current altered transactions need to be synchronized with the Server set this option to YES.

Synchronize Over Slow Connection

Can be set to YES while synchronizing through the DialUp connection. Accept the Rule.

Once client rule is created, switch back to the Synchronization menu and opt for Synchronize. A request would be sent to the server from the client machine for creating a Server Rule corresponding to the Client Rule. A user can never create a Server Rule manually. A Server Rule gets created implicitly whenever a Client Rule tries to synchronize with the server.

If you don't receive any error message in the calculator pane of Tally in the client machine, then it is confirmed that the Server Rule has been created successfully on the server machine.

ACTIVATING THE SERVER RULE FROM THE SERVER MACHINE

Gateway of Tally > Import of Data > Synchronization > Server Rules > Activate. You will get a list containing the GUID and name of the company on Client that requested the synchronization. A client cannot exchange data with the server unless a user on the server activates a server rule. This is required for enforcing security. You can have more than one server rule as a result of multiple client requests.

Name of Rule shows the GUID of the client company that requested synchronization.

Company Name on Client shows the name of the company in the Client that has sent the request for synchronization.

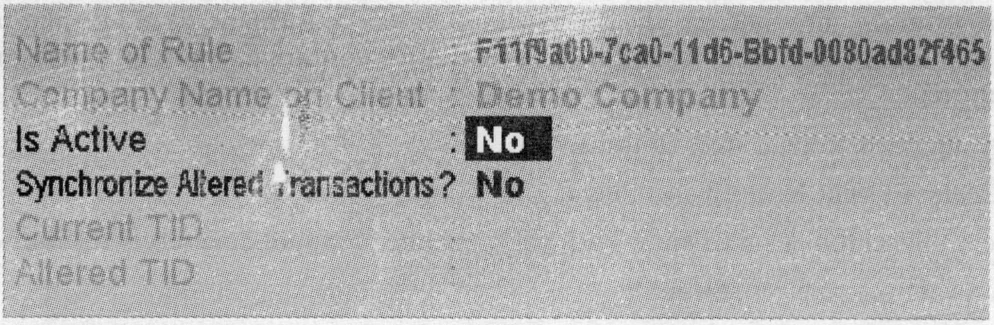

Select the appropriate server rule and set Yes for is Active.

The GUID (Globally Unique Identifier) is a 16-byte value that uniquely identifies a company created in Tally. Technically, a GUID is a very large, statistically unique identifier generated from the address of the Ethernet card in the current machine, the current time since 1582 (10 bits), etc. No two Ethernet cards anywhere should have the same address. If the machine has no network card, another number is synthesized that will almost certainly be unique to the machine. It is very unlikely that duplicate GUIDs will ever be created. GUIDs are useful because they ensure that there will be no naming clashes within the companies created in Tally. Tally assigns a GUID to every company while creating it.

Once a server rule has been activated, data can now be exchanged between the two hosts. Now from the TallyClient machine, click on Synchronize again. All the data from the client gets posted to the server and all data from the server get saved in the client.

To sum it up, setting up synchronization can be done by performing the following steps:

1. Define the Client / Server parameters in the Tally.ini on the TallyServer and TallyClient machines.
2. Create a client rule in TallyClient machine.
3. Select Synchronize menu option. The client connects to the server and creates a Server Rule
4. Activate the Rule on the TallyServer.
5. Click on the option "Synchronize" in TallyClient machine again.
6. The data will be synchronized.

SYNCHRONIZING BACK-DATED VOUCHERS

If you have set up synchronization between 2 companies having large amount of data, the initial synchronization can take a large amount of time over the Internet. The client can also display an out of memory error. The recommended way to start synchronization in this scenario is to export data from the source company to a disk file and import the data into the target company.

However, since Tally maintains the last ID of the remote company along with the rules, you have to make sure that the ID gets updated when you import data into the target company. To ensure proper update of Remote Ids in the corresponding rules – perform the following steps.

Client is supposed to send data to the server:

- Create a Client Rule on the Client
- Select Synchronize on Client – This will create the corresponding server rule on Server
- Activate the rule on server
- DON'T synchronize again.
- Export all masters in XML format from the client company to disk file
- Export all vouchers in XML format from the client company to disk file
- Import the masters into the server company from disk file
- Import the transactions into the server from disk file
- The TID of the last imported voucher gets updated in the Server Rule
- Subsequent syncs would be incremental

OR

- If you want to sync over LAN / Internet, you can choose to send one transaction at a time by selecting Sync Over Slow Connection in the client rule. This will ensure that the XML for 1 transaction is created and sent at a time avoiding any "out of memory" errors. Note: This works ONLY for client sending data to the server. The server always creates and sends the entire XML to the Client.

Client is supposed to retrieve data from the server:

- Create a Client Rule on the Client
- Select Synchronize on Client – This will create the corresponding server rule on Server
- Activate the rule on server
- DON'T synchronize again.
- Export all masters in XML format from the server company to disk file
- Export all transactions in XML format from the server company to disk file
- Import the masters into Client Company

Use the Select Import Initial Option to import the transactions and NOT the regular Import Transaction.

E-CAPABILITIES

Tally has extensive internet capabilities. E-mail, Web-publishing and data interchange over the Internet are all easily achieved from within Tally.

Pre-requisites to using E-capabilities of Tally:

You should have an internet connection accessible from your computer. This could be through a direct dial-up modem or through the network.

For E-mail - an E-mail account.

For Web Publishing - you should know the sites URL (address) and have authority to upload files on the sites.

E-mail

The E-mail is the most widely used facility on the Internet. It saves time and cost of postage. Use the email feature in Tally to:

- E-mail any Tally report or document like invoices or purchase orders
- Post reminder letters and statement of accounts

The following example illustrates the use of this feature in Tally:

- E-mail a Reminder Letter

To send a reminder letter to a customer by email:

1. Go to Gateway of Tally > Display > Statements of Accounts > Outstandings > Ledger
2. Select the customer's/company's ledger from the List of Ledgers
3. Click on Email from the button bar or press Alt+M
4. The fields on the Mailing Ledger Outstanding form are automatically completed if you have given the required information during creation of the master records. Select No or press Backspace to change/modify the entries. Select Yes to accept.
5. The E-mail Server field is highlighted next. This is a mandatory field. The first time you use this feature in Tally, enter the name of your SMTP server, example: mail.btinternet.com. Subsequently, Tally will automatically display the SMTP server name. Refer to your Internet Service Provider (ISP) or network administrator for further queries.
6. The From field displays the name of your company entered in the Company Creation screen and stored in the Company Information Master records. You can also modify the default information. Press Enter.
7. The From E-mail Address field displays the e-mail address entered in the Company Information Master data. Enter your email address, if you have not done so while creating a company, or if you want to change the id.
8. Enter the user name and password in Authentication User Name (Only if required) and Password field respectively if the mail server requires authentication.

Mailing Ledger Outstanding

E-Mail Server	: *yourdomain.com*
From	: *ABC Company*
From E-Mail Address	: *you@yourdomain.com*
Authentication User Name	: **username**
(Only if required)	
Password	: *****
Format	: *HTML (Web-Publishing)* Resolution : *1024 x 768*
To E-Mail Address	: **Party1@domain.com**
CC To (if any)	: **[None**
Subject	: **Party1 (Bill-wise Details)**
Additional Text (if any)	: **Payment overdue by five days**

Include Post-Dated Transactions ? **No**
Show overdue using Bill Date ? **No**

Range of Bills to show : **Overdue Bills**
Format : **Detailed**
Show Qty Info in Detailed Format ? **Yes**
Show bills of following type : **All Bills**
Show Bills in Foreign Exchange? **No**

Mail ?
Yes or **No**

9. In the Format field a pop-up screen lists the three formats in which you can generate your email:

   ASCII (Comma-delimited)

   HTML (Web-publishing)

   XML (Data-Interchange)

   Select the type that suits your recipient.

10. To E-mail Address field is a mandatory field.

    It displays the recipient's email address as entered in the Mailing and Related details during ledger creation. Enter the address if you have not done so while creating the ledger or if you want to modify the information.

11. Type the email address of another recipient to whom you want to send a carbon copy of the email in the CC (if any) field.

12. The Subject field is filled by default and displays the subject of your mail. You can change it to a subject of your choice.

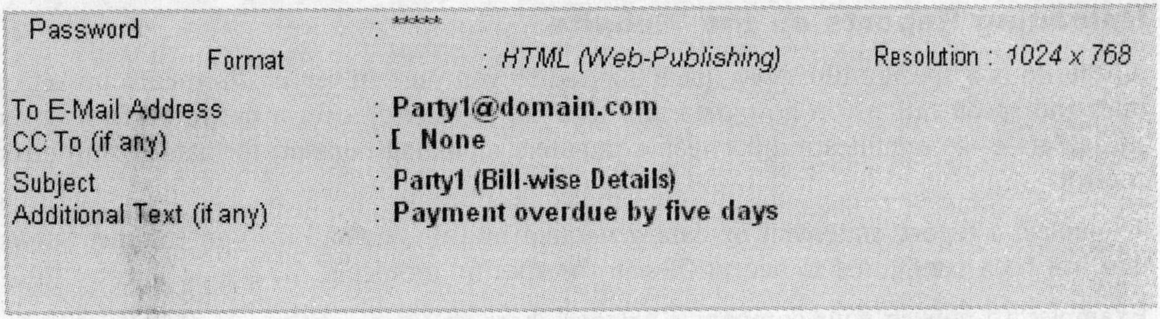

13. Any text you enter in the Additional Text field precedes the report in the recipient's mail program. You can use this field to type a message to the recipient.

14. Additional Options provided in the form are:
    - *Include Post-Dated Transactions*?: Set this option to Yes to include post-dated transactions.
    - *Show Overdue using Bill Date*?: Set this option to Yes to show bill date in report.
    - *Range of Bills to Show*: Select all bills or overdue bills to display.
    - *Format*: Select condensed or detailed format for your reminder letter.
    - *Show Qty Info in Detailed Format*?: This option is selected for the detailed format mode and displays quantity.
    - *Show Bills of the Following Type*: Select the types of bills from all, credit or debit bills.

    Additional Options may vary depending upon the type of report you want to email.
15. Print Preview: Use the Print Preview screen to view the document before emailing. This shows how the document appears in the recipient's email.

WEB PUBLISHING

All reports and documents generated in Tally can be published on your website. Tally can create reports in HTML format and upload the same directly to your website. For example, use this feature to inform your customers about the new price-range and stocks available for sale on your website. Tally uses the highest standard of data encryption methods to ensure security of data.

Uploading Reports on the Website

A website is a specific directory space allotted to you on that server. Protocols are set of rules and specifications on how data and files are transferred over a network. They cover all aspects of communication between computers including content, formatting and error control.

To publish a report, statement or data generated in Tally, upload it to an Internet Server that has been configured to accept files in the specific protocols.

Example: To publish your company's balance sheet on your website:

1. Go to Gateway of Tally > Balance Sheet.
2. Click the Upload button from the button bar or press Alt+O.
3. The first time you upload, you will have to enter the required information on the screen displayed. The field Upload to has two options:

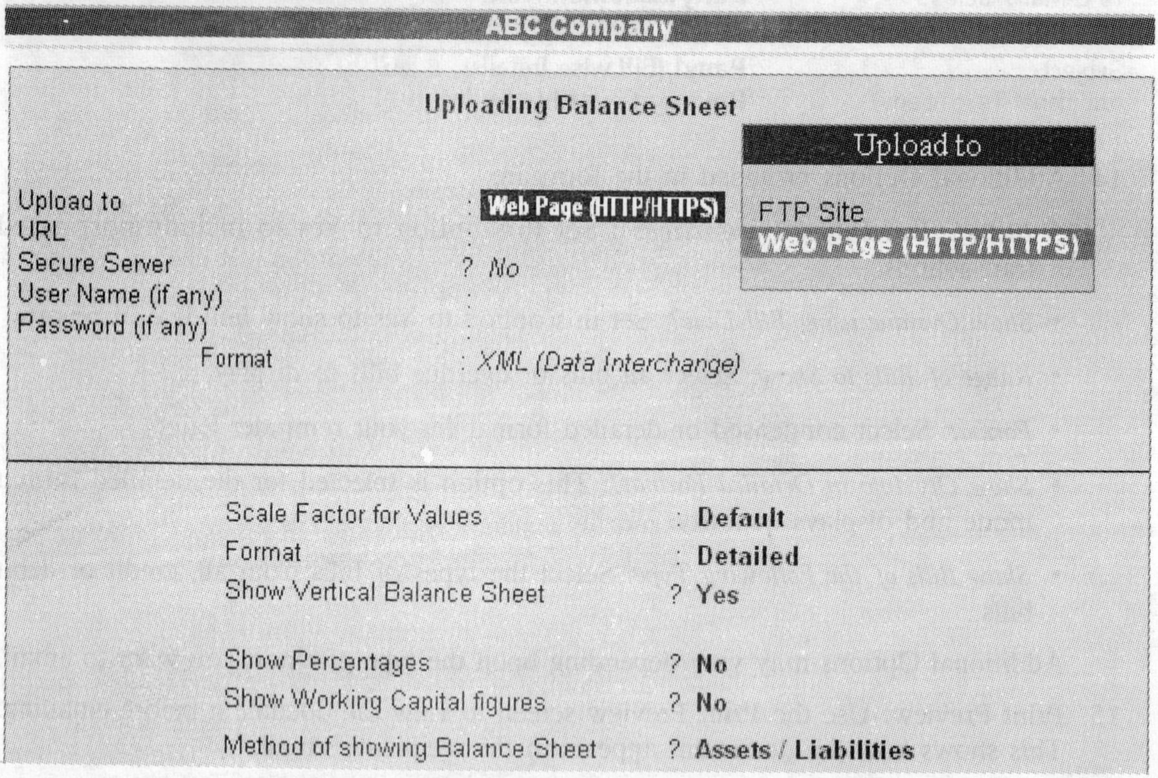

FTP Site

Web Page (HTTP/HTTPS)

This site accepts files transfers in File Transfer Protocol (FTP). FTP is a common choice for data or file transfer to a website. Select this option unless your site accepts HTTP or HTTPS uploads. Hyper Text Transfer Protocol (HTTP) is the standard for

ABC Company

Uploading Balance Sheet

Upload to	: **FTP Site**
URL	: *http://subdomain.domainname.com*
User Name (if any)	: *username*
Password (if any)	: *****
Format	: *HTML (Web-Publishing)* Resolution : *1024 x 768*
Destination File	: *BSheet.htm*

transferring HTML files over the Internet. HTTP Servers are pre-programmed to accept HTTP connections. HTTPS sites are servers configured to accept secure connections. They conform to standard security protocols (example: SSL and SET) to ensure that your data and files are not tampered during an upload.

Uploading Balance Sheet

Upload to	: **Web Page (HTTP/HTTPS)**
URL	: *www.yourdomain.com*
Secure Server	? *No*
User Name (if any)	: *username*
Password (if any)	: *****
Format	: *HTML (Web-Publishing)* Resolution : *1024 x 768*

4. URL: Universal Resource Locator (URL) is the server address where you want to publish your report. For FTP, you will need to know the FTP server name and directory path. The FTP server name is the domain name of the Web server (example: ftp.server.com). The directory path is the folder on the server where the report is stored (example: /public_html). For a web page, an URL is typically in the form www.myweb.com/.
5. Secure Server: This option displays when you select Web Page in Upload to field. Use a secure connection when the data is sensitive and your server is configured for it. A secure site is one that has alphabet s following http (https) and the URL in the address bar of your browser displays https://www.______.com.
6. User Name (if any): Enter the user-name you need to access the server for uploading.
7. Password (if any): Enter the password. Internet servers authenticate your identity before you can put data and files on the site. If you are unsure about your user name, password, or FTP location, contact your Internet Service Provider (ISP).
8. Format: You can generate your reports in three formats. To know more about these formats, click on the links given below:

ASCII (Comma delimited) HTML (Web-publishing) XML (data interchange)

Select the type that suits your requirement.

9. Destination File: This option displays on selecting an FTP Site in Upload to field. The default names are displayed. Modify if necessary. Additional options may vary depending on the type of report you want to upload.
10. Print Preview: Use the Print Preview screen through the Print option to view the document before you upload.

Descriptive Type Questions

1. In what forms data can be exported from Tally?
2. How would you use ODBC?
3. What are Client Rules?
4. How would you send Tally data in the form of e-mail?
5. How would you upload from Tally?
6. How would you use Web browser from Tally?

12 The Administrative Tally

SECURITY LEVELS – TYPES OF SECURITY

Tally has a very customizable security system. You can set up authority levels and users who are placed at these levels. The authority levels or Types of Security decide the rights of the users – what they can or cannot do when using Tally.

Tally has two security types already set up. One is Owner and the other Data Entry. Owner has full access and rights to all parts of Tally, except Tally Audit & Company Alteration screen which are reserved for the Administrator alone. Data Entry has restricted rights. You are allowed to create other security types based on these predefined types and allow more or less rights as required.

Gateway of Tally > [ALT]+F3:Create Cmp >Security Control

Types of Security (Security or Authority Levels)

Owner has full access rights. The other predefined type, Data Entry, is based on owner but is restricted by default. The default settings for Data Entry are as follows. You can change them to allow more or less rights as necessary.

Types of Security [Enter] > Data Entry[Enter]

Create a New Security Level

Types of Security > Data Entry > [Down Arrow]

(Press the down arrow key at the option data entry.)

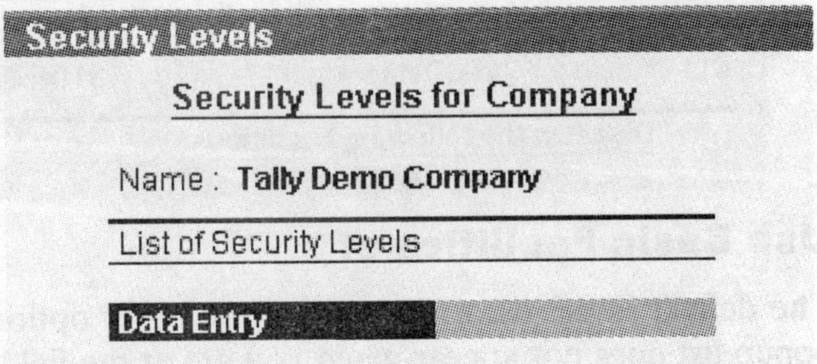

This is one of the few places in Tally where you create a new entry in this fashion.

Type the new security level, e.g. Manager

Press [enter] to bring up the Level Definition screen

The Level Definition Screen

The level of security.

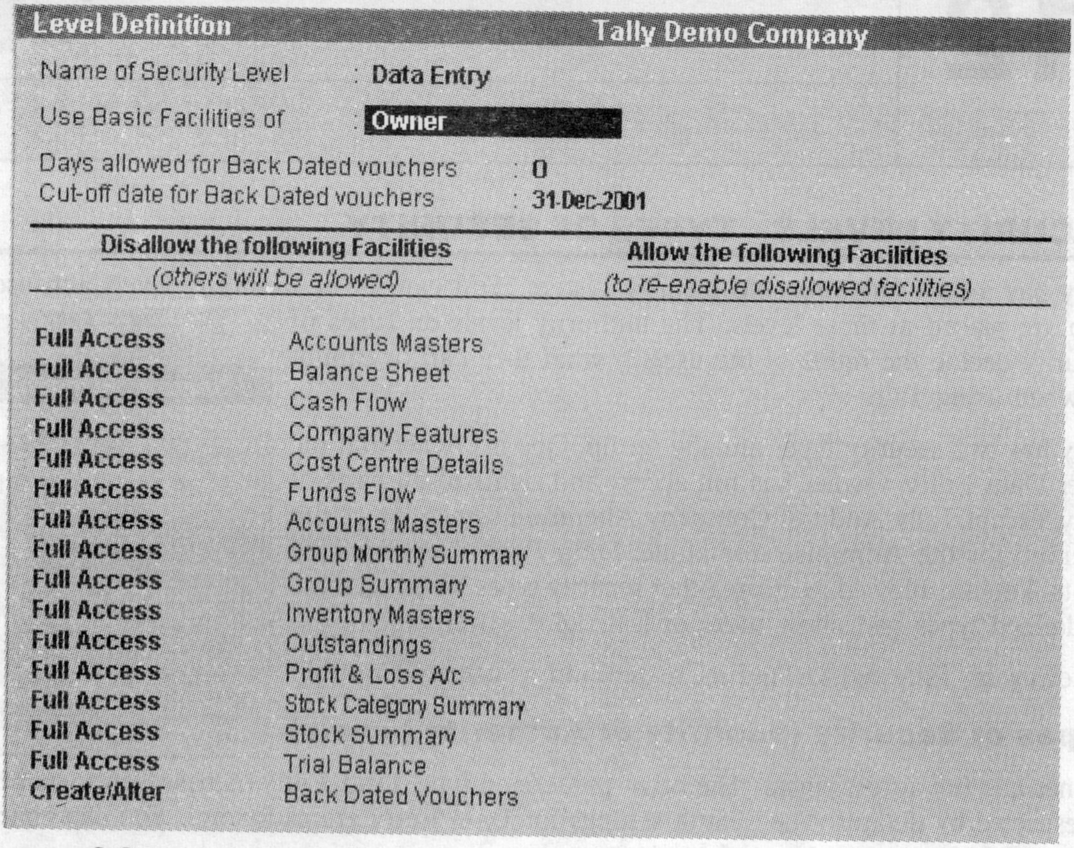

Name of Security Level

This defaults to the name you have created.

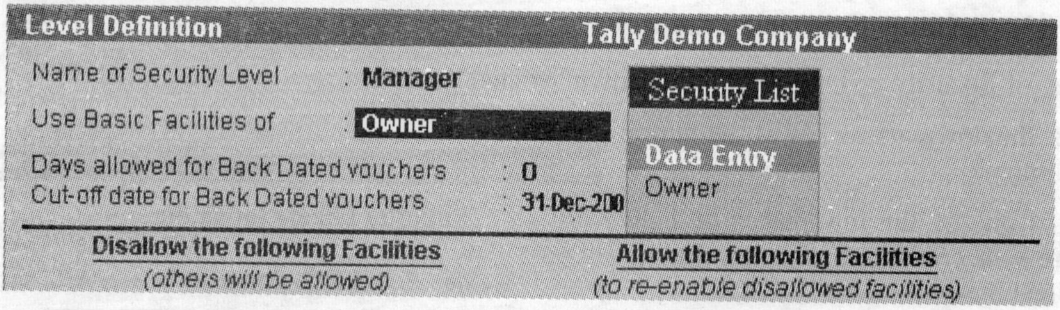

Use Basic Facilities of

The default is the owner. However, the other option is also available – Data Entry. If the popup list does not appear when you are at the field, press D – beginning to type the word. Going back from the next field will also pop it up. The new level Manager will, likewise, be available when you create a next level.

Days Allowed for Back-dated Vouchers

This is the number of days the users of this level are allowed to create back-dated vouchers.

Specifying 0 will indicate that back-dated vouchers are not allowed, and 7 will allow the user at this level to insert vouchers going back 7 days.

Cut-off Date for Back-dated Vouchers

Specify the date before which users of this profile or security level may not create or alter vouchers. This is additional control over and above the previous 'days allowed'. This is useful in cases where you have completed your Tax Assessment for a period and no changes are desired in the data for that period.

Disallow the Following Facilities/Allow the Following Facilities

The screen is now divided into two broad columns each have two sub-columns. The left side is to disallow access to the various options of the system. The right side allows the security level the different facilities. The different access rights options – Types of Access - are available in a pop-up list when the cursor is on an access rights field (the first left column in the screen above). The options sought to be controlled, are on the right (the second column from the left). To disallow access to different options; First select the type of access and then select the option. Options may be selected from the popup list of Reports. Repeat the procedure till you have set access rights for the different options. Note the bracketed sentence in italics. When you select a type of access, this type would be disallowed for the option. Hence, if you select Full Access for Balance Sheet, you want to prevent any access to Balance Sheet by this security level. Conversely, under 'Allow the following facilities', if you select Full Access for Balance Sheet, you want to allow full access. Full access incorporates all rights.

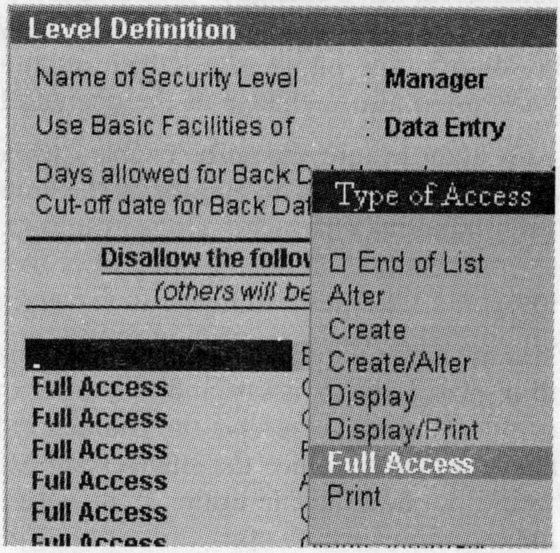

Select [End of List] at the Type of Access field to complete the definition.

You are taken back to the screen 'Security Levels for Company' at a blank field following the one you just created, viz., Manager. If you have any other level to create, simply type the name and follow the same procedure. Otherwise press [enter] at the blank field to accept and return from this screen.

USERS AND PASSWORDS

You would need to create different users who belong to one or more different security levels or types of security. Select the option at the Security control menu to define users, give their passwords and their security levels. Only the administrator can assign users and their passwords.

You need to create security levels first and then users

Alter/Display a User or Type of Security

There is no separate menu option to alter or display a security option. Use the same menu to display or alter user or security level set-up. To delete a user, simply blank out the user name and accept the screen. Do the same for a security level. Obviously, if you have defined a user under a security level, then the security level cannot be deleted before deleting the users under it.

TALLY AUDIT

TallyAudit provides the capability to the administrator/auditor to track changes in the accounts following his previous review. Changes of two areas are important – changes in transactions or vouchers and changes in ledger masters. Only material changes are considered, i.e., a change in the narration does not affect the integrity of a transaction, hence it would not be considered as changed. Any other change in a voucher is material and would be logged. The name of a ledger account if changed, it is material, hence it would be tracked. So also a change in the opening balance of a ledger master.

TallyAudit feature should be enabled while creating the company and authority lists. Only a user designated as an auditor or the administrator can view the audit list and act upon it. Tally tracks all changes made to vouchers that are more than 30 days old. Hence, changes to vouchers that are less than 30 days old are not reported. This is to allow adequate time to correct mistakes. A change includes insertion of new transactions or accounts.

You are not required to make any additional input of data. The authorised user simply needs to display TallyAudit lists and may print out the lists. If he is satisfied with the authenticity of the changes, he accepts the changes either selectively or all of them (by clicking on the relevant button). Once the changes are accepted, they are removed from the audit list and would not be available again. If, however, a change is repeated, it is reflected in the audit list.

How to View Tally Audit Lists

For this do the following:

Gateway of Tally > Display > Statement of Accounts > Tally Audit

Display Vouchers Audit List

Gateway of Tally > Display > Statements of Accounts > TallyAudit > Vouchers

Note the three buttons relevant to the audit list.

F7: Accept one

F7: Accept All

F12: Configure

Audit listing of changes to vouchers with names of users

F12: Configure

The listing now incorporates the user's name.

Now print the list for records. Assess each or all the entries for authenticity and accept. F7:Accept One can be pressed after placing the cursor bar on the relevant voucher. This would accept the voucher as valid and remove from this exception list. If you are satisfied that all the vouchers are valid then press F7:Accept All to accept them all together.

Once you accept an entry it is not available for listing. Hence it is recommended that you take a print before acceptance.

It is recommended that the very first time you use Tally Audit, go through the list and accept all the vouchers. Do a disciplined verification of the list so that it is periodically cleared and only vouchers that are concerned remain.

Display Ledgers Audit List

To display the changes to ledger masters, follow the same steps as for vouchers. The listing here differs from the vouchers in two ways namely:

It allows you to display all ledger accounts and with a toggle the ones that have been changed – (by pressing the toggle button F6:All Accts/Audit List)

The F12:Configure button is not available; but the list always displays user names if available. (If you activate TallyAudit sometime after you are well through the accounts, the user names will not be displayed. In such cases, accept the list after verification. Any changes henceforth, would give the user names).

The first audit list below shows all accounts and there are no accounts that were modified or created after the last review. The second audit list below shows ledger accounts that were either modified since last review or created. The modification could be in the name or in the opening balance. The name is considered important as a creditor's name could be changed to some other name with malafide intentions.

Please note that you need to identify a change even in cases where two names are interchanged. This would enable identification of fraudulent transfer of account balances. You are able to make the identification through the ID assigned to each ledger account. Of course, you must first take a print of all the ledger accounts with their original ID with which to match subsequent audit lists.

TALLY VAULT

The Security of Data, Financial or otherwise, has always been a matter of concern. Most businesses depend on the confidentiality of information. TallyVault is an enhanced security system which allows for encryption of the company data with the most secure method of encryption being used.

TallyVault ensures, that under no circumstances, the original information is available in any form. The technique could be likened to "encryption-decryption-on-the-fly", and the decrypted form of data is never stored in the system. Apart from this, it uses the "non-stored password" mechanism. By using highly advanced mechanisms to validate a new user without any prior knowledge of the original password. The combination of these facilities means, that **TallyVault** becomes one of the most secure means of information storage.

How to Use TallyVault?

TallyVault password can be given at the time of company creation. For existing companies, the procedure is:

Load the desired company and using Alt+F3 proceed to the Company Information screen.

Go to Change Tally Vault. You will be required to select the company name once again (this incase you have more than one company loaded). Give the new TallyVault password and confirm it.

Once you encrypt the data, the result is that the company name no longer becomes visible to anyone.

Select the company and Tally will prompt you for the Tally Vault password.

By the above procedure, once can ensure that data is kept confidential and is available only to administrator (initiator of the TallyVault).

BACKUP

Tally has a flexible back-up mechanism where in you can take a backup of the data from virtually any storage medium into any other medium. The more commonly used media are floppy drive, hard disk drive, zip drive, tape drive, etc - installed either locally or on a network. In the backup screen, the source of the backup and the destination of where it has to be stored has to be given, Tally will do as required.

How to Take a Backup?

Start Tally - If the Company Information screen is loaded first – there is a menu option "Backup". Select this to get the "Select Companies to Backup" screen. However, if the Gateway of Tally Loads – use Alt+F3 to get the option Backup. Note that this option is available only on the Company Information screen

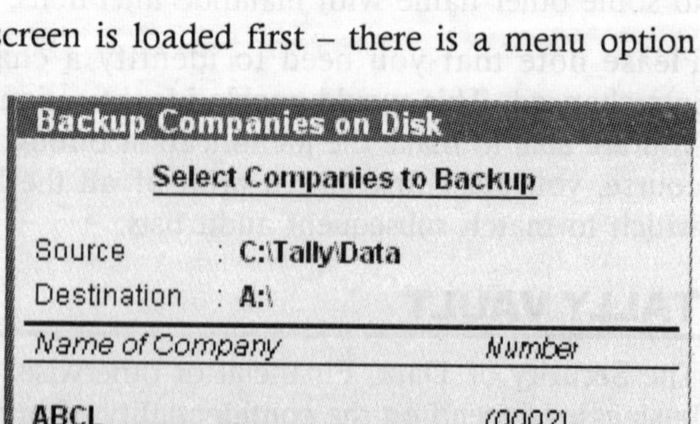

To change either the source or the destination paths, use the Backspace key and change the path as required. Let us say we want to backup the data to a directory Tally backup in the D Drive – change the path to D:\Tallybackup and choose the companies as required. Incase we want to take a backup onto another person's system – the path will be \\machinename\\drivename\directoryname

The process of backing up data begins when at least one company is selected for the same. To stop selecting companies, select the option "End of List" which appears at the top of the selection list.

Note: This option appears only after one company is selected for backup.

The backup file is stored as TBK500.001. If the backup is taken in a medium likely to extend more than one – for example, floppy, then the extension digits (001, 002) will be stored accordingly.

Backup Precautions

As we are already aware, data on a computer is vulnerable to all types of difficulties. Considering the same, it is important that we do not overlook the importance of regular backing-up of data, however strong the database may be. With a little planning and forethought, we can ensure that maintenance of the important data is continuous and hassle-free.

Depending on the volume of data entry, an appropriate backup mechanism will have to be devised. One method to achieve the same will be by maintaining a backup directory in the local hard disk or the server (external storage media such as the floppy disk, zip diskette can also be used). We can have sub-directories for every day of the week under the main backup directory and regularly take data backups in the following manner depending on the day of the week.

Monday – C:\TallyBackup\Monday

Tuesday – C:\TallyBackup\Tuesday

Wednesday – C:\TallyBackup\Wednesday and so on till Saturday.

The above procedure ensures that there exists a reliable data backup at any given time. In order to use that reliable data backup or bring back the data from that existing data backup we have to use the "Restore" option.

RESTORE

Restore literally means 'to bring back'. Similar to backing up of data, Tally allows restoring of data from any medium into any other storage medium. In Tally's context restore means – we have a Tally backup and we wish to work on the data backup instead of the current data – this can be achieved by simply restoring from the existing data backup.

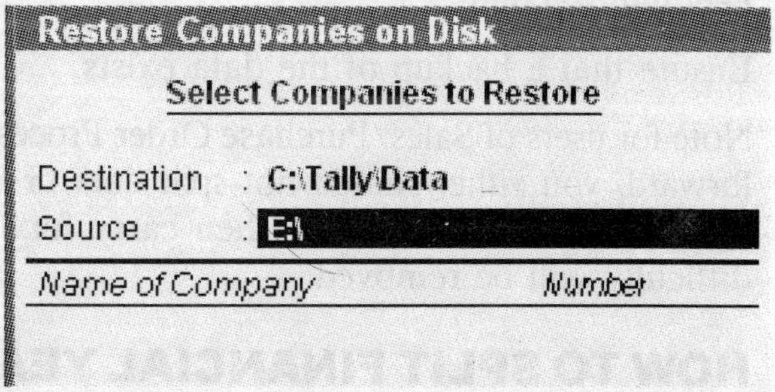

How to Restore?

Start Tally If the Company Information screen is loaded first – there is a menu option "Restore". Select this to get the "Select Companies to Restore" screen. However, if the

Gateway of Tally Loads – use Alt+F3 to get the option Restore. Note that as in the case of backup - this option is available only on the Company Information screen.

The Source and Destination paths displayed here are those that were used last.

The source field has to have the appropriate path from which we intend to bring back the previous data. Accepting the path will read the contents of the particular file and will then display the list of companies available.

Select as required and restore the data accordingly.

Restore Precautions

It is preferable NOT to restore a backup on the original data directory – primarily to ensure that No data is unintentionally overwritten.

SPLIT FINANCIAL YEARS

Tally's flexible period-less accounting permits entry of data for any number of years. This in itself has tremendous benefits. However, presence of old data in cases where they are voluminous, causes greater overhead on the system. Splitting financial years enables you to retain most benefits while overcoming this overhead.

When you split the data, two things happen:

New companies are created for the respective split periods.

Full data is retained in the original company.

Important Pre-split Activity

(Not carrying out these will result in mismatched information.)

Before you split data, ensure that:

All unadjusted forex gains/losses have been fully adjusted by journal entries. Verify that the item does not appear in the Balance Sheet. There are no Purchase Bills/Sales Bills to come.Check the Profit & Loss Account and Inventory Statements – Purchase/Sales Bills Pending. You may account them to the respective party accounts or to respective 'Bills Pending' Account.

Ensure that a backup of the data exists.

Note for users of Sales/Purchase Order Processing features: Since open orders are not carried forward, you either should not split data or if you do be aware that you have to enter the outstanding orders afresh. When carry forward of orders become available in Tally, this difficulty will be removed.

HOW TO SPLIT FINANCIAL YEARS?

1. At the Gateway of Tally, Select [ALT]+F3: Cmp Info (Create Cmp in earlier releases).
2. Select Split Company Data.

3. Select the Company whose data is to be split.
4. Tally recommends the split-off date based on the data existing. It is recommended that the Split Point is set as the beginning of the latest financial year though Tally permits any date as the split point.
5. Splits occur in sets of two periods. Hence, start with the latest. For example assuming that three years data – from 1-1-96 to 31-12-98 for a company and you want them split into three separate 'companies' each with a financial year. First, select the beginning of the latest financial year (this is what Tally would prompt you to do).
6. On confirming the activity, two new companies will be created – one with data from 1-1-96 to 31-12-97, i.e., two years, and the other for 1-1-98 to 31-12-98.

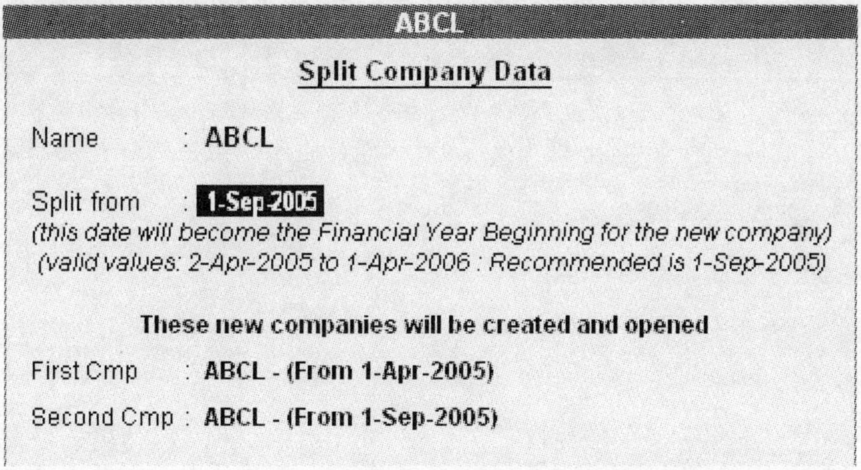

Typically, this is all you need to do. Your historical data, whether of 1 or more financial years, will be preserved as one company, and your current financial year, as another. There is, normally, no reason or benefit to split the prior years again into separate years. However, should you wish to do so, repeat the above steps for the prior period company.

All the companies are full companies in their own right. Data can be entered, displayed and altered. Please display or print out the key financial reports (Trial Balance, Balance Sheet, Profit & Loss, Stock Summary etc.) from each of the companies for the relevant periods and compare them for accuracy.

Once you are satisfied that you have a successful split, it is advisable to backup the original company onto diskettes and permanently delete its data from your hard-disk. This will ensure that you do not accidentally use it to enter fresh data. To delete a company, press Alt+F3 at the Gateway of Tally, select to Alter it, and at the point where you can modify the Company Information, press Alt+D.

You will also need to alter the names of the two freshly created companies to suit you.

Descriptive Type Questions

1. Define the various types of security levels provided by Tally.
2. How would you create a new security level?
3. Define password security.
4. What is TallyAudit?
5. What is TallyVault?
6. How would you take a Backup?
7. How would you restore the data?

A Fundamentals of Accounting and Inventory

FUNDAMENTALS OF ACCOUNTING

This section tells you about the basic accounting features and how Tally handles them. Those of you who have accounting background must be very clear about these concepts and would probably find the following information quite childish but it is important for us to give these information specially for those of you who do not have the accounting background.

Let us start with some definitions.

Debit

It is what you receive.

Credit

It is what you give.

Debtor

It is that person who owes money to the business on account of credit sale of goods or advance given or services rendered to him.

Creditor

It is that person to whom the business owes money on account of credit purchase of goods or loan taken or services received from him.

Transactions

It means transfer of money or money's worth from one party to another.

Drawing

It means withdrawal. The amount of money or the value of goods taken by the proprietor from the business for his personal use.

Liability

It is that sum of money which the business owes to outsiders. Capital is that part of wealth which is contributed by the proprietor to start, run and further expand the business.

Assets

These are the things of value owned by the company. Cash, unsold stock, furniture, money due from the debtors fall under the category of assets.

ACCOUNTING SYSTEMS

There are two main accounting systems: Cash and Mercantile. In cash system enteries in the book are done only when the amount due has been received. It is not shown as due at any stage.

On the other hand in mercantile system, a record is made on the basis of amounts having become due for payment or receipt.

Transactions are also of two types: Double and Single entry. The double entry system is based on the fact that a transaction is a double-sided affair. If one receives something, somewhere something must have been reduced, or some service must have been rendered.

A single entry system on the other hand is concerned with only one side of the transaction, either you pay someone or you receive from someone.

The double entry system is more accurate, scientific and systematic.

JOURNAL ACCOUNTS

Debiting and crediting each and every individual account for every transaction is very time consuming. This is overcome by recording the debit and its corresponding credit or the credit and its corresponding debit in a subsidiary book. Each journal transaction is recorded in the form of a voucher. A voucher is supposed to have the following information:

Date

It records the date of transaction with its month and year.

Particulars

This is what is usually known as narration. You can write here the details of the transactions in plain English.

Ledger Folio

Posting in the ledger accounts is done on the basis of journal entries. It is therefore, necessary that there should be certain reference to the page number of ledger, where the account in journal is being posted.

Debit

This contains the amount debited under a transaction.

Credit

This contains the amount credited under a transaction.

CASH BOOK

For a big company it is not possible to have only one journal to carry all the accounting information. So for this we have different books for different accounts. That is why we have Purchase Books, Purchase Return Books, Sales Books, Sales Return Books, Bill Receivable Books and Bills Payable Books. You will read about them later in the book.

Cash book records all the cash transactions. Cash does not mean hard cash only. It also means notes, coins, bank drafts, cheques and postal orders too. As in other transactions, here too you have Receipts and Payments. There are various types of cash books which the company's maintain depending upon the type of business that they have.

Simple Cash Book

It is the simplest form of the cash book, where all the cash transactions are recorded. It does not even records the banking and cash discount transactions. The following may represent a format of the same:

Dr.	Receipts				Payments		Cr.
Date	Particulars	L.F.	Amount Rs. P.	Date	Particulars	L.F.	Amount Rs. P.

Remember the cash book is maintained date wise and all the entries are totalled as per the date, i.e., the balance is found out at the end of each date.

Petty Cash Book

It is a usual practice for a company to withdraw cash from the bank and then keep on using it for various purposes like Travelling, Postage, Carriage, Stationery, etc. So when the cash level reaches a minimum level more cash is added and thus this book keeps on working. This book is called the Petty Cash Book since it takes care of the cash transactions which are very petty in nature.

In this case the ledger has the various heads under which the usual amount is spent. The first column is receipt of the cash and then day to day cash activities are noted as per the details. At the end of week/month the totals are done and balance taken.

A possible example of the petty cash book can be:

Receipts	*Date*	*Particulars*	*V no.*	*Total*	*Conveyance*	*Stationary*	*Postage*	*Others*
100.00	1.2.00	To cash A/c.						
	2.2.00	By conveyance		15.00	15.00			
	5.2.00	By Stationary		19.00		19.00		
	7.2.00	By Postage		22.00			22.00	
	10.2.00	By telephone		6.00				6.00

100.00	Total	62.00	15.00	19.00	22.00	6.00
	By balance C/d	38.00				
38.00	By balance B/d					

Next in line is the Ledger and Ledger accounts.

LEDGER AND LEDGER ACCOUNTS

These reflect the main accounting picture of a company. All transactions dealing with a particular account are reflected here.

The ledger shown here is divided into two parts. The left hand side is debit side and right hand side is the credit side. Each side is further divided into 4 sections namely: Date, Particulars, Folio and Amount.

Dr.							Cr.
Date	Particulars	Folio	Amount	Date	Particulars	Folio	Amount

Date

These columns record the date of the transaction. The date of transaction is first recorded in the journal book, from the journal it is brought to the ledger account.

Particulars

As usual this column records the details of the transaction, i.e., the name of the account in which the corresponding debit or credit is found.

Folio

This column works as reference. Here we write the Journal Page No. of the account which is being written in the Particulars column of ledger.

Amount

This is the amount which is debited or credited and is entered in this column.

Following is the example of an account where some transactions have taken place between the company and Sachin in the form of sale. Let us see how they are first recorded into journal, then into the accounts of Sachin and the cash account.

Date	*Particulars*	*Amount (in Rs.)*
2-1-01	Goods sold to Sachin	10,000
4-1-01	Received cash from Sachin	8,000

6-1-01	Brought goods on cash	20,000
8-1-01	Paid cartage	100
10-1-01	Goods returned by Sachin	2,000
12-1-01	Goods sold to Sachin	4,000
15-1-01	Received cash from Sachin	3,000

These entries in the journal will look like this.

Date	*Particulars*		*L.F.*	*Debit (Rs.)*	*Credit (Rs.)*
2-1-01	Cash Account	Dr.		10,000	
					10,000
	(being the sale of goods on cash)				
4-1-01	Cash Account	Dr.		8,000	
					8,000
	(being receipt of cash)				
6-1-01	Goods Account	Dr.		20,000	
					20,000
	(purchase of goods)				
8-1-01	Goods Account	Dr.		100	
					100
	(cartage on goods)				
10-1-01	Goods Account	Dr.		2,000	
	To Sachin Account				2,000
	(being the value of goods returned)				
12-1-01	Sachin Account	Dr.		4,000	
	To Goods Account				4,000
	(being the sale of goods on credit)				
15-1-01	Cash Account	Dr.		3,000	
	Sachin Account				3,000
	(being receipt of cash)				

Let us now see how the individual ledgers would look like.

Dr. **Cash Account** **Cr.**

Date	*Particulars*	*J.F.*	*Amount (Rs.)*	*Date*	*Particulars*	*J.F.*	*Amount (Rs.)*
2-1-01	To Goods A/c		10,000	6-1-01	By Goods A/c		20,000

4-1-01	To Sachin A/c		8,000	8-1-01	By Goods A/c		100
15-1-01	To Sachin A/c		3,000				
							20,100
					By Balance C/d 900		
			21,000				21,000
	To Balance b/d		900				

Dr. **Goods Account** **Cr.**

Date	*Particulars*	*J.F.*	*Amount (Rs.)*	*Date*	*Particulars*	*J.F.*	*Amount (Rs.)*
6-1-01	To Cash A/c		20,000	2-1-01	By Cash A/c		10,000
8-1-01	To Cash A/c		100	12-1-01	By Sachin A/c		4,000
10-1-01	To Sachin A/c		2,000				
					By Balance C/d		8,100
			22,100				22,100
	To Balance b/d		8,100				

Dr. **Sachin Account** **Cr.**

Date	*Particulars*	*J.F.*	*Amount (Rs.)*	*Date*	*Particulars*	*J.F.*	*Amount (Rs.)*
12-1-01	To Goods A/c		4,000	15-1-01	By Cash A/c		3,000
					By Balance C/d		1,000
			4,000				4,000
	To Balance b/d		1,000				

TRIAL BALANCE

At the end of an accounting period all the accounts are balanced and the balances listed. The total on both the sides of this, called the trial balance, should balance. Since we are working on the concept of every debit entry having a contra credit entry and vice versa. Thus the trial balance is an arithmetic check that all the double entries have been completed.

A company's trail balance could look like this:

Particulars	*Debit (Rs.)*	*Credit (Rs.)*
Cash Account	30,000	
Bank Account	4,000	
Goods Account	5,000	
Discount Account		200

Machinery Account	8,000	
Capital Account		50,000
Sachin Account	1,000	
Salary Account	3,000	
Rent Account		1,500
Interest Account	700	
	51,700	51,700

The total on the debit side equals the total of credit side, indicating that there are no mistakes in the calculations.

TRADING AND PROFIT AND LOSS ACCOUNT

The result of all financial accounting amounts to two parts: income statements and position statements. The term income statement is better known as Trading and Profit & Loss Account and position statement is known as Balance Sheet.

Before you go any further you must understand the following terms:

Gross Profit = Net Sales – Cost price of goods sold

Net sales = Sales – Goods returned

Cost of goods sold = Sales – Gross profit

or in other words this can be written as:

Cost of goods sold = Opening stock + Net purchases + Direct Expenses – Closing stock

Gross loss = Cost of goods sold - Net sales

Net Purchases = Purchases – Purchases returned

Let us now take another example and try to calculate the profit from the following information about a company

	Amount (Rs.)
Opening Stock	20,000
Purchases	4,000
Sales	40,000
Salaries	5,000
Fuel	2,000
Closing Stock	4,000
Purchase returned	1,500

Sales returned	1,000
Transportation	1,500
Octroi	600

On the basis of above information, we can generate the following results:

Direct expenses = Fuel + Transportation + Octroi

= 2000 + 1500 + 600

= 4100

Net Purchases = Purchases – Purchases returned

= 4000 – 1500

= 2500

Net Sales = Sales – Sales Returned

= 40000 – 1000

= 39000

Cost of goods = Opening stock + Net Purchases + Direct expenses – Closing stock

= 20000 + 2500 + 4100 – 4000

= 22600

Gross Profit = Net Sales – Cost of gocds

= 39000 – 22600

= 16400

Proforma of a Trading Account

The trading account of a company would look like the one shown below. Let me explain the various heads used in this.

Dr. **Trading Account** **Cr.**

Particulars	*Amount (Rs.)*	*Particulars*	*Amount (Rs.)*
To opening stock		By Sales Less: Sales return By closing stock	
To Purchases		By gross loss - transferred to Profit/Loss account (if debit side exceeds the credit side)	
To Carriage or Cartage			

To Octroi or Local Taxes

To Wages

To Fuel

To Royalty

To any other expenses related to purchases on production.

To gross profit (transferred to Profit/Loss A/c if credit side exceeds the debit side)

Firstly the ones on the left hand side of the account.

Opening Stock

It is the stock available with the company on the opening day of the accounting period. This stock is available from the debit side of trial balance, therefore it is shown on the debit side of the trading account. The opening stock does not exist for a newly started business but if the company has existed for more than one year it will definitely have an opening stock.

Purchases

This account includes all cash as well as credit purchases of goods made during the year. Two important points need to be mentioned here.

Firstly, we have to show net purchases in the trading account, hence we deduct here the purchases returned.

Secondly, it needs to be emphasized that the only purchases transferred to this account are the one in which business is being carried. The account does not include purchase of assets.

Carriage or Cartage

All expenses incurred during the purchase of goods are direct expenses and add to the cost of goods purchased.

Wages

Companies involved in manufacturing have to pay wages to the labour. These expenses are the part of the value of goods manufactured by the company. It is therefore necessary that these expenses are added to the cost of goods produced and debited to trading account.

Fuel

Just like cartage expenses, the amount of money spent on fuel which is used to fetch the raw material for producing goods adds up to the cost of goods and must be accounted for.

Royalty

It is the amount payable to the landlord of mines and tea gardens for the right to work at his place, or any other similar thing. In case of foreign collaboration it is the amount given to foreign principals as part of the agreement for the consultancy. It is paid by the company and is treated as direct expenses.

Now we come to the right hand side of the trading account.

Sales

It includes the total of both the cash and credit sales made during a financial year. As before two points have to be emphasized, first sale does not include the sales of assets and second the amount of net sales, goods sold-goods returned, is recorded here.

Closing Stock

It is the value of goods on the closing date of an accounting period. Stock is valued at cost price or market price, whichever is lower. Usually, the closing stock is not given in the trial balance but is given among other adjustments outside the trial balance. In order to bring the closing stock into account, it is necessary to pass an adjustment entry debiting stock account and crediting trading account. The following is the example of a trading account of a company.

	Amount (Rs.)
Opening Stock	60,000
Sales A/c	80,000
Purchases return	4,000
Royalty A/c	8,000
Fuel	2,000
Wages	5,000
Sales return	1,000
Purchase A/c	10,000
Closing Stock as on 31st Dec, 2001	4,000

This when put into the trading account would look like as shown below.

Dr. Trading Account Cr.

Particulars	*Amount (Rs.)*	*Particulars*	*Amount (Rs.)*
		By Sales	80,000
To opening stock	60,000	Less: Sales return	1,000

To Purchases	10,000	By gross loss - transferred to Profit/Loss account (if debit side exceds the credit side)	
Purchase return	4,000		
	6,000	Closing Stock	6,000
To Wages	5,000		
To Fuel	2,000		
To Royalty	8,000		
To gross profit (transferred to Profit/Loss A/c if credit side exceeds the debit side)	4,000		
	85,000		85,000

Profit and Loss Account

It is prepared to calculate the net profit or net loss of the business for a given accounting period. As expected it is the summary of all income and expenses.

On the income side, you can have the entries like:

Dividend received

Interest earned

Discount and commission received

Whereas on the expenses side you can have expenses like:

Selling Expenses

Such as rent for office premises, advertising expenses, travelling allowance, commission, etc.

Distributive Expenses

Such as packing charges, vehicle maintenance, outward cartage, etc.

Administrative Expenses

Such as staff salary, electricity bill and other office expenses.

Closing Entries

The entries that have to be made in the journal for preparing the trading account and profit & loss account are known as closing entries. Follow the steps mentioned below to make the necessary entries:

- In order to close the accounts of expenses or loses, debit the profit and loss account and credit the corresponding expense account. This entry will close all the expenses account in the ledger.

- In order to close the accounts of income or profit, debit the corresponding income account and credit the profit and loss account. This entry will close the income account in the ledger.
- In order to transfer the balance of profit and loss account, debit the profit and loss account and credit the capital account if there is net profit, otherwise credit the profit and loss account and debit the capital account.

On the basis of these available figures we would prepare the Trading Account and then Profit and Loss Account. So let's do it.

Trial Balance

Debit Balances	*Debit (Rs.)*	*Credit Balances*	*Credit (Rs.)*
		Capital Account	50,000
Stock Account	6,000		
Cash at Bank	10,000		
Cash in Hand	7,000		
Machinery Account	5,000		
Furniture Account	3,000		
Purchases Account	4,000		
Wages Account	6,000		
Fuel Account	6,000		
Electricity Bill Account	5,000		
Salaries Account	2,000		
Discount Allowed Account	8,000		
		Discount Receivd Account	1,000
Advertising Account	2,000	Sales Account	50,000
		Adjustments	
		(i) stock on 31st March	10,000
		(ii) Depreciation on Machinery & Furniture	10%
		(iii) Rent outstanding	1,000

Adjustment Entries

Stock (closing Account)	Dr.	10,000	
To Trading Account			10,000
(being the amount of closing stock brought into account)			
Profit & Loss A/c	Dr.	1,000	
To Outstanding Rent A/c			1,000

Dr. Trading Account Cr.

Particulars	*Amount (Rs.)*	*Particulars*	*Credit (Rs.)*
To Stock A/c	6,000	By Sales A/c	50,000
To Purchase A/c	4,000	By Closing Stock	10,000
To Wages A/c	6,000		
To Fuel A/c	6,000		
To Electricity Bill A/c	5,000		
To Gross Profit transferred to Profit & Loss A/c	33,000		
	60,000		60,000

Dr. Profit & Loss A/c Cr.

Particulars	*Amount (Rs.)*	*Particulars*	*Credit (Rs.)*
To Salaries A/c	2,000	By Gross profit transferred from the Trading A/c	33,000
To Discount Allowed A/c	8,000	By Discount Received A/c	1,000
To Advertising A/c	2,000		
To Net Profit transferred to Capital A/c	22,000		
	34,000		34,000

BALANCE SHEET

A balance sheet is a statement of the financial position of the company, in terms of capital, assets and liabilities. Let us see what goes into the balance sheet and what it reflects.

Assets – Liabilities = Capital

The two sides of the balance sheet show the following:

Left Hand Side	*Right Hand Side*
Capital and Liabilities	**Assets**
Sources	Uses
Where the finances came from	Where the finances went to
What the business owes	What the business owns

A balance sheet of the company may have the following information.

Balance Sheet

Liabilities	*Amount (Rs.)*	*Assets*	*Amount (Rs.)*
Sundry or Trade Creditors		Cash in Hand	
Bills Payable		Petty Cash	
Bank Overdraft		Cash at Bank	
Employees Provident Fund		Bills Receivable	
Loans (Cr.)		Sundry Debtors	
Mortage		Loans (Dr.)	
Reserve/Res. Fund Capital			
Capital		Closing Stock	
Add Interest on Capital		Investments	
Add Net Profit		Furniture and Fittings	
Less Drawings		Loose Tools	
Less Income Tax		Plant & Machinery	
Less Interest on Drawings		Horses & Carts	
Less Net Loss		Land and Buildings	
Outstanding Expenses		Freehold/Leasehold Land	

FUNDAMENTALS OF INVENTORY

In the last section you read about Accounting. But, Tally is not about Accounting only, it takes care of the Inventory too. By inventory we mean the stocks and items. Before you go deep into understanding Tally for Inventory you must understand the basics of Inventory specially if you are a non-accounting person.

You can enter inventory details while entering Vouchers. For convenience of entry, Tally also permits to enter in invoice format where computation of Taxes, Duties or other charges can be automated. You can organize items into Groups and optionally Categorize them for better organization and reporting. You get numerous Reporting options on diverse parameters. To enter and maintain inventory details, in the Company Info screen, you should opt for Maintaining Accounts with Inventory option.

Let us understand the various inventory terms.

Stock Items

What you receive or issue, Sell or purchase, each item is a Stock Item. For example, for the Bookshop from you buy this book, this book is a Stock item. Similarly stock items can be clubbed together and can be called Stock groups. For example, in a department store of clothes, Gents clothes can be a group having Pants, Shirts, Coats, etc., for under that category. Similarly for Ladies and Children.

Usually Stock Items are measured in a Unit, e.g., Pcs, Kg, Ltr, etc. Different items may be measured in different units. You can create Unit of Measurement as per your business need. You can specify the Unit in which the item is transacted—normally one Unit. However, some items may be transacted in 12 units also called dozens.

Tally allows you to specify upto 2 Units for a single Stock Item, one as Unit and the other as Alternate Unit, you define relationship between the two Units.

A company has usually many places to store inventory items, they are called Godowns normally. Each godown has its inventory and that when combined with inventory of other godowns give the complete picture of the company's inventory. This helps in locating an item which may not be there at one location, then, it can be transfered from other godown where it is there.

Tally allows you to create Stock items as per your requirement, its alternate Name (Aliases), Part Numbers, Description, Remarks, etc. You can optionally maintain Batchwise details, enter Purchase and Sale prices, specify Stock Valuation Method for an item.

Stock Group

As mentioned earlier, stocks items can be clubbed together to form stock groups. We had taken the example of Gents clothing. Normally thousands of Stock items are traded in an Organization. It may become unmanagable if the items are not properly grouped. You can arrange all Stock items into Stock Groups based on common features (e.g., based on Brand, Quality, Specification, etc.) You can nest Groups to any depth, as such.

Gents Clothing:

- Pants
- Shirts
- Coats, etc.

Women Clothing:

- Sarees
- Dresses

- Other accessories, etc.

Children Clothing:

- Toddler items
- Children clothing
- Toys, etc.

Grouping of stock items helps to get Group specific report. In above example, to get a Stock report of Sarees only, you cn conveniently get it by selecting Saree Group. In fact Stock Group provides similar advantages as Account Groups provide for organization of Accounts.

Stock Categories

Stock Categories offer the benefit of classifying an item in another dimension - thus at any moment you can find similar items. In the above example, gents shirts may be of different types, for example, of brands like Live-in, Newman, Provouge, etc.

Such additional information for item help when a customer asks for one item which is not available in Stock or enquiries about similar items.

Godowns

It has been mentioned earlier while talking about Stock items, Godown (or Location) is a place to store materials. It may be a Warehouse, Rack, Shell, BIN or anything. You can extend this concept even to materials issued to Jobbers or Principal's goods held on Consignment basis. To monitor Locationwise movement of Stock, you may create Multiple Godowns and while entering transactions, specifications, specify the Godown.

On activating Godown option, Tally creates a default godown main Location under primary, you can alter its Name but cannot delete. Godowns can be nested to any level. So you can logically build Warehouses, Shed No., Godown Number, Rack Number, BIN Number, etc., to organize Godowns to get summarized totals for each level.

You can treat the Godwons as stockable/non-stockable. Non-stockable godowns does not appear in the List of Godowns in Voucher to prevent data entry errors.

Unit of Measure

As mentioned earlier, a stock item is measured in a Unit, e.g., Piece, Litre, Metre, etc. Select one of this option to create all such units. Many items are measured by a combination of 2 units (e.g., Box of 100 pcs, strip of 4 capsules) which is termed as Compound Units.

MARKET VALUATION METHOD

Inventory costing methods are various as per Tally. You can choose any one of them. A brief explation of the various options are:

FIFO

The full form is First In First Out. Tally considers oldest stock moved first.

LIFO Annual

LIFO is the abbreviation for Last In First Out. Tally considers movement of latest goods first, taking into account the current financial year.

LIFO Perpetual

It is similar to LIFO Annual but last purchase continues from previous Financial year.

Average Cost

The weighted average for the whole year is computed considering all Purchases.

Monthly Avg. Cost

It is similar to Average Cost but weighted average is computed for the month instead of whole year.

Last Purchase Cost

Values at latest Purchase Cost.

Standard Cost

At the rate that you entered in Stock item at Standard Purchase Cost applicable for the date of Report.

At Zero Cost

Cost of such item is considered at zero. For example, for defective items of no commerical value.

REORDER LEVELS

Reorder Level report is helpful for Manufacturing organisation or Assembling industry for timely procurement of materials (to ensure no production loss due to non-availability of raw materials or component). Traders will also be able to identify items for which order to be placed in time to ensure no cusotmer is returned due to non-availability of Stock.

Besides specifying absolute quantity, you can also base re-order level on previous consumption during a specific period and ask Tally to compute whichever lower or higher with option for Rounding Off.

Many vendors fix a minimum ordering quantity which too you can specify for each item. In many trade, it becomes economical to buy a larger lot as compared to immediate requirement - you can specify such quantity to achieve economy of scale. All these helps placement of Purchase Order in time.

What is a Reorder Level?

Reorder level is the quantity for a Stock item, when stock-in-hand reaches that quantity, you should place order for supplies. Every organization desires to execute customer orders in time and have sufficient stock to serve them but at the same time over-stocking costs hight (in terms of blocked money, interest cost and space to store). Thus, re-order level figure is computed in such a manner that neither stock for an item becomes NIL at any point of time nor unwanted stock is carried.

MULTIPLE PRICE LIST

During Stock item creation, you learned how to enter Standard Sales Price for each Stock item. Many organisation have different Price Lists for different class of Nuyers, for example, one Price List for Retail Customers and another for Wholesale Customer. Some Organization also offer different discount on different volume. With a single Standard Price List you cannot address all these issues. Besiders Cost and Sales Prices for Stock items. Tally provides you with the option of having multiple Price Lists.

INVENTORY TRASACTIONS

Like accounting, inventory too has vouchers with the help of which you can enter the information to Tally. All stock items information whether the item is going in or going out is given to Tally with the help of vouchers.

You can also give information with the help of invoice, order or challans.

Vouchers

Various voucher which are used in inventory are:

Stock Journal Vouchers

This voucher is used for transfer of materials. It allows you to move stock items from one godown to another without affecting the financial accounts.

Recipt Note Vouchers

Whenever you buy goods, you pass a purchase voucher. However, if you have not received a bill then you can simply pas a Receipt Note. This updates the stock of that item but does not afffect the financial accounts. When yu receive the bill, you can adjust it against the Receipt Note.

Rejections-in Vouchers

Sometimes the party to which you sell goods you can send them as rejections. If the buyer does not immediately send you a debit note, then you can pass Rejections in voucher to bring the goods back into your stock.

Delivery Note Vouchers

When you sell goods to a customer, you generally raise an invoice. However, sometimes you send goods out with a Delivery Note and later raise an invoice against this delivery note.

Rejections-out Vouchers

Sometimes, you reject some items from the goods you purchased but send its debit note to the seller later. In this case, you can pass a Rejection Out voucher and raise a Debit Note against this rejection note.

Physical Stock Vouchers

This voucher at any given date represents the confirmation of actual stock on that date. Whenever you check the actual stock, you pass a Physical Stock voucher to specify the corect stock value. The stock value at this point is considered the stock-in-hand and all the calculations are based on this value.

INVOICE

Invoice entries are similar to Vouchers, the prime difference may be listed as under:

In Voucher you first enter Accounts allocation, then Inventory allocation. In Invoice, it is just the reverse, i.e., first inventory allocation, then accounting details. In Vouchers, you have to pre-compute the item transaction value, duties and taxes, etc., in order to compute the amount to debit/credit the party account. In Invoice, all the computation is done by the software Tally, you have to just enter the basic figures of quantity, rate, etc.

ORDER

Orders are optional documents of pre-invoice stage. You can prepare invoices even without incorporating ordering system. Orders do not affect inventory.

Tally provides you the following options for Purchase and Order Acceptance:

1. Entry and printing of Purchase and Sales Order Acceptance.
2. Staggering Deliver Time for the same item.
3. Item specific & common Rates for Discount, Tax and Other Billing Terms.
4. Bypassing of Orders, i.e., Sales & Purchase transaction entry with & without orders.
5. Tracking of Outstanding Order status.
6. Other Terms and Conditions for Sales & Purchase.

CHALLANS

Normally inventory tansaction comprises of 2 principal elements, Movement of Materials and Financial Transactions. Thus, the Inventory and Accounting vouchers reflecing the transaction may be like:

1. Movement of Goods and Financial Trasaction simultaneously.
2. Movement of Goods and Financial Transaction are separate events.

INVENTORY REPORTS

Following reports can be generated from Tally with respect to inventory.

Movement Analysis — Stock Group Analysis

Movement Analysis of a selected stock group brings up the Total Inward and Outward movement of all the items in which slected Stock Group. The Quantaties shown are acual Quantaties of movement (which is some cases, may be different from the billed Qty in the transactions). The inward detail shows the Effective Rate or Final Landed Cost of the materials, after considering all overhead costs.

In case the Effective Rate is different from the basic invoice rate of the materials, it is shown in Bold — to highlight a possible candidate for further study. The Outward detail shown the Basic Invoice Rate and Value of Goods sold/transferred out.

Item Movement Analysis

Item Movement Analysis is the next level of information (press Enter on the stock item or Display Inventory - Books Stock Item Analysis). This brings up the Party-wise/Transfer wise detail of Movement In and Out. The inward details show the Basic Invoice Rate as well as the Effective Rate.

This is a greate comparative report to view the effect of Purchase costs from different suppliers. For example, Supplier A may have a lower Basic Invoice Rate as compared to Supplier B, but the Effective Rate may be higher — (perhaps due to differences in Taxes, Packaging Costs, Freight Costs, etc.)

Similarly, in context where a material is both manufactured in-house, as well as purchased — the difference in Purchase Costs and In-house Costs can be compared. Lastly, by selecting multiple columns for different periods, you would get to see the changes in Effective Rate for your purchases. The next level of information (press Enter on the Party Name or Stock Journal Name), gives the transaction level detail of information.

Here, the Date of goods received/sold, the Quantities, Basic Rates, Addl. Costs and Effective Rate for each transaction may be viewed pressing Enter expands into the Date, Type and Number of the Vouchers which have contributed to this transaction.

Ledger Analysis

Ledger Analysis is similar to Movement Analysis, except for bringing up the movements of the items for the selected Ledger (Party). Thus, you get an analysis of all purchases made from a supplier or all items sold to a customer. The next level of information brings up the transaction level detail.

Transfer Analysis

Transfer Analysis gives the movement details of each type of Stock Journal. This can be used powerfully by following a simple discipline of using different Stock Journal types for each nature of trnasaction. For example, item A Prod item B can be used for the production of items A and B respectively.

In this scenario, the report then represents the total of item A produced, as well as the Raw Materials used for its production, with overhead costs (as entered). This becomes a very useful costing and waste analysis too. In non-manufacturing segments, but with Multiple Godown, this report becomes a quick check to verify that all transfer have been entered correctly - since the Total Movement In and Out must watch.

Aged Stock Analysis (Ageing Analysis)

A very important function of Working Capital management is monitoring stocks. Money locked up in stocks can adversely affect the liquidity of company and every company strives or should strive to reduce stock levels to the optimum.

Every business (except perhaps the liquor and antiques dealers) would prefer to dispose of older stocks as they might deteriorate with time, go out of fashion or simply get forgotten. Tally's aged stock analysis or Stock agening enables you to know the age of stocks in hand according to when they were received and the purchase value.

Stock Transfers

This report displays the number of stock journal vouchers for the month.

Physical Stock Register

This report displays the monthly sotck transfer vouchers in a register format.

Godown Summary (Location Summary)

The Godown/Location Summary statement shows the Stock Summary for different Godown/Locations. While the main Stock Summary shows the stock position for the entire company on a given date, the Godown/Location Summary is a statement of stock in hand at each location on a particular date.

As with all Tally statements, it is updated with every transaction so that it provides current stock position for any godown/location at any time.

Views of Godown/Location Summary Statement

Use options in the button bar to set up different information views. The Godown/Location Summary shows stocks at each location.

Godown/Location Stock Flow/Reconciliation

The reconciled flow of goods at each location is available.

EXCEPTION REPORTS

Excetion reports are reports that track transactions or balances. The different Exception reports are:

Negative Stock

This a list of all stock items that have a negative balance at the end of the period of display. If a negative balance occurs within the period but is adjusted by a purchase so that the balance is not negative at the end of the display period, the item will not be listed.

Change the period or select multi-column display, via auto-column and see the negative items.

Negative Ledgers

This is a list of ledger accounts that have observer balances, i.e., balances that are opposite to the nature of the account. For example, a creditor amount having a debit balance and an asset account having a credit balance.

Overdue Receivables

This is list of all invoices that are overdue on the current date.

Overdue Payables

This is a list of all purchae bills that are overdue on the current date.

List of Memorandum Vouchers

This a list of Memorandum Vouchers entered during a period. Change the period as required.

List of Reversing Journals

This is a list of Reversing Journals entered during a period. Change the period as required.

List of Optional Vouchers

This is a list of vouchers marked as Optional during a period. This list includes all types of vouchers that are marked Optional.

Post-dated Vouchers

This is a list of vouchers that are marked Post-dated within a given period. This list includes all types of vouchers that are marked Post-dated.

B Keyboard Shortcuts

SHORTCUT KEYS IN TALLY

The shortcut keys appear in button names in the button bar (right side of the Tally screen). You can either click the button from the button bar or press the relevant function key or character underlined/double-underlined.

The buttons have a function key before the button names (Eg. F1: Select Cmp) which means you need to press F1 key (Function Key) to select the 'Select Company' screen

The buttons have an underlined character (Eg:F3:Cmp Info) which means you need to press A lot + F3 to select the 'Company Info' Screen.

Some buttons have a double-underlined character (Eg: As Voucher) which means you need to press Ctrl + V to select the 'Voucher' in voucher mode.

The shortcut keys available in Tally are listed in the below table:

Function Key Combination

Windows	*Functionality*	*Availability*
F1	To select a company	At all masters menu screen
F1	To select the Accounts Button	At the Accounting Voucher creation and alteration screen
F1(Alt+F1)	To select the Inventory Button	At the Inventory Voucher creation and alteration screen
F2	To change the date	At almost all screens in Tally
F3	To select the company	At almost all screens in Tally
F4	To select the Contra voucher	At Accounting / Inventory Voucher creation and alteration screen
F5	To select the Payment voucher	At Accounting / Inventory Voucher creation and alteration screen
F6	To select the Receipt voucher	At Accounting / Inventory Voucher creation and alteration screen
F7	To select the Journal voucher	At Accounting / Inventory Voucher creation and alteration screen

	deleted subject to conditions, as explained in the manual.	At Stock Groups/ Stock Categories/ Stock Items/ Reorder Levels/ Godowns/ Voucher Types / Units of Measure (Inventory Info) creation/ alteration screen
Ctrl+E	To select the Currencies	At Groups/Ledgers/Cost Centres/ Budgets/Scenarios/Voucher Types/ Currencies (Accounts Info) creation and alteration screen
Ctrl+G	To select the Group	At Groups/Ledgers/Cost Centres/ Budgets/Scenarios/Voucher Types/ Currencies (Accounts Info) creation and alteration screen
Ctrl+I	To select the Stock Items	At Stock Group/ Stock Categories/ Stock Items/ Reorder Levels/ Godowns/ Voucher Types / Units of Measure (Inventory Info) creation/ alteration screen
Ctrl+L	To select the Ledger	At Groups/Ledgers/Cost Centres/ Budgets/Scenarios/Voucher Types/ Currencies (Accounts Info) creation and alteration screen
Ctrl+O	To select the Godowns	At Stock Group/ Stock Categories/ Stock Items/ Reorder Levels/ Godowns/ Voucher Types / Units of Measure (Inventory Info) creation/ alteration screen
Ctrl+Q	To abandon a form – wherever you use this key combination, it quits that screen without making any changes to it.	At almost all screens in Tally.
Ctrl+Alt+R	Rewrite data for a Company	From Gateway of Tally screen
Ctrl+S	Allows you to alter Stock Item master	At Stock Voucher Report and Godown Voucher Report
Ctrl+U	To select the Units	At Stock Groups/ Stock Categories/ Stock Items/ Reorder Levels/ Godowns/ Voucher Types / Units of Measure (Inventory Info) creation/ alteration screen
Ctrl+V	To select the Voucher Types	At Groups/Ledgers/Cost Centres/ Budgets/Scenarios/Voucher Types/

		Currencies (Accounts Info) creation and alteration screen

Special Function Key Combinations

Windows	*Functionality*	*Availability*
Alt+F1	To close a company	At all menu screens
	To view detailed report	At almost all report screens
	To explode a line into its details	At almost all screens in Tally
Alt+F2	To change the period	At almost all screens in Tally
Alt+F3	To select the company info menu	At Gateway of Tally screen
	To create/alter/shut a Company	
Alt+F4	To select the Purchase Order Voucher Type	At Accounting / Inventory Voucher creation and alteration screens
Alt+F5	To select the Sales Order Voucher Type	At Accounting / Inventory Voucher creation and alteration screens
	To view monthly and quarterly report	At almost all report screens in Tally
Alt+F6	To select the Rejection Out Voucher Type	
	To change the Sales Order Voucher Type	At Accounting / Inventory Voucher creation and alteration screens
Alt+F7	To select the Stock Journal Voucher Type	To accept all the Audit lists
		At Accounting / Inventory Voucher creation and alteration screens
		At TallyAudit Listing screen
Alt+F8	To select the Delivery Note Voucher Type	At Accounting / Inventory Voucher creation and alteration screens
	To view the Columnar report	At Ledger Voucher screen
Alt+F9	To select the Receipt Note Voucher Type	At Accounting / Inventory Voucher creation and alteration screens
Alt+F10	To select the Physical Stock Voucher Type	At Accounting / Inventory Voucher creation and alteration screens
Alt+F12	To filter the information based on monetary value	At almost all report screens
Ctrl+Alt+F12	Advanced Config	At Gateway of Tally

Key Combination Used for Navigation

Windows	*Functionality*	*Availability*
PgUp	Display previous voucher during voucher entry/alter	At voucher entry and alteration screens
PgDn	Display next voucher during voucher entry/alter	At voucher entry and alteration screens
Enter	To accept anything you type into a field.	You have to use this key at most areas in Tally
	To accept a voucher or master	
	To get a report with further details of an item in a report.	At the receivables report – press Enter at a pending bill to get transactions relating to this bill (e.g., original sale bill, receipts and payments against this bill, etc)
Esc	To remove what you typed into a field	
	To come out of a screen	At almost all screens in Tally.
	To indicate you do not want to accept a voucher or master.	
Shift+Enter	Collapse next level details	At Voucher Register screen and Trial Balance report
Shift+Enter	To explode a line into its details	In almost all Reports:
		At a Group/Stock Group/Cost Category/Godown/Stock Category – displays Sub Groups and Ledgers/Stock Items/Cost Centres/Secondary Godowns/Secondary Stock Categories
		At a Voucher – displays its entries and narration
		At a Stock Item- displays its godowns and batch details
		At Voucher Register screen – displays the next level details
		At Trial Balance report - displays the next level details
Ctrl+Enter	To alter a master while making an entry or viewing a report	At voucher entry and alteration screens
		At all reports

FIREWALL MEDIA

(An imprint of Laxmi Publications Pvt. Ltd.)

Computer Books *for School, BCA, MCA, IGNOU, DOEACC and Engineering Students and Professionals*

ISBN	TITLE	AUTHOR	PRICE	PAGES
	.NET			
8170087155	**Building Business Intelligence Applications with .Net**	Robert Ericsson	Rs. 295.00	404
8170083567	**Learning VB.Net Through Applications**	Clayton Crooks	Rs. 295.00	450
8131800865	**Magic of C# with .Net Frame Work**	Shibi Panikkar, Kumar Sanjeev	Rs. 495.00	950
8170082471	**Magic of ASP.Net with C#**	Shibi Panikkar, Kumar Sanjeev	Rs. 395.00	828
8170089662	**ASP.Net Interview Questions and Answers**	J. Rajaram	Rs. 95.00	175
	A TO Z SERIES			
8170083214	**Access 2002 from A to Z**	Julia Kelly, Stephen L. Nelson	Rs. 75.00	185
8170083222	**Excel 2002 from A to Z**	Stephen L. Nelson	Rs. 75.00	193
8170083230	**Front Page 2002 from A to Z**	Heather Williamson	Rs. 85.00	219
8170083249	**Outlook 2002 from A to Z**	Stephen L. Nelson	Rs. 75.00	202
8170083257	**Page Maker 7 from A to Z**	Marc Campbell	Rs. 75.00	202
8170083265	**PowerPoint 2002 from A to Z**	Stephen L. Nelson	Rs. 75.00	202
8170083273	**Windows XP from A to Z**	Pat Coleman	Rs. 95.00	249
8170083281	**Word 2002 from A to Z**	Stephen L. Nelson	Rs. 75.00	199
817008329X	**XML from A to Z**	Heather Williamson	Rs. 75.00	200
8170083303	**Dreamweaver 4 from A to Z**	Heather Williamson	Rs. 85.00	215
	BEGINNERS & GENERAL INTEREST			
817008248X	**Shortcuts to Success in Computing**	Dheeraj Mehrotra	Rs. 55.00	110
8170083311	**Pictorial Computer Dictionary**	Dheeraj Mehrotra	Rs. 45.00	156
8170083486	**Pocket Net Browser**	Dheeraj Mehrotra	Rs. 95.00	302
8170084261	**1000 IT Quizzes**	Dheeraj Mehrotra	Rs. 75.00	120
8131800679	**Information Technology Bible**	Remesh Bangia	Rs. 295.00	567
8131800377	**Fundamentals of Information Technology Including MS Office**	Dinesh Maidasani, Jai Narayan Yadav	Rs. 175.00	356
813180089X	**Fundamentals of Information Technology Including MS Office (Hindi Medium)**	Dinesh Maidasani, Jai Narayan Yadav	Rs. 175.00	425
8170089719	**Foundations of Computer Science**	Ashok Arora	Rs. 250.00	386

Please write for a free color Firewall Media Catalog for details on the above books.

ISBN	TITLE	AUTHOR	PRICE	PAGES
	CALL CENTERS			
8170082196	**Call Centers Made Easy**	Stephen Medcroft	Rs. 195.00	310
	CISCO			
8170087481	**Enabling IP Routing with Cisco Routers**	R. Das, K. Chakrabarty	Rs. 295.00	486
817008749X	**Designing Networks with Cisco**	H. Pasricha, D. Jagu	Rs. 195.00	316
8170087503	**Cisco IP Routing Protocols: Troubleshooting Techniques**	V. Anand, K. Chakrabarty	Rs. 295.00	409
	DATABASES			
8170089530	**DBMS—Complete Practical Approach**	Sharad Maheshwari, Ruchin Jain	Rs. 350.00	656
8170082404	**Learn to Program Visual Basic-Examples**	John Smiley	Rs. 295.00	482
8170082412	**Learn to Program Visual Basic-Databases**	John Smiley	Rs. 325.00	653
8170082420	**Learn to Program Visual Basic-Objects**	John Smiley	Rs. 325.00	670
817008475X	**IT Resources-Access 2002 VBA Programming Access**	Michele Amelot	Rs. 195.00	424
8170084512	**The Power of Oracle 9i**	Rajiv Parida, Vinod Sharma	Rs. 475.00	1035
8170088518	**Principles and Implementation of Data Warehousing**	Rajiv A. Parida	Rs. 295.00	487
817008864X	**DBA Study Guide OCP Prep Guide**	Nazar Abdul	Rs. 295.00	474
8170088658	**Oracle 11i—The Complete Reference**	Rashmi Anandi	Rs. 495.00	975
8131800067	**Toxonomy of Database Management System**	Aditya Kumar Gupta	Rs. 75.00	146
8131800385	**Introduction to SQL and PL/SQL**	Sharad Maheshwari, Ruchin Jain	Rs. 200.00	389
	DOEACC 'O' LEVEL			
8170088089	**DOEACC 'O' Level Model Test Papers**	Ramesh Bangia	Rs. 175.00	296
8170089115	**DOEACC 'O' & 'A' Level Programming & Problem Solving Through 'C' Language (Model Test Paper with Solutions)**	Mukesh Sharma	Rs. 95.00	213
8170089069	**DOEACC 'O' & 'A' Level Business Systems (Model Test Paper with Solutions)**	Mukesh Sharma	Rs. 100.00	252
8170085640	**Programming and Problem Solving Through "C" Language**	Harsha Priya, R. Ranjeet	Rs. 95.00	306

Please write for a free color Firewall Media Catalog for details on the above books.

ISBN	TITLE	AUTHOR	PRICE	PAGES
8170084474	**IT Tools and Applications**	Ramesh Bangia	Rs. 145.00	370
8170085594	**Business Systems**	Ramesh Bangia	Rs. 175.00	452
8170089514	**Internet & Web Design**	Ramesh Bangia	Rs. 150.00	300
	ELECTRONIC COMMERCE			
8170085497	**Electronic Commerce**	Pete Loshin, John Vacca	Rs. 295.00	472
817008119X	**E-Commerce**	Mamta Bhusry	Rs. 95.00	215
8170083524	**Marketing in the Cyber Age**	Kurt Rohner	Rs. 295.00	223
	HARDWARE/EMBEDDED SYSTEMS			
8170087473	**Essential Electronics for PC Technicians**	John W. Farber	Rs. 295.00	546
8170086264	**Grid Computing: A Practical Guide to Technology and Applications**	Ahmar Abbas	Rs. 295.00	408
8170088186	**CD Cracking Uncovered Protection Against Unsanctioned CD Copy**	Kris Kaspersky	Rs. 295.00	422
8170083435	**Practical Linux Programming: Device Drivers, Embedded Systems and the Internet**	Ashfaq A. Khan	Rs. 295.00	420
8170083575	**TCP/IP Application Layer Protocols for Embedded Systems**	M. Tim Jones	Rs. 295.00	460
8131800520	**PC Repair and Maintenance : A Practical Guide**	Joel Rosenthal, Kevin Irwin	Rs. 195.00	362
8131800768	**The A+ Certification and PC Repair Handbook**	Christopher A Crayton, Joel Z. Rosenthal	Rs. 495.00	888
	INTERNET & WEB TECHNOLOGY			
8170083206	**The Internet Handbook for Writers, Students and Teachers**	Mary McGuire, Linda Stilborne	Rs. 195.00	276
8170084776	**Way in-Internet Getting Started**	Elizabeth Bramire	Rs. 95.00	165
8170088976	**Web Technology**	Ramesh Bangia	Rs. 250.00	560
8170087163	**Web Design with Macromedia Studio MX 2004**	Eric Hunley	Rs. 295.00	558
8170083400	**Professional Web Design (Techniques and Templates)**	Clint Eccher	Rs. 295.00	425
8170088046	**HTML, XHTML, CSS and XML**	Teodoru Gugoiu	Rs. 195.00	355
8170083583	**FrontPage 2000 for Visual Learners**	Chris Charuhas	Rs. 95.00	200
8170083591	**HTML & Java Script for Visual Learners**	Chris Charuhas	Rs. 95.00	200

ISBN	TITLE	AUTHOR	PRICE	PAGES
8170083605	**The Visual Learners Guide to Managing Web Projects**	Chris Charuhas	Rs. 95.00	130
8170083613	**Dreamweaver 4 for Visual Learners**	Chris Charuhas	Rs. 95.00	200
8170084768	**IT Resource-Implementing XML: Managing and Formatting Data**	Johhny Brochard	Rs. 125.00	279
8170089476	**Design Your Web World**	Sunil Jalota	Rs. 75.00	146

KEEPING AHEAD SERIES

ISBN	TITLE	AUTHOR	PRICE	PAGES
8170084652	**Keeping Ahead-Exchange 2000 Server**	Philippe Levesque	Rs. 145.00	285
8170084660	**Keeping Ahead-Windows 2000 Professional**	Jose Dardoigne	Rs. 175.00	388
8170084679	**Keeping Ahead-Windows 2000 Server**	Philippe Mathon	Rs. 175.00	360
8170084687	**Keeping Ahead-Linux Administration Kernel Version 2.0 to 2.2**	Bruno Guèrin	Rs. 125.00	240
8170084695	**Keeping Ahead-Using Linux Kernel Version 2.0 to 2.2**	Bruno Guèrin	Rs. 125.00	258
8170084709	**Keeping Ahead-Java 2**	Benjamin Aumaille	Rs. 145.00	284
8170084717	**Keeping Ahead-SQL Server 7**	Joelle Mosset	Rs. 145.00	329
8170084725	**Keeping Ahead-JavaScript and VBScript**	Benjamin Aumaille	Rs. 145.00	313
8170084733	**Keeping Ahead-C++ Programming Language**	Bruno Dubois	Rs. 125.00	234
8170084741	**Keeping Ahead-TCP/IP in the NT Environment**	Bruno Ferec	Rs. 125.00	230

MCSE

ISBN	TITLE	AUTHOR	PRICE	PAGES
817008489X	**MCSE-Administering SQL Server 7.0**	Jerome Gabillaud	Rs. 295.00	580
8170084903	**MCSE-Networking Essentials**	Jose Dordoigne	Rs. 245.00	453
8170084911	**MCSE-Windows 2000 Professional**	Jose Dordoigne	Rs. 325.00	665
817008492X	**MCSE-Windows 2000 Server**	Phillippe Mathon	Rs. 345.00	712

MULTIMEDIA AND ANIMATION

ISBN	TITLE	AUTHOR	PRICE	PAGES
8170088208	**3DS Max 6 Animation with Character Studio 4 and Plug-Ins**	Boris Kulagin, Dmitry Morozov	Rs. 175.00	216

Please write for a free color Firewall Media Catalog for details on the above books.

ISBN	TITLE	AUTHOR	PRICE	PAGES
8170088216	**Adobe Audition: Soundtracks for Digital Video**	Roman Petelin, Yury Petelin	Rs. 195.00	278
8170086205	**Building A Digital Human**	Ken Brilliant	Rs. 295.00	380
8170086213	**Making Digital Videos**	Ben Long	Rs. 295.00	284
8170087171	**Illustrating with Macromedia Flash ™ MX2004**	Robert Firbaugh	Rs. 245.00	366
8170082439	**Multimedia Basics-Technology (Vol. I)**	Andreas Holzinger	Rs. 195.00	312
8170082447	**Multimedia Basics-Learning (Vol. II)**	Andreas Holzinger	Rs. 195.00	326
8170082455	**Multimedia Basics-Design (Vol. III)**	Andreas Holzinger	Rs. 195.00	280
8170083532	**Maya Feature Creature Creations**	Todd Palamar	Rs. 295.00	376
8170083540	**Sound Forge Power**	Scott R. Garrigus	Rs. 195.00	344
8131800288	**Multimedia and Web Technology**	Ramesh Bangia	Rs. 395.00	878
813180044X	**Photoshop CS**	Shruti Lal	Rs. 195.00	434

NETWORKING

ISBN	TITLE	AUTHOR	PRICE	PAGES
817008721X	**Networking Essentials**	Jose Dordoigne	Rs. 195.00	453
8170089328	**TCP/IP Distributed System**	Vivek Acharya	Rs. 250.00	474
8170087023	**Computer Networks**	Ajit Kumar Singh	Rs. 95.00	181
8131800148	**The Real—world Network Troubleshooting Manual**	Alan Sugano	Rs. 295.00	396
817008203X	**Telecom & Networking Glossary**	Robert Mastin	Rs. 300.00	250
8170082048	**Data Networking Made Easy**	Karen Patten	Rs. 360.00	350
8170082056	**Digital Convergence**	Andy Covell	Rs. 300.00	234

OFFICE AUTOMATION

ISBN	TITLE	AUTHOR	PRICE	PAGES
8170089891	**Desk Top Publishing**	Dinesh Maidasani	Rs. 150.00	311
8170087805	**Learning Computer Fundamentals, MS Office and Internet & Web Technology**	Dinesh Maidasani	Rs. 95.00	301
8170087686	**MS-Word 2000 Thumb-Rules and Details**	Snigdha Banerjee	Rs. 175.00	390
8170089239	**Computer Accounting with Tally 7.2**	Firewall Media	Rs. 195.00	330

ON YOUR SIDE SERIES

ISBN	TITLE	AUTHOR	PRICE	PAGES
8170084830	**On your Side-Powerpoint 2002**	Andrew Blackburn	Rs. 145.00	282
8170084849	**On your Side-Excel 2002**	Adrienne Tommy	Rs. 125.00	275

ISBN	TITLE	AUTHOR	PRICE	PAGES
8170084857	**On your Side-Word 2002**	Adrienne Tommy	Rs. 125.00	289
8170084865	**On your Side-Access 2002**	Adrienne Tommy	Rs. 125.00	303
8170084873	**On your Side-Frontpage 2002**	Andrew Blackburn	Rs. 95.00	245
8170084881	**On your Side-Windows XP**	Adrienne Tommy	Rs. 125.00	310

OPERATING SYSTEMS

ISBN	TITLE	AUTHOR	PRICE	PAGES
8170087236	**Linux—A Practical Approach**	B. Mohamed Ibrahim	Rs. 95.00	187
8170088623	**Red Hat Linux Study Guide**	Vijay Shekhar	Rs. 350.00	635
8170088631	**Red Hat Linux-The Complete Bible**	Vijay Shekhar	Rs. 545.00	1176
8170089581	**Unix and Shell Programming**	Archana Verma	Rs. 80.00	137
8170089131	**Operating System Concepts**	P.S. Gill	Rs. 95.00	181
8170083427	**The MS-Windows XP Professional Handbook**	Louis Columbus	Rs. 295.00	330
8170084784	**Way in-Windows XP Home Edition**	Andrew Blackburn	Rs. 95.00	183
8170086221	**Cyber Rookies—Operating System Fundamentals**	D. Irtegov	Rs. 295.00	498

PROGRAMMING

ISBN	TITLE	AUTHOR	PRICE	PAGES
8170087791	**The Art of Programming Through Flowcharts & Algorithms**	Anil Bikas Chaudhuri	Rs. 95.00	160
8170086248	**Preventative Programming Techniques: Avoid and Correct Common Mistakes**	Brian Hawkins	Rs. 295.00	322
8170083443	**Learning Computer Programming : It's not about Languages**	Mary Farrell	Rs. 295.00	375
8170086256	**Object-Oriented Programming: From Problem Solving to Java**	José M. Garrido	Rs. 295.00	360
817008931X	**Object-Oriented Programming-Concept and Implementation**	A. Rajesh	Rs. 95.00	182
8170089107	**Java: J2SE-5 A Practical Approach**	B. Mohammad Ibrahim	Rs. 175.00	332
8170089409	**Advance Java**	Gajendra Gupta	Rs. 175.00	305
8170088038	**Assembly Language Programming for Intel Processors Family**	Vasile Lungu	Rs. 295.00	577
8170088178	**The Assembly Programming Master Book**	Vlad Pirogov	Rs. 395.00	726
813180075X	**Java Messaging**	Eric Bruno	Rs. 295.00	480

Please write for a free color Firewall Media Catalog for details on the above books.

ISBN	TITLE	AUTHOR	PRICE	PAGES

PROGRAMMING - C#, C, C++

ISBN	TITLE	AUTHOR	PRICE	PAGES
8170083702	**The Power of C#**	Rajiv Parida	Rs. 295.00	576
8170085632	**Mastering Graphics Programming in 'C'**	Sudhir Dawra	Rs. 145.00	286
8170088879	**Programming in C and Numerical Analysis**	J.B. Dixit	Rs. 350.00	355
8170087074	**Mastering C Programs**	J.B. Dixit	Rs. 195.00	434
8170081262	**Programming in C**	J.B. Dixit	Rs. 295.00	506
8170087619	**Unix and C Programming**	Ashok Arora, Shefali Bansal	Rs. 295.00	606
817008878X	**C Interview Questions and Answers**	J. Rajaram	Rs. 75.00	139
8170089034	**Pragmatic C**	R.K. Jangda	Rs. 150.00	258
8170086140	**Data Structure for 'C' Programming**	Ajay Kumar	Rs. 145.00	290
8170081270	**Programming in C++**	J.B. Dixit	Rs. 260.00	602
8170088194	**Hackish C++ Pranks & Tricks**	Michael Flenov	Rs. 245.00	326
8170082889	**Basics of C++ Programming**	Nishant Kundalia	Rs. 95.00	168
8170083648	**Mastering C++ Programs**	J.B. Dixit	Rs. 295.00	598
817008623X	**Cyber Rookies—C++ Programming Fundamentals**	Chuck Easttom	Rs. 295.00	417
8131800202	**Data Structure using C++**	N. Jayalakshmi	Rs. 65.00	126
8170089123	**C++ Made Easy**	T.D. Malhotra	Rs. 250.00	449
8131800393	**C++ & Introduction to C#**	T.D. Malhotra, Rajeev A. Parida, A. Rajesh	Rs. 200.00	440
8131800350	**OOPS with C++**	M. Jaya Prasad	Rs. 150.00	317

SECURITY

ISBN	TITLE	AUTHOR	PRICE	PAGES
8170083419	**Computer Forensics : Computer Crime Scene Investigation**	John Vacca	Rs. 445.00	731
8131800156	**Computer Evidence (Collection and Preservation)**	Christopher L.T. Brown	Rs. 295.00	394
8170083494	**Firewall Architecture for the Enterprise**	Norbert Pohlmann, Tim Crothers	Rs. 295.00	480
8170086272	**Net Spies**	Andrew Gauntlett	Rs. 195.00	210
3826607546	**Firewall Systems**	Norbert Pohlmann	Rs. 1630.00	544
8131800504	**Homeland Security Techniques and Technologies**	Jesus Mena	Rs. 295.00	346

ISBN	TITLE	AUTHOR	PRICE	PAGES

ENGINEERING AND TECHNOLOGY

ISBN	TITLE	AUTHOR	PRICE	PAGES
817008718X	**Human Aspects of Software Engineering**	James E. Tomayko, Orit Hazzan	Rs. 195.00	338
8131800032	**Management Information Systems**	Avdhesh Gupta, Anurag Malik	Rs. 195.00	400
8170087953	**Human Computer Interaction**	Rajendra Ranjan Kumar	Rs. 95.00	210
8170088097	**Structured System Analysis and Design**	Preeti Gupta	Rs. 125.00	192
817008802X	**Autocad 2005 for Engineers**	Ionel Simion	Rs. 175.00	271
8170088054	**Digital Signal Processing Fundamentals**	Ashfaq A. Khan	Rs. 295.00	391
8131800164	**Digital Communication System Using System VUE**	Dennis Silage	Rs. 295.00	365
8170089719	**Foundations of Computer Science**	Ashok Arora	Rs. 250.00	386
817008363X	**Practical Project Management**	Ivan Bayross	Rs. 195.00	342
8131800806	**Digital Signal Processing using MATLAB and Wavelets**	Michael Weeks	Rs. 350.00	452
8131800792	**Classical Electrodynamics**	Hans C. Dhanian	Rs. 395.00	620
8131800512	**The Software Vulnerability Guide**	Herbert H. Thompson, Scott G. Chase	Rs. 195.00	368
8131800776	**Robot Modelling and Kinematics**	Rachid Manseur	Rs. 295.00	380
8131800369	**System Software**	M. Joseph	Rs. 95.00	185

STRAIGHT TO THE POINT SERIES

ISBN	TITLE	AUTHOR	PRICE	PAGES
8170084601	**STTP : Word 2002**	Corinne Hervo	Rs. 45.00	154
817008461X	**STTP : Excel 2002**	Corinne Hervo	Rs. 45.00	153
8170084628	**STTP : Dreamweaver 4**	Corinne Hervo	Rs. 45.00	135
8170084636	**STTP : Flash 5**	Corinne Hervo	Rs. 45.00	183
8170084644	**STTP : Photoshop 6**	Corinne Hervo	Rs. 45.00	152
817008881X	**STTP : MS Office 2000**	Dinesh Maidasani	Rs. 125.00	290
8170086100	**STTP : MS Office 2003**	Dinesh Maidasani	Rs. 145.00	288
8170087651	**STTP : MS Word 2003**	Firewall Media	Rs. 60.00	150
8170088011	**STTP : Photoshop CS**	Firewall Media	Rs. 60.00	150
8170088143	**STTP : MS Excel 2003**	Firewall Media	Rs. 60.00	150
8170088151	**STTP : CorelDraw 12**	Firewall Media	Rs. 60.00	150
8131800105	**STTP : 3ds MAX 7**	Dinesh Maidasani	Rs. 95.00	182
8131800083	**STTP : Auto CAD 2006**	Dinesh Maidasani	Rs. 95.00	190
8131800245	**STTP : CorelDraw X3**	Dinesh Maidasani	Rs. 75.00	188

ISBN	TITLE	AUTHOR	PRICE	PAGES
8131800253	**STTP : Dreamweaver 8**	Dinesh Maidasani	Rs. 75.00	148
8131800237	**STTP : Photoshop CS2**	Dinesh Maidasani	Rs. 75.00	172
8170088380	**STTP : Tally 7.2**	Firewall Media	Rs. 175.00	322
8131800091	**STTP : Flash 8**	Dinesh Maidasani	Rs. 95.00	180
8131800407	**STTP : My SQL 5.0**	Dinesh Maidasani	Rs. 85.00	166
8131800458	**STTP : Microsoft Power Point 2003**	Dinesh Maidasani	Rs. 75.00	142

STUDIO FACTORY

ISBN	TITLE	AUTHOR	PRICE	PAGES
8170084792	**Studio Factory—Photoshop 6**	Christophe Aubry	Rs. 175.00	364
8170084806	**Studio Factory—Flash 5**	Sami Ben Yahiya	Rs. 145.00	314
8170084814	**Studio Factory—Dreamweaver Ultradev 4**	Phillippe Chatellier	Rs. 95.00	240
8170084822	**Studio Factory—Dreamweaver 4**	Christophe Aubry	Rs. 175.00	373
8170087643	**Studio Factory—Dreamweaver MX**	Christophe Aubry	Rs. 195.00	407
8170087627	**Studio Factory—Flash MX**	Arnaud Blanche	Rs. 145.00	337
817008766X	**Studio Factory—Photoshop 7**	Cyril Guerin	Rs. 195.00	420

LAXMI PUBLICATIONS (P) LTD

113, Golden House, Daryaganj, New Delhi-110002
Phone : **011 - 43 53 25 00**
Fax : **011 - 43 53 25 28**
EMAIL : info@laxmipublications.com
Website : www.laxmipublications.com

BRANCHES

- 129/1, IIIrd Main Road, IX Cross, Chamrajpet, **Bangalore** (*Phone* : 080-26 61 15 61)
- 26, Damodaran Street, T. Nagar, **Chennai** (*Phone* : 044-24 34 47 26)
- 43/1394D, St. Benedict's Road, Ernakulam North, **Cochin** (*Phone* : 0484-239 70 04)
- Pan Bazar, Rani Bari, **Guwahati** (*Phones* : 0361-254 36 69, 251 38 81)
- 4-2-453, Ist Floor, Ramkote, **Hyderabad** (*Phone* : 040-24 75 02 47)
- Adda Tanda Chowk, N.D. 365, **Jalandhar City** (*Phone* : 0181-222 12 72)
- 106/A, Ist Floor, S.N. Banerjee Road, **Kolkata** (*Phones* : 033-22 27 37 73, 22 27 52 47)
- 18, Madan Mohan Malviya Marg, **Lucknow** (*Phone* : 0522-220 95 78)
- 142-C, Victor House, Ground Floor, N.M. Joshi Marg, Lower Parel (W), **Mumbai** (*Phones* : 022-24 91 54 15, 24 92 78 69)
- Radha Govind Street, Tharpagna, **Ranchi** (*Phone* : 0651-230 77 64)